THE CO
OXFORD

THE COLLEGES OF OXFORD:

THEIR HISTORY AND TRADITIONS.

XXI CHAPTERS
CONTRIBUTED BY MEMBERS OF THE
COLLEGES.

EDITED BY
ANDREW CLARK, M.A.,
FELLOW OF LINCOLN COLLEGE, OXFORD.

PREFACE.

The history of any one of the older Colleges of Oxford extends over a period of time and embraces a variety of interests more than sufficient for a volume. The constitutional changes which it has experienced in the six, or four, or two centuries of its existence have been neither few nor slight. The Society living within its walls has reflected from age to age the social, religious, and intellectual conditions of the nation at large. Its many passing generations of teachers and students have left behind them a wealth of traditions honourable or the reverse. Yet it seems not impossible to combine in one volume a series of College histories. What happened in one College happened to some extent in all; and if, therefore, certain periods or subjects which are fully dealt with in one College are omitted in others, a single volume ought to be sufficient, not merely to narrate the salient features of the history of each individual College, but also to give an intelligible picture of College life generally at successive periods of time.

This is what the present volume seeks to do. Brasenose and Hertford chapters give a hint of the multiplicity of halls for Seculars out of which the Colleges grew; in Trinity and Worcester chapters we have a glimpse of the houses for Regulars which for a while mated the Colleges, but disappeared at the Reformation. In Queen's College, early social conditions are described; in New College, early studies. Balliol College gives prominence to the Renaissance movement; Corpus Christi to the consequent changes in studies. In Magdalen College we see the divisions and fluctuations of opinions which followed the Reformation; in S. John's, the golden age of the early Stuarts; in Merton, the dissensions of the Civil War; in Exeter College, the strong contrast between Commonwealth and Restoration. University College naturally enlarges on the Romanist attempt under James II. The bright and dark sides of the eighteenth century are exhibited in Pembroke and Lincoln. To Corpus, which had described the Renaissance, it belongs almost of right to depict the renewed love of letters which distinguishes the present century. And as with successive phases of social and intellectual life, so with other matters of interest. Oriel College gives a full account of the different books of record of a College, and of the long warfare of contested elections. Lincoln College sets forth the constitutional arrangements of a pre-Reformation College. Lincoln and Worcester show through what uncertainties projected Colleges have to pass before they are legally settled. Christ Church suggests the architectural and artistic wealth of Oxford.

It is only fair to the writers of the separate chapters to say that the limits of length imposed on them, and the selection of subjects for special treatment, are not of their own choosing. Space for fuller treatment in each case is of necessity wanting; but somewhat greater latitude has been allowed to those less fortunate Colleges which have no history of their own, extant or in prospect. Colleges which have found their historian, will not, it is hoped, grudge their sisters this consolation.

A. C.

August 1891.

I.
UNIVERSITY COLLEGE.

BY F. C. CONYBEARE, M.A., SOMETIME FELLOW OF UNIVERSITY COLLEGE.

The popular mind concerning the origin of University College is well exampled in the form of prayer which after the reform of religion was used in chapel on the day of the yearly College Festival, and which begins in these words—

"Merciful God and loving Father, we give Thee humble and hearty thanks for Thy great Bounty bestow'd upon us of this place by Alfred the Great, the first Founder of this House; William of Durham, the Restorer of it; Walter Skirlow, Henry Percy, Sir Simon Benet, Charles Greenwood, especial Benefactors, with others, exhibitors to the same."[1]

However, Mr. William Smith, Rector of Melsonby, and above twelve years Senior Fellow of our Society, who in the year 1728 published his learned Annals of the College, sets it down that King Alfred was not mentioned in the College prayers as chief founder until the reign of Charles I., and he relates how "that Dr. Clayton, after he was chosen Master (in 1665), when he first heard King Alfred named in the collect before William of Durham, openly and aloud cried out in the chapel, '*There is no King Alfred there.*'"

For at an earlier date it had been of custom to pray indeed for the soul of King Alfred, but only in the following order—

"I commend also unto your devout Prayers, the souls departed out of this world, especially The Soul of William of Durham, our chief Founder. The Soul of Mr. Walter Skirlaw, especial Benefactor. The Soul of King Alfred, Founder of the University. The Soul of King Henry the 5th. The Souls of Henry Percy, first Earl of Northumberland; Henry the 2nd Earl, and my Ladies their Wives, with all their Issue out of the World departed.... The Souls of all them that have been Fellows, and all good Doers. And for the Souls of all them that God would have be prayed for."

The date of this form of prayer is concurrent with Philip and Mary; between whose reign and that of Charles I. it is therefore certain that King Alfred was lifted in our prayers from being Founder only of the University to the being Founder of our College. And in so much as during many generations the belief that this college was founded by King Alfred has, by all who are competent to judge, been condemned for false and erroneous, I will follow the example of the learned antiquarian already mentioned, and recount its true foundation by William of Durham; eschewing the scruples of those brave interpreters of the law, who in the year 1727 said in Westminster Hall, "that King Alfred must be confirmed our Founder, for the sake of Religion itself, which would receive a greater scandal by a determination on the other Side, than it had by all the Atheists, Deists, and Apostates, from Julian down to Collins; that a succession of Clergymen for so many years should return thanks for an Idol, or mere Nothing, in Ridicule and Banter of God and Religion, must not be suffered in a court of Justice."[2]

The historical origin of University College dates from the thirteenth century, and was in this wise. There was in the year 1229, so Matthew Paris relates, a great falling out between the students and citizens of Paris, and, as was usual for Academicians then to do, all the scholars removed to other places, where they could have civiller usage, and greater privileges allowed them, as the Oxonians had done in King John's time, when three thousand removed to Reading and Maidstone (and as some say to Cambridge also). It appears that the English king, Henry III., was not blind to the advantages which would accrue to his country from an influx of scholars, and therefore published Letters Patent on the 14th July, of that very year, to invite the masters and scholars of the University to England; and foreseeing they would prefer Oxford before any other place, the said king sent several Writs to the Burgers of Oxon, to provide all conveniences, as lodgings, and all other good Entertainment, and good usage to welcome them thither.[3] Among other Englishmen who left Paris in consequence of these dissensions, was Master William of Durham, who repaired at first to Anjou only. But we may well suppose that his attention was drawn by the fostering edicts of the English king to Oxford as a centre of schools. It is certain that when he died, at Rouen, on his way home from Rome, twenty years later, in 1249, "abounding in great Revenues, eminently learned, and Rector of that noble Church of Weremouth, not far from the sea," he bequeathed to the University of Oxford the sum of three hundred and ten marks, for purchase of annual rents, unto the use of ten or eleven or twelve, or more Masters, who should be maintained withal.

The above information is derived from a report drawn up in 1280, by certain persons delegated by the University of Oxford to enquire into the Testament of Master William of Durham; which report is still kept among the muniments of the College, and constitutes our earliest statutes.

In the thirteenth century there was not the same choice of investments as to-day. The best one could do was to lend out one's money to the nobles and king of the Realm, or to purchase houses therewith. The former security corresponded to, but was not so secure as, the consolidated funds of a later age. Nor was house property entirely safe. For in an age when communication between different parts of the country was slow and insecure, it was not of choice, but of necessity, that one bought house property in one's own city; since farther afield and in places wide apart one lacked trusty agents to collect one's rents; but in a single city a plague might in one year lay empty half the houses, and so forfeit to the owners their yearly monies.

In laying out William of Durham's bequest, the University had recourse to both these kinds of security. As early as the year 1253, a house was bought for thirty-six marks from the priors and brethren of the hospital of Brackle; perhaps for the reception of William of Durham's earliest scholars. This house stood in the angle between School Street and St. Mildred's Lane (which to-day is Brazenose Lane), and corresponded therefore with the north-east corner of the present Brazenose College. Two years later, in 1255, was purchased from the priors of Sherburn, a house in the High Street, standing opposite the lodge of the present college, where now is Mr. Thornton's book-shop. For this piece of property the University paid, out of William of Durham's money, forty-eight marks down.

This house, the second purchase made out of the founder's bequest, after belonging to the College for upwards of six hundred years, was lately sold to Magdalen College instead of being exchanged as it should have been, if it was to be alienated at all, with a house belonging to Queen's College, numbered 85 on the opposite side of the street. And at the same time, all properties and tenements, not already belonging to us, except the aforesaid No. 85, intervening between Logic Lane and the New Examination Schools, were purchased, to give our College the faculty of some day, if need be, extending itself on that side.

The third house bought out of the same bequest adjoined (to the south) the former of the two already mentioned, and fronting on School Street, was called as early as A.D. 1279, Brazen-Nose Hall. It cost £55 6s. 8d. sterling, and on its site stands to-day Brazen-nose College gate and chapel. The purchase was completed in 1262. The last of the early purchases made by the University for the College consisted of two houses east of Logic Lane on the south side of the High Street. (The old Saracen's Head Inn on the same side of Logic Lane only came to the College in the last century by the bequest of Dr. John Browne, who became master in 1744.) These two houses paid a Quit Rent of fifteen shillings, for which the University gave, A.D. 1270, seven pounds of William of Durham's money, proving, as Mr. Smith notes, that in the thirteenth century houses were purchased in Oxford at ten years' purchase, so that you received eleven per cent. interest on your money.

The rents of all these houses, so we learn from the Inquisition of the year 1280 already mentioned, amounted to eighteen marks. As to the rest of the money bequeathed, the Masters of Arts appointed by the University in 1280 to enquire found, "That the University needing it for itself, and other great men of the Land that had recourse to the University; the rest of the money, to wit, one hundred Pounds and ten Marks, had been made use of, partly for its own necessary occasions, and partly lent to other persons, of which money nothing at all is yet restored."

The barons to whom the University thus lent money had long been at strife with King Henry for his extortions, and in May of 1264 won the Battle of

Lewes against him. With them the University took side against the king, so far at least as to advance them money out of William of Durham's chest. It is not certain—though it seems probable—that some few scholars were as early as 1253 invited by the University to live together, as beneficiaries of William of Durham, in the Hall which was in that year purchased out of his bequest. If it be asked how were they supported, it may be answered: with the interest paid by the nobles upon the hundred pounds lent to them; for, since the capital sum was afterwards repaid, it is fair to suppose that the interest was also got in year by year from the first. Although the University drew up no statutes for William of Durham's scholars till the year 1280, yet his very will—which is now lost—may have served as a prescription ruling their way of life, even as it was made the basis of those statutes of 1280. Perhaps, however, his scholars were scattered over the different halls until 1280, when, after the pattern of the nephews and scholars of Walter de Merton, they were gathered under a single roof for the advancement of their learning and improvement of their discipline. Even if they lived apart, the title of college can hardly be denied to them, for—to quote Mr. William Smith—"taking it for granted and beyond dispute, that William of Durham dyed A.D.1249, and that several purchases were bought with his money shortly after his death, as the deeds themselves testifie; all the doubt that can afterwards follow is, whether William of Durham's Donation to ten, eleven, or twelve masters or scholars, were sufficient to erect them into a society? and whether that society could properly be called a college?" And the same writer adds that a college "signifies not a building made of brick or stone, adorned with gates, towers, and quadrangles; but a company, or society admitted into a body, and enjoying the same or like privileges one with another." Such was a college in the old Roman sense.

We will then leave it to the reader to decide whether University College is or is not the earliest college in Europe, even though its foundation by King Alfred is mythical, and will pass on to view the statutes made in the year 1280. In that year at least the Masters delegated by the University "to enquire and order those things which had relation to the Testament of Master William of Durham," ordained that "The Chancellor with some Masters in Divinity, by their advice, shall call other masters of other Faculties; and these masters with the Chancellor, bound by the Faith they owe to the University, shall chuse out of all who shall offer themselves to live of the said rents, four Masters, whom in their consciences they shall think most fit to advance, or profit in the Holy Church, who otherwise have not to live handsomely without it in the State of Masters of Arts.... The same manner of Election shall be for the future, except only that those four that shall be maintained out of that charity shall be called to the election, of which four one at least shall be a Priest.

"These four Masters shall each receive for his salary fifty shillings sterling[4] yearly, out of the Rents bought....

"The aforesaid four masters, living together, shall study Divinity; and with this also may hear the Decretum and Decretalls, if they shall think fit; who, as to their manner of living and learning, shall behave themselves as by some fit and expert persons, deputed by the Chancellor, shall be ordered. But if it shall so happen, that any ought to be removed from the said allowance, or office, the Chancellor and Masters of Divinity shall have Power to do it."

By the same Statutes a procurator or Bursar was appointed to take care of rents already bought and procure the buying of other rents. This Bursar was to receive fifty-five shillings instead of fifty. He was to have one key of William of Durham's chest, the Chancellor another, and a person appointed by the University Proctors the third.

Three points are evident from these statutes: firstly, that in its inception the College of William of Durham was entirely the care of the University, which thus held the position of Visitor. Secondly, theology was to be the chief, if not sole study of the beneficiaries. Perhaps the founder viewed with jealousy the study of Roman law, which was beginning to engross some of the best minds of the age. Thirdly, only Masters were admissible as Fellows. It was the custom at the time to have graduated in Arts before proceeding to teach Divinity.

After a lapse of twelve years, A.D. 1292, at the Procurement of the Executors of the Venerable Mr. William of Durham, who were, it seems, still living, the University made new statutes for the College. In these new statutes we hear for the first time of a Master of the College, of commoners, and of a College library. The Senior Fellow was to govern the Juniors, and get half a mark yearly for his diligence therein. Thus the headship of the College went at first by succession, and not until 1332 by election; after which date the master was required to be cæteris paribus proxime Dunelmiam oriundus, or at least of northern extraction.

The first alien to the College who was elected Master was Ralph Hamsterley, in 1509. Previously he was a fellow of Merton College, where in the chapel he was buried. (Brodrick, *Memorials of Merton College*, p. 240.) He was "nunquam de gremio nostro neque de comitiva," and was therefore chosen Master conditionally upon the visitors granting a dispensation to depart from the ordinary rule. (W. Smith's MSS., xi. p. 2.)

The Master had until lately as much or as little right to marry as any of the Fellows, and in 1692 the Fellows, before electing Dr. Charlet, exacted from him a promise that he would not marry, or, if he did, would resign within a year. It seems that in old days Fellows of Colleges who were obliged to be in Holy Orders were free to marry after King James the I.'s parliament had sanctioned the marriage of clergymen. Already in 1422 the Master is called the custos, but he was till 1736, when new statutes made a change, called *"the Master or Senior Fellow, Magister vel senior socius."* He had the key of the College, but in time delegated the function of letting people in and out to a statutory porter. The introduction of commoners or scholars not on the foundation is thus referred to in these statutes of 1292: "Since the aforesaid scholars have not sufficient to live handsomely alone by themselves, but that it is expedient that other honest persons dwell with them; it is ordained that every Fellow shall secretly enquire concerning the manners of every one that desires to sojourn with them; and then, if they please, by common consent, let him be received under this condition, That before them he shall promise whilst he lives with them, that he will honestly observe the customs of the Fellows of the House, pay his Dues, not hurt any of the Things belonging to the House, either by himself, or those that belong to him."

In the year 1381 we find from the Bursar's roll that the students not on the foundation paid £4 18*s.* as rents for their chambers, a considerable sum in those days.

As to the books of the College, it was ordained that there be put one book of every sort that the House has, in some common and secure place; that the Fellows, and others with the consent of a Fellow, may for the future have the benefit of it.

For the rest it was ordained that the Fellows should speak Latin often, and at every Act have one Disputation in Philosophy or Theology, and have one Disputation at least in the principal Question of both Faculties in the Vespers, and another in the Inception in their private College. In these disputations it is clear that rival disputants sometimes lost their tempers from the following ordinance—

"No Fellow shall under-value another Fellow, but shall correct his Fault privately, under the Penalty of Twelve-pence to be paid to the common-Purse; nor before one that is no Fellow, under the Penalty of two shillings; nor publickly in the Highway, or Church, or Fields, under the penalty of half a mark; and in all these cases, he that begins first shall double what the other is to pay, and this in Disputations especially."

In those days a lesson was read during dinner. In these degenerate days all the above salutary rules are inverted, and it is customary for the senior scholar to sconce in a pot of beer any junior member who quotes Latin during the Hall-dinner.

In the year 1311 fresh statutes were ordained by convocation for the College, which, however, add little to the former ones. Of candidates for a Fellowship, otherwise duly qualified, he was to be preferred who comes from near Durham. After seven years a Fellow was to oppose in the Divinity Schools, which was equivalent to nowadays taking the degree of Doctor of Divinity. Each Fellow or past-Fellow was to put up a mass once a year for the Repose of the soul of William of Durham; and all alike were to cause themselves to be called, so far as lay in their power, the scholars of William of Durham. Lastly, the Senior Fellow was to be in Holy Orders. This, however, must not be taken to mean that the other Fellows were not to be so likewise. They were till recently expected to be ordained within four years of their degree, and the Statutes of 1311 A.D. were reaffirmed in that sense by the visitors under the chancellorship of Dr. Fell, 1666 A.D., when it was sought to remove Mr. Berty, a Bennet Fellow, because he had not taken orders.

In or about the year 1343 the scholars of William of Durham removed to the present site of the College, where a house called Spicer's Hall, occupying the ground now included in the large quadrangle, had been bought for them. At the same time White Hall and Rose Hall, two houses facing Kybald Street—which joined the present Logic Lane and Grove Street half-way down each—were bought, and made part of the College. Ludlow Hall, on the site of the present east quadrangle, was bought at the same time, and a tenement, called in 1379 Little University Hall, and occupying the site of the Lodgings of the Master (which in 1880, on the completion of the Master's new house, were turned into men's rooms), was bought in 1404. But Ludlow Hall and Little University Hall were not at once added to the College premises.

During the first hundred years of the life of the College its members were called simply *University Scholars*, and the ordinance of A.D. 1311, that they should call themselves *the Scholars of William of Durham*, proves that that was not the name in common vogue. Their old house at the corner of what is to-day Brazen-nose College was called the *Aula Universitatis in Vico Scholarum* (the Hall of the University in School Street). After 1343, the probable year of their migration, until at least 1361, the College was called as before *Aula Universitatis*, only *in Alto Vico*, i. e. in High Street. After 1361 they assumed the official title of *Master and Fellows of the Hall of William of Durham*, commonly called *Aula Universitatis*. It was not till 1381 that the present title *Magna Aula Universitatis*, or Mickle University Hall, was used, in distinction from the *Little University Hall*, which was only separated from it by Ludlow Hall. But the nomenclature was not uniform, and in Elizabeth's reign, as in Richard II.'s, it was called *the College of William of Durham*.

The legend of the foundation of the College by King Alfred has been mentioned, and here is a convenient place to conjecture how and when it arose. The first mention of it we meet with in a petition addressed in French to King Richard II., A.D. 1381, by his "poor Orators, the Master and Scholars of your College, called Mickil University Hall in Oxendford, which College was first founded by your noble Progenitor, King Alfred (whom God assoyle), for the maintenance of twenty-four Divines for ever." Twenty years before, in 1360, Laurence

Radeford, a Fellow, had bought for the College various messuages, shops, lands and meadows yielding rents of the yearly value of £15. This purchase was made out of the residuum of William of Durham's money, now all called in. But it turned out that the title to the new property was bad, and, after forging various deeds without success, the College appealed in the above petition to the king, Richard II., to exercise his prerogative, and take the case out of the common courts, in which—so runs the petition—the plaintiff, Edmond Frauncis, citizen of London, "has procured all the Pannel of the Inquest to be taken by Gifts and Treats."

The petition prays the king to see that the College be not "tortiously disinherited," and appeals to the memory of the "noble Saints John of Beverley, Bede, and Richard of Armagh, formerly scholars of the College." A petition so full of fictions hardly deserved to lead to success, and the College was eventually compelled to redeem its right to the estate by payment of a large sum of money to the heirs of Frauncis. The interest of this petition, however, lies in the fact that in 1728, on the occasion of a dispute arising for the mastership between Mr. Denison and Mr. Cockman, it formed the ground upon which, in the King's Bench at Westminster, it was held that the College is a Royal foundation, and the Crown the rightful visitor; the truth being that the whole body of Regents and non-Regents of the University were and always had been the true and rightful visitor.

But the French Petition to Richard II. was not the only fabrication to which William of Durham's unworthy beneficiaries had recourse in order to establish a fictitious antiquity and deny their real founder. About the same time they stole the chancellor's seal and affixed its impress to a forged deed purporting to have been executed inA.D. 1220, the 4th of Henry III., May 10th, by Lewis de Chapyrnay, Chancellor. This false deed records the receipt of four hundred marks bequeathed by William, Archdeacon of Durham, for the maintenance of six Masters of Arts, and the conveyance of certain tenements to Master Roger Caldwell, Warden and senior Fellow of the great hall of the University. The reader will the more agree that this forgery was worthier of Shapira than of "honest and holy clerks," when he reads in Antony à Wood (*City of Oxford*, ed. Andrew Clark, vol. i. p. 561)— who was not deceived by it—that it was written "on membrane cours, thick, greasy, whereas, in the reign of Henry III. parchment was not so, but fine and clear." There never were such persons as Chapyrnay and Caldwell, and William of Durham did not die till 1249, and then left only three hundred and ten marks. Mr. Twine, the author of the *Apology for the Antiquity of Oxford*, said of this deed, "mentiri nescit, it cannot lie." "But," says quaintly Mr. William Smith, "if ever there was a lie in the world, that which we find in that Charter is as great a one as ever the Devil told since he deceived our first Parents in Paradise."

It would oppress the reader to detail all the other fictions which followed on this early one. One lie makes many, and as time went on outward embellishments were added to the College commemorative of its mythical founder. Thus a picture of King Alfred was bought in the year 1662 for £3—perhaps the same which one now sees in the College library. There was—so Mr. Smith relates— an older picture of him in the Masters' lodgings.

A statue of Alfred also stood over the chapel door, and was removed by Mr. Obadiah Walker, Master in 1676, to a niche over the hall door to make place for a statue of St. Cuthbert, the patron saint of Durham, on whose day the gaudy used to be celebrated until 1662, at which date it was changed to the day of Saints Simon and Jude, out of respect to the memory of Sir Simon Benet, who had lately bequeathed four Fellowships, four scholarships, and various other benefits. This was the real cause of the 28th of October being chosen for the gaudy, although afterwards the Aluredians absurdly pretended that it was the day of King Alfred's obit. The statue of Alfred above-mentioned was given by Dr. Robert Plot, the well-known author of *The Natural History of Oxfordshire*, who was a Fellow-commoner of the College, and it cost £3 1*s.* 5*d.* to remove it, as related, in the year 1686. A hundred years later a marble image of Alfred was given to the College by Viscount Folkestone, which is now set up over the fireplace in the oak common-room. A relief of him is also set over the fireplace in the college-hall, and was given by Sir Roger Newdigate, a member of the

College, and founder of the University annual prize for an English poem.

A picture of St. John of Beverley, mentioned in the French petition to Richard II., was, we learn from Gutch's edition of Antony Wood's *Colleges and Halls* (ed. 1786, p. 57), set in the east window of the old chapel in the beginning of the seventeenth century. The same authority assures us that until Dr. Clayton's time (Master, 1605) there were in a window on the west side of the little old quadrangle pictures of King Alfred kneeling and St. Cuthbert sitting, … the king thus bespeaking the saint in a pentameter, holding the picture of the College in his hand, "Hic in honore tui collegium statui," to whom the saint made answer, in a scroll coming from his mouth—"Quæ statuisti in eo pervertentes maledico."

In a window of the outer chapel were also the arms of William of Durham, which were, "Or, a Fleur de lis azure, each leaf charged with a mullet gules." Round these arms was written on a scroll: "Magistri Willielmi de Dunelm … huius collegii"; the missing word, so Wood had been informed, was "Fundatoris," erased, no doubt, by an Aluredian. The arms of the College to-day are those of Edward the Confessor, to wit—"Azure, a cross patonce between five martlets Or." We would do well to resign our sham royalty, and return to the arms of William of Durham, our true founder.

The crowning fiction was the celebration in the year 1872 of the millennium of the College, during the mastership of the Rev. G. G. Bradley, afterwards

Dean of Westminster. It is said that a distinguished modern historian ironically sent him a number of burned cakes, purporting to have been dug up at Athelney, to entertain King Alfred's scholars withal. It is not recorded if they were served up or no to the guests, among whom were Dean Stanley and Mr. Robert Lowe, both past tutors of the College. At the dinner which graced this festal occasion, the late Dean of Westminster is said to have ridiculed the idea of King Alfred having bestowed lands and tenements on scholars in Oxford, which place was in A.D. 872 in possession of Alfred's enemies the Danes; whereupon Mr. Lowe made the happy answer, that this latter fact was itself a confirmation of the legend, for King Alfred was a man much before his time, who in the spirit of some modern leaders of the democracy took care to bestow on his followers, not his own lands, but those of his political opponents.

This legend of King Alfred sprang up in the fourteenth century, when people had forgotten the Norman Conquest and time had long healed all the scars of an alien invasion. Then historians began to feel back to a more remote period for the origin of institutions really subsequent. In so doing they fed patriotic pride by establishing an unbroken continuity of the nation's life. So to-day we see asserting itself, and with better historical warranty, a belief in the antiquity of English ecclesiastical institutions. The best minds are no longer content with that idol of the Evangelicals, a parliamentary church dating back no more than three centuries. It may be even that a good deal of the Aluredian legend was earlier in its origin than the fourteenth century, and shaped itself at the first out of anti-Norman feeling. In the reign of King Richard, anyhow, all sections of the now united nation accepted it, and not only have we the writ of King Richard II., dated May 4th, 1381 (in answer to the French petition), setting down the College to be "the Foundation of the Progenitors of our Lord the King, and of his Patronage,"[5] but in that very reign, if not later, a passage was interpolated in MSS. of Asser's *Life of Alfred*, identifying the schools—which Alfred undoubtedly maintained—with the schools of Oxford. The Fellows of University only took advantage of a feeling which was abroad, and by which they were also duped, when they declared themselves in the French petition to be a royal foundation. Antony Wood was not deceived by the legend, though he credits it in regard to the University. It is strange to find Hearne the antiquary, and Dr. Charlet, Master, 1692-1722, both acquaintances of Mr. W. Smith, adhering to the belief. Mr. Smith declares that Dr. Charlet did so from vanity, because he thought that to be head of a royal foundation added to his dignity. Obadiah Walker had sided with the Aluredians, because he was a papist, and because Alfred had been a good Catholic king and faithful to the Pope. What is most strange of all is that, although the king's attorney and solicitor-general, being duly commissioned to inquire, had, in October 1724 pronounced that the College was not a royal foundation, nor the sovereign its legitimate visitor, yet the Court of King's Bench three years after decided both points in just the opposite sense. It is an ill wind that blows no one any good. We then lost the University as our visitor, but have since obtained gratis on all disputed points the opinion of the highest law officer of the realm, the Lord Chancellor.

Between the years 1307 and 1360 as many as sixteen halls in the parishes of St. Mary, St. Peter, St. Mildred, and All Hallows were bought for the College. They were no doubt let out as lodgings to University students, and were in those days, as now, a remunerative form of investment; some of them standing on sites which have since come to be occupied by colleges.

It was not till the fifteenth century that the College acquired property outside Oxford, and then not by purchase, but by bequest. In those days locomotion was too difficult for a small group of scholars to venture on far-off purchases. But in 1403 Walter Skirlaw, Bishop of Durham, left to our College the Manor of Mark's Hall, or Margaret Ruthing, in Essex. The proceeds were to sustain three Fellows "chosen out of students at Oxford or Cambridge, and if possible born in the dioceses of York and Durham." It has already been remarked how closely connected was the College with the North of England. No other conditions were attached to the benefaction save this, that "all the Fellows shall every year, for ever, celebrate solemn obsequies in their chapel upon the day of the Bishop's death, with a Placebo and Dirige, and a Mass for the dead the day after." Is it altogether for good that we have outgrown those customs of pious gratitude to the past? Bishop Skirlaw's Fellowships, it may be added, figure in the Calendar as of the foundation of Henry IV., because the lands were passed as a matter of legal form through the sovereign's lands in order to avoid certain difficulties connected with mortmains.

The next great benefactor of the College after Bishop Skirlaw was Henry Percy, Earl of Northumberland, who in 1442 left property and the advowson of Arncliffe in Craven in Yorkshire. Three Fellows drawn from the dioceses of Durham, Carlisle, and York were to be sustained out of his benefaction. The next chief benefaction was that of John Freyston or Frieston, who in 1592 bequeathed property in Pontefract for the support of a Fellow or Exhibitioner, who should be a Yorkshire man, and also by his will made the College trustee to pay certain yearly sums to the grammar schools of Wakefield, Normanton, Pontefract, and Swillington.

Coming to the seventeenth century, we find a Mr. Charles Greenwood, a past-Fellow, leaving a handsome bequest to the College, out of which, however, only £1500 was secured from his executors, which money paid for the present fabric to be partially raised; the north side of the quadrangle, the chapel, and hall and old library being first begun A.D. 1634. The present library was partly built out of money given by the executors and trustees of the second Lord Eldon, past-Fellow of the College. It shelters the colossal twin-image of his kinsmen, and was designed by Sir G. G. Scott, and is better suited to be a chapel than a library. Then in 1631, Sir Simon Bennet, a relative and college pupil of Mr. Greenwood's, left lands in Northampton to maintain eight Fellows and eight scholars; though they turned out sufficient to maintain but four of each sort. The last great benefactor of this century was the famous Dr. Radcliffe, formerly senior scholar, of whom the eastern quadrangle, built by his munificence, remains as a monument. Beside completing the fabrics he founded two medical Fellowships, and, dying in 1734, bequeathed in trust to the College for its uses his estate of Linton in Yorkshire.

It is beyond the limits of a short article to narrate all the vicissitudes which during the epochs of the Reformation and Commonwealth the College underwent. In the reign of Elizabeth it sided with the Roman Catholics, and the Master and several Fellows were ejected on that account. Later on, in 1642, the College *lent* its plate, consisting of a silver flagon, 8 potts, 9 tankards, 18 bowles, one candle-pott, and a salt-sellar to King Charles I., one flagon alone being kept for the use of the Communion. The gross weight as weighed at the mint was 738 oz. The Fellows and commoners also contributed on 30th July, 1636, the sum of 19li. 10s. for entertaining the king; and again on 17th Feb., 1636, 4li. 17s. 6d. Subsequently the College sustained for many months 28 soldiers at the rate of 22li. 8s. per month. After all this show of loyalty we expect to learn that Cromwell ejected the Master, Thomas Walker, and instituted a Roundhead, Joshua Hoyle, in his place.

Another member of the College of the same name, but who achieved more fame, was Obadiah Walker, who was already a Fellow under Thomas Walker's mastership, and was ejected by the Long Parliament along with him, and also with his old tutor, Mr. Abraham Woodhead. Woodhead and O. Walker retired abroad and visited Rome and many other places. At the Restoration they both regained their Fellowships, but Woodhead never more conformed to the English Church. O. Walker, however, continued to take the Sacrament in the College chapel, and after that he was elected Master distributed it to the other Fellows, till, on the accession of James II., he "openly declared himself a Romanist, and got a dispensation from his Majesty for himself and two Fellows, his converts, who held their places till the king's flight, notwithstanding the laws to the contrary." William Smith, who was a resident Fellow at the time, has "many good things to say of Obadiah Walker, as that he was neither proud nor covetous, and framed his usual discourse against the Puritans on one side, and the Jesuits on the other, as the chief disturbers of the peace, and hinderers of all concessions and agreement amongst all true members of the Catholic Church." He complains, however, that "as soon as he declared himself a Roman Catholic, he provided him and his party of Jesuits for their Priests; concerning the first of which (I think he went by the name of Mr.

Edwards) there is this remarkable story, that having had mass said for some time in a garret, he afterwards procured a mandate from K. James to seize on the lower half of a side of the quadrangle, next adjoining to the College chapel, by which he deprived us of two low rooms, their studies and their bed-chambers; and after all the partitions were removed, it was someway or other consecrated, as we suppose, to Divine services; for they had mass there every day, and sermons at least in the afternoons on the Lord's Day."

Smith goes on to relate how the Jesuit chaplain was one day preaching from the text, "So run that you may obtain," when one of many Protestants, who were harkening at the outside of the windows in the quadrangle, discovering that the Jesuit was preaching a sermon of Mr. Henry Smith, which he had at home by him, went and fetched the book, and read at the outside of the window what the Jesuit was preaching within. For this it seems the particular Jesuit got into trouble. Smith complains also that by mandate of the king, Walker sequestred a Fellowship towards the maintenance of his priest, and incurred the College much expense in putting up the statue of James II., presented by a Romanist,[6] over the inside of a gate-house. He adds that "Mr. Walker that had the king's ear, and entertained him at vespers in their chapel, and shewed the king the painted windows in our own, so that the king could not but see his own statue in coming out of it, never had the Prudence nor kindness to the College, as to request the least favour to the society from him."

That Mr. William Smith, who writes the above, could also make himself a *persona grata* to the great men of State who came to Oxford to attend on the king, we see from the following letter written by Lord Conyers, who in 1681 lodged with his son in University College, on the occasion of the Parliament meeting in Oxford. It is dated Easter Thursday, London, 1681, and is as follows (MSS. Smith):—

"Sir,

I cannot satisfy my wife without giving you this trouble of my thanks for your very greate kindnesse to me and my sonn: we gott hither in v. good time on Thursday to waite on ye king before night; who was in a course of physick, but God be praised is v. well & walked yesterday round Hide Parke. My son also desires his humble services to you: And we both of us desire our services & thanks to Mr. Ledgard & Mr. Smith for y^r great civilities to us; & whenever I can serve any of you or the College, be most confident to find me

"Y^r most affect. friend &

"humble Servant

"Conyers."

In 1680, March 30, London, Lord Conyers writes to O. Walker about sending his son to the College, "who is growne too bigge for schoole tho' little I fear in scholarship … he is very towardly & capable to be made a scholar." He desires [letter of London,

April 9, 1682] Mr. Walker to provide a tutor for "his young man."

Smith's account of Obadiah Walker's doings at the College is fitly completed by the following passage from a letter sent by a Romanist priest at Oxford, Father Henry Pelham, to the Provincial of the Jesuits, Father John Clare (Sir John Warner, Bart.), preserved in the Public Record Office in Brussels, and given in Bloxam's *Magdalen College and James II.* (p. 227)—

"Oxford, 1690, May 2.—Hon. Sir, You are desirous to know how things are with us in these troublous times, since trade (*religion*) is so much decayed. I can only say that in the general decline of trade we have had our share. For before this turn we were in a very hopeful way, for we had three public shops (*chapels*) open in Oxford. One did wholly belong to us, and good custom we had, viz. the University (*University College Chapel*); but now it is shut up. The Master was taken, and has been ever since in prison, and the rest forced to abscond."

Thus ended the last attempt to force the Romanist religion upon Oxford. In the following December we find "Obadiah Walker" in the list of prisoners remaining at Faversham under a strong guard until the 30th of December, and then conducted some to the Tower, some to Newgate, and others released. Mr. Obadiah Walker lived for many years afterwards, and added to the literary work he had already accomplished in Oxford a history of the Ejected Clergy. His memory long survived in

Oxford, and with the mob was kept alive in a doggrel ballad which bore the refrain, "Old Obadiah sings Ave Maria."

In University College, under Obadiah Walker, were focussed all the propagandist influences of the time. Dr. John Massey, Dean of Christchurch, 1686, referred to in Pelham's letter, was originally a member of University College, and was converted by Obadiah Walker. There was also a printing press kept going in University to publish books of a Romanist tendency, which the University would not authorize to be printed by its Press.

The official College record (in the Register of Election) of the deposition of Mr. Obadiah Walker from the headship of the College is as follows (MSS. of Will. Smith, vol. vii. p. 113)—

"About the middle of Dec., A.D. 1688, Mr. Obadiah Walker attempted to flee abroad, but was taken at Sittingbourne in Kent, and carried to London, and there lodged in the Tower on a charge of high treason.

"On Jan. 7, 1689, the Fellows of University deputed Master Babman to go to him and ask him if he would resign his post, to whom, after deliberation lasting many days, Walker answered that he would not.

"On Jan. 22, after this answer had been brought to Oxford and conveyed to the Vice-Chancellor, the latter summoned the Fellows to appear before the

Visitors on Jan. 26, in the Apodyterium of the Venerable House of Convocation.

"Where on Jan. 26, between 9 and 10 a.m., there appeared in person and as representing the College the following Fellows—Mr. Will. Smith, Tho. Babman, Tho. Bennet, Francis Forster, and besought the Vice-Chancellor, Proctors, and Doctors of Divinity representing Convocation to remedy certain grievances in the College, specially concerning the Master and two Fellows. To them a citation was then issued by the Vice-Chancellor, Proctors, Doctors of Divinity, and others, as the ordinary and legitimate patrons and visitors of the College, to appear before them in the College Chapel on Monday, Feb. 4 following between 8-9 a.m.

"On the appointed day there met in the chapel between 8-9 a.m. the Vice-Chancellor, Gilbert Ironsyde, S.T.P., Rob. Say, Byron Eaton, Master of Oriel, W. Lovett, Tho. Hyde, Chief Librarian, Tho. Turner, President of C.C.C., Jonath. Edwards, S.T.P., Thom. Dunstan, Pres. of Magdalen College, Will. Christmas, Jun. Proctor, and others. After the Litany had been repeated, the Vice-Chancellor prorogued the meeting to the common-room, where were present the afore-mentioned Fellows, and in addition Edw. Farrar, Jo. Gilve, Jo. Nailor, Jo. Hudson. The Fellows preferred a complaint that the statutes of the Realm, of the University, and of the College had been violated by Obadiah Walker, Master or Senior Fellow of the College. They objected in particular that he had left the religion of the Anglican Church, established and confirmed by the statutes of this Realm, and betaken himself to the Roman or papistical religion; that he had held, fostered, and frequented illegal conventicles within the aforesaid College; that he had procured to be sequestred unto wrong uses and against the statutes the income and emoluments of the Society; also that he had had printed books against the Reformed religion, and that within the College, and had published the same unto the grave scandal as well of the University as of the College. All these charges were amply proved by trustworthy witnesses, whereupon the visitors decreed that the post of Mr. Obadiah Walker was void and vacant. At the same time, at the instance of the said Fellows, Masters Boyse and Deane, Fellows of the College, who had left the religion of the reformed Anglican Church, were ordered to be proceeded against so soon as a new Master or Senior Fellow was chosen."

Mr. Obadiah Walker lived for many years after the accession of William and Mary. He was a man of great piety and vast and varied learning, as is shown by his books upon Religion, Logic, History, and Geography. He wrote a book upon Greenland, and made experiments in physics. A near friend of the great benefactor of the College, Dr. John Radcliffe, he sought to convert that famous physician to the Roman faith, but found him as little inclined to believe in transubstantiation as "that the phial in his hand was a wheelbarrow." In spite of their want of religious sympathy, however, the two men liked each other's society, and the great physician, who respected Walker's learning, gave him a competency during the latter years of his life. In the College archives is an elegant letter addressed by O. Walker, then Master, to Radcliffe, thanking him for his gift of the east window of the College chapel. It runs thus:

"Sir, we return you our humble and hearty thanks for your noble and illustrious benefaction to this ancient foundation; your generosity hath supplied a defect and covered a blemish in our chapell; the other lesse eminent windows seemed to upbraid the chiefest as being more adorned and regardable than that which ought to be most splendid; till you was pleased to compassionate us and ennoble the best with the best work. Other benefactions are to be sought out in registers and memorialls, yours is conveyed with the light. The rising sun displays the gallantry of your spirit, and withall puts us in mind as often as we enter to our devotions to remember you and your good actions towards us. Nor can we salute the morning light without meditating on ye Shepherds and y^{e}Angells adoring the true Sun. And y^r holy praise and prostration by your singular favour is continually proposed, as to our sight and consideration, so to our example also. And so we do accept and acknowledge it, not only as an object moving our devotions, but as praise of ye artificer who hath not only observed much better decorum and proportion in his figures, but hath all so ingeniously contrived that the light shall not be hindred as by ye daubery of ye others."—The letter concludes with a prayer that Dr. Radcliffe may prosper in his profession.

The following quaint "letter sent by the College to begge contributions towards the building the East Side of the quadrangle about yᵉ end of 1674 or beginning of 1675 to the gentlemen in the North Parts" may fitly conclude our notice of this college (*vide* MSS. W. Smith, x. 239).

"Gentlemen,

"Your aged mother, and not yours alone, but of this whole University, if not all other such nurseries of Learning, at least in this nation, craves your assistance in the Time of her Necessity. It is not long since her walls Ruining and her Buildings, almost, after so many years, decayed; It pleased God to excite two of her sonnes in especiall manner, Mʳ Charles Greenwood, the tutor, and Sʳ Simon Benett, his pupill, to compassionate her decay, Repair her Ruins and Renew with Great Augmentation her former glory. But the late civil warrs and other alterations intervening not only interrupted that progresse which in a small time would have finished the work; But also disappointed her of the Assistance of Diverse, who were willing to contribute to her repairs.

"And we have very good Hopes that you will not be wanting to us in this our Necessity; this being a college designed for and most of the preferment in it limitted to Northern Scholars. A college which hath had the felicity to be herselfe at this present time

DCCC. years old.... In recompense she may justly expect that as she hath fostered your youths, so you would cherish her age."

Additional Notes.

p. 9. On Clerical Fellows.—It should be added that the statutes of 1736 provided that the two senior Fellows of the foundation of Sir Simon Bennet might study Medicine or Law. In 1854 the general ordinances of the Commissioners provided that there should be six (*i. e.* half of the) Fellows in Holy Orders. More recently clerical Fellowships have been practically abolished in the College.

p. 14. Anti-Norman feeling.—A spirit of Rivalry with Cambridge may with more reason be alleged in explanation of the acceptance of the Aluredian Legend.

p. 14. On the Legend of King Alfred.—The Court of King's Bench only decided that the College is a Royal Foundation, not that it was actually founded by King Alfred. Cp. the Preamble of Statutes of 1736: "it manifestly appears by a Judgement lately given in our Court of Kings Bench that the college of the great Hall of the University, commonly called University College, in Oxford, is of the foundation of our Royal Progenitors."

p. 23. On Northern Scholars.—The College lost its one-sided Northern character in 1736, when new statutes ordained that Sir Simon Bennet's Fellows were to come from the Southern Province of Canterbury (in partibus regni nostri Australibus oriundi).

II.
BALLIOL COLLEGE.[7]

By Reginald L. Poole, M.A., Balliol College.

The precedence of Balliol over Merton College depends upon the fact that John Balliol made certain payments not long after 1260 for the support of poor students at Oxford, while Walter of Merton's foundation dates from 1264; but it was not until the example had been set by Merton that the House of Balliol assumed a corporate being and became governed by formal statutes. The "pious founder" too was at the outset an involuntary agent, for the obligation to make his endowment was part of a penance imposed on him together with a public scourging at the Abbey door by the Bishop of Durham.[8] John Balliol, lord of Galloway, was the father of that John to whom King Edward the First of England adjudged the Scottish crown in 1292. His wife, the heiress, was Dervorguilla, grandniece to King William the Lion. It is to her far more than to her husband that the real foundation of the College bearing his name is due, and husband and wife are rightly coupled together as joint-founders, the lion of Scotland being associated with the orle of Balliol on the College shield. A house was first hired beyond the city ditch on the north side of Oxford, hard by the church of St. Mary Magdalen, and here certain poor scholars were lodged and paid eightpence a-day for their commons.[9] It was in the beginning a simple almshouse, founded on the model already existing at Paris, it depended for its maintenance upon the good pleasure of the founder, and possessed (so far as we know) no sort of organization, though customs and rules were certain to shape themselves before long without any positive enactment.

This state of things lasted until 1282, when Dervorguilla,—her husband had died in 1269,—took steps to place the House of Balliol upon an established footing. By her charter deed[10] she appointed two representatives or "proctors" (one, it seems probable, being always a Franciscan friar, and the other a secular Master of Arts) as the governing body of the House. The Scholars were, it is true, to elect their own Principal, and obey him "according to the statutes and customs approved among them," but he and they were alike subordinate to the Proctors or (as they came to be distinguished) the Extraneous Masters. The Scholars, whose number is not mentioned, were to attend the prescribed religious services and the exercises at the schools, and were also to engage in disputations among themselves once a fortnight. Three masses in the year were to be celebrated for the founders' welfare, and mention of them was to be made in the blessing before and grace after meat. Rules were laid down for the distribution of the common funds; if they fell short it was ordered that the poorer Scholars were not to suffer. The use of the Latin language (apparently at the common table) was strictly enjoined upon the Scholars. Whoever broke the rule was to be admonished by the Principal, and if he offended twice or thrice was to be removed from the common table, to eat by himself, and be served last of all. If he remained incorrigible after a week, the Proctors were to expel him. One feature of the Balliol Statutes which deserves particular notice is that none of them, until we reach the endowments of the sixteenth century, placed any sort of local restriction upon those who were capable of being elected to the Foundation.

This charter was plainly but the giving of a constitution to a society which had already formed for itself rules and usages with respect to discipline and other matters not referred to in it. The "House of the Scholars of Balliol" was placed on a still more assured footing when its charter was confirmed by Bishop Sutton of Lincoln two years later,[11] in which year the Scholars removed to a house bought for them by the foundress in Horsemonger-street, a little to the eastward of their previous abode;[12] and soon afterwards the Bishop permitted them to hold divine service, though they still attended their parish Church of St. Mary Magdalen on all great festivals.[13]Before the middle of the fourteenth century the society had considerably enlarged its position. It had bought houses on both sides of its existing building, so that it now occupied very nearly the site of the present front-quadrangle.[14] It received from private benefactors endowment for two Chaplains; and in 1327, with help furnished through the Abbot of Reading,[15] the building of a Chapel dedicated to Saint Catherine—the special patron whom we find first associated with the College in the letter of Bishop Sutton—was carried into effect. But the College remained dependent upon its parish Church for the celebration of the Mass until the Chapel was expressly licensed for the purpose by Pope Urban the Fifth in April 1364. As early as 1310 the College had become possessed of a messuage containing four schools on the west side of School-street, which were, according to the usual practice, let out to those who had exercises to perform, and thus added to the resources of the College.[16]Some unused land on this property was afterwards conveyed to the University to form part of the site of the Divinity School, and the University still pays the College a quitrent for it.[17]

During this time there seems to have been an active dispute among the Scholars as to the studies which they were permitted to pursue. Bishop Sutton had expressly ordained that they should dwell in the House *until they had completed their course in Arts*. It seemed naturally to follow that it was not lawful for them to go on to a further course of study, for instance, in Divinity, without ceasing their connection with the House. At length in 1325 this inference was formally ratified by the two Extraneous Masters in the presence of all the members as well as four graduates who had formerly been *Fellows* (a title which now first appears in our muniments as a synonym for Scholars) of the House.[18] One of the Extraneous Masters was Nicolas Tingewick, who is otherwise known to us as a benefactor of the Schools of Grammar in the University;[19] and one of the ex-Fellows was Richard

FitzRalph, afterwards Vice-Chancellor of the University and Archbishop of Armagh, the man to whom above all others John Wycliffe, a later member of Balliol, owed the distinguishing elements of his teaching.[20] It was thus decided that Balliol should be a home exclusively of secular learning; and it reads as a curious presage, that thus early in the history of the College the field should be marked out for it in which, in the fifteenth century and again in our own day, it was peculiarly to excel.

But the theologians soon had some compensation, for in 1340 a new endowment was given to the College by Sir Philip Somerville for their special benefit. From the Statutes which accompanied his gift[21] we learn that the existing number of Fellows was sixteen; this he increased to twenty-two (or more, if the funds would allow), with the provision that six of the Fellows should, after they had attained their regency in Arts, enter upon a course of theology, together with canon law if they pleased, extending in ordinary cases over *not more* than twelve or thirteen years from their Master's degree in Arts. Such was the rigour of the demands made upon the theological student in the University system of the middle ages; with what results as to solidity and erudition it is not necessary here to say.

Somerville's Statutes further made several important changes in the constitution of the Hall or House, as it is here called. The Principal still exists, holding precedence among the Fellows, much like that of the President in some of the Colleges at

Cambridge; but he is subordinate to the Master, who is elected by the society subject to the approval of a whole series of Visitors. After election the Master was first to present himself and take oath before the lord of Sir Philip Somerville's manor of Wichnor, and then to be presented by two of the Fellows and the two Extraneous Masters to the Chancellor of the University, or his Deputy, and to the Prior of the Monks of Durham at Oxford. By these his appointment was confirmed. There was thus established a complicated system of a threefold Visitatorial Board. The powers of the lords of Wichnor were indeed probably formal; but those of the Extraneous Masters subsisted side by side by, and to some extent independently of, the Chancellor and the Prior. The former retained their previous authority over the Fellows of the old foundation; they were only associated with the Chancellor and Prior with respect to the new theological Fellows. Finally, over all the Bishop of Durham was placed, as a sort of supreme Visitor, to compel the enforcement of the provisions affecting Somerville's bequest. One wonders how this elaborate scheme worked, and particularly how the society of Balliol liked the supervision of the Prior of Durham College just beyond their garden-wall. But the curious thing is that the benefactor declares that in making these Statutes he intends not to destroy but to confirm the ancient rules and Statutes of the College, as though some part of his extraordinary arrangements had been already in force.[22]

It is easy to guess that the scheme was impracticable, and in fact so early as 1364 a new code had to be drawn up. This was given, under papal authority, by Simon Sudbury, Bishop of London, afterwards Archbishop of Canterbury; but unfortunately it is not preserved. We can only gather from later references that it changed more than it left of the existing Statutes, and that it established Rectors (almost certainly the old Proctors or Extraneous Masters under a new name[23]) to control the Master and Fellows, and possibly a Visitor over all. But the one thing positive is that a right of ultimate appeal was now reserved to the Bishop of London, who thus came to exercise something more than the power which was in later times committed to the Visitor. It was by his authority that in the course of the fifteenth century the property-limitation affecting the Master was abolished, and he was empowered to hold a benefice of whatever value;[24] and that Chaplains were made eligible, equally with the Fellows, for the office of Master.[25] On the one hand the dignity of the Master was increased; on the other the ecclesiastical element was brought to the front.

The latter point becomes more than ever clear in the Statutes which were framed for the College in 1507, and which remained substantially in force until the Universities Commission of 1850. The cause of their promulgation is obscurely referred to the violent and high-handed action of a previous— possibly the existing—Visitor. The matter was laid before Pope Julius the Second, and he deputed the

Bishops of Winchester and Carlisle, or one of them, to draw up an amended body of Statutes which should preclude the repetition of such misgovernment. The Statutes[26] themselves are the work of the Bishop of Winchester, the same Richard Fox who left so enduring a monument of his piety and zeal for learning in his foundation of Corpus Christi College. That foundation however was ten years later, and Fox had not yet, it should seem, formed in his mind the pattern according to which a College in the days of revived and expanded classical study should be modelled. In Balliol he saw nothing but a small foundation with scanty resources and without the making of an important home of learning. The eleemosynary character of its original Statutes he left as it was, only slightly increasing the commons of the Fellows.[27] The Master was to enjoy no greater allowance than Fellows who were Masters of Arts, but he retained the right to hold a benefice. He was no longer necessarily to be chosen from among the Fellows. The unique privilege of the College to elect its own Visitor—how the privilege arose we know not—is expressly declared. But the essential changes introduced in the Statutes of 1507 are those which gave the College a distinctively theological complexion, and those which established a class of students in the College subordinate to the Fellows.

We have seen how the Chaplains had been long rising in dignity, as shown by the fact that, though not Fellows, they had since 1477[28] been equally eligible with the Fellows for the office of Master. By the new Statutes two of the Fellowships were to be filled up by persons already in Priest's orders to act as Chaplains. This was in part a measure of economy, since Fellows could be found to act as Chaplains, but the increased importance of the latter is the more significant since these same Statutes reduced the number of Fellows from at least twenty-two to not less than ten. Besides this, every Fellow of the College was henceforth required to receive Priest's orders within four years after his Master's degree. Doubtless from the beginning all the members of the foundation had been—as indeed all University students were—*clerici*; but this did not necessarily imply more than the simple taking of the tonsure. The obligation of Priest's orders was something very different. The Fellows were as a rule to be Bachelors of Arts at the time of election. Their studies were limited to logic, philosophy, and divinity; but they were free to pursue a course of canon law in the long vacation. The Master's degree was to be taken four years after they had fulfilled the requirements for that of Bachelor. It may be noticed that, instead of their having, according to the modern practice, to pay fees to the College on taking degrees, they received from it on each occasion a gratuity varying according to the dignity of the degree.

The reduction in the number of Fellowships was evidently made in order to provide for the lower rank of what we should now-a-days call Scholars. In the Statutes indeed this name is not found, for it was not forgotten that Fellow and Scholar meant the same thing: and so the old word *scholasticus*, which was often used in the general sense of a "student," was now applied to designate those junior members of the College for whom Scholar was too dignified a title. They were to be "scholastics or servitors," not above eighteen years of age, sufficiently skilled in plain song and grammar. One was assigned to the Master and one to each graduate Fellow, and was nominated by him; he was his private servant. The Scholastics were to live of the remnants of the Fellows' table, to apply themselves to the study of logic, and to attend Chapel in surplices. They had also the preference, in case of equality, in election to Fellowships. We may add that, although the position of these Scholars (as they came to be called) unquestionably improved greatly in the course of time, the Statute affecting them was not revised until 1834.[29]

The Statutes throw a good deal of light on the internal administration of the College at the close of the middle ages. Of the two Deans, the senior had charge of the Library, the junior of the Chapel; they were also to assist the Master generally in matters of discipline. The Master, Fellows, and Scholastics were bound on Sundays and Feast-days to attend matins, with lauds, mass, vespers, and compline; and any Fellow who absented himself was liable to a fine of twopence, while Scholastics were punished with a flogging or otherwise at the discretion of the Master and Dean. The senior Dean presided at the disputations in Logic, which were held on Saturdays weekly throughout the term, except in Lent, and attended by the Bachelors, Scholastics, and junior Masters. The more important disputations in philosophy were held on Wednesdays, and were not intermitted in Lent. They were even held during the long vacation until the 7th September. At these all the Fellows were to be present, and the Master or senior Fellow to preside. Theological disputations were also to be held weekly or fortnightly in term so long as there were three Fellows who were theologians to make a quorum. The College was empowered to receive boarders not on the foundation—what we now call commoners or persons who pay for their commons,—on the condition of their following the prescribed course of study (or in special cases reading civil or canon law); and the fact of their paying seems to have given them a choice of rooms.

The Bible or one of the Fathers was to be read in hall during dinner, and all conversation to be in Latin, unless addressed to one—presumably a guest or a servant—ignorant of the language. French was not permitted, as it was at Queen's,[30] but the Master might give leave to speak English on state occasions,—evidently on such a feast as that of Saint Catherine's day, when guests were invited and an extraordinary allowance of 3s. 4d. was made. The condition of residence was strictly enforced; nevertheless *in order that when, as ofttimes comes to pass, a season of pestilence rages, the Muses be not silent nor study and teaching of none effect by reason of the strength of fear and peril*, it was permitted that the members of the College should withdraw into the country, to a more salubrious place not distant more than twelve miles from Oxford, and there dwell together and carry on their life of study and their accustomed disputations so long as the plague should last.[31] The gates of the College were closed at nine in summer and eight in winter, and the keys deposited with the Master until the morning. Whoever spent the night out of College or entered except by the gate, was punished, a Fellow by a fine of twelve pence, a Scholastic by a flogging.

Having now sketched the constitutional history of the College to the end of the middle ages, we have now to mention a few facts of interest during that time. These group themselves first round the name of John Wycliffe the reformer of religion, and then round the band of learned men and patrons of learning, the reformers of classical study, in the century after him.

In 1360 and 1361 John Wycliffe is mentioned in the College muniments as Master of Balliol. That this was the famous teacher and preacher is not disputed, but there has been much controversy as to his earlier history. That he began his University life at Queen's is indeed known to be a mistake; but the entry of the name in the bursar's rolls at Merton under the date June 1356 has led many to believe that he was a Fellow of that College. It seems nearly certain that there were two John Wycliffes at Oxford at the time; and since the Master of Balliol could only be elected from among the Fellows, the inference seems clear that the Wycliffe who was Master of Balliol cannot have been Fellow of Merton. Besides, it has been pointed out that Wycliffe the reformer's descent from a family settled hard by Barnard Castle, the home of the Balliols, would naturally lead him to enter the Balliol foundation at Oxford; there was another Wycliffe also at Balliol, and three members of the College—one himself Master—were given the benefice of Wycliffe-upon-Tees between 1363 and 1369. Fellowships were obtained by personal influence, and ties of this kind would easily help his admission. Moreover, it was not common for a northerner to enter a College like Merton, which appears in fact to have formed the head-quarters of the southern party at Oxford.[32]

Whatever be the truth in this matter, Wycliffe's connection with Balliol is scarcely a matter of high importance. Men did not in those days receive their education within the College walls. The College was the boarding-house where they dwelt, where they were maintained, and where they attended divine service. It is true that disputations were required to take place within the House; but this was only to ensure their regularity. It was an affair of *discipline*, not of tuition, for the College tutor was an officer undreamt of in those days; the duty of the Principal on these occasions was only to announce the subject, to preside over the discussion, and to keep order. Nor again was Wycliffe Master for more than a short time. He was elected after 1356, and he resigned his post shortly after accepting the College living of

Fillingham in 1361. When in later years he lived in Oxford he took up his abode elsewhere than in Balliol; perhaps at Queen's, then, according to many, at Canterbury Hall, finally at Black Hall: Balliol, it should seem, at that time had room only for members of the foundation. The chief interest residing in his connection with the College lies in the fact, to which we have alluded, that his great exemplar, Richard FitzRalph, had been a Fellow of it about the time of Wycliffe's birth, and was probably still resident in Oxford when Wycliffe came up as a freshman.

The age succeeding Wycliffe's death is the most barren time in the history of the University. Scholastic philosophy had lost its vitality and become over-elaborated into a trivial formalism. Logic had ceased to act as a stimulus to the intellectual powers, and had rather become a clog upon their exercise; and men no longer framed syllogisms to develop their thoughts, but argued first and thought, if at all, afterwards. When, however, towards the middle of the fifteenth century, the revival of learning which we associate with the name of humanism began to influence English students, it was not those who stayed in England who caught its spirit, but those who were able to pursue a second student's course in Italy, and there devote their zeal to the half-forgotten stores of classical Latin literature and the unknown treasure-house of Greek. It was only the ebb of the humanistic movement which in England, as in Germany, turned to refresh and invigorate the study of theology. In the earlier phase, so far as it affected England, Balliol College took a foremost position, though indeed there is less evidence of this activity among the resident members of the House than among those who had passed from it to become the patrons and pioneers of a younger generation of scholars. They were almost all travelled men, who collected manuscripts and had them copied for them, founded libraries and sowed the seed for others to reap the fruit.

First among these in time and in dignity was Humphrey Duke of Gloucester, the Good Duke Humphrey, by whose munificence the University Library grew from a small number of volumes chained on desks in the upper chamber of the Congregation House at Saint Mary's,[33] into a collection of some six hundred manuscripts, of unique value, because, unlike the existing cathedral and monastic libraries, it was formed at the time when attention was being again devoted to classical learning and with the help of the foreign scholars, whose work the Duke loved to encourage, and whom he employed to transcribe and collect for him. His library contained little theology; it was rich in classical Latin literature, in Arabic science (in translations), and in the new literature of Italy, counting at least five volumes of Boccaccio, seven of Petrarch, and two of Dante.[34] Unhappily the whole library was wrecked and brought to nothing in the violence of the reign of King Edward the Sixth, and the three volumes which are now preserved in the re-founded University Library of Sir Thomas Bodley were recovered piecemeal from those who had obtained possession of them in the great days of plunder.[35] That Duke Humphrey was a member of Balliol College is attested by Leland[36] and Bale,[37] but further evidence is wanting.

Almost at the same time as the University Library was thus enriched, five Englishmen are mentioned as students at Ferrara under the illustrious teacher Guarino:[38]four of the five are claimed by our College, William Grey, John Tiptoft, John Free, and John Gunthorpe. Of these, two were men of letters and munificent patrons of learning, the third was himself a scholar of high repute, and the last combined, perhaps in a lesser degree, the characteristics of both classes. William Grey stands in a peculiarly close relation with the College. A member of the noble house of Codnor, he resided for a long time at Cologne in princely style, and maintained a magnificent household. Here he studied logic, philosophy, and theology. He was Chancellor of the University of Oxford from 1440 to 1442, and then went forth again for a more prolonged course of study in Italy, at Florence, Padua, and Ferrara. Removing in 1449 to Rome, as proctor for King Henry the Sixth, he lived there an honoured member of the learned society in the papal city, and continued to collect manuscripts and to have them transcribed and illuminated under his eyes, until he was recalled in 1454 to the Bishopric of Ely. It was his devotion to humanism and his patronage of learned men that naturally found favour with Pope Nicolas the Fifth, and his elevation to the see of Ely was the Pope's act. After his return to England he was not regardless of the affairs of State,—indeed for a time in 1469 and 1470 he was Lord Treasurer,—but his paramount interest still lay in his books and his circle of scholars, himself credited with a knowledge not only of Greek but of Hebrew. It was his desire that his library should be preserved within the walls of his old College. One of its members, Robert Abdy, heartily coöperated with him, and the books—some two hundred in number, and including a *printed* copy of Josephus,—were safely housed in a new building erected for the purpose, probably just before the Bishop's death in 1478. Many of the codices were unhappily destroyed during the reign of King Edward the Sixth, and by Wood's time few of the miniatures in the remaining volumes had escaped mutilation.[39] But it is a good testimony to the loyal spirit in which the College kept the trust committed to them, that no less than a hundred and fifty-two of Grey's manuscripts are still in its possession.[40]

Part of the building in which the library was to find a home was already in existence. The ground-floor, and perhaps the dining-hall (now the library reading-room) adjoining, are attributed to Thomas Chase, who had been Master from 1412 to 1423, and was Chancellor of the University from 1426 to 1430. It was the upper part of the library which was expressly built for the purpose of receiving Bishop Grey's books, and it was the work of Abdy, who as Fellow and then, from 1477 to 1494, as Master devoted himself to the enlargement and adornment of the College buildings, Grey helping him liberally with money. On more than one of the library windows their joint bounty was commemorated:—

> Hos Deus adiecit, Deus his det gaudia celi:
> Abdy perfecit opus hoc Gray presul et Ely.

And again:—

> Conditor ecce novi structus huius fuit Abdy:
> Presul et huic Hely Gray libros contulit edi.

The bishop's coat of arms may still be seen on the panels below the great window of the old solar, now the Master's dining-hall; and elsewhere in the new buildings might be seen the arms of George Nevill, Archbishop of York, the brother of the King-Maker, who was also a member, and would thus appear to have been a benefactor, of the College.[41] The future Archbishop was made Chancellor of the University in 1453 when he was barely twenty-two years of age.[42] His installation banquet, the particulars of which may be read in Savage's *Balliofergus*,[43] was of a prodigality to which it would be hard to find a parallel: it consisted of nine hundred messes of meat, with twelve hundred hogsheads of beer and four hundred and sixteen of wine; and if, as it appears, it was held within the College, the resources of the house must have been severely taxed to make provision for the entertainment of the company, which included twenty-two noblemen, seventeen bishops and abbots, a number of noble ladies, and a multitude of other guests, not to speak of more than two thousand servants.

The other Balliol scholars who followed the instruction of Guarino at Ferrara were a good deal younger than Grey; for Guarino lived on until 1460, when he died at the age of ninety. Tiptoft, who was created Earl of Worcester in his twenty-second year, in 1449, was an enthusiastic traveller. He set out first to Jerusalem; returned to Venice, and then spent several years in study at Ferrara, Padua, and Rome.[44] During this time he collected manuscripts wherever he could lay hands on them, and formed a precious library, with which he afterwards endowed the University of Oxford: its value was reckoned at no less than five hundred marks.[45] His later career as Treasurer and High Constable belongs to the public history of England. It is to be lamented that he brought back from the Italian *renaissance* a spirit of cruelty and recklessness of giving pain, unknown to the humaner middle ages, which made him one of the first victims of the revolution that restored King Henry the Sixth to the throne. But in his death the cause of letters received a blow such as we can only compare with that which it suffered by the execution of the Earl of Surrey in the last days of King Henry the Eighth. It is a strange coincidence that one of the leaders of the restoration movement, one of those chiefly chargeable with Tiptoft's death, was his own Balliol contemporary, Archbishop Nevill, the new Lord Chancellor.[46]

John Free, who graduated in 1450,[47] was a Fellow of Balliol College, and was afterwards a Doctor of Medicine of Padua. During a life spent in Italy he became famous as a poet and a Greek scholar, a civilist and a physician.[48] Pope Paul the Second made him Bishop of Bath and Wells, but he died almost immediately, in 1465.[49] Gunthorpe was his companion in study at Ferrara, and he too became distinguished as a scholar: but he was still more a collector of books, some of which he gave to Jesus College, Cambridge—at one time he was Warden of the King's Hall in that University,—while others came to several libraries at Oxford. Gunthorpe is best known as a man of affairs, a diplomatist and minister of state. He became Dean of Wells, and is still remembered in that city by the *guns* with which he adorned the Deanery he built.[50] He survived all his fellow-scholars we have named, and died in 1498.[51]

From the end of the middle ages down to the present century Balliol College presents none of those characteristics of distinction which we have remarked in the fifteenth century. During this time, indeed, although in the nature of things a large number of men of note continued to receive their education at Oxford, there was no College or Colleges which could be said to occupy anything like a position of peculiar eminence or dignity. In the general decline of learning, education, and manners, Balliol College appears even to have sunk below most of its rivals, and its annals show little more than a dreary record of lazy torpor and bad living.[52] The Statutes of the College received no alterations of importance. Its power to choose its own Visitor was indeed for a time overridden by the Bishop of Lincoln, who was considered *ex officio* Visitor until Bishop Barlow's death in 1691;[53] and the *Scholastici* became distinguished as *Scholares* from an inferior rank of *Servitores* with which the Statutes of 1507 had identified them. Another lower class of students, called Batellers, also came into existence. Every Commoner was required by a rule of 1574 to be under the Master or one of the Fellows as his Tutor;[54] Scholars being apparently *ipso facto* subject to the Fellows who nominated them. In 1610 it was ordered, with the Visitor's consent, that Fellow Commoners might be admitted to the College and be free from "public correction," except in the case of scandalous offences; they were not bound to exhibit reverence to the Fellows in the quadrangle unless they encountered them face to face,—*reverentiam Sociis in quadrangulo consuetam non nisi in occursu praestent*. Every such Commoner was bound to pay at least five pounds on admission for the purchase of plate or books for the College.[55] The sum was in 1691 raised to ten pounds.[56] As the disputations in hall tended to become less and less of a reality, and the lectures in the schools became a pure matter of routine for the younger Masters, provision had to be made for something in the way of regular lectures, but fixed tuition-fees were not yet invented, and so the richest living in the gift of the College—that of Fillingham in Lincolnshire, which had been usually held by the Master and was now attached to his office—was in 1571 charged with the payment of £8 13*s*..4*d*. to three Prelectors chosen by the College who should lecture in hall on Greek, dialectic, and rhetoric.[57] The lectures, it was soon after decided, were to be held at least thrice a week during term, except on Feast Days or when the lecturer was ill.

Any one who failed to fulfil his duty—either in person or by a deputy—was to pay twopence *to be consumed by the other Fellows at dinner or supper on the Sunday next following.*[58] In 1695 the famous Dr. Busby, who had before shown himself a friend to the College,[59] established a Catechetical Lecture to be given on thirty prescribed subjects through the year, at which all members of the College were bound to be present.[60] This Lecture was maintained until recent years.

During the two centuries following the reign of King Edward the Third the College had received little or no addition to its corporate endowments, though, as we have seen, it had been largely helped by donations towards its buildings, and above all by the foundation of its precious library.[61] Between the date of the accession of Queen Elizabeth and the year 1677, in the renewed zeal for academical foundations which marked that period, the College received a number of new benefactions; and these introduced a new element into its composition. Hitherto all the Fellowships had been open without restriction of place of birth or education; and although it is likely that the College in its earlier days drew its recruits mainly from the north of England, yet there was nothing in the Statutes to authorize the connection. The College, it is true, was a very close corporation, for Fellow nominated Scholar, and out of the Scholars the Fellows were generally elected. Still, in contradistinction to the majority of Colleges, there were no local limitations upon eligibility to Scholarships. The new endowments, on the other hand, with the exception of those of the Lady Periam, were all so limited. First, by a bequest of Dr. John Bell, formerly Bishop of Worcester, two Scholarships confined to natives of his diocese were founded in 1559,[62] and in 1605 Sir William Dunch established another for the benefit of Abingdon School.[63] A little later Balliol nearly became possessed of the much larger endowment, of seven Fellowships and six Scholarships, attached to the same school by William Tisdale. Indeed part of the money was paid over, six Scholars were appointed, and Cesar's lodgings—of which more hereafter—were bought for their reception.[64] But a subsequent arrangement diverted the endowment, which in 1624 helped to change the ancient Broadgates Hall into Pembroke College.[65] In the meanwhile a more considerable benefaction, also connected with a local school, accrued to Balliol between 1601 and 1615, when in execution of the will of Peter Blundell one Fellowship and one Scholarship were founded to be held by persons educated at Blundell's Grammar School at Tiverton, and nominated by the Trustees of the School.[66] The next endowment in order of time was that of Elizabeth, widow of Chief Baron Periam and sister of Francis Bacon. The nomination to the Fellowship and two Scholarships which she founded in 1620, she reserved to herself for her lifetime; afterwards they were to be filled up in the same manner as the other Fellowships of the College.[67]

After the Restoration two separate benefactions set up that close connection between the College and

Scotland which saved Balliol from sinking into utter obscurity in the century following, and which has since contributed to it a large share of its later fame. Bishop Warner of Rochester, who died in 1666, bequeathed to the College the annual sum of eighty pounds for the support of four scholars from Scotland to be chosen by the Archbishop of Canterbury and the Bishop of Rochester; and about ten years later certain Exhibitions were founded by Mr. John Snell for persons nominated by Glasgow University. The latter varied in number according to the proceeds of Mr. Snell's estate; at one time they were as many as ten and of the yearly value of £116, but their number and value have since been reduced. Both of these foundations were expressly designed to promote the interests of the Episcopal Church in Scotland.[68] Their importance in the history of the College cannot be overestimated, and it is to them that it owes such names among its members as Adam Smith, Sir William Hamilton, and Archbishop Tait, to say nothing of a great company of distinguished Scotsmen now living. The Exhibitioners have also as a rule offered an admirable example of frugal habits and hard work; and perhaps it was in consideration of their national thriftiness that the rooms assigned them are noticed in 1791 as mean and incommodious.[69]

Among more recent benefactions to the College the most important is that of Miss Hannah Brakenbury who, besides the questionable service of contributing towards the rebuilding of the front quadrangle, endowed eight Scholarships for the encouragement of the studies of Law and Modern History. Nor should we omit to mention the two Exhibitions of £100 a-year each, founded under the will of Richard Jenkyns, formerly Master, which are awarded by examination to members of the College, and the list of holders of which is of exceptional brilliancy. But in recent years the number of Scholarships and Exhibitions has been most of all increased not by means of any specific endowment but by savings from the annual internal income of the College. In pursuance of the ordinances of the Universities' Commission of 1877, Balliol became the owner of New Inn Hall on the death of its late Principal; and the proceeds of the sale of the Hall, when effected, are to be applied to the establishment of Exhibitions for poor students.

We now resume the history of the College buildings. We have seen that the Chapel was built early in the reign of King Edward the Third, and that the hall and library buildings were added in the following century.[70] A new Chapel was built between 1521 and 1529,[71] which lasted until the present century. It contained a muniment-room or treasury, "which," says Anthony Wood, "is a kind of vestry, joyning on the S. side of the E. end of the chappel;"[72] and there was a window opening into it, as at Corpus, from the library.[73] With the present Chapel in one's mind it is hard to estimate the loss which from a picturesque point of view the College has suffered by the destruction of its predecessor. In modern times Oxford has ever been a prey to architects. The rebuilding of Queen's is an example of what happily was not carried into effect at Magdalen and Brasenose in the last century; but in the present, Balliol is almost peculiar in the extent to which these depredations have run, and those who remember the line of buildings of the Chapel and library as they looked from the Fellows' garden say that for harmony and quiet charm they were of their kind unsurpassed in Oxford. Among the special features of the old Chapel were the painted windows, particularly the great east window given by Lawrence Stubbs in 1529. The fragments of this are distributed among the side windows of the modern Chapel, and even in their scattered state are highly regarded by lovers of glass-painting.[74]Of the later buildings of the College, "Cesar's lodgings" must not pass without notice. It had its name from Henry Caesar, afterwards Dean of Carlisle—the brother of Sir Julius Caesar, Master of the Rolls (1614-1636),—and stood opposite to where the "Martyrs' Memorial" now is. Being currently known as *Cesar*, an opposite stack of buildings to the south of it was naturally called *Pompey*. The two were pulled down, not before it was necessary, in the second quarter of the present century.[75]Hammond's lodgings, which came to the College in Queen Elizabeth's time, and stood on the site of the old Master's little garden and the present Master's house, were occupied by the Blundell and Periam Fellows.[76]

Before the front of the College was a close, planted with trees like that in front of St. John's.

"Stant Baliolenses maiore cacumine moles,
Et sua frondosis praetexunt atria ramis;

Nec tamen idcirco Trinam sprevere minorem
Aut sibi subiectam comitem sponsamve recusant—"

ran some verses of 1667.[77] But if we may judge from a story to be told hereafter of the respective prosperity of the two Colleges, it was rather Trinity which had the right to look down upon its rival at that time. In the eighteenth century the buildings of Balliol were considerably enlarged by the erection of two staircases westward of the Master's house, by Mr. Fisher of Beere, and of three running north of these over against St. Mary Magdalen Church. The fronts of the east side of the quadrangle, reputed to be the most ancient part of the College, and of part of the south side adjoining it, were rebuilt.[78] The direction of the hall was reversed, so that instead of the passage into the garden, the entrance to the hall, and the buttery being beneath the Master's lodgings, they were placed on the northern extremity of the hall.[79] In the present reign a further addition to the College was made in the place of the dilapidated "Cesar," and with it a back porch with a tower above it was built. Then followed the rebuilding of the Chapel and, after an interval, of two sides of the front quadrangle and of the Master's house. A little later the garden was gradually enclosed by buildings on the north side, which were completed in 1877 by a hall with common room, buttery, kitchen, and a chemical laboratory beneath it.

It is very difficult to obtain any accurate knowledge of the number of persons ordinarily inhabiting a College in past times. A few lists happen to have been preserved, but their accuracy is not free from suspicion. Thus, a census of 1552 enumerates under the head of Balliol seven Masters, six Bachelors, and seventeen others, these seventeen including the manciple, butler, cook, and scullion.[80] In ten years this list of thirty names has grown to sixty-five: six Masters, thirteen Bachelors, and forty-six others, eight of whom were Scholars, five "poor scholars"—presumably batellers,—and four servants.[81] By 1612 the number appears to have nearly doubled, and comprises the Master and eleven Fellows, thirteen Scholars, seventy commoners, twenty-two "poor scholars," and ten servants; in all a hundred and twenty-seven:[82] a total the magnitude of which is the more perplexing since the College matriculations between 1575 and 1621 averaged hardly more than fifteen a-year.[83] No doubt, in the days when several students shared a bedroom, it was possible even for a small College to give house-room to a far larger number than we can imagine at the present time; but still it is hard to understand how so many as a hundred and twenty persons could be accommodated in the then existing buildings of Balliol. According to the procuratorial cycle of 1629, Balliol ranks with University, Lincoln, Jesus, and Pembroke, among the smallest Colleges.[84] In recent times, taking years by chance, we find the number of Fellows, Scholars, and Commoners in the *University Calendar* for 1838 to be 102, in that for 1859 to be 122, in 1878 about 195, and in 1891 about 187.[85] That the College has been able to count so many resident members is partly owing to the extension of the College buildings, but much more to the modern

Statute whereby all members of the College are not necessarily required to live within the College walls.

Notices of the domestic history of Balliol during the sixteenth, seventeenth, and eighteenth centuries are surprisingly scanty. In the following pages we have gathered together such particulars as we have thought of sufficient interest to be recorded in a brief sketch like the present. Early in the seventeenth century the life of the College was varied by the presence of two Greek students, sent over by Cyril Lucaris, the Patriarch of Constantinople, to whom England owes the gift of the Codex Alexandrinus. One of these, Metrophanes Critopulos, became Patriarch of Alexandria. The other, Nathaniel Conopios, we are told "spake and wrote the genuine Greek (for which he was had in great Veneration in his Country), others using the vulgar only," and was a proficient in music. He took the degree of B.D., and was made Bishop of Smyrna. Evelyn remarks that he was the first he "ever saw drink coffee, wch custom came not into England until 30 years after."[86] Our next note is of a different character. Soon after the Scholars endowed by Tisdale[87] were established in Cesar's lodgings, a dispute arose between one of them, named Crabtree, and Ferryman Moore, a freshman of three weeks' standing. Crabtree called Moore an "undergraduate" and pulled his hair; whereupon Moore drew his knife and stabbed him so that he died. In the trial that followed Moore pleaded benefit of clergy and was condemned to burning in the hand, but at the petition of the Vice-Chancellor, Mayor, and other Justices, received the Royal pardon on the 19th November, 1624,—the very year in which the benefaction that had brought his victim to Balliol was settled in its lasting home in Pembroke College.[88] A little later, in 1631, we find one Thorne, a member of Balliol, preaching at St. Mary's against the King's Declaration on Religion of 1628: he was expelled the University by Royal order.[89] The famous John Evelyn, who was admitted a Fellow Commoner of the College in May 1637, being then in his seventeenth year, tells us that "the Fellow Com'uners in Balliol were no more exempt from Exercise than the meanest scholars there, and my Father sent me thither to one Mr. George Bradshaw," who was Master from 1648 to 1651. "I ever," he adds, "thought my Tutor had parts enough, but as his ambition made him much suspected of yᵉ College, so his grudge to Dr. Lawrence, the governor of it (whom he afterwards supplanted), tooke up so much of his tyme, that he seldom or never had the opportunity to discharge his duty to his scholars. This I perceiving, associated myself with one Mr. James Thicknesse, (then a young man of the Foundation, afterwards a Fellow of the House,) by whose learned and friendly conversation I received great advantage. At my first arrival, Dr. Parkhurst was Master; and after his discease, Dr. Lawrence, a chaplaine of his Ma'ties and Margaret Professor, succeeded, an acute and learned person; nor do I much reproach his severity, considering that the extraordinary remissenesse of discipline had (til his coming) much detracted from the reputation of that Colledg." Later Evelyn mentions that his Tutor managed his expenses during his first year. In January 1640 "Came my Bro. Richard from schole to be my chamber-fellow at the University," so that even Fellow Commoners did not always have rooms to themselves. It is noticeable that the chief studies which Evelyn speaks of engaging in are those of "the daucing and vaulting Schole" and music; and one is not surprised to read that when he quitted Oxford in April 1640, without taking a degree, and made his residence in the Middle Temple, he should observe, "My being at the University, in regard of these avocations, was of very small benefit to me."[90]

When King Charles was at Oxford, Balliol, with the great majority of Colleges, handed over its plate to him, 20 January 1642/3. The weight of the metal was only 41*lb.* 4 *oz.*, less than that of any other College recorded.[91] When the Parliamentary Visitation began in 1647. Thomas Lawrence was Master and also Margaret Professor of Divinity. After a while he submitted to the Visitors' authority and then resigned his offices. In the Mastership he was succeeded by George Bradshaw, Evelyn's tutor.[92] Apparently about half the members of the College in time made their submission.[93] From 1651 the Mastership was held by Henry Savage, a man of cultivation, who had travelled in France, and here at least deserves to be remembered as the author of the first and only history of his College, a work to which we have been constantly indebted for its transcripts and extracts from the muniments.[94] On his death in 1672 he was succeeded by Thomas Good,—one of the first of those who submitted to the Parliamentary

Visitors[95]—whom Wood describes as when resident in College "a frequent preacher, yet always esteemed an honest and harmless puritan."[96] He is best known from the stories which Humphrey Prideaux tells about him. According to him the Master "is a good honest old tost, and understands business well enough, but is very often guilty of absurditys, which rendreth him contemptible to the yong men of the town."[97] One of these stories he does "not well beleeve; but however you shall have it. There is over against Baliol College a dingy, horrid, scandalous alehouse, fit for none but draymen and tinkers and such as by goeing there have made themselves equally scandalous. Here the Baliol men continually ly, and by perpetuall bubbeing ad art to their natural stupidity to make themselves perfect sots. The head, beeing informed of this, called them togeather, and in a grave speech informed them of the mischiefs of that hellish liquor cald ale, that it destroyed both body and soul, and adviced them by noe means to have anything more to do with it; but on of them, not willing soe tamely to be preached out of his beloved liquor, made reply that the Vice-Chancelour's men drank ale at the Split Crow,[98] and why should not they to? The old man, being nonplusd with this reply, immediately packeth away to the Vice-Chancelour,[99] and informed him of the ill example his fellows gave the rest of the town by drinkeing ale, and desired him to prohibit them for the future; but Bathurst, not likeing his proposall, being formerly and [sic] old lover of ale himselfe, answered him roughly, that there was noe hurt in ale, and that as long as his fellows did noe worse he would not disturb them, and soe turned the old man goeing; who, returneing to his colledge, calld his fellows again and told them he had been with the Vice-Chancelour, and that he told them there was noe hurt in ale; truely he thought there was, but now, beeing informed of the contrary, since the Vice-Chancelour gave his men leave to drinke ale, he would give them leave to; soe that now they may be sots by authority."[100]

Another story of the same time connecting Balliol and Trinity Colleges is told of Dr. Bathurst, President of Trinity and the "Vice-Chancelour" named in the foregoing quotation. "A striking instance," says Thomas Warton, "of zeal for his college, in the dotage of old age, is yet remembered. Balliol College had suffered so much in the outrages of the grand rebellion, that it remained almost in a state of desolation for some years after the restoration: a circumstance not to be suspected from its flourishing condition ever since. Dr. Bathurst was perhaps secretly pleased to see a neighbouring, and once rival society, reduced to this condition, while his own flourished beyond all others. Accordingly, one afternoon he was found in his garden, which then ran almost contiguous to the east side of Balliol-college, throwing stones at the windows with much satisfaction, as if happy to contribute his share in completing the appearance of its ruin."[101]

Indeed, that Balliol was by no means in a state of prosperity after the Restoration may be gathered from the facts that it is described as possessing but half the income of Exeter, Oriel, and Queen's, and containing but twenty-five commoners;[102] and that in 1681 the College was taken by the opposition Peers for lodgings during the Oxford Parliament.[103] In January the Earl of Shaftesbury, together with the Duke of Monmouth, the Earls of Bedford and Essex, and twelve other Peers, subscribed a petition praying that the Parliament should sit not at Oxford but at Westminster; and when they found they could not move the King, Shaftesbury promptly set about securing rooms at Oxford. John Locke, who conducted negotiations for him, reported on the 6th February that the Rector of Exeter would be happy to place three rooms in his house at his Lordship's disposal, "but that the whole college could by no means be had." Dr. Wallis's house was also inspected, and it was soon discovered that Balliol College was at the Peers' service. From a letter however from Shaftesbury to Locke, of the 22nd February, it seems that he himself and Lord Grey occupied Wallis's house, and "dieted" elsewhere, no doubt at Balliol.[104] On their departure Shaftesbury and fourteen other Peers—almost exactly the same list as that of the petitioners of the 25th January— presented to the College "a large bole, with a cover to it, all double guilt, 167 *oz.* 10 *dwts*,"[105] which was melted down into tankards many years since.

The history of the College during the greater part of the eighteenth century coincides with the life of Dr. Theophilus Leigh, who took his Bachelor's degree from Corpus in 1712, was appointed Master of Balliol fifteen years later, and held his office until 1785. Hearne records the circumstances of his election in a way which implies that he owed his success to an informality, with more than a hint of nepotism on the part of the Visitor.[106] Six years after his death Martin Routh was elected President of Magdalen College. He died in 1855; so that the academical lives of these two men overlapping just at the extremities cover a period of not less than a hundred and forty-six years. In Leigh's days Balliol was sunk in the heavy and sluggish decrepitude which characterized Oxford at large. The *Terrae Filius*—doubtless an authority to be received with caution—reviles the Fellows for the perpetual fines and sconces with which they burthened the undergraduates;[107] and it is stated that Adam Smith, when a member of the College, was severely reprimanded for reading Hume.[108] It is certain that, at least when Leigh was first a Fellow, the College did not even trust the undergraduates with knives and forks, for these, we are assured, were chained to the table in hall, while the trenchers were made of wood.[109] There was "a laudable custom" which lasted on to a later generation "of the Dean's Visiting the Undergraduats Chambers at 9 o' Clock at Night, to see that they kept good hours."[110]

It was before nine o'clock on the 23rd February 1747-8 that a party was gathered there which led to serious consequences. In spite of the failure of the rebellion of 1745 the zealous ardour of some Jacobite members of the College waxed so warm that they and their guests paraded down the Turl shouting *G—d bless k—g J——s*, until they reached Winter's coffee-house near the High Street, where Mr. Richard Blacow, a Canon of Windsor, was sitting "in company with several Gentlemen of the University and an Officer in his Regimental Habit," about seven o'clock in the evening. Mr. Blacow tells us with righteous indignation how he not only heard treasonable and seditious expressions in favour of the exiled family, but also such cries as *d—n K—g G——e.* Being a young Master of Arts and very much on his dignity, he went forth into the street to check the outrage, but was only met by a rough handling on the part of the rioters, who stood shouting in St. Mary Hall Lane in front of Oriel College; so that Mr. Blacow was glad to make good his retreat within the College gate. Reappearing after a while he was on the point of being attacked, when his assailant was carried off by the Proctor. Another, Luxmoore, B.A. of Balliol, took to his heels. After this the loyal Canon sought in vain to induce the Vice-Chancellor to take steps for the trial of the offenders; but he could by no means be prevailed upon. At length, as the scandal spread abroad, the Secretary of State, the Duke of Newcastle, requested Mr. Blacow to lay an information before him; and three members of the University were tried for treason in the King's Bench. Of the two who belonged to Balliol one, Luxmoore, was acquitted; the other Whitmore, with Dawes of St. Mary Hall,— both undergraduates barely twenty years of age,— were sentenced to a fine, to two years' imprisonment, to find securities for their good behaviour for seven years, "to walk immediately round Westminster Hall with a libel affixed to their foreheads denoting their crime and sentence, and to ask pardon of the several courts."[111]

The letters of Robert Southey, who entered Balliol as a commoner in 1792, do not give an unfavourable impression of the condition of the College just after Leigh's death. His own peculiarities of taste and temper placed him doubtless in uncongenial surroundings,—he refused the assistance of the College barber and wore his curly hair long,—but his complaint is not of the College but of the University system in general. The authorities are "men remarkable only for great wigs and little wisdom." "With respect to its superiors, Oxford only exhibits waste of wigs and want of wisdom; with respect to the undergraduates, every species of abandoned excess." In his second year, with the haughty air of a senior man, he found the freshmen "not estimable"; but he made friends in College, and two of his first four comrades in the great Pantisocratic scheme were Balliol men. Even his tutor, Thomas Howe, delighted him by being "half a democrat," and still more by the remark—"Mr. Southey, you won't learn any thing by my lectures, Sir; so, if you have any studies of your own, you had better pursue them." Rowing and swimming, Southey used to say, were all he learned at Oxford; but with two years' residence, and a term missed in them, with Pantisocracy and *Joan of Arc*, we may doubt whether it was all Oxford's fault.[112]

The real revival of Balliol College began after the election of John Parsons as Master in 1798. He succeeded to the Vice-Chancellorship in 1807 unexpectedly, on the death of Dr. Richards, Rector of Exeter, after a single year of office. "He was a good scholar," says Bedel Cox, "and an impressive preacher, though he did not preach often; above all, he was thoroughly conversant with University matters, having been for several years the leading, or rather the working, man in the Hebdomadal Board. Indeed, he had the great merit of elaborating the details of the Public Examination Statute at the end of the last century. His subsequent promotion" to the Bishopric of Peterborough "was considered as the well-earned reward of that his great work. Dr. Parsons had also the credit of laying the foundation of that collegiate and tutorial system which Dr. Jenkyns afterwards so successfully carried out."[113] Those who may think the establishment of the examination system a questionable benefit may be comforted by knowing that for many years it was conducted entirely *vivâ voce*, while the requirements for degrees in the time preceding the change were so notoriously perfunctory that the old method could not possibly be maintained. In the Colleges too the tutorial system, in its principle—as still at Cambridge—a disciplinary system, had long outlived its vitality; and Dr. Parsons deserves credit not merely for invigorating it, but for setting on a firm foundation an organization for teaching undergraduates as well as for keeping them in order.

But it was not to be expected that these reforms should bear full fruit for many years. Sir William Hamilton, who was at Balliol from 1807 to 1810, describes himself as "so plagued by these foolish lectures of the College tutors that I have little time to do anything else—Aristotle to-day, ditto to-morrow; and I believe that if the ideas furnished by Aristotle to these numbskulls were taken away, it would be doubtful whether there remained a single notion. I am quite tired of such uniformity of study."[114] He was however unfortunately placed under an eccentric tutor named Powell, who lived furtively in rooms over the College gate and was never seen out except at dusk. "For a short time Hamilton and his tutor kept up the formality of an hour's lecture. This however soon ceased, and for the last three years of his College life Hamilton was left to follow his own inclinations."[115] But, as Dr. Parsons said, "he is one of those, and they are rare, who are best left to themselves. He will turn out a great scholar, and we shall get the credit of making him so, though in point of fact we shall have done nothing for him whatever."[116] Yet in later years the philosopher speaks of the "College in which I spent the happiest of the happy years of youth, which is never recollected but with affection, and from which, as I gratefully acknowledge, I carried into life a taste for those studies which have contributed the most interesting of my subsequent pursuits."[117]

Hamilton's freshman's account of the daily life and manners of the College deserves quotation: its date is 13 May, 1807. "No boots are allowed to be worn here, or trousers or pantaloons. In the morning we wear white cotton stockings, and before dinner regularly dress in silk stockings, &c. After dinner we go to one another's rooms and drink some wine, then go to chapel at half-past five, and walk, or sail on the river, after that. In the morning we go to chapel at seven, breakfast at nine, fag all the forenoon, and dine at half-past three."[118]

Under Dr. Parsons as Master, and Mr. Jenkyns as Tutor and then Vice-Master on the Head's elevation to the see of Peterborough, the College continued steadily to improve. Mr. Jenkyns succeeded to the Mastership on the Bishop's death in 1819. But there were still two points in the constitution of the College which were felt to be out of keeping with the spirit of modern education. One was the direct nomination of each Scholar, except those on the Blundell Foundation, by a particular Fellow in turn; and the other, the obligation under which all the Fellows lay of taking Priest's orders. The former arrangement was revised by a new Statute sanctioned by the Visitor in 1834, which placed all the Scholarships, with the exception named, in the appointment of the Master and Fellows after examination. At the same time the College yielded to the tendency of the time which brought undergraduates to the University older than formerly, and raised the age below which candidates were admissible to scholarships from eighteen to nineteen.[119] The other question was settled by a decision in 1838 that the obligation of Fellows to take holy orders did not debar candidates from election who had no such purpose in mind, provided of course that their tenure of Fellowships terminated at the date by which according to the Statutes they were bound to be ordained.[120]

In the same year that this decision was given Mr. Benjamin Jowett, afterwards Regius Professor of Greek and since 1870 Master of the College, was elected to a Fellowship. He has committed to writing in a most interesting letter to the son of William George Ward, famous for his share in the Oxford Movement and for his degradation by Convocation in 1845, his recollections of the Fellows as they were when he was elected to their membership; but we have only room here for a short extract from his account of Master Jenkyns, "who was very different from any of the Fellows, and was held in considerable awe by them. He was a gentleman of the old school, in whom were represented old manners, old traditions, old prejudices, a Tory and a Churchman, high and dry, without much literature, but having a good deal of character. He filled a great space in the eyes of the undergraduates. 'His young men,' as he termed them, speaking in an accent which we all remember, were never tired of mimicking his voice, drawing his portrait, and inventing stories about what he said and did…. He was a considerable actor, and would put on severe looks to terrify Freshmen, but he was really kind-hearted and indulgent to them. He was in a natural state of war with the Fellows and Scholars on the Close Foundation; and many ludicrous stories were told of his behaviour to them, of his dislike to smoking, and of his enmity to dogs.... He was much respected, and his great services to the College have always been acknowledged."[121]

When we consider the progress made by Balliol College during the years between 1813, when Jenkyns became Vice-Master, and 1854, when he died, we may perhaps venture to question whether the balance between "old manners, old traditions, old prejudices," and new manners, new traditions, new prejudices, does not hang very evenly. But into this we are not called upon to enter. The Statutes made by the University Commission of 1850 made fewer changes in the condition of Balliol than of most Colleges, because the most inevitable reforms had been carried into effect already. The Close Fellowships were opened, and the majority of the Fellowships were released from clerical obligations. The moment which witnessed the promulgation of the new Statutes witnessed also the death of Dean Jenkyns and the succession of Robert Scott. But here we may well conclude the story of the Balliol of the past. To carry it down further would require much more space than the limits of this chapter permit; and besides, the Balliol of the present is a new College in a different sense from perhaps any other College in Oxford. No other College has so distinctly parted company with its traditions beyond the lifetime of men now living. The commemoration of founders and benefactors on St. Luke's Day has long been given up, and the Latin grace in hall has not been heard for many years. The College buildings are for the greater part the work of the present reign. In the new hall the portraits which strike the eye behind the high table are all those of men who were alive when the hall was opened in 1877. Bishop Parsons and Dean Jenkyns are seen above them, while in the obscurity of the roof may be discerned the pictures— unhistorical, as in other Colleges, it need not be said—of John Balliol and Dervorguilla his wife. A visitor from the last century would see little that he could recognize; but when he entered the common room after dinner he would notice one highly conservative custom revived. In 1773 it had been the lament of older men, that

> "Nec Camerae Communis amor, qua rarus ad alta
> Nunc tubus emittit gratos laquearia fumos;"[122]

but in late years the practice of smoking has been regularly admitted even in those sacred precincts.

Every College has its own ideal, and that of Balliol has been by a steady policy adapted to the modern spirit of work, employing the best materials not so much for learning as an end in itself as a means towards practical success in life. In this field, in the distinctions of the schools, of the courts, and of public life, it has been seldom rivalled by any other College. But it is remarkable that in the long and distinguished list of its men of mark we find, speaking only of the dead, no Statesman and not many scholars of the first rank. The College has excelled rather in its practical men of affairs, diplomatists, judges, members of parliament, civil service officials, college tutors, and schoolmasters. At the present moment it counts among former members no less than seven of her Majesty's Judges and seven Heads of Oxford Colleges. But to show that another side of culture has been represented at Balliol in the present reign, we must not forget the band of Balliol poets, Arthur Hugh Clough, Matthew Arnold, and Algernon Charles Swinburne.

III.
MERTON COLLEGE.[123]

BY THE HON. GEORGE C. BRODRICK, D.C.L.,
WARDEN OF MERTON COLLEGE.

In the year 1274, "the House of the Scholars of Merton," since called Merton College, was solemnly founded, and settled upon its present site in Oxford, by Walter de Merton, Chancellor to King Henry III. and King Edward I. Ten years earlier, in the midst of the Civil War, this remarkable man had already established a collegiate brotherhood, under the same name, at Malden, in Surrey, but with an educational branch at Oxford, where twenty students were to be maintained out of the corporate revenues. The Statutes of 1264 were very slightly modified in 1270; the Statutes of 1274, issued on the conclusion of the peace, and sealed by the King himself, were a mature development of the original design, worked out with a statesman-like foresight. These statutes are justly regarded as the archetype of the College system, not only in the University of Oxford, but in that of Cambridge, where they were adopted as a model by the founder of Peterhouse, the oldest of Cambridge Colleges. In every important sense of the word, Merton, with its elaborate code of statutes and conventual buildings, its chartered rights of self-government, and its organized life, was the first of English Colleges, and the founder of Merton was indirectly the founder of Collegiate Universities.

His idea took root and bore fruit, because it was inspired by a true sympathy with the needs of the University, where the subjects of study were then as frivolous as it was the policy of Rome to make them, where religious houses with the Mendicant Friars almost monopolized learning, and where the streets were the scenes of outrageous violence and license. To combine monastic discipline with secular learning, and so to create a great seminary for the secular clergy, was the aim of Walter de Merton. The inmates of the College were to live by a common rule under a common head; but they were to take no vows, to join no monastic fraternity, on pain of deprivation, and to undertake no ascetic or ceremonial obligations. Their occupation was to be study, not the *claustralis religio* of the older religious orders, nor the more practical and popular self-devotion of the Dominicans and Franciscans, "the intrusive and anti-national militia of the Papacy." They were all to read Theology, but not until after completing their full course in Arts; and they were encouraged to seek employment in the great world. As the value of the endowments should increase, the number of scholars was to be augmented; and those who might win an ample fortune (*uberior fortuna*) were enjoined to show their gratitude by advancing the interests of "the house." While their duties and privileges were strictly defined by the statutes, they were expressly empowered to amend the statutes themselves in accordance with the growing requirements of future ages, and even to migrate from Oxford elsewhere in case of necessity. The Archbishop of Canterbury, as Visitor by virtue of his office, was entrusted with the duty of enforcing statutable obligations.

The Merton Statutes of 1274, as interpreted and supplemented by several Ordinances and Injunctions of Visitors, remained in force within living memory, and the spirit of them never became obsolete. The Ordinances of Archbishop Kilwarby, issued as early as 1276, with the Founder's express sanction, chiefly regulate the duties of College officers, but are interesting as recognizing the existence of out-College students. Those of Archbishop Peckham, issued in 1284, are directed to check various abuses already springing up, among which is included the encroachment of professional and utilitarian studies into the curriculum of the College; the admission of medical students on the plea that Medicine is a branch of Physics is rigorously prohibited, and the study of Canon Law is condemned except under strict conditions and with the Warden's leave. The Ordinances of Archbishop Chicheley, issued in 1425, disclose the prevalence of mercenary self-interest in the College, manifested in the neglect to fill up Fellowships, in wasteful management of College property, and so forth. The ordinances of Archbishop Laud, issued in 1640, are specially framed, as might be expected, to revive wholesome rules of discipline, entering minutely into every detail of College life. Chapel-attendance, the use of surplices and hoods, the restriction of intercourse between Masters and Bachelors, the etiquette of meals, the strength of the College ale, the custody of the College keys, the costume to be worn by members of the College in the streets, and the careful registration in a note-book of every Fellow's departure and return—such were among the numerous punctilios of College economy which shared the attention of this indefatigable prelate with the gravest affairs of Church and State. A century later, in 1733, very similar Injunctions were issued by Archbishop Potter; and on several other occasions undignified disputes between the Wardens and Fellows called for the decisive interference of the Visitor. But the general impression derived from a perusal of the Visitors' Injunctions is, that a reasonable and honest construction of the Statutes would have rendered their interference unnecessary, and that it was a signal proof of the Founder's sagacity to provide such a safeguard against corporate selfishness and intestine discord, in days when public spirit was a rare virtue.

While the University of Oxford has played a greater part in our national history than any other corporation except that of the City of London, the external annals of Merton, as of other Colleges, are comparatively meagre and humble. The corporate life of the College, dating from the Barons' War, flowed on in an equable course during a century of French Wars, followed by the Wars of the Roses. We know, indeed, that in early times Merton was sometimes represented by its Wardens and Fellows in camps and ecclesiastical synods, as well as in Courts, both at home and abroad. For instance, Bradwardine, afterwards Archbishop, rendered service to Edward III. in negotiations with the French King; Warden Bloxham was employed during the same reign in missions to Scotland and Ireland; two successive Wardens, Rudborn and Gylbert, with several Fellows, are said to have followed Henry V. as chaplains into Normandy, and to have been present at Agincourt; Kemp, a Fellow and future Archbishop, attended the Councils of Basle and Florence; and Abendon, Gylbert's successor in the Wardenship, earned fame as delegate of the University at the Council of Constance. But the College, as a body, was unmoved either by continental expeditions, or by the storms which racked English society in the Middle Ages; and its "Register," which commences in 1482, is for the most part ominously silent on the great political commotions of later periods. During the reign of Henry VII., indeed, occasional mention of public affairs is to be found in its pages. Such are the references to extraordinary floods, storms, or frosts; to the Sweating Sickness; to the Battle of Bosworth Field; to Perkin Warbeck's Revolt, and other insurrectionary movements of that age; to notable executions; to the birth, marriage, and death of Prince Arthur; to the death of Pope Alexander VI., and to Lady Margaret's endowment of a Theological Professorship. After the reign of Henry VII. the brief entries in this domestic chronicle, like the monotonous series of cases in the Law Reports, almost ignore Civil War and Revolution, betraying no change of style or conscious spirit of innovation; and it is from other sources that we must learn the events which enable us to interpret some passages in the Register itself.

Whether John Wyclif was actually a Fellow of Merton is still an open question, though no sufficient evidence has been produced to rebut a belief certainly held in the next generation after the great Reformer's death. That his influence was strongly felt at Merton is an undoubted fact, and the liberal school of thought which he represented had there one of its chief strongholds until the Renaissance and the Reformation. Being anti-monastic by its very constitution, and having been a consistent opponent of Papal encroachments, Merton College might naturally have been expected to cast in its lot with the Protestant cause at this great crisis. A deed of submission to Henry VIII. as Supreme Head of the Church, purporting to represent the unanimous voice of the College, and professing absolute allegiance not only to him, but to Anne Boleyn and her offspring, is preserved in the Public Record Office. This deed bears the signatures of the Sub-Warden and fifteen known Fellows, besides those of three other persons who were perhaps Chaplains, but not that of Chamber, the Warden, though his name is expressly included in the body of the deed. Nevertheless, the sympathies of the leading Fellows appear to have been mainly Catholic. William Tresham, an ex-Fellow, zealous as he was in the promotion of learning, was among the adversaries of the Reformation movement, and was rewarded by Queen Mary with a Canonry of Christ Church. Though he signed the acknowledgment of the Royal

Supremacy, Richard Smyth was a still more active promoter of the Catholic re-action. He also received a Canonry of Christ Church, with the Regius Professorship of Divinity, and preached a sermon before the stake when Ridley and Latimer were martyred, on the unhappy text—"Though I give my body to be burned, and have not charity, it profiteth me nothing." Dr. Martiall, another Fellow of Merton, acted as Vice-Chancellor on the same occasion, and his brother Fellow, Robert Ward, appears on the list of Doctors appointed to sit in judgment on the doctrines of the Protestant bishops. Parkhurst, afterwards Bishop of Norwich, is the only Fellow of Merton recorded by Anthony Wood to have sought refuge beyond the seas during the Marian persecution. On the other hand, four only, including Tresham, are mentioned as having suffered the penalty of expulsion for refusing the Oath of Supremacy under Elizabeth, though Smyth was imprisoned in Archbishop Parker's house, and Raynolds, the Warden, on refusing that Oath, was deposed by order of a new Commission.

A more important place was reserved for Merton College in the great national drama of the following century. Having been one of the Colleges in which members of the Legislature were lodged during the Oxford Parliament of 1625, and upon which the officers of a Parliamentary force were quartered in 1641, it was selected, in July 1643, for the residence of Queen Henrietta Maria, who then joined the King at Oxford, and remained there during the autumn and winter. She occupied the present dining-room and drawing-room of the Warden's house, with the adjoining bedroom, still known as "the Queen's Room." The King, who held his Court at Christ Church, often came to visit her by a private walk opened for the purpose through Corpus and Merton gardens; and doubtless took part in many pleasant re-unions, of which history is silent, though a graphic picture of them is preserved in the pages of *John Inglesant*.

It does not follow that Royalist opinions preponderated among the Merton Fellows, and there is clear evidence that both sides were strongly represented in the College. Sir Nathaniel Brent, the Warden, being a Presbyterian, and having openly espoused the Parliamentary cause, absented himself, and was deposed in favour of the illustrious Harvey, Charles I.'s own physician, recommended by the King, but duly elected by the College. Ralph Button, too, a leading Fellow and Tutor, quitted Oxford, when it became the Royal head-quarters, lest he should be expected to bear arms for the King. On the other hand, Peter Turner, one of the most eminent Mertonians of his day, accompanied a troop of Royalist horse as far as Stow in the Wold, was there captured, and was committed to Northampton Gaol. A third Fellow, John Greaves, Savilian Professor of Astronomy, drew up and procured signatures to a petition for Brent's deposition; and two more, Fowle and Lovejoy, actually served under the Royal standard. But we search the College Register in vain for any formal resolution on the subject of the Civil War. It is certain that Merton gave up the whole of its plate for the King's use in 1643, and no silver presented at an earlier date is now in the possession of the College. But it is interesting, if not consolatory, to know that in the previous reign a large quantity of old plate had been exchanged for new, so that, from an antiquarian point of view, the sacrifice made to loyalty was not so great as might be imagined. No College order directing the surrender is extant, and two of the Fellows afterwards mutually accused each other of having thus misappropriated the College property.

Other notices of the great struggle then convulsing the nation are few and far between in the minutes of the College Register. It is remarkable that, so far back as August 1641, the College directed twelve muskets and as many pikes to be purchased, *bello ingruente*, for the purpose of repelling any roving soldiers who might break in for the sake of plunder. Anthony Wood particularly observes, that during the Queen's stay at Merton there were divers marriages, christenings, and burials in the Chapel, of which all record has been lost, as the private register in which the Chaplain had noted them was stolen out of his room when Oxford was finally surrendered to Fairfax. The confusion that prevailed during the Royalist occupation of Oxford is, however, officially recognized by the College. It is duly chronicled, for instance, that on August 1st, 1645, the College meeting was held in the Library, neither the Hall nor the Warden's Lodgings being then available for the purpose; and several entries attest the pecuniary straits to which the College was reduced. At last it is solemnly recorded, under the date of October 19th, 1646, that by the Divine goodness the war had at last been stayed, and the Warden (Brent) with most of the Fellows had returned, but that as there were no Bachelors, hardly any Scholars, and few Masters, it was decided to elect but one Bursar and one Dean. It is added that, as the Hall still lay *situ et ruinis squalida*, the College meeting was held in the Warden's Lodgings.

When the scenes were shifted, and a solemn Visitation of the University was instituted by "The Lords and Commons assembled in Parliament," Merton College may be said to have set the example of conformity to the new order in Church and State. Sir Nathaniel Brent himself was President of the Commission. Among his colleagues were three Fellows of Merton, Reynolds, Cheynell, and Corbet, who had already been appointed with four other preachers to convert the gownsmen through Presbyterian sermons. The earlier sittings of the Commission were held in the Warden's dining-room, or, during his absence, in Cheynell's apartments. When the members of the College, including servants, were called before the Visitors and required to make their submission, about half of them, according to Anthony Wood, openly complied: most of the others made answers more or less evasive, declaring their readiness to obey the Warden, or submitting in so far as the Visitors had authority from the King. French, who, as official guardian of the University Register, had refused to give it up, now made his submission, but justified it on the strange ground that he was bound by the capitulation of Oxford to Fairfax. One Fellow only, Nicholas Howson, boldly refused submission, declaring that he could not reconcile it with his allegiance to the King, the University, and the College. He was of course removed; and the same fate befell Turner, Greaves, French, and one other Fellow, with a larger number of Postmasters, of whom, however, some were condemned as improperly elected, and some were afterwards restored through Brent's influence. Even while the Commission was sitting, a Royalist spirit must have lingered in the College, since we read that four of the Fellows, three of whom had submitted, were put out of commons for a week and publicly admonished by the Warden for drinking the King's health with a *tertiavit*, and uncovered heads. Brent resigned the Wardenship in 1651; whereupon the Parliamentary Visitors proceeded to appoint, by their own authority, but on the express nomination of the Protector, Dr. Jonathan Goddard, who had been head physician to Cromwell's army in Ireland and Scotland—thereby improving on Charles I.'s paternal but constitutional recommendation of Harvey.

With the suspension of this great Visitation, shortly to be followed by the Restoration of Charles II., the short-lived connection of Merton College with general history may be said to have closed. It had the honour of lodging the Queen and favourite ladies of Charles II. in the plague-year, 1665; it cashiered a Probationer-Fellow in 1681 for maintaining that Charles I. died justly; it took part in the enlistment of volunteers for the suppression of Monmouth's rebellion; and it joined other Colleges in the half-hearted reception of William III. But its records are devoid of political interest, except so far as it became a chief stronghold of Whig principles in the University during the Jacobite re-action which followed the Revolution, was encouraged by the avowed Toryism of Queen Anne, and almost broke out into civil war on the accession of George I. Charles Wesley expressly mentions it with Christ Church, Exeter, and Wadham, as an anti-Jacobite society; and Meadowcourt, a leading member of the College, was the hero of a famous scene at the Whig "Constitution Club," when the Proctor, breaking in, was reluctantly obliged to drink King George's health. Shortly afterwards the following entry appeared in the University "Black Book":—"Let Mr. Meadowcourt, of Merton College, be kept back from the degree for which he next stands, for the space of two years; nor be admitted to supplicate for his grace, until he confesses his manifold crimes, and asks pardon on his knees"—a penalty, however, which he managed to evade, being afterwards thanked for his loyalty by the Whig government.

In the absence of contemporary letters or biographies, it is only from casual notices in Visitors' Injunctions, Bursars' Rolls, and (after 1482) the College Register, that we can obtain any light on the life and manners of Merton scholars, whether senior or junior, before the Reformation-period. That it was a haven of rest for quiet students, and a model of academical discipline to extra-collegiate inmates of halls and lodgings, during the incessant tumults of the fourteenth century, admits of no doubt whatever. A notable proof of this is the special exemption of Merton *"et aularum consimilium"*—probably University, Balliol, Exeter, Oriel, and Queen's Colleges—from the general rustication of students which followed the sanguinary riot on St. Scholastica's day in 1354. But the rules laid down by the Founder, and enforced by successive Visitors, were expressly directed to secure good order in the Society. By the Statutes of 1274, summary expulsion was to be the penalty of persistence in quarrelsome or disorderly behaviour. By the Ordinances of Archbishop Peckham and several other Visitors, the inmates of the College are strictly prohibited from taking meals in the town or entering it alone, and enjoined always to walk about in a body, returning before nightfall. Other Regulations, of great antiquity, but of somewhat uncertain date, emphatically warn the Fellows against aiding and abetting, even in jest, the squabbles between the Northern and Southern "Nations," or between rival "Faculties." In 1508, the College itself legislated directly against the growing practice of giving out-College parties in the city and coming in late, "even after ten o'clock." By the Injunctions of Archbishop Laud, it was ordered that the College gates should be closed at half-past nine and the keys given to the Warden, none being allowed to sleep in Oxford outside the College walls, or even to breakfast or dine, except in the College

Hall, carefully separated according to their degrees. Whether the scholars of Merton, old and young, originally slept in large dormitories, or were grouped together by threes and fours in sets of rooms, like those occupied singly by modern students, is a question which cannot be determined with certainty. The structure of "Mob Quadrangle," however, together with the earliest notices in the Register, justifies the belief that most of them lived in College rooms, and that in those days the College Library, far larger than could be required for the custody of a few hundred or thousand manuscripts, was the one common study of the whole College, perhaps serving also as a covered ambulatory. This building is known to have been constructed, or converted to its present use, about 1376; but the dormer windows in the roof were not thrown out until more than a century later; and in the meantime readers can scarcely have deciphered manuscripts on winter-days, in so dark a chamber, without the aid of oil lamps. Fires were probably unknown, except in the Hall, whither inmates of the College doubtless resorted to warm themselves at all hours of the day. It is to be hoped that, at such casual gatherings, they were relieved from the obligation to converse in Latin imposed upon them during the regular meals in Hall. But intimacy between juniors and seniors was strictly prohibited; and though Archbishop Cranmer allowed the College to dispense with the practice of Bachelors "capping" Masters in the Quadrangle, it was thought necessary to revive it. As for manly pastimes, which occupy so large a space in modern

University life, they are scarcely to be traced in the domestic history of Merton, though a ball-court is known to have existed at the west-end of the Chapel. Football, cudgel-play, and other rough games, were certainly played by the citizens in the open fields on the north of Oxford; but if Merton men took part in them, it was against the spirit of Merton rules, since these playful encounters were a fertile source of town and gown rows. There seem to have been no academical sports whatever; rowing was never practised, cricket was not invented, archery was cultivated rather as a piece of warlike training; and it is to be feared that poaching in the great woods then skirting Oxford on the north-east was among the more favourite amusements of athletic students.

It must not be forgotten, however, that, by the original foundation, all the members of the College were both Scholars and Fellows, of equal dignity, except in standing, the Scholar being nothing but a junior Fellow, and the Fellow nothing but an elder Scholar. There were a few boys of the Founder's kin, for whom a separate provision was made; and "commoners" were admitted from time to time at the discretion of the College, but these were mere supernumeraries, at first of low degree, afterwards of higher rank, and on the footing of fellow-commoners. It was not until the new order of Postmasters (*portionistae*) was founded by Wylliott, about 1380, that a second class of students was recognized by the College; and this institution of College "scholarships," in the modern sense, long remained a characteristic feature of Merton. Unlike the young "Scholares," the Postmasters did not rise by seniority to what are now called Fellowships, and were, in fact, the humble friends of the Master-Fellows who had nominated them. It would appear that at the end of the fifteenth century, if not from the first, each Master-Fellow had this right; and the number of Postmasters was always to be the same as that of the Master-Fellows. Until that period they seem to have been lodged in the separate building, opposite the College gate, long known as "Postmasters' Hall." It is not clear whether they took meals in the College Hall, or lived on rations served out to them; but it is perfectly clear that they fared badly enough until their diet was improved in the reign of James I. by special benefactions of Thomas Jessop and others. In the previous reign, they had been removed into the College itself; and thenceforward for several generations they slept, probably on truckle-beds, in the bedrooms of their respective "Masters." Indeed, a College-order of 1543 leads us to suppose that some of them were expected to wait upon the Bachelor-Fellows in Hall.

Another institution characteristic of Merton in the olden times is one now obsolete, but formerly known as the "Scrutiny." The Founder had expressly ordained in his statutes that a "Chapter or Scrutiny" should be held in the College itself thrice a year—a week before Christmas, a week before Easter, and on July 20; and that on these occasions a diligent enquiry should be made into the life, behaviour, morals, and progress in learning of all his scholars, as well as into all matters needing correction or improvement. He also decreed that, once a year, the Warden, bailiffs of manors, and all others concerned in the management of College property, should render a solemn account of their stewardship before the Vice-Warden and all the Scholars, assembled at "one of the manors." The bailiffs and other agents of the College were to resign their keys, without reserve, into the hands of the Warden; but the Warden himself was to undergo a like inquisition into his own conduct, and was apparently to be visited with censure or penalties, in case of delinquency, by the College meeting. It is by no means easy to understand why this annual audit, for such it was, should not have been appointed to be held at one of the stated "Chapters or Scrutinies," or why "one of the manors" should have been designated as the lawful place for it. At all events, the distinction between a Scrutiny and an Audit-meeting seems to have been lost at a very early period. Scrutinies, or Chapters, were held frequently, though at irregular intervals; but at least once a year the Scrutiny assumed the form of an Audit, not only into accounts, but into conduct, being sometimes held in the College Hall, and sometimes at Holywell Manor. The earliest notice of such a Scrutiny in the College Register is under the date 1483, when three questions were propounded for discussion:—(1) the conduct of College servants; (2) the number of Postmasters; and (3) the appointment of College officers. Two years later, however, we find three other questions laid down as the proper subjects for consideration:—(1) the residence and conduct of the

Warden; (2) the condition of the manors; and (3) the expediency of increasing the number of Fellows. At a later period, the regular questions were—(1) the expediency of increasing the number of Postmasters; (2) the conduct of College servants (as before); and (3) the appointment of a single College officer, the garden-master. Practically, the Scrutiny often resolved itself into a sort of caucus, at which a free and easy altercation took place among the Fellows upon all the points of difference likely to arise in a cloistered society absorbed in its own petty interests. In Professor Rogers' interesting record of a Scrutiny held in 1338-9, long before the College Register commences, every kind of grievance is brought forward, from the Warden's neglect of duty to the slovenly attire of the Chaplain, the excessive charge for horses, and the incessant squabbles between three quarrelsome Fellows. The same freedom of complaint shows itself in the briefer notices of later Scrutinies to be found in the Register. Undue indulgence in games of ball, loitering about the town, the introduction of Fellow-commoners into Hall, the prevalence of noise in the bed-chambers at night, as well as enmities among the Fellows, and abuses in the estate-management, were among the stock topics of discussion at Scrutinies; and in 1585 complaints were made at a Scrutiny against suspected Papists. It is evident that reflections were often cast upon the Warden; but it was known that he could only be deposed by the Visitor after three admonitions from the Sub-Warden; and, though in one case these admonitions were given, the Visitor,

Archbishop Sancroft, declined to adopt the extreme course. The practice of reviewing the conduct of the Warden at Scrutinies appears, indeed, to have been finally dropped under Warden Chamber, who, as Court physician to King Henry VIII., had a good excuse for constantly absenting himself; but the practice of inviting personal charges against Fellows survived much longer, and Scrutinies were nominally held in the last century.

A third institution distinctive of Merton was the system of "Variations," or College disputations, of the same nature as the exercises required for University degrees. This custom is thus described by John Poynter, in a little work on the curiosities of Oxford, published in 1749. "The Master-Fellows," he says, "are obliged by their Statutes to take their turns every year about the Act time, or at least before the first day of August, to vary, as they call it, that is, to perform some public exercise in the Common Hall, the Variator opposing Aristotle in three Latin speeches, upon three questions in Philosophy, or rather Morality; the three Deans in their turns answering the Variator in three speeches in opposition to his, and in defence of his Aristotle, and after every speech disputing with him syllogistically upon the same. Which Declamations or Disputations were amicably concluded with a magnificent and expensive supper, the charges of which formerly came to £100, but of late years much retrenched." He adds that the audience was composed of the Vice-Chancellor and Proctors, with several Heads of Houses, besides the Warden and all the members of the College. As Variations were still in force when Poynter wrote, we may accept his description of them as tolerably accurate; but he is evidently wrong in supposing them to have taken place at one season of the year only, for the College Register clearly proves the actual date of them to have been moveable, so long as they were performed within the two years of "Regency" following Inception. By the old rule of the University, all Regent-Masters were obliged to give "ordinary" lectures during that period. This obligation was enforced at Merton by the oath required of Bachelor-Fellows before their Inception; and by the same oath they bound themselves during the same period, not only to engage in the logical and philosophical disputations of the College, but also to "vary twice." The system was regularly established, and is mentioned as of immemorial antiquity, before the end of the fifteenth century. From that time forward Variations are frequently and fully recorded in the Register; and, whenever dispensations were allowed, the fact is duly noted. In 1673 a Fellow was fined £12—a large sum in those days—for neglecting his second Variations; and the significant comment is appended:—"we acquitted him, so far as we could, of his perjury." Even the subjects chosen by the Variators are carefully specified, and astonish us by their wide range of interest. At first, metaphysical and logical questions predominate; but there is a large admixture of ethical questions, and a few bearing on natural philosophy. At the end of the sixteenth and throughout the seventeenth century, politics enter largely into the field of disputation; while in the eighteenth century a more discursive and literary tone of thought makes itself clearly felt. Upon the whole, we can well believe that, in the age before examinations, these intellectual trials of strength played no mean part in education, quickening the wits of Merton Fellows, if they did not encourage the cultivation of solid knowledge.

It is to be hoped, no doubt, that they were preceded and supplemented by sound private tuition; but upon this, unhappily, the Merton records throw no light. It seems to be assumed in the original Statutes that Scholars of Merton, though bound to study within the House, will receive their instruction outside it. The only exception was the statutable institution of a grammar-master, who was to have charge of the students in grammar, and to whom "the more advanced might have recourse without a blush, when doubts should arise in their faculty." This institution was treated by Archbishop Peckham as of primary importance; and he specially censures the College for practically excluding boys who had still to learn the rudiments of grammar. There is good reason to believe that John of Cornwall, who is mentioned as the first to introduce the study of English in schools, and to abandon the practice of construing Latin into French, actually held the office of grammar-master in Merton College. These Merton grammar-masters (who continued to be appointed in the sixteenth century) were probably the earliest type of College tutors—an order which inevitably developed itself at a later period, but of which the history remains to be evolved from very scanty materials. The medical lectures founded by Linacre, and the Divinity lectures founded by Bickley, in the sixteenth century, as well as the lectures delivered by Thomas Bodley on Greek, were essentially College lectures, but seem to have been professorial rather than tutorial. A College order of June 9th, 1586, the first year of Savile's wardenship, requires the Regent-Masters to deliver twenty public lectures to the Postmasters on the Sphere or on Arithmetic, as the Warden should think fit. Probably this rule was soon neglected; and it is not until a much later period that we find the modern relation of tutor and pupil a living reality in Colleges.

We may pass lightly over some other strange, though not unique, customs of Merton which fill a large space in the Register and the pages of Anthony Wood. One of these was the annual election of a *Rex Fabarum*, or "Christmas King," on the vigil of St. Edmund (Nov. 19th), under the authority of sealed letters, which "pretended to have been brought from some place beyond sea." This absurd farce, reminding us of the rough burlesques formerly practised on board ship in crossing the Equator, was solemnly enacted year after year, and recorded in the Register with as much gravity as the succession of a Warden. The person chosen was the senior Fellow who had not yet borne the office; and, according to Wood, his duty was "to punish all misdemeanours done in the time of Christmas, either by imposing exercises on the juniors, or putting into the stocks at the end of the Hall any of the servants, with other punishments that were sometimes very ridiculous." This went on until Candlemas (Feb. 2nd), "or much about the time that the *Ignis Regentium* was celebrated." The *Ignis Regentium* seems to have been nothing more than a great College wine-party round the Hall fire, attended with various traditional festivities, and provided at the cost of all the Regent-Masters, or only of the Senior Regent, whose munificent hospitality is sometimes expressly commended. Of a similar nature were the practical jokes and rude horse-play described by Anthony Wood as carried on, by way of initiating freshmen, on All Saints Eve and other Eves and Saints' Days up to Christmas, as well as on Shrove Tuesday, when the poor novices were compelled to declaim in undress from a form placed on the High Table, and rewarded, or punished with some brutality, for their performances. It is significant that, under the Commonwealth, these old-world jovialities were disused, and soon afterwards died out. The old custom of singing Catholic hymns in the College Hall, on the Eves and Vigils of Saints' Days between All Saints and Candlemas Day, had been modified at the Reformation by the substitution of Sternhold and Hopkins' Psalms, which continued to be sung in Anthony Wood's times. Not less curious, and more important, are the detailed regulations made for the health of the College during frequent outbreaks of the plague, when the majority of Fellows and students migrated to Cuxham, Stow Wood, Islip, Eynsham, or elsewhere, and communication between the College and the town was strictly limited.

Were it possible for a Merton Fellow of the Plantagenet, Tudor, or Stuart period to revisit his College in our own day, he would find but few survivals of the quaint usages once peculiar to it. The recitation of a thanksgiving prayer for benefits inherited from the Founder at the end of each chapel-service, the time-honoured practice of striking the Hall table with a wooden trencher as a signal for grace, and the ceremonies observed on the induction of a new Warden, are perhaps the only outward and visible relics of its ancient customary which the spirit of innovation has left alive. But he would feel himself at home in the noble choir of the Chapel, with its stonework and painted glass almost untouched by the lapse of six centuries; in the Library, retaining every structural feature of Bishop Rede's original work down to its minutest detail; in the Treasury, with its massive high-pitched roof, under which the College archives have been preserved entire since the reign of Edward I., together with a coeval inventory of the documents then deposited there; in the College Garden, surrounded on two sides by the town-wall of Henry III., extended eastward since the close of the Middle Ages by purchases from the City, but curtailed westward by sales of land for the site of Corpus. Perhaps, on reviewing the unbroken continuity of College history through more than twenty generations, crowded with vicissitudes in Church and State, with transformations of ancient institutions, and with revolutions in human thought, he would cease to repine over changes which the

Founder himself foresaw as inevitable, and would rather marvel at the vitality of a collegiate society, which can still maintain its corporate identity, with so much of its original structure, in an age beyond that which mediæval seers had assigned for the end of the world.

IV.
EXETER COLLEGE.

BY THE REV. CHARLES W. BOASE, M.A., FELLOW
OF EXETER COLLEGE.

In 1314 Walter de Stapeldon, Bishop of Exeter, founded Stapeldon Hall, soon better known as Exeter College, for "Scholars" (*i. e.* Fellows), born or resident in Devon and Cornwall, eight from the former and four from the latter county; and he also founded a grammar-school at Exeter, to prepare boys for Oxford. He had, at first, bought ground in and near Hart Hall (now Hertford College); but this site not proving large enough, he removed the students to St. Stephen's Hall in St. Mildred's parish, and gave them Hart Hall, that by its rent their rooms might be kept in repair and be rent-free.

The object of the early founders of Colleges was to pass as many men as possible through a course of training that would fit them for the service of Church or State: and so Stapeldon fixed fourteen years as the outside period of holding his scholarships; he had no idea of giving fellowships for life. The twelve scholars were to study Philosophy; and a thirteenth scholar was to be a priest studying Scripture or Canon Law. Aptness to learn, good character, and poverty were the qualifications required of them; and they were to be chosen without regard to favour, fear, relationship, or love. They were kept in order by punishments, increasing from a stoppage of commons to expulsion, at the discretion of the Rector, who was chosen annually after the audit in October. The Rector also looked after the money, and rooms, and servants; but, if two Fellows demanded the expulsion of a servant he was to appoint another. The Rector must have been always under thirty; it was the younger Masters of Arts that then directed education in the University. Disputations were held twice a week, and of three disputations, two were in Logic, one in Natural Science. Tenpence a week was allowed for commons, and each scholar received in addition the sum of ten shillings a year, the Rector and the Priest twenty shillings each. If any scholar was away for more than four weeks his commons were stopped; and by an absence of five months he forfeited his scholarship.

Stapeldon endowed his Hall with the great tithes of Gwinear in Cornwall, and of Long Wittenham in Berks; and any surplus or legacy was to go to public purposes, such as increasing the number of scholars or buying books. There was a common chest with three keys, kept by the Rector, the senior Scholar, and the Priest; and the audit-rolls (*computi*) are extant from 1324, though with gaps, as for instance during the Black Death (1349). There is something touching in the number of legacies which Stapeldon left to individual poor scholars in his will.

The scholars were very poor; and to relieve them, Ralph Germeyn (Precentor of Exeter), Richard Greenfield (Rector of Kilkhampton in Cornwall), and Robert Rygge (Fellow 1362-1372; afterwards Canon and Chancellor of Exeter), at several times founded "chests" for making loans to them without interest, on security of books or plate; but all such funds have now disappeared, having been, it seems, absorbed in Charles I's war-chest. The College itself sometimes borrowed; in 1358 the College accounts show a payment of "£3 for a Bible redeemed from Chichester chest"; in 1374, of "four marks to our barber for a Bible pledged to him in the time of Dagenet" (John Dagenet had been Rector in 1371-1372).

The life was simple. Besides the "commons" (*i. e.* allowances for food), "liveries" (*i. e.* clothes) were supplied about once in three years. The scholars were to wear black boots (*caligæ*); and conform to clerical manners according to their standing as Sophists, Bachelors, or Masters. Meals were taken in the hall (which stood a little north of the present hall), where there was always a large bason with hanging towels. A charcoal fire burned in the middle of the hall, under an opening to let out the smoke; but men were not allowed to linger round the fire, and they went off to bed early because candles were dear, nearly 2*d.* a pound, *i. e.* 2*s.* of our money— they lacked therefore the genial inspiration of writing by good candle-light. All had to be in College by nine o'clock in the evening; and the key of the gate was kept in the Rector's room, which was over the gate. Lectures began at six or seven in the morning; dinner was at ten; supper at five. Of the servants, the manciple received five shillings a term, the cook two, barber twelvepence, washerwoman fifteen pence. The barber was the newsmonger of that as of other ages.

The scholars might by common consent make any new statutes, not contrary to the Founder's ordinances; and were to refer all doubts to the Visitor.

The Bishops of Exeter were kind Visitors; and gave books and money several times. Gradually more halls and lodging-houses were obtained, some lying on the lane[124] which ran all along inside the city wall, others along St. Mildred's (now Brasenose) lane, and others along the Turl. A tower was built on the site of St. Stephen's Hall, with a gate opening into the lane under the city wall; two windows of this tower survive in the staircase of the present Rector's house. The present garden is on the site of some of the old buildings, but the ivy-clad buttresses of the Bodleian and the great fig-trees along the College buildings, which make such a show in summer, of course do not date from such early times.

An agreement had to be made with the Rector of St. Mildred's parish, who feared lest the College-chapel should interfere with his rights. This early chapel had rooms under it, and a porch. The *computus* for building a library in 1383, shows that the building cost £57 13s. 5½d., the leaded roof costing £13 13s. 4d.; and it was completed between Easter and Michaelmas, before the beginning of the Academic year. The timber came from Aldermaston in Berks, the stone from Taynton in Gloucestershire and Whatley near Frome—the latter corresponding to our present Bath stone. Carpenters and masons were paid 6*d.* a day, and the masons had breakfast and dinner (*merenda* and *prandium*). David, the foreman, had 6*d.* a week for "commons," and he held the place of a modern architect.

The regard paid to poverty brought forward some distinguished men, such as Walter Lihert (Fellow 1420-1425), Bishop of Norwich, a miller's son from Lanteglos by Fowey in Cornwall. This consideration for poor scholars did not often fail. Long afterwards John Prideaux (Fellow 1601, Rector 1612-1642) used to say, "If I could have been parish clerk of Ubber (Ugborough in Devon), I should never have been Bishop of Worcester." Benjamin Kennicott was master of a charity school at Totnes till friends helped him to come to Oxford, where (in 1747) he obtained a Fellowship in Exeter College, and became a great Hebrew scholar. William Gifford, the critic, was apprentice to a shoemaker at Ashburton, where a surgeon helped him to gain a Bible clerkship at Exeter (1779); when he became a leader in the literary world, he remembered his own rise in life, and founded an Exhibition at Exeter for poor boys from Ashburton school. Thus the Universities had formerly something of the character of popular bodies in which learning and study were recommendations, and the avenues of promotion were not closed even to the poorest.

The Wiclifite movement largely influenced Exeter College, and a number of the Fellows suffered in the cause. But, mixed with this, was a wish to uphold the independence of the University, as against the Archbishop of Canterbury's power of visitation; and perhaps a feeling for the *lay* government, as against the clergy. A former Fellow, Robert Tresilian, was among Richard II's chief supporters; and his fate is the first legend in *The Mirror for Magistrates*, written by William Baldwin in 1559. Later on several Fellows were connected with the House of Lancaster. Michael de Tregury (Fellow 1422-1427) was in 1431 made Rector of the new University, set up at Caen by the English during their rule in France. The physicians of Henry VI. and Margaret were both Fellows. But when Margaret was at Coventry in 1459, levying an army for the War of the Roses, she took "Queen's gold" from the College, *i. e.* a tenth of an old fine paid the King for ratifying the grant of a house.

The College was favourably known in the Revival of Learning. William Grocyn taught Greek in the hall; and Richard Croke and Cornelius Vitelli lodged in rooms in the College. Some of the Fellows too were connected with Wolsey; but the College on the whole sided with the opposition to Henry VIII's measures, like their friends in the West. John Moreman (Fellow 1510-1522) opposed Catherine's divorce, and was imprisoned under Edward VI. The Cornish insurgents in 1549 demanded that "Dr. Moreman and Dr. Crispin should be safely sent to them." Moreman was also famous as a schoolmaster;

and as Vicar of the College living of Menheniot, he taught the Creed, Lord's Prayer, and Commandments in English, the people having hitherto used only the old Cornish tongue.

The *Valor Ecclesiasticus* of 1535 states the College revenues at only £83 2s. But Sir William Petre, a statesman trained under Thomas Cromwell, wishing to benefit his old College, gave it some lands and advowsons which he bought of Queen Elizabeth, and added eight Fellowships for the counties in which his family held or should hold land. Elizabeth's Charter of Incorporation is dated 22nd March, 1566.

New Statutes were then framed by Petre and the Visitor. The Rectorship had already been made perpetual. Petre allowed the Fellows to retire to the Vicarage of Kidlington in time of plague, an oft-recurring trouble. Under a later ordinance a Fellow was allowed, with Lord Petre's approval, to travel abroad for four years to study Medicine or Civil Law.

Petre also gave the College a curious Latin Psalm-book, which had been the family Bible of the Tudors, the most learned royal family in Europe. It is from it that we know the birthday of Henry VII., 28th Jan. 1457.

Exeter was still in sympathy with the old faith. Ralph Sherwine (Fellow 1568-1575) was hanged by the side of Edmund Campian of St. John's, in 1581; and several Fellows fled abroad, such as Richard

Bristowe, the chief of the translators who put forth the Douai Bible. Elizabeth remedied this by getting two loyal men appointed Rectors successively, Thomas Glasier in 1578, and Thomas Holland in 1592—the latter was one of the translators of the Authorised Version. Under them Exeter became remarkable for discipline and learning, tinged by Puritan views.

John Prideaux was an equally well-known Rector under Charles I., and came into conflict with Laud. There was more intercourse then between English and foreign Protestant Universities than there is now; and Sixtinus Amama, the Dutch Hebraist, speaks in the most grateful terms of the kindness he received from Prideaux and the Fellows. Exeter was now training men like Sir John Eliot, William Strode, William Noye, and John Maynard. Maynard afterwards gave his old College money to found a Catechetical and a Hebrew lectureship. In 1612 the members included 134 commoners, 37 poor scholars, and 12 servitors—the number of the whole University was 2920. Western friends, the Aclands, Peryams, and others, now built a new hall; and John Peryam also built the rooms between the hall and the library, while George Hakewill, a Fellow, gave money to build a new chapel in 1623.

As to the life of the place, Shaftesbury, the famous statesman, who was a member of the College in 1637, gives an amusing account of "coursing" (now become a sort of free fight) in the schools; of how he stopped the evil custom of "tucking" freshmen (*i. e.*

grating off the skin from the lip to the chin); and how he prevented the Fellows "altering the size of" (*i. e.* weakening) "the College beer." Shaftesbury's future colleague in the Cabal, Clifford, was also at Exeter.

Charles I., in 1636, gave an endowment out of confiscated lands to found Fellowships for the Channel Islands at Exeter, Jesus, and Pembroke, that men so trained might devote themselves to work in the Islands. He made John Prideaux (Rector 1612-1642) and Thomas Winniff (Fellow 1595-1609), Bishops, the former of Worcester, the latter of Lincoln, when he at last tried to conciliate the gentry, who were almost all opposed to Laud's innovations.

In the Civil War most of the Fellows took the King's side, and Archbishop Usher sojourned in some wooden buildings then known as Prideaux Buildings, situated behind the old Rector's house, buildings now partly re-erected in the Turl. The College plate was taken by Charles, although the Fellows had redeemed it by a gift of money; but the King's needs were overwhelming.

Under the Commonwealth John Conant became Rector, and increased the fame of the College for learning and discipline. "Once[125] a week he had a catechetical lecture in the Chapel, in which he went over Piscator's *Aphorisms* and Woollebius' *Compendium Theologiæ Christianæ*; and by the way fairly propounded the principal objections made by the Papists, Socinians, and others against the orthodox doctrine, in terms suited to the understanding and capacity of the younger scholars. He took care likewise that the inferior servants of the College should be instructed in the principles of the Christian religion, and would sometimes catechise them in his own lodgings. He looked strictly himself to the keeping up all exercises, and would often slip into the hall in the midst of their lectures and disputations. He would always oblige both opponents and respondents to come well prepared, and to perform their respective parts agreeably to the strict law of disputation. Here he would often interpose, either adding new force to the arguments of an opponent, or more fullness to the answers of the respondent, and supplying where anything seemed defective, or clearing where anything was obscure in what the moderator[126] subjoined. He would often go into the chambers and studies of the young scholars, observe what books they were reading, and reprove them if he found them turning over any modern author, and send them to Tully, that great master of Roman eloquence, to learn the true and genuine propriety of that language. His care in the election of Fellows was very singular. A true love of learning, and a good share of it in a person of untainted morals and low circumstances, were sure of his patronage and encouragement. He would constantly look over the observator's roll and buttery-book himself, and whoever had been absent from chapel prayers or extravagant in his expenses, or otherwise faulty, was sure he must atone for his fault by some such exercise as the Rector should think fit to set him, for he was no friend to pecuniary mulcts, which too often punish the father instead of the son. The students were many more than could be lodged within the walls: they crowded in here from all parts of the nation, and some from beyond the sea. He opposed Cromwell's plan of giving the College at Durham the privileges of a University, setting forth the advantages of large Universities and the dangers which threaten religion and learning by multiplying small and petty Academies. He was instrumental in moving Mr. Selden's executors to bestow his prodigious collection of books, more than 8000 volumes, on the University. In his declining age he could scarce be prevailed upon by his physicians to drink now and then a little wine. He slept very little, having been an assiduous and indefatigable student for about threescore years together. Whilst his strength would bear it, he often sat up in his study till late at night, and thither he returned very early in the morning."

The Restoration put an end alike to learning and to discipline, to the grief of a few good men, such as Ken, though the Royalists in general issued numerous squibs and satires against the Puritans, which still impose on some writers. Anthony Wood, a strong Royalist and constant resident in Oxford, makes frequent allusion in his diaries to the disastrous effects of the Restoration. "Some cavaliers that were restored," he says in one place, "were good scholars, but the generality were dunces." "Before the war," he says in another place, "we had scholars that made a thorough search in scholastic and polemical divinity, in humane learning, and natural philosophy: but now scholars study these things not more than what is just necessary to carry them through the exercises of their respective Colleges and the University. Their aim is not to live as students ought to do, viz. temperate, abstemious, and plain and grave in their apparel; but to live like gentry, to keep dogs and horses, to turn their studies into places to keep bottles, to swagger in gay apparell and long periwigs." The difference between a Puritan and a Restoration Head of a House is strongly set out by the contrast between Conant's government of Exeter and that of Joseph Maynard, who was elected on Conant's ejection for refusing submission to the Act of Conformity (1662). Wood says—"Exeter College is now (1665) much debauched by a drunken governor; whereas before in Dr. Conant's time it was accounted a civil house, it is now rude and uncivil. The Rector (Maynard) is good-natured, generous, and a good scholar; but he has forgot the way of a College life, and the decorum of a scholar. He is given much to bibbing; and when there is a music-meeting in one of the Fellows' chambers, he will sit there, smoke, and drink till he is drunk, and has to be led to his lodgings by the junior Fellows."

In 1666 pressure was put upon Maynard to resign, and he did so on advice of the Visitor and his brother, Sir John Maynard. The resignation was made smooth for him by the understanding that he should be appointed Prebendary of Exeter in room of Dr. Arthur Bury, who was now elected Rector of

Exeter. Dr. Bury wrote a book, famous in the Deist controversy, called *The Naked Gospel*, which had the distinction of being impeached by several Masters of Arts, and formally condemned and burnt by order of the Convocation of the University. About the time of its publication, Bury got into trouble with Trelawney the Visitor, the same whose name became a watchword in the West ("and shall Trelawney die"), over questions of discipline and jurisdiction. The Visitor expelled Bury and his supporters, July 1690; the decision was appealed against in the Court of King's Bench, and in the House of Lords, but was finally upheld.

The evil effects of the Restoration in studies and in morals continued. Later on, Dean Prideaux can still say, "There is nothing but drinking and duncery. Exeter is totally spoiled, and so is Christ Church. There is over against Baliol, a dingy, horrid, scandalous ale-house, fit for none but dragooners and tinkers. Here the Baliol men, by perpetual bubbing, add art to their natural stupidity to make themselves perfect sots."

Exeter and Christ Church were both reformed by John Conybeare,[127] a writer famous for his answer to the *Christianity as old as the Creation* of Matthew Tindal, also an Exeter man.

Jacobite feeling was strong in Oxford, and at the election of county members in 1755, when the Jacobites guarded the hustings in Broad Street, twenty men deep, the Whigs passed through Exeter and succeeded in voting. The Vice-Chancellor, a strong Jacobite, remarked on "the infamous behaviour of one College"; and this led to a war of pamphlets. Christ Church, Exeter, Merton, and Wadham were the four Whig Colleges.

Early in the eighteenth century the front gate and tower and the buildings between this and the Hall were erected by the help of such friends as Narcissus Marsh, Archbishop of Armagh, formerly a Fellow. But in 1709 the library was burnt. The fire began "in the scrape-trencher's room. This adjoining to the library, all the inner part of the library was destroyed, and only one stall of books or thereabouts secured." The wind was west, and the smoke must have reached the nostrils of Hearne as he lay abed at St. Edmund Hall, for "he was strangely disturbed with apprehensions of fire." The library was rebuilt in 1778, and had many gifts of books and manuscripts, and a fund for buying more was established by Dr. Hugh Shortridge.

When the time of religious revival came, John Wesley influenced some members of the College, such as Thomas Broughton (Fellow 1733-1741). During the present century other Fellows were noted in the Evangelical movement; and in the Tractarian movement the names of William Sewell, John Brande Morris, and John Dobree Dalgairns (better known as Father Dalgairns), were conspicuous.

Nor did the College lack among the fellows and scholars names in Science, such as Milman and Rigaud; or in Oriental Learning, as Kennicott and Weston; or in Classics and Literature, as Stackhouse and Upton; or in Law, as Judge Coleridge; or in Theology, as Forshall the editor of Wiclif's Bible, and Milman, Bishop of Calcutta, and Jacobson, Bishop of Chester; while among its other members it counted Sir Gardner Wilkinson and Sir Charles Lyell. Of the living men who uphold the repute of the College, this is not the place to speak.

In 1854 the Commissioners threw the Fellowships open, and turned eight of them into scholarships, ten open, ten for the diocese of Exeter, and two for the Channel Islands. In the same year new buildings were begun facing Broad Street, and next year a library, and the year after a chapel and a rectory. Since the chapel absorbed the site of the former rector's house (east of the old chapel), the new house was built on the site of St. Helen's quadrangle. The liberality of the members was conspicuous on the occasion of these buildings. Stained-glass and carved oak stalls have been since given to the chapel, and some fine tapestry, representing the Visit of the Magi, executed by Burne Jones and William Morris, old members of the College.

Many changes have been made in old arrangements, but the foundation of the new scholarships carried out the real spirit of the Founder's views, in passing men rapidly through a University training. It is hoped that Walter de Stapeldon would, if now living, approve of the care for educating scholars which he had so much at heart.

V.
ORIEL COLLEGE.

By C. L. Shadwell, M.A., Fellow of Oriel College.

Adam de Brome, the actual, though not the titular, founder of Oriel College, was at the beginning of the fourteenth century a well-endowed ecclesiastic, in the service of King Edward the Second. He held the living of Hanworth, Middlesex; he was Chancellor of Durham and Archdeacon of Stow; he held the office of almoner to the King; and in 1320 he was presented by the King to the Rectory of St. Mary the Virgin, Oxford.

The College of Walter de Merton had then been in existence nearly half a century; and the type which he had created, a self-governing, independent society of secular students, well lodged and well endowed, was that to which the aims of the struggling foundations of William of Durham, Devorguilla of Balliol, and Bishop Stapeldon were directed. The poor masters established out of William of Durham's fund, and now beginning to be known as the scholars of University Hall, were still subject to Statutes issued by the University, and had not yet attained to an independent position. It was not till 1340 that the scholars of the Lady Devorguilla were set free from the authority of extraneous Procuratores, and allowed to be governed by a Master of their own choosing. The office of Rector of Stapeldon Hall was an annual one; he was appointed by the scholars from among themselves, or if they disagreed, by the Chancellor of the University, and his principal duties were bursarial. But for the standard set by the completely organised House of Merton, the development of these infant societies might have taken a very different direction.

Adam de Brome appears to have chosen Merton as his model, and his foundation was from the first intended to be styled a College, a title perhaps till then exclusively enjoyed by Merton.[128]

By Letters Patent, dated at Langley, 20th April, 1324, he obtained the royal license to purchase a messuage in Oxford or its suburbs, and therein to establish "quoddam collegium scolarium in diversis scientiis studentium," to be styled the College of St. Mary in Oxford, with power to acquire lands to the annual value of thirty pounds. In the course of the same year he purchased the advowson of the church of Aberford, in Yorkshire; and, in Oxford, Perilous Hall, in St. Mary Magdalen parish, and Tackley's Inn in the High Street; and by his charter dated 6th December at Oxford, and confirmed by the King, 20th December, 1324, at Nottingham, he founded his College of scholars "in sacra theologia & arte dialectica studentium," appointing John de Laughton as their Rector, and assigning to them Tackley's Inn as their residence. This Society, if it ever came into actual existence at all, lasted only a little more than a twelvemonth; and on the first of January, 1325-6, its possessions were surrendered by Adam de Brome into the King's hands, as a preliminary to its re-establishment under the King's name. Edward the Second had already shown an interest in the maintenance of academical students at the sister University; and the scholars whom he supported there were the germ of the institution afterwards developed by his son under the name of King's Hall. He also founded the Cistercian house at Oxford. He lent himself readily to the suggestion of his Almoner; and by his Letters Patent, dated at Norwich, 21st January, 1325-6, he refounded the College, with Adam de Brome as its head with the title of Provost, restoring the old endowments, further augmented by the grant of the advowson of St. Mary's. Leave was given to appropriate the church to the use of the College on condition of maintaining four chaplains for the performance of daily service. License was given to take and hold lands in mortmain to the annual value of sixty pounds. The original statutes are dated on the same day as the charter of foundation. By these statutes, nearly all the provisions of which are taken verbatim from the Merton statutes of 1274, the College was to consist of a Provost, and ten scholars to be nominated in the first instance by Adam de Brome, and thereafter to be elected by the whole body. The ten first nominated were to study Theology; those elected in future were to study Arts and Philosophy, until they were allowed to pass to the study of Theology or (to the number of five or six out of ten) of Civil or Canon Law. The Provost was to be chosen by the whole body of scholars from among themselves and presented to the King's Chancellor for admission. The second officer of the College was the Dean, corresponding to the Sub-Warden at Merton, filling the Provost's place in his absence, and acting with him at all times in the College government. Provision was made, similar to that at Merton, for the appointment of other subordinate Deans, such as were established elsewhere and in later foundations; this power has however never been exercised, and the Dean of Oriel, alone of all who bear that title, is in power and dignity second only to the head of the College. The scholars were to be chosen from among Bachelors of Arts, without preference for any locality, place of birth, or kindred. Three chapters were to be held in the year, at the same times as those appointed at Merton, Christmas, Easter, and St. Margaret's day, at which inquiry was to be made into the conduct of the members, and newly elected scholars were to be admitted.

The foundation was now in contemplation of law, complete. The new Society was a corporate body, having a license to hold land, and with a common seal.[129] It probably was at first established either in St. Mary's Hall, the Manse or Rectory House of St. Mary's Church, or in Tackley's Inn, a large messuage in the High Street, on the site now occupied by the house No. 106.

But the College had not long been founded before Adam de Brome perceived that the protection afforded by the King's name would be insufficient, unless he could also obtain the support of the Bishop of Lincoln, Henry de Burghash. The Bishop's approbation of the foundation was not given until a new body of statutes had been drafted, differing in many important particulars from the Foundation Statutes, and placing the College under the control not of the Crown but of the Bishop. The Provost when elected is to be presented to the Bishop for approval or confirmation. Only three of the Fellows may be allowed to study Civil or Canon Law, all the rest being required to betake themselves to Theology. The Bishop is everywhere substituted for the King or his Chancellor; his approval is required for alterations in the statutes; the power of interpreting them on the occasion of any dispute is vested in him; and he is constituted the sole and final judge in the removal of a Provost or scholar for misconduct. Prayers are to be said for the Bishop's father and mother, Robert Lord Burghash and Matilda his wife, his brothers Robert and Stephen, as well as for the King and Adam de Brome; the name of Hugh le Despenser is significantly omitted. These statutes were issued by the College 23rd May, and confirmed by the Bishop 11th June, 1326; the Bishop's charter approving the foundation was first given on 13th March, but apparently was kept back until the constitution of the College had been settled to his satisfaction, and was only finally granted on 19th May. In the course of the same year the appropriation of the church of St. Mary was approved by the Bishop and the Dean and Chapter of Lincoln; and on Adam de Brome's resignation, the

College was duly inducted by the Prior of St. Frideswide (August 10).

By the close of the year the Queen's party, to which Bishop Burghash belonged, had triumphed over the Despensers, the deposition of the King following in January 1327. The Bishop made use of the favour in which he stood with the new government to obtain some substantial benefits for the College which he had taken under his protection. The advowson of Coleby, Lincolnshire, purchased by Adam de Brome, was secured to the College by a Royal grant, with a view to its ultimate appropriation. The Hospital of St. Bartholomew, near Oxford, and of Royal foundation, was annexed to the College. The maintenance of the almsmen was provided by a charge on the fee farm rent of the city; but the possessions of the Hospital, consisting principally of tenements and rents in Oxford, went to augment the slender endowments of the College.[130] But the most important accession which the institution now received was by the grant of a messuage, called "La Oriole," the nucleus of the site of the present College buildings. This messuage stood in St. John Baptist's parish, fronting Schidyard Street and St. John Street, and occupying nearly the whole of the southern half of the present quadrangle; the south-east corner, the site of the present chapel, was not acquired till later. It had anciently been known as Senescal Hall, but had since acquired the name of La Oriole. Queen Eleanor, wife of Edward the First, had granted it to her chaplain and kinsman James of Spain, and the reversion was now (Dec.

1327) conferred upon the College. The life interest was surrendered in 1329, and the Society probably removed there in that year.[131]

The increase in the College revenues since its first establishment was probably the occasion of issuing some further supplementary statutes, 8th December, 1329. The commons or weekly allowance was raised from twelve to fifteen pence a week for each scholar. The stipend of the Provost was increased to ten marks. Ten shillings were allowed to the Dean; five shillings apiece to the two Fellows, "collectores reddituum," who collected the income derived from the oblations in St. Mary's Church, and the rents of house and other property in Oxford; five shillings to the collector of the Littlemore tithes; pittances were allowed to the Fellows at Christmas, Easter, and Whitsuntide. The Provost was allowed to keep a separate table, and to maintain a private servant. By a more important provision, ex-Fellows were made eligible to the office of Provost. These statutes were confirmed by the Visitor 26th Feb. 1330, and with those of May 1326, by Royal Letters Patent, 18th March, 1330.

The first chapter in the history of the College, recording the birth and establishment of Adam de Brome's foundation, closes with the Papal Bulls ratifying and confirming the acts of the King and the Bishop, and authorising the appropriation of the three benefices of St. Mary's, Aberford, and Coleby. These were obtained in answer to a letter of the King, dated 4th December, 1330, in which the design of the foundation is becomingly set forth. In a postscript to this letter the King calls the Pope's attention to another matter, the inconvenience arising from the frequent occurrence of disturbances in St. Mary's Church and Churchyard, arising from the gatherings that habitually took place there, and which led to "effusiones sanguinis" within the consecrated precincts, calling for the Bishop's sentence of reconciliation. This was not always easily to be obtained, the Bishop being engaged elsewhere in his extensive diocese; and the King suggests that the Pope should authorise the Bishop to give a standing commission to the Abbots of Oseney and Rewley to act for him whenever occasion should require, and effect the necessary reconciliation. The Pope, having taken six months to consider this application, issued on the 23rd June, 1331, four separate Bulls, three of which provided for the appropriation to the College of the three churches, and the fourth dealt with the matter last referred to, the use of St. Mary's Church for secular assemblies, but very differently from the King's expectations. Instead of acceding to the proposal that a simple and expeditious machinery should be provided for the reconciliation of the Church, on the not unusual occurrence of a riot within its walls, he proceeded to forbid, under penalty of excommunication, the holding of any meetings whatever, "mercationes aliquas emendo vel vendendo seu conventiculas illicitas," in the church or churchyard. The Bulls authorising the appropriations asked for were promptly put into execution, and the benefices secured to the College, though Aberford did not fall vacant till 1341, and Coleby not till 1346. But the fourth Bull was suffered to lie unemployed in the College custody, until an opportunity[132] arose in which it was thought likely to prove serviceable.

Adam de Brome died 16th June, 1332, on which day his obit. was long observed by the College. By his will, proved in the Mayor of Oxford's Court, certain houses in Oxford—Moses Hall in Penyferthyng Street, and Bauer Hall in St. Mary Magdalen parish—which he had acquired for the further endowment of his College, were devised to Richard Overton, clerk, his executor. Overton may have been one of the Fellows; at all events he was intimately associated with Adam de Brome in the establishment of the College and in the acquisition of its endowments; and the property now left to him, and other property afterwards acquired, were all ultimately secured to Oriel.

Adam de Brome was succeeded in the Provostship by William de Leverton, Fellow and Master of Arts, unanimously elected by the College, and instituted by the Bishop, 27th June. Leverton died 21st Nov. 1348, and William de Hawkesworth, Doctor in Theology, was elected in his place. The Bishop annulled this election on the ground of informality, and himself appointed Hawkesworth to be Provost by his own authority.[133] Hawkesworth's tenure of the Provostship was short, and it is chiefly memorable for the part he played in the disputed election to the Chancellorship of the University, which occurred early in 1349. Hawkesworth, who had already acted as the Chancellor's Commissary, was the candidate of the Northerners, the party with which the College appears throughout to be connected; John Wylliot, Fellow of Merton, was the candidate of the Southerners. On the 19th of March 1349, Hawkesworth, as Chancellor, with his Proctors proceeded to St. Mary's for the performance of Divine service, and they were there attacked by Wylliot and his party. It was then that Hawkesworth had recourse to the neglected Bull of Pope John XXII., which had hitherto lain unused in the College Treasury. It was now produced and publicly read in the Church, with what immediate result does not appear, though Wylliot's action was complained of to the King, and a Commission sent to inquire into the matter. Hawkesworth's death followed soon after, April 8th; he was buried in St. Mary's, where an inscription still remains to his memory. Before the election of his successor, an order was received from the Bishop, prescribing the procedure to be followed, probably with the object of preventing the irregularities which had vitiated the last election. William de Daventre, who was now chosen, had been an active member of the College for some years; his name occurs frequently in deeds relating to the Oxford property. In 1361 the College found itself rich enough to obtain the King's license to add to its possessions divers messuages and small pieces of ground in Oxford, which had been accumulating since the foundation, and which were, up to this time, held in the name of members of the society in trust. The earliest roll of College property, the rental for the year 1363-4, was drawn up shortly after the license had been obtained and acted upon; and as a consequence of this increase in their corporate revenues, a new ordinance or statute was issued in 1364, augmenting the weekly commons, and assigning additional stipends to the Provost, and to certain College servants.

Daventre died in June 1373, and was succeeded by John de Colyntre, then one of the Fellows, and for some years past one of its leading members. The entry of his election in the Lincoln Register records the names of the electing Fellows, eight besides Colyntre himself, and describes him in eulogistic language, "virum in spiritualibus et temporalibus plurimum circumspectum literarum sciencia vita et moribus merito commendandum scientem et valentem jura domus nostrae efficaciter prosequi et tueri quin immo propter vite sue munditiam et excellentiam virtutum apud omnes admodum gratiosum." It was long before the Fellows were again as completely in harmony upon the choice of their head. Colyntre's rule lasted till his death in 1385 or 1386.

All through the latter part of the fourteenth century the College was engaged in increasing its scanty endowment, by the purchase, as opportunity offered, of houses, quit-rents, and other property in Oxford, contiguous to or in the neighbourhood of La Oriole. The chantry of St. Mary in the church of St. Michael Southgate, founded by Thomas de la Legh, was annexed to the College in 1357; as was also the chantry of St. Thomas in the church of St. Mary the Virgin in 1392. Other acquisitions were secured by successive licenses in mortmain, granted in 1376, in 1392, and in 1394. In this way the greater part of the ground lying between La Oriole and St. Mary's Hall was acquired and appropriated to the enlargement of the College buildings and garden.

The name of St. Mary's College, the legal description of the College, seems to have been little used: the Society is sometimes described as the King's Hall, or the King's College, but it was more generally known by the old name of the mansion in which it was lodged. The first instance of the use of the name "Oriel" by the College itself in a formal document is in 1367; but it was no doubt a popular designation at a much earlier date.

In 1373 license was granted by the Bishop for the celebration of masses and other divine offices in a chapel constructed, or to be constructed, within the College. Previous to this the church of St. Mary had been resorted to for all purposes. The legends on the painted glass windows in this chapel, preserved by Wood, record its erection by Richard Earl of Arundel, and by his son Thomas Arundel, about the year 1379.

Next in importance for the society of students which Adam de Brome had founded, after providing them with a house to lodge in, a church or chapel to worship in, and means to maintain them, was books for them to study; and this he had, as he believed, secured in the infancy of the foundation, by acquiring the library which Thomas Cobham, Bishop of Worcester, had brought together, and which he had placed in the new building he had erected adjoining St. Mary's Church. The building and the books placed in it were intended by the Bishop to be made over to the University for the use of all its students; but his intention was frustrated by his premature death; and his executors, finding his estate unequal to the payment of his debts and funeral expenses, were driven to pawn the books for the sum of fifty pounds. Adam de Brome, who, as Rector of the church, had allowed the building to be erected on his ground, pressed for the completion of the Bishop's undertaking; and the executors, unable otherwise to help him, told him to go in God's name, and redeem the books and hold them for the use of his College. Acting upon this permission, he redeemed the books, brought them to Oxford, and gave them, with the building which had been built for their reception, to his newly founded Society. This account of the transaction was not acquiesced in by the University; and in the Long Vacation of 1337, five years after Adam de Brome's death, the Chancellor's Commissary, at the head of a body of students, made forcible entry into the building, and carried off the books, the few Fellows who were then in residence not daring, as the College plaintively records, to offer any resistance. Thirty years later, proceedings were taken in the Chancellor's Court to recover possession of the building itself; and notwithstanding an urgent petition of the College imploring the Bishop of Lincoln to interfere on its behalf, the University took possession, and established, in the upper story of what is still known as the Old Congregation House, the nucleus of its first library. The College continued for a long time to assert its claim; and it was not till 1410 that the dispute was finally set at rest. But although disappointed in this quarter, other donors and benefactors rapidly came forward to compensate the College for its loss. Adam de Brome probably gave largely. Master Thomas Cobildik appears in the earliest catalogue as the donor of a considerable part of the then recorded collection. William Rede, Bishop of Chichester, who died in 1385, left ten books to Oriel, and made a similar bequest to most of the then existing Colleges. Provost Daventre, who died in 1373, left the residue of his books to the College. Two Fellows, Elias de Trykyngham and John de Ingolnieles, whose names occur together in a deed of 1356, gave books which are still in the College library. In 1375 a catalogue was compiled, which is still preserved;[134] this comprises about one hundred volumes, arranged according to the divisions of academical study, the Arts, the Philosophies, and lastly, the higher departments of Law—Civil and Canon—and Theology.

The Society for whose use it was intended was still a small one; the number of Fellows remained, as Adam de Brome had left it, at no more than ten. The average tenure of a Fellowship was about ten years. The requirement to proceed to the higher faculties produced little result; either it was disregarded, or the Fellowship was vacated from other causes before the time came for obeying it. By the statutes a vacancy was caused by entering religion, obtaining a valuable benefice, or ceasing to reside and study in the College. Marriage must always have been reckoned as a variety of the last disqualification; and it is especially enumerated in a deed of 1395 reciting the various causes which might bring about the avoidance of a Fellowship.

The Provost, on the other hand, generally held his office till his death. This is the case during the whole of the first century of the College (1326-1425).

Besides the members of the corporate society, room appears to have been found in the Oriole for a few other members, graduates, scholars, bible-clerks, commensales. Thomas Fitzalan, or Arundel, afterwards Archbishop of Canterbury, is the most eminent name recorded in the fourteenth century.

It is perhaps worth while here to dispose of the claim of the College to be connected with the authorship of *Piers Ploughman*. The real name of the author of this remarkable poem was, no doubt, William Langlande; but a misunderstanding of a passage in the opening introduction led Stowe hastily to infer that it was written by one John Malverne; and a name something like this, John Malleson, or Malvesonere, occurring as that of one of the Fellows of Oriel in deeds of the year 1387 and subsequently, was sufficient ground for identification. It is enough now to say that the poem was not written by any John Malverne, and that no person of that name was ever Fellow of Oriel; that the only Fellow with a name at all resembling it first appears some time after the date of the poem (*c.* 1362); and that the internal evidence makes it highly improbable that the writer was ever at any University. There has been, however, this indirect advantage to the College, that, on the ground of its supposed connexion, a valuable MS. of the poem was presented to its library in the seventeenth century, which ranks among the best authorities for the text.

On the death of Provost Colyntre in 1386 began the first of a long series of disputes concerning the election of a head. The Fellows were divided in their choice between Dr. John Middleton, Fellow and Canon of Hereford, and Master Thomas Kirkton. Middleton had the support of five, Kirkton of four of the Fellows. An attempt was made, though whether before or after the election does not clearly appear, to deprive Master Ralph Redruth, B.D., of his Fellowship, though on appeal to the King he succeeded in retaining his place. Kirkton presented himself to the Bishop of Lincoln, and was confirmed. From the Bishop appeal was made to the Archbishop of Canterbury, and to the King. On the 18th of April, 1386, Letters Patent were issued, ordering two of the Fellows, John Landreyn, D.D., and Master Ralph Redruth, to assume the government of the College, pending the termination of the dispute; and by other letters of May 23rd, the Archbishop, Robert Rugge, Chancellor of the University, and John Bloxham, Warden of Merton, were commissioned to hear the parties and give final judgment and sentence. Under this commission some sentence may have been given in favour of Kirkton, though of this no record has been discovered. At all events the King's Sergeant-at-arms was ordered, October 26th, to put him in peaceable possession of the Provostship. This order was again, January 4th, 1386-7, revoked by Letters Patent, reciting that Kirkton had before Arundel, then Chancellor and Bishop of Ely, renounced all his claims. Meanwhile the Archbishop had proceeded independently and more slowly. On the 4th of May he had commissioned Master John Barnet, official of the Court of Canterbury, and Master John Baketon, Dean of Arches, to hear Middleton's appeal; and a like commission to Barnet alone was issued on the 21st of November. Under the last commission sentence was given in favour of Middleton, and an order was sent, 26th February, 1386-7, to the Chancellor of Oxford, and to John Landreyn for his due induction.

Middleton died at Hereford, 27th June, 1394, and was succeeded by John Maldon, M.A., B.M., and Scholar in Divinity, "nuper & in ultimis diebus consocius et conscolaris juratus." In the record of the election in the Lincoln Register, the names of twelve other Fellows appear as electors. The most important memorial of his period of office now preserved is the Register of College muniments, compiled in 1397, perhaps under the hand of Thomas Leyntwardyn, Fellow, and afterwards Provost. This valuable record consists of a carefully arranged catalogue of all the deeds, charters, and muniments of title then in the College possession. Prefixed to the Register is a Calendar, noting the anniversaries, obits, and other days to be observed in the College in commemoration of its founders and benefactors. Maldon died early in 1401-2. By his will, dated January 21st, he made various bequests to the College, and to individual Fellows. One book, at least, belonging to him is still in the library.

Hitherto the materials for the history of the College have mainly consisted of the title-deeds relating to the property from time to time acquired, the purchases being in the first instance made in the names of a certain number of the Fellows, these again handing it on to some of their successors, until the College felt itself in a position to apply for a license in mortmain to enable it to hold the property in its corporate character. In this way it is possible to make out a tolerably full list of the early members of the College. From about the time of the compilation of the earliest Register, in 1397, this source of information is no longer very productive. Compared with the abundance of deeds of the fourteenth century, which are catalogued in the Register of 1397, the fifteenth century is singularly deficient. Fortunately, however, the want is supplied by other sources of information of more interest. The earliest book of treasurer's accounts, still preserved, extends from 1409 to 1415. The income of the College was made up of the rents of Oxford houses, about £53; the tithes of its three churches, Aberford, Coleby, and Littlemore, belonging to St. Mary's, about £35;

and the proceeds of offerings in St. Mary's Church, about £28. The net income, after deducting repairs and other outgoings on property, was between £80 and £90. The principal items of expenses were (1) the commons of the Provost and Fellows, at the rate of 1*s*. 3*d.* per week per head; (2) battells, the charge for allowances in meat and drink to other persons employed in and about the College, servants, journeymen, labourers, tilers, and the like, including also the entertainment of College visitors, the clergy of St. Mary's, or the city authorities; (3) exceedings, "excrescentiae," the cost incurred on any unusual occasion of College festivity, wine drunk on the feasts of Our Lady, pittances distributed among the members of the College on certain prescribed days, and similar extraordinary expenses. The amounts expended are accurately recorded for each week, the week ending, according to the practice which continues at Oriel to the present day, between dinner and supper on Friday. The total of these charges amounted to about £40. The stipends of the Provost and of the College officers, the payments to the Vicar of St. Mary's and the four chaplains, the wages of College servants, and the ordinary cost of the College fabric, are the principal other items of expenditure.

In 1410, the long-standing dispute with the University as to Cobham's library was set at rest, through the mediation of Archbishop Arundel. Not long afterwards a sum of money was raised by contributions from members of the College, and from parishioners of St. Mary's, for renewing the internal fittings of the church, the University giving £10 *pro choro*. On the completion of the work, the Chancellor and the whole congregation of regents and non-regents were regaled with wine, at a cost of eight shillings, including oysters for the scrutineers.

It would not be easy to discover in the dry pages of the College accounts, any indication of the domestic quarrels which at this time violently divided the Society. The attempts made by the Archbishop, with the support of the King, to suppress the Lollard doctrines, aroused considerable opposition in the University. In 1395, Pope Boniface IX. had issued a Bull, in answer to a petition from the University, by which the Chancellor was confirmed as the sole authority over all its members, to the exclusion of all archbishops and bishops in England. This Bull, though welcome to the majority of the Congregation, consisting largely of Masters of Arts, was resisted by the higher faculties, and especially by the Canonists; and the King, at the instance of the Archbishop, compelled the University, by the threat of withdrawing all its privileges, to renounce the exemption. Another burning question was the condemnation of the heretical doctrines of Wycliffe. Under considerable pressure from Archbishop Arundel, the University appointed twelve examiners to search Wycliffe's writings, and extract from them all the erroneous conclusions which deserved condemnation. This task was performed in 1409; but the recalcitrant party among the residents continued to throw considerable difficulty in the way of the Archbishop's wishes; and

Oriel seems to have been an active centre of resistance. In 1411, the Archbishop visited the University, with the double object of asserting his metropolitical authority, which had been threatened by the Papal Bull of exemption, and of crushing out the Lollard heresies. He was not immediately successful; but he had behind him the support of the King, and by the end of the year the obnoxious Bull was revoked, and order was restored. It was probably after this settlement that an enquiry was held at Oriel into the conduct of some of the Fellows who had taken an active part in opposition. William Symon, Robert Dykes, and Thomas Wilton, all Northerners, are charged with being stirrers up and fomenters of discord between the nations; they frequent taverns day and night, they come into College at ten, eleven, or twelve at night, and if they find the gate locked, climb in over the wall. Wilton wakes up the Provost from his sleep, and challenges him to come out and fight. On St Peter's Eve, 1411, when the College gate was shut by the Provost's order, he went out with his associates, attacked the Chancellor in his lodgings, and slew a scholar who was within. One witness deposed to seeing him come armed into St. Mary's Church, and when his sword fell out of his hand, crying out, "There wyl nothing thryve wyt me." In support of the charge that Oriel College suffered in reputation by reason of the misbehaviour of its Fellows, Mr. John Martyll, then Fellow, deposes that many burgesses of Oxford and the neighbourhood are minded to confiscate the College lands, rents, and tenements. Upon these general charges of domestic misconduct, follow others against Symon and against Master John Byrche of more public importance. Byrche was Proctor in 1411, and Symon in 1412.[135] Both appear to have taken an active part in opposing the attempt of the Chancellor and the Archbishop to correct the ecclesiastical and doctrinal heresies of the University. Byrche as Proctor contrived to carry in the Great Congregation a proposal to suspend the power of the twelve examiners appointed to report on Wycliffe's heresies; and when the Chancellor met this by dissolving the Congregation, Byrche next day summoned a Small Congregation, and obtained the appointment of judges to pronounce the Chancellor guilty of perjury, and by this means frightened him into resigning his office. When the Archbishop arrived for his visitation, Byrche and Symon held St. Mary's Church against him, and setting his interdict at naught, they opened the doors, rang the bells, and celebrated high mass. When summoned in their place in College to renounce the Papal Bull of Exemption, they declined to follow the example of their elders and betters, and flatly refused to comply.

Upon these charges a number of witnesses were examined; some, possibly townsmen, giving evidence as to the disturbances in the streets between the Northern and Southern nations; others, notably John Possell, the Provost, Mr. John Martyll, and Mr. Henry Kayll, Fellows, Mr. Nicholas Pont, and Mr. John Walton, speaking to the occurrences in College and in the Convocation House. It does not seem that any very serious results followed from the inquiry;

Symon, and a young bachelor Fellow, Robert Buckland, against whom no specific charge was made, confessed themselves in fault; as to the others, nothing more is recorded. A number of further charges were prepared against a still more important member of the College, the Dean, John Rote (or Root), who by his connivance, and by his refusal to support the Provost's authority, made himself partaker in the misconduct of the younger Fellows, and was justly held to be the "root" of all the evil. Such was the weight of his character in College, that none would venture to go against his opinion; his refusing to interfere, his sitting still and saying nothing when these enormities were reported to the Provost, was a direct encouragement to the offenders. At other times, in Hall, and in the company of the Fellows, he uttered the rankest Lollardism. "Are we to be punished with an interdict on our church for other people's misdoings? Truly it shall be said of the Archbishop, 'The devil go with him and break his neck.' The Archbishop would better take care what he is about. He tried once before to visit the University, and was straightway proscribed the realm. I have heard him say, 'Do you think that Bishop beyond the sea'—meaning the Pope—'is to give away my benefices in England? No, by St. Thomas.'" What was this but the battle-cry of the new sect, "Let us break their bonds asunder, and cast away their cords from us"? But no evidence was offered on these charges, and Root remained undisturbed in his College eminence.

Possell, who is stated to have been sixty years of age at the time of the commission of enquiry, seems to have died in September 1414; and the proceedings which followed further illustrate the divided condition of the College. A prominent candidate for the Provostship was Rote, already conspicuous for his outspoken Lollardism, and who, by his adversaries' own admissions, was of far more weight and influence in the College than the old and timid Provost. An election was held, seemingly in the following October, at which he was chosen; and he obtained confirmation from the Bishop of Lincoln on November 17th. But the validity of the proceedings was at once contested by Mr. John Martyll, one of the Fellows, on the ground of want of notice; and Rote's claim to the office was kept in suspense, pending an appeal to Rome. From the College accounts, the payments due to the Provost seem to have been made to Rote, under a salvo, pending the appeal. Archbishop Courtenay, who had lately succeeded Arundel, interfered, and summoned the parties before him at Lambeth, where on 14th February, 1415, Rote renounced his claims. A new election took place, at which Dr. William Corffe was chosen; and he was confirmed by the Bishop of Lincoln, on the 16th of March following, by John Martyll, his proxy. He appears then to have been absent from England, representing the University at the Council of Constance. From this embassy he perhaps never returned; the proceedings of the Council record him as present in June 1415; and a note in a MS. in the College library states that he died at Constance. His name occurs as Provost in a deed dated 14th May, 1416; and he is mentioned as "in remotis agens" 3rd April, 1417. His death may be presumed to have occurred about September 1417.

The period from 1429 to 1476, during which the College was under the rule of its four great provosts—John Carpenter, Walter Lyhert, John Hals, and Henry Sampson—was one of exceptional brilliance and prosperity. Hitherto the College had been one of the most slenderly endowed; but during this period a stream of benefactions flowed in upon it, which materially altered its position. The first and most considerable addition which it received was the legacy of John Frank, Master of the Rolls, who left the sum of £1000 for the support of four additional Fellows. The money was judiciously invested in the purchase of the Manor of Wadley, near Faringdon, once the property of the Abbey of Stanley, Wilts, and which had lately been forfeited to the Crown. This property was acquired in 1440, and the statute providing for the enlargement of the Foundation is dated 13th May, 1441. The adjoining estate of Littleworth was purchased some time later by Hals, then Bishop of Lichfield, and also given to the College. The manors of Dene and Chalford,[136] in the parishes of Spelsbury and Enstone, Oxon, were acquired by Carpenter, who had become Bishop of Worcester in 1443, and were given by his will to the College, for the support of a Fellow from the diocese of Worcester. Somewhat later William Smyth, Bishop of Lincoln, and afterwards one of the founders of Brasenose College, founded another Fellowship for his own diocese, and endowed the College with the manor of Shenington, near Banbury. The last considerable addition to the College property was made by Richard Dudley, sometime Fellow, who in 1525 gave the manor of Swainswick, near Bath, to maintain two Fellows. The whole of these new endowments, which exceed many times over the value of the original possessions of the College, were acquired in a period of less than a hundred years, and they are the lasting memorial of what until recent times must be considered the most splendid period in the College history.

By these benefactions the number of Fellows, fixed at ten in the Foundation Statutes, was raised to eighteen, at which it remained down to the changes of recent times. Four of these, founded by John Frank, were to be chosen out of the counties of Wilts, Dorset, Somerset, and Devon; one, founded by Bishop Carpenter, from the diocese of Worcester; and one, founded by Bishop Smyth, from the diocese of Lincoln. The two Fellowships founded by Dudley were not made subject to any restriction; but the College bound itself, in acknowledgment of Carpenter's benefaction, to assign one of the original Fellowships also to the diocese of Worcester. This provision was repealed in 1821. There were therefore from the reign of Henry VIII. onwards seven Fellowships limited in the first instance to certain counties and dioceses, and eleven which were subject to no restriction. And there never grew up at any time any class of junior members of the Foundation, entitled by statute or custom to succeed to Fellowships, or indeed any class whatever, corresponding to the scholars, postmasters or demies, to be found at most other Colleges. Certain Exhibitions were indeed established by Bishop Carpenter and Bishop Lyhert, and charged upon lands given by them to St. Anthony's Hospital in London. Others, again, were founded by Richard Dudley. But neither the Exhibitions of St. Anthony nor the Dudley Exhibitions ever grew to the least importance. The small stipends originally assigned to them were never increased; and with the change in the value of money, they sank into complete insignificance.

New statutes to regulate these additions to the Foundation were enacted in 1441, 1483, and in 1507. From another statute in 1504 dates the establishment of the College Register, which thenceforward becomes the sole authentic record of the history of the College. This Register is directed to be kept not by the Provost, but by the Dean; and a similar practice was established about the same time in several other Colleges, such as Merton, where the Register begins in 1482, Magdalen, Brasenose, and others. It was probably thought that the duty would be better discharged by a subordinate officer, who could be called to account by his superior, than by the Head himself, whose negligence it was no one person's business to correct. The Oriel Register, though first instituted by the statute of 1504, contains also the record of some transactions of earlier date; and the statute was probably intended to put upon a regular footing a practice which had already begun, and which was found to be of service. If this Register had been employed as the statute directed, in recording "omnia acta et decreta, per Praepositum et Scholares capitulariter facta," it would be invaluable for the history of the College; but unfortunately the tendency soon showed itself to confine the entries to a limited number of cases, such as the elections and admissions of the Provost and Fellows, and to leave unnoticed many matters belonging to the ordinary daily life of the Society, for the insertion of which no exact precedent was found. When at a later time the character of the College changed from a small Society of graduate students to an educational institution, receiving undergraduate members, scarcely any notice is to be discovered in the Register which betrays the existence of tutors or pupils, or of any other members of the Society besides the Provosts and Fellows.

Another important source of information is the series of Treasurer's accounts, known as the Style. These begin in 1450, almost immediately after the election of Provost Sampson, and the plan then introduced, of which he may possibly have been the author, has lasted in unbroken continuity to the present time. For some time this account records the whole of the pecuniary transactions of the College; but after the act of Elizabeth (18 Eliz. c. 6) came into operation, and the surplus revenue of each year became divisible among the Provost and Fellows, the practice soon established itself of excluding from both sides of the account items of a novel or exceptional character. The rents of the College estates are given in the fullest detail; but no mention is made of the fines taken on the renewal of leases, although these began very early to form an important part of the College revenue. The whole of the domestic side of the account, the charges upon members outside the Foundation, and the cost of their maintenance, the fees paid by undergraduates to tutors and College officers, servants' wages, and other similar items, are nowhere noticed. When in the seventeenth century the whole fabric of the College was pulled down and rebuilt, it would be difficult to find in the pages of the Style any entry which would give a hint that any unusual outlay was in progress.

The century which followed the resignation of Provost Sampson in 1475, presents very little of general interest. At the visitation of the College by Atwater, Bishop of Lincoln, in 1520, among other matters of minor consequence, occurs the first recorded instance of an abuse which was probably then and for long afterwards not unfrequent. Thomas Stock had resigned his Fellowship in favour of John Throckmorton, keeping back his resignation until he was sure that Throckmorton would be elected. "Hoc potest trahi in exemplum perniciosum. Ita quod in posterum socii resignabunt loca sua quibus voluerint. Dominus injunxit ne deinceps aliquis talia faceret in electionibus ibidem." The Injunctions of Bishop Longland, following on his visitation in 1531, seem to show a growing laxity of discipline. The Provost, then Thomas Ware, is admonished to be personally resident in the College, and to attend more diligently to his duties. The Bachelors are to observe the regular hours of study in the library at night, and not to introduce strangers into their sleeping-rooms. The new classical learning ("recentiores literae, lingua Latina, et opera poetica") is not to be pursued to the prejudice of the older studies, the "Termini Doctorum antiquorum." The disputations and exercises are to be kept up as in former times; the Provost, Dean, and senior masters are to attend the disputations, and to be ready to solve the doubtful points. No Fellow is to go out of residence without the leave of the Provost or the Dean, and then only for a limited time, whether in term or vacation. The vacant Fellowships are to be filled up in a month's time, and no Fellowship to remain vacant in future longer than one month.

Fifteen years later another set of Injunctions was issued by the same Bishop. The Fellows are again enjoined to be diligent in their studies, giving themselves to philosophy for three years following their admission, and then going on to divinity. The unseemly behaviour of Mr. Edmund Crispyne calls for special reprimand; he is to give up blasphemy and profane swearing; he is not to let his beard grow, or to wear plaited shirts, or boots of a lay cut; he is to be respectful and obedient to the Provost and Dean, on pain of excommunication and deprivation of his Fellowship. Mention is made of St. Mary Hall as a place of education under the control of the College, but distinct from it. The door opening from the College into the Hall is to be walled up, and no communication between the two to be allowed henceforth. The College is to appoint a fit person to be Principal of the Hall, who is to provide suitable lectures for the instruction of the students there.

The Reformation makes but little mark in the recorded history of the College. No difficulty was met with by the King's Commissioner, Dr. Cox, when he came in 1534 to require the acknowledgment of the Royal supremacy. Four years later came the orders for depriving Becket of the honours of saintship, and for removing his name from all service-books. The thoroughness with which these orders were carried out is remarkably illustrated at Oriel, where even in so obscure a place as the Calendar prefixed to the Register of College Muniments, the days marked for the observance of St. Thomas have been carefully obliterated. There was, however, one member of Oriel, Edward Powell, who distinguished himself by his opposition to the King's policy. He had been Fellow of the College from about 1495 to 1505; afterwards he became Canon of Salisbury, and also held other ecclesiastical preferments. On the first appearance of Luther's writings he was selected by the University as one of the defenders of orthodoxy, and recommended as such to the King. When, however, the question of the King's divorce arose, Powell was retained by Queen Katherine as her ablest advocate; and from that time he was conspicuous by his resistance to the King. In 1540 he was hanged, drawn, and quartered at

Smithfield for denying the Royal supremacy, and for refusing to take the oath of succession.

In the pages of the College Register the affairs of St. Bartholomew's Hospital play a much more important part than any changes in religion. It was in 1536 that the long-standing dispute between the College and the City respecting the payment appropriated to the support of the almsmen was finally settled. The charge, £23 0*s*. 5*d*., out of the fee farm rent of the town, had been granted by Henry I. on the first establishment of the Hospital; but ever since the annexation to the College by Edward III., great difficulty had been experienced in obtaining punctual payment. Charters confirming the charge had been obtained from nearly every sovereign through the fourteenth and fifteenth centuries; but the City persevered in disputing its liability. In 1536 both parties agreed to stand to the award of two Barons of the Exchequer, and by their decision the payment was settled at the reduced amount of £19 a year, and the nomination of the almsmen was transferred to the city.

On the resignation of Provost Haynes in 1550, the King's Council endeavoured to procure the election of Dr. William Turner, a prominent Protestant divine, honourably known as one of the fathers of English Botany. The Fellows, perhaps anticipating interference, held their election on the day of Haynes' resignation, and chose Mr. John Smyth, afterwards Margaret Professor of Divinity. Smyth was promptly despatched to the Bishop of Lincoln for confirmation, and on his return to the College was duly installed Provost. Some days afterwards the Dean was summoned to attend the Council and to give an account of the College proceedings. His explanations were apparently accepted, and no further action was taken. Smyth retained his place through all the changes of religion under Edward, Mary, and Elizabeth. On his resignation in 1565, Roger Marbeck of Christchurch, and Public Orator, was chosen, although not statutably qualified, having never been a Fellow. It is possible, though not hinted at in the account of the election, that he was recommended either by the Queen or by some other powerful personage; and a dispensation was obtained from the Visitor authorising a departure from the regulations of the Statutes. Marbeck held the office only two years, and was succeeded by John Belly, Provost 1566 to 1574.

The long reign of the next Provost, Anthony Blencowe, covers the period of transition from the old to the new era. The College of the medieval type consisted of the Fellows only. Already Bachelors of Arts at the time of their election, they carried on their studies under the direction of the Head and seniors, proceeding to the higher degrees, and ultimately passing from Oxford to ecclesiastical employment elsewhere. William of Wykeham had indeed made one important innovation on the type which Walter de Merton had created; for the younger members of his foundation were admitted direct from school, and only obtained their first University degree after they had been some years at College.

The example of New College was followed at Magdalen and Corpus; but in these cases, as at New College, the admission of undergraduates was only introduced as part of the regulations for members of the Foundation, and it was not in contemplation to make the College a school for all comers. No doubt a few *extranei*, graduate or undergraduate, were occasionally admitted to share the Fellows' table, and to profit by their advice and companionship; but the bulk of the younger students remained outside the Colleges, lodging in the numerous Halls in the town, and subject only to the discipline of the University. Instances of such *extranei* are Thomas Arundel, already mentioned as a member of Oriel in the fourteenth century; Henry, Prince of Wales, afterwards Henry V., at Queen's College; Doctor Thomas Gascoigne, who at different times resided at Oriel, at Lincoln, and at New College. This class survived to recent times in the Fellow commoners, or gentlemen commoners, whose connexion with the Colleges is historically older than the more numerous and important class of commoners, which has overshadowed and ultimately extinguished them. It is worth observing that the three Colleges of William of Wykeham's type, New College, Magdalen, and Corpus, although they received gentlemen commoners, did not admit ordinary commoners until the changes which followed on the University Commission of 1854. All Souls has remained to the present day a College of Fellows alone.

The religious changes of the sixteenth century were followed by great alterations in the discipline of the University. Acting on pressure from without, a Statute was passed in 1581 requiring all matriculated students to reside in a College or Hall. The old Halls had nearly all disappeared; of the few remaining most were connected more or less closely with one of the Colleges. Queen's College claimed, and was successful in retaining, St. Edmund's Hall. Merton had purchased Alban Hall in the earlier part of the century. Magdalen Hall was dependent on Magdalen College. The connexion between Oriel and St. Mary Hall was older and closer than any. The Principal was, invariably, chosen or appointed from among the Fellows. The holders of the small Exhibitions founded by Bishop Carpenter and Dr. Dudley were lodged not in the College but in the Hall; in times of plague the members of the Hall were allowed to remove to St. Bartholomew's Hospital, for a purer air. In the census of the University, taken in 1572, Oriel appears to have numbered forty-two members; of these the Provost and Fellows account for nineteen; three were servants; the remaining twenty, one of whom may be perhaps identified with Sir Walter Raleigh, represent the favoured class of *extranei*, of which we have already spoken. In the same year the members of St. Mary Hall numbered forty-six. The next half century sees this proportion completely reversed. The matriculations at Oriel from 1581 to 1621 average a little over ten a year; those at St. Mary Hall sink to five. The control over the Hall was taken away by the Chancellor, Lord

Leicester, though the College might well have made out as good a claim as that successfully asserted by Queen's College over St. Edmund's Hall. But the Principals continued to be chosen from among Fellows of Oriel down to the time of the Commonwealth.

As has been already stated, the Register contains but few notices from which it could be gathered that any great change in the character of the College took place at this time. In 1585 the Provost admonishes the Fellows as to the behaviour of their scholars, and they are ordered to be responsible to the butler for the battels of their scholars or pupils. In 1594 an order was made that no Fellow should have more than one poor scholar under the name of batler. In 1595 the Dean is invested with the power of catechising. In 1606 one of the Fellows is appointed public catechist for the instruction of the youth, as required by University Statute. In 1624 a Mr. Jones, not a Fellow, is appointed, on his own application, Praelector in Greek. A Register of the admission of commensales, that is the members of the higher order only, or Fellow commoners, was begun in 1596, and continued to 1610. It contains eighteen names only, the first being that of Robert Pierrepont, afterwards Earl of Kingston. With this exception the admissions into the College have to be collected from the University Matriculation Register, supplemented from about 1620 by the Caution Book.

It was this enlargement of its numbers that made it necessary for the College to take in hand the question of rebuilding the fabric in a manner suitable to the new requirements. The buildings then existing had been erected at different times, and had gradually been brought into the form of a quadrangle, occupying the site of the older part of the present College. These are shown in Neale's drawing, made in 1566. The chapel on the south side was that built by Richard, Earl of Arundel, about 1373. The Hall on the north side had been rebuilt about the year 1535, partly by the contributions of former Fellows. Provost Blencowe died in 1618, and was succeeded by Mr. William Lewis, Chaplain to Lord Bacon, and afterwards Master of St. Cross, and Prebendary of Winchester. Lewis' election was not unanimous, and though he was duly presented to the Bishop of Lincoln and confirmed by him, he thought it necessary to obtain a further ratification of his title from his patron. This proceeding is remarkable, as it is almost the solitary instance in which the original statutes of January 1326, superseded almost immediately after their issue by the Lincoln statutes of May in the same year, were quoted or acted upon. The Chancellor, assuming cognizance of the case as of an election in discord, pronounced in favour of Lewis, and by an order entered in the College Register and authenticated by his own hand, confirmed Lewis in his place. Lewis held the office for three years only, during which time, however, the design of the new building was determined upon, and the first part completed. Blencowe had left the sum of £1300 to be applied in the first instance to the west side—"the primaria pars Collegii." This was undertaken in 1619, and in the following year the south side was also taken down and rebuilt. Besides Blencowe's legacy, £300 was forthcoming from a College fund, and plate was sold to the value of £90. The College groves at Stowford and Bartlemas supplied some of the timber; the stone came from the College quarry at Headington. Timber was also sold from other College estates. But it was in obtaining contributions from former members, and from great people connected with Oriel, that Provost Lewis' talent was most remarkable. His skill in writing letters—"elegant, in a winning, persuasive way"— was long quoted as an example to other heads of Colleges. This "art, in which he excelled," had recommended him to Lord Bacon, and it was by his patron's advice that he employed it in the service of the College. Among those whom he laid under contribution were the Earl of Kingston and Sir Robert Harley, whose arms are still to be seen in the windows of the Hall. Lewis resigned the Provostship in 1621, and was succeeded by John Tolson. The completion of the new quadrangle was postponed for some years, though the design had probably been determined on from the first. In 1636 large sums of money were again raised by contributions from present and former members, and the north and east sides of the quadrangle were erected.

The plan of the new College is in its main features similar to that of Wadham, erected 1613, and of University, which was built some years after Oriel. In all of these the chapel and hall stand together opposite to the gateway, and form one side of a quadrangle. The other three sides are of uniform height, consisting of three stories, containing chambers for the Fellows and other members. In Oriel the library occupied a part of the upper story on the north side. The hall is approached by a flight of steps under a portico on the centre of the east side; above this portico are the figures of the Virgin and Child, to whom the College is dedicated, and of King Edward II., the founder, and King Charles I. in whose reign it was set up. Round the portico ran the legend in stone—"Regnante Carolo." By an unaccountable blunder, this last figure has been described in all accounts of the College as being that of King Edward III.; but there can be no doubt, both from the dress and from the features, that it represents King Charles, and no one else. Over the doorways round the quadrangle were stone shields bearing the arms of the four great benefactors— Frank, Carpenter, Smyth, and Dudley, and of the three Provosts—Blencowe, Lewis, and Tolson— under whom the new building was planned and executed. Blencowe's are also to be seen in the treasury in the tower, and upon the College gate. The whole building was completed in 1642, when the chapel was first used for divine service.

This great work had scarcely been completed when the Civil War broke out. In January 1642-3, the King being at Oxford, the College plate was demanded: 29 lbs. 0 oz. 5 dwt. of gilt, and 52 lbs. 7 oz. 14 dwt. of white plate was given, the College retaining only its founder's cup, and two other small articles—a mazer bowl and a cocoa-nut cup, believed to have been the gift of Bishop Carpenter. A few days afterwards a weekly contribution of £40 was assessed upon the Colleges and Halls for the expenses of fortifying the city; the charge upon Oriel was fixed at £1. This charge was joyfully acquiesced in by the College, "ita quod faxit Deus Musae una cum Rege suo contra ingrassantes hostium turmas tutius agant ac felicius." But these hopes were not to be realised; and the hardships of the siege soon came to tell heavily on the College finances. The high price of provisions, the difficulty of getting in rents, the debts incurred for the College building, must have seriously crippled their resources; and grievous complaints of their inability to complete the October audit occur in the years 1643, 1644, and 1645. In the last of these years extraordinary expedients had to be resorted to in order to maintain even the common table; leases were renewed or promised in reversion on almost any terms; the Oxford tenants were solicited to pay their rents in advance, on the promise of considerate treatment at their next renewal; all the timber at Bartlemas was felled at one stroke and converted into money. Even these heroic remedies were inadequate; and in March 1645-6 the commons' allowance was reduced to one-half, and the elections to vacant Fellowships suspended. The surrender of the city to the Parliament in the summer of 1646 must have been felt as a great relief. From that time, although the times were not altogether prosperous, the distress of the years of siege never reappeared with the same acuteness. The numbers of the undergraduate members, which had sunk to almost nothing, soon revived; and the College was able to build a Ball Court for their diversion in the back part of their premises. The Hospital of St. Bartholomew was rebuilt in 1651. Although now converted to other uses, this good gray stone house, with its eight chambers for the eight almsmen, still stands and bears its history on its face. On the several doorways, and also on the chapel, which, though not rebuilt, was refitted and beautified, are the date of the work, and the initials of the College,[137]the Provost, and the Treasurers.

The Parliamentary Visitation which descended upon Oxford in the year following the siege dealt on the whole very tenderly with Oriel. It is possible that Prynne, an old Oriel man, who was an active member of the London Committee, may have stood its friend. The answers of the Provost and Fellows to the Visitors' questions were in almost every case such as merited expulsion; but in the result only five Fellows were removed, and of these two were soon afterwards allowed to return to their place. Two Fellowships were suspended by the Visitors' order, in order to pay off the debts under which the College lay. Others were filled up by the Visitors or the London Committee during the years 1648 and 1652. After the latter year no further interference seems to have taken place, and on the death of Saunders, in 1652-3, Robert Say was elected in the accustomed form, and admitted without any confirmation from external authority. He held office till 1691, when he died after a long but uneventful reign of nearly forty years.

Of the Fellows of the College during the seventeenth century, not many achieved any distinction. Humphrey Lloyd, elected Fellow in 1631, and removed by the Visitors in 1648, became Bishop of Bangor. William Talbot, successively Bishop of Oxford, Salisbury, and Durham; Sir John Holt, who, after the Revolution, became Lord Chief Justice of England; and Sir William Scroggs, one of his predecessors, who gained an unenviable reputation in the political trials which arose out of the Popish Plot, were educated at Oriel, but were not Fellows. The most eminent name among the Fellows is undoubtedly John Robinson, Bishop of Bristol and afterwards of London, Lord Privy Seal, and the chief negotiator of the Peace of Utrecht. Soon after his election in 1675, he obtained leave to reside abroad, as chaplain to the English Minister at Stockholm. His benefactions to the College will be more conveniently mentioned later. With these exceptions the list of Fellows contains very few eminent names; and the same remark continues to be true in the main throughout the eighteenth century. The truth probably is that the system of election to Fellowships was tainted with corruption. Buying and selling of places was a common practice in the age of the Restoration, and it has survived to our own time in the army. In many Colleges this evil was to some extent kept in check by the establishment of a regular succession from Scholars to Fellows; but at Oriel, as has been already observed, the choice of the electors was absolutely free, and, valuable as this freedom may be when honestly exercised, it is capable of leading to corruption of the worst kind. In 1673 a complaint was made to the Bishop of Lincoln, the Visitor, by James Davenant, Fellow, against the conduct of the Provost at a recent election. The Bishop issued a commission to the Vice-Chancellor (Peter Mews, Bishop of Bath and Wells), Dr. Fell (Dean of Christ Church), and Dr. Yates (Principal of Brasenose), to visit the College. The conduct of the business seems to have been chiefly in Fell's hands; and in his letters to the Bishop he expresses in strong terms his opinion of the state of things he found in Oriel. He writes, 1st Aug. 1673—"When this Devil of buying & selling is once cast out your Lordship will I hope take care that he return not again lest he bring seven worse than himself into the house after 'tis swept and garnisht." He recommends various regulations for checking the evil; among them that the election be by the major part of the whole Society, "else 'twill always be in the Provost's power to watch his opportunity & when the house is thin strike up an election"; also that the successor be immediately admitted, "for there is a cheat in some houses by keeping the successor out for a good while after the election." The Bishop on this report issued a decree, 24th Jan., 1673-4, prescribing the proceeding in elections. Not to be baffled, the Provost, Say, hit upon the ingenious device of obtaining a Royal letter of recommendation for the candidate whose election he desired, and a letter was sent in favour of Thomas Twitty for the next vacancy. He was probably elected and admitted upon this recommendation;

though the Vice-Chancellor refused to allow him to subscribe as Fellow. The Bishop made his remonstrances at Court, and obtained the withdrawal of the King's letter, and Twitty's election was annulled before it had been entered in the College Register. The Provost seems to have written an insolent letter to the Bishop, such (says Fell) "as in another age a valianter man would not have written to a Visitor." Fell goes on—"Though I am afraid that with a very little diligence the being a party to Twitty's proceedings may be made out, yet it will not be safe to animadvert on that act, however criminal, as a fault, for notwithstanding the present concession, the Court will never endure to have the prerogative of laying laws asleep called in question. As to the letter I think 'twill be much the best way not to answer it. It is below the dignity of a Visitor to contest in empty words. If the Provost goes on with his Hectoring 'tis possible he may run himself so in the briers that 'twill not be easy for him to get out."

The regulations of Bishop Fuller were more fully established by a statute made by the College with the Visitor's approval in 1721, when the day of election was fixed to the Friday in Easter week, and the examination on the Thursday before. But new disputes had already begun which led to unexpected but most important consequences. At the Fellowship election in July 1721, Henry Edmunds, of Jesus, the hero of the ensuing struggle, received the votes of nine Fellows against those of three other Fellows and the Provost. The Provost rejected Edmunds and admitted his own candidate. Edmunds appealed to the Visitor, who upheld the Provost. On the Friday after Easter, 1723, Edmunds stood again, and he and four other candidates were chosen by a majority of the electors into the five vacant Fellowships. The Provost refused to admit them, and was again upheld by the Visitor, who claimed that the right of filling up the vacancies had devolved upon himself. Three places he proceeded to fill up at once; as to the other two he seems to have been in consultation with the Provost as to his choice, but not to have made any nomination. At the election in the following April 1724, two candidates received the votes of eight of the Fellows, against the votes of the Provost and of one other Fellow only, Mr. Joseph Bowles. The Provost as before refused to admit them. Edmunds now brought his action in the Common Pleas on behalf of himself and his four companions, claiming to have been legally elected. He took his stand on the original Foundation Statutes of January 1326, and claimed that the Crown and not the Bishop of Lincoln was the true and lawful Visitor of the College. These statutes, as has been already mentioned, were superseded within six months of their issue, and although in a few rare instances, questions had been brought before the King or his Chancellor, the Visitatorial authority of the Bishop had never before been disputed, but had been repeatedly exercised and acquiesced in for four hundred years. The case was tried at bar, before Chief Justice Eyre, and the three puisne judges, and a special jury; and on the 14th May, 1726, judgment was given in Edmunds' favour. The authority of the statutes of Jan. 1326 was established, and the Crown declared to be the sole Visitor. Edmunds and his four co-plaintiffs, as also the two candidates chosen in 1724, were admitted to their Fellowships in July 1726 by the Dean, the Provost refusing, on the ingenious plea that if the Crown was Visitor, it was for the Crown and not for the Common Pleas to decide on the validity of the election.

Dr. Carter died in September 1727, and notwithstanding his disagreement with the Fellows, he showed his affection for the College by leaving to it his whole residuary estate. He had already, by the help of Bishop Robinson, obtained the annexation to his office of a prebend at Rochester, and he provided for its further endowment by leaving £1000 for the purchase of a living to be held by the Provost. With this money the living of Purleigh, in Essex, was bought in 1730. Hitherto the Provostship had been but scantily endowed. The Parliamentary Visitors in 1648 had scheduled it as one of the Headships that required augmentation. The fixed stipend and the allowances prescribed by the statutes had, with the change in the value of money, shrunk to small proportions; the principal part of his income was derived from the dividend and the fines.

Both these sources of income were of modern growth. By the Act 18 Eliz., leases of College estates were limited to twenty-one years, and one-third of the old rent was to be reserved in corn. House property might be let for not longer than forty years. The beneficial effect of these Acts on the corporate revenue was not immediate; in many cases long terms had been granted shortly before, which did not expire for many years. Notably the College estate at Wadley had been let in 1539 for 208 years; and in 1736, when this long period was approaching its end, the lessees petitioned Parliament to interfere and prevent them being deprived of what they had so long treated as their own property. But few leases were of this extravagant duration; and in the course of the seventeenth century the College income was considerably increased. The Provost, however, received no more than one Fellow's share and a half in the dividend, *i. e.* the surplus income of the year, and one share only of the fines. The ecclesiastical preferment which Provost Carter secured to the Headship resulted in making it one of the best endowed places in Oxford, without imposing any additional charge on the College.

Bishop Robinson, who obtained the Rochester stall for the Provost, was also a benefactor in other ways. He founded three Exhibitions, to be held by bachelor students; and he also erected at his own expense an additional building on the east side of the College garden, containing six sets of chambers, three of which were to be occupied by his Exhibitioners. Dr. Carter erected at the same time a similar building on the west side.

The effect of the decision given in the Court of Common Pleas, was to restore the authority of the Foundation Statutes of January 1326. Under these Statutes only an actual Fellow could be chosen

Provost, and the election must be unanimous. On Dr. Carter's death, Mr. Walter Hodges was chosen by a majority of votes only, but he was confirmed by the Lord Chancellor, Lord King, upon whom, under these circumstances, the election had devolved. Henceforward, the Fellows agreed to make the formal election unanimous in every case, and no further instance of a disputed election occurred.

The history of the College during the remainder of the eighteenth century was quiet, decorous and uneventful. Its undergraduate members were drawn from all classes, but always included many young men of rank and family. Some of these showed their affection for the College in after life by benefactions more or less important. Henry, fourth Duke of Beaufort, founded four exhibitions for the counties of Gloucester, Monmouth and Glamorgan. Mrs. Ludwell, a sister of Dr. Carter, gave an estate in Kent for the support of two exhibitioners from that county. Edward, Lord Leigh, who died in 1786, bequeathed to the College the entire collection of books in his house at Stoneleigh. For the reception of this bequest, the new Library was built in the following year at the north end of the College garden.

Of the few eminent names connected with the College in the last century, that of Bishop Butler is the greatest. He entered Oriel in 1715, and his early rise in his profession was in a great measure due to the acquaintance he there made with Charles Talbot, afterwards Lord Chancellor, who recommended him to the patronage of his father, the Bishop of Durham, also an old member of the College. William Hawkins, elected Fellow in 1700, was an eminent lawyer, whose treatise of the Pleas of the Crown still keeps its place as a standard legal work. William Gerrard Hamilton, admitted in 1745, is still remembered as an early patron of Burke, and for his speech in the great debate in Nov. 1755, by which he gained his nickname. Gilbert White, of Selborne, among all the Fellows of Oriel of this period, has left the most lasting name. Yet his College history is in curious contrast to the reputation which is popularly attached to him. Instead of being, as is often supposed, the model clergyman, residing on his cure, and interested in all the concerns of the parish in which his duty lay, he was, from a College point of view, a rich, sinecure, pluralist non-resident. He held his Fellowship for fifty years, 1743-1793, during which period he was out of residence except for the year 1752-3, when the Proctorship fell to the College turn, and he came up to claim it. In 1757 he similarly asserted his right to take and hold with his Fellowship the small College living of Moreton Pinkney, Northants, with the avowed intention of not residing. Even at that time the conscience of the College was shocked at this proposal, and the claim was only reluctantly admitted. White continued to enjoy the emoluments of his Fellowship and of his College living, while he resided on his patrimonial estate at Selborne; and although it was much doubted whether his fortune did not exceed the amount which was allowed by the Statutes, he acted on the maxim that anything can be held by a man who can hold his tongue, and he continued to enjoy his Fellowship and his living till his death.

It was not till near the close of the century that the College took the decisive step which at once lifted it above its old level of respectable mediocrity, and gave it the first place in Oxford. As has been already shown, the election to Fellowships was singularly free from restriction; for most of them there was no limitation of birth, locality, or kindred; and no class of junior members had any title to succession or preference. When in 1795 Edward Copleston was invited from Corpus to stand for the vacant Fellowship, the first precedent was set for making the Oriel Fellowship the highest prize of an Oxford career. The old habit of giving weight to personal recommendations was not at once immediately laid aside. Even when Thomas Arnold was elected in 1815, it was still necessary for the Fellows to be lectured against allowing themselves to be prejudiced by the reports in Oxford that the candidate was a forward and conceited young man. But the better principle had the victory: the last election in which the older motives were allowed to prevail was in 1798, and from that time the College continued year after year to renew itself without fear or favour out of the most brilliant and promising of the younger students.

It was the head of Oriel, Provost Eveleigh, who, backed by the growing reputation of his College, induced the Hebdomadal Board to institute the new system of examination for honours. Under this system Oriel soon took and long retained the first place. It was an Oriel Fellow who, as Headmaster of the Grammar School at Rugby, succeeded, as was foretold of him, in changing the whole face of Public School Education in this country. It was another Fellow who brought about that religious movement which has worked a still greater change in the Church of England.

List of Provosts.

- 1326. Adam de Brome: first Provost under Charter of 21 Jan. 1325-6: died 16 June 1332.
- 1332. William de Leverton: instituted 27 June 1332: died 21 Nov. 1348.
- 1348. William de Hawkesworth: election confirmed 20 Dec. 1348: died 8 April 1349.
- 1349. William de Daventre: elected 1349: died June 1373.
- 1373. John de Colyntre: elected 8 July 1373: died c. 1385.
- 1385. [Headship in dispute between Thomas Kirkton and John de Middleton.]
- 1387. John de Middleton: confirmed 26 Feb. 1386-7: died 27 June 1394.
- 1394. John de Maldon: elected 3 July 1394: died Jan. 1401-2.
- 1402. [Headship in dispute between John Paxton and John Possell.]
- 1402. John Possell: died Sept. 1414.
- 1414. [John Rote: elected and confirmed 17 Nov. 1414, but resigned his claim 14 Feb. 1414-15.]
- 1415. William Corffe: confirmed 16 March 1414-15: died about Sept. 1417.

- 1417. [Headship in dispute between Richard Garsdale and Thomas Leyntwardyn.]
- 1419. Thomas Leyntwardyn: died 1421.
- 1421. Henry Kayle: confirmed 3 Dec. 1421: died 1422.
- 1422. [Headship in dispute between Nicholas Herry and another.]
- 1426. Nicholas Herry: first decision in his favour given 30 July 1424: final decision given 29 Jan. 1425-6: died 1427.
- 1427. John Carpenter: resigned 1435.
- 1435. Walter Lyhert: elected 3 June 1435: resigned 28 Feb. 1445-6.
- 1446. John Hals: elected 24 March 1445-6: resigned 4 March 1448-9.
- 1449. Henry Sampson: resigned 1475.
- 1475. Thomas Hawkyns: elected Nov. 1475: died Feb. 1477-8.
- 1478. John Taylor: elected 8 Feb. 1477-8: died 23 Dec. 1492.
- 1493. Thomas Cornysh: elected 5 Feb. 1492-3: resigned 26 Oct. 1507.
- 1507. Edmund Wylsford: elected 30 Oct. 1507: died 3 Oct. 1516.
- 1516. James More: elected 14 Oct. 1516: resigned 12 Nov. 1530.
- 1530. Thomas Ware: elected 16 Nov. 1530: resigned 6 Dec. 1538.
- 1538. Henry Mynne: elected 6 Dec. 1538: died 13 Oct. 1540.
- 1540. William Haynes: elected 18 Oct. 1540: resigned 17 June 1550.
- 1550. John Smyth: elected 17 June 1550: resigned 2 March 1564-5.
- 1565. Roger Marbeck: elected 9 March 1564-5: resigned 24 June 1566.

- 1566. John Belly: elected 25 June 1566: resigned 3 Feb. 1573-4.
- 1574. Antony Blencowe: elected 10 Feb. 1573-4: died 25 Jan. 1617-18.
- 1618. William Lewis: elected 28 March 1618: resigned 29 June 1621.
- 1621. John Tolson: elected 5 July 1621: died 16 Dec. 1644.
- 1644. John Saunders: elected 19 Dec. 1644: died 20 March 1652-3.
- 1653. Robert Say: elected 23 March 1652-3: died 24 Nov. 1691.
- 1691. George Royse: elected 1 Dec. 1691: died 23 April 1708.
- 1708. George Carter: elected 6 May 1708: died 30 Sept. 1727.
- 1727. Walter Hodges: elected 24 Oct. 1727: died 14 Jan. 1757.
- 1757. Chardin Musgrave: elected 27 Jan. 1757: died 29 Jan. 1768.
- 1768. John Clarke: elected 12 Feb. 1768: died 21 Nov. 1781.
- 1781. John Eveleigh: elected 5 Dec. 1781: died 10 Dec. 1814.
- 1814. Edward Copleston: elected 22 Dec. 1814: resigned 29 Jan. 1828.
- 1828. Edward Hawkins: elected 31 Jan. 1828: died 18 Nov. 1882.
- 1882. David Binning Monro: elected 20 Dec. 1882.

VI.
QUEEN'S COLLEGE.

By J. R. Magrath, D.D., Provost of Queen's.

It is now just five centuries and a half since Robert of Eglesfield founded "the Hall of the scholars of the Queen" in Oxford. The Royal license for its foundation was sealed in the Tower of London on the eighteenth of January, and the statutes of the founder were corrected, completed and sealed in Oxford on the tenth of February in the year 1340 as men then reckoned, or as we should say 1341.

Eglesfield was chaplain and confessor to Philippa, Queen of Edward III. He came of gentle blood in Cumberland, and had ten years before received from the King the hamlet and manor of Ravenwyk or Renwick, forfeited through rebellion by Andrew of Harcla. This and the property he had purchased in Oxford as a site for his hall was all that Eglesfield was able of himself to contribute to its maintenance. His relations with the Queen and the King were, however, of priceless service to the new foundation.

Eglesfield seems to have continued for the remainder of his life to have fostered by his presence and influence the institution he had founded. In the earliest of the "Long Rolls," or yearly accounts of the College, which are preserved, that of 1347-8, his name appears at the head of the list of the members. In that year sixteen pence is paid for the hire of a horse for six days, that he may visit London on the Thursday after the feast of St. Augustine, bishop of the English; twenty-three shillings is paid for a horse for him to go to Southampton about the time of the festival of St. Peter *ad vincula*; William of Hawkesworth, Provost of Oriel, a former Fellow, lends him a horse, and a penny is put down for a shoe for the same, and a halfpenny for parchment bought for him for documents executed on the feast of Saints Cosmo and Damian.

His funeral is celebrated in 1351-2. They made a "great burning for him," as of seventeen and a quarter pounds of wax, costing nine shillings, expended during the year, eleven pounds were used at the funeral of the founder. Fourpence halfpenny only seems to have been spent on wine on the same occasion.

A casket containing his remains was transferred from the old chapel to the vault under the new chapel when the latter was built.

His horn is still used on gaudy-days as the loving-cup. It must have been mounted in something like its present condition almost from the beginning, as in the Long Roll of 1416-7 sixteen pence is paid "pro emendatione aquilae crateris fundatoris." Other repairs are mentioned later as in 1584-5, "pro reparatione particulae coronae quae circumdat operculum cornu xii d.; item, pro reparandis aliis partibus cornu xviii d."

His name is also kept alive by the "canting" custom observed in the College on New Year's Day, when after dinner the Bursar presents to each guest a needle threaded with silk of a colour suitable to his faculty (*aiguille et fil*), and prays for his prosperity in the words "Take this and be thrifty."[138]

The object with which the College was founded is set forth in the statutes as "the cultivation of Theology to the glory of God, the advance of the Church, and the salvation of souls." It was to be a Collegiate Hall of Masters, Chaplains, Theologians, and other scholars to be advanced to the order of the priesthood. It was founded in the name of the Holy and Undivided Trinity, to the Glory of our Lord and of His Mother and of the whole Court of Heaven, for the benefit of the Universal Church and especially of the Church of England, for the prosperity of the King and Queen and their children, and for the salvation of their souls and the souls of their progenitors and successors, and of the souls of the founder's family and his benefactors, especially William of Muskham, Rector of the Church of Dereham, and for the "*salutare suffragium*" of all the living and the dead.

The benefactions of Muskham do not seem to have ceased with the foundation of the College. In 1347 Roger Swynbrok goes to Dereham on behalf of the College to get money from Muskham, and the hire of his horse costs eightpence, and there are entries of money received from Muskham in later years. Other persons besides the members of the College were interested in him, as in 1362 the oblations for his soul and the soul of John de Hotham the second Provost amounted to £29 16s. 11½d.

The statutes lay down with considerable minuteness of detail the course of life which Eglesfield expected the members of his foundation to follow, and, in connection with the early accounts of the College, which have been preserved with tolerable completeness, give us some materials for an account of the social life in the College during the earlier portion of its history.

It is probable, indeed, that the large and complex establishment, whose details are developed in Eglesfield's statutes, rather represent what he wished for and aimed at than the actual condition of the College at any time; but there seems to have been always in the College a sincere desire to carry out, so far as was possible, the prescriptions of the founder; and, as we shall see, some of his minutest directions have regulated the practice of the College ever since his days.

The patronage of the Hall, "the advowson" as he calls it, was to be vested in his Royal mistress Philippa, and in the Queens consort of England who shall succeed her. He adds the characteristic detail that, if a king dies before his successor is married, the patronage shall be continued to the widow till a Queen consort comes into being.

Philippa had already procured from her husband for the infant College the Church of Brough under Staynesmore, and this was to be only an earnest of the benefits the College was to derive from the lofty patronage the founder thus secured to it. She was the first queen to be distinguished as patroness and foundress of a Collegiate Hall.

In 1353-4, which seems to have been a year of unusual expense to the College, among the donations received xxvj pounds iiij shillings is credited to "domina Regina."

It was doubtless through the Queen's influence that the King in 1343 endowed the College with the advowson of Bletchingdon, and in the following year with the Wardenship of St. Julian's Hospital, commonly called God's House, in Southampton.

The College seems always to have been careful to secure the patronage of the Queens consort of England. In the muniment room is preserved a letter from Anne, Richard II.'s queen, to her husband, asking him to grant letters patent to the College.

In 1603, on the 3rd of August, 48*s.* 6*d.* is allowed to the Provost for his journey "ad solicitandam dominam reginam pro patronatu collegii." This was another Anne, James I.'s wife. A bible was presented to the Queen which cost 42*s.* 4*d.*

It was through Henrietta Maria—Queen Mary, as the College delights to call her—that Charles I. was supplicated for the advowsons in Hampshire given by the King to the College in 1626. Caroline, George II.'s queen, gave £1000 towards the rebuilding of the College in the eighteenth century; and promised another £1000, which, owing to her death, still (as the Benefactors' Book says) remains "unpaid but not unhoped for." Charlotte, George III.'s consort, heads the list of those who subscribed towards the rebuilding of the south-west wing after the fire of 1778. Queen Adelaide was the last queen entertained within the walls of the College.

The community was to consist of a Provost and twelve Fellows, incorporated under the name of "the Hall of the Queen in Oxford," with a common seal.

The original body was nominated by the founder, and their names are set forth in his statutes.

The number thirteen was chosen with reference to the number of our Lord and His Apostles, "sub mysterio decursus Christi et Apostolorum in terris."

Richard of Retteford, Doctor of Divinity, was the first Provost, and the thirteen came from ten different dioceses. Several of them were, or had been, Fellows of Merton; one, a Fellow of Exeter.

It was some years before the revenues of the College allowed of the maintenance of so large a number of Fellows. The first "long roll" preserved mentions only five persons, including Eglesfield himself, as receiving a Fellow's allowance; and eight is the largest number of Fellows named in any account up to the end of the century. In the early part of the sixteenth century the numbers rose to about ten, but dwindled again in the disturbed periods about the middle of the century. Twelve Fellows first appear in the Long Roll for 1590; and soon after the number was increased to fourteen, at which the number of the Fellows on the original foundation seems to have remained till the first of the two University Commissions of the present century.

By the ordinance of 1858, the number of Fellows of the Consolidated Foundation was fixed at nineteen; and by the statutes of 1877, the Fellowships are to be not less in number than fourteen and not more than sixteen. The actual number is fourteen.

From the earliest times down to the legislation of 1858 the body of Fellows seems to have been recruited from the junior members of the foundation, and ordinarily by seniority.

It seems to have soon become a rule that no one should be admitted to a Fellowship till he had proceeded to his Master's degree. The University was often appealed to to grant dispensations to Queen's men to omit some of the conditions generally required for that degree in order to enable them to be elected Fellows.

In 1579 some Bachelors were elected Fellows: "electi socii dum Domini fuere; sed irrita facta est electio: postea vero electi."

The names given to the different orders of foundationers perhaps deserve a passing notice. The Fellows, as we should call them, were the "Scholares," who, with the "Praepositus," or Provost, constituted the Corporation. They are in the original statutes called indifferently "Scholares" and "Socii." The first name under which other recipients of Eglesfield's bounty appear is that of "Pueri," or "Pueri eleemosynarii." By the end of the fourteenth century the name "Servientes" came to be applied to an intermediate order, between the "socii" and the "pueri," recruited from the latter. In 1407, for instance, Bell is a "pauper puer"; in 1413 Ds. Walter Bell is a "serviens"; and in 1416 Mr. Walter Bell, who was for the previous Michaelmas Term, and for the first term of the year, still "serviens" and chaplain, becomes a Fellow. A candidate for the foundation seems to have entered the College as a "pauper puer"; to have become a "serviens" on taking his Bachelor's degree; and to have been eligible to a Fellowship as soon as he had proceeded to the degree of M.A.

The distinction between the three orders seems to have been maintained, though with some variety in the names given to the orders and some laxity in their application. Chaplains who are Masters are sometimes loosely called "pueri" even as early as the middle of the fifteenth century; and about 1570 the term "servientes" seems to have gone out of use and the name "pueri" to have been transferred to the Bachelors.

Soon after this a fourth order appears intermediate between the first and second, of "magistri non-socii," or Masters on the foundation. It might often be convenient for a B.A. to proceed to his M.A. degree before a Fellowship was ready for him. The Chaplains were generally appointed from among these Masters. In the University Calendar of 1828 there appear as many as nine of these expectants.

Before the end of the fifteenth century we find the lowest order called "pueri domus," and then "pueri de taberta" or "taberto" or "tabarto." The first appearance of this famous appellation seems to be in the Long Roll for 1472. The tabard from which the Taberdars, as we now call them, derived their name appears early in the accounts of the College. Under the expenses of the boys in 1364-5 occurs:—"Item, cissori pro cota Ad. de Spersholt cum capic. tabard. et calig. xii d."

The livery of the boys seems always to have been a special part of the provision made by the College for them: 25*s.* 4*d.* is expended in 1407 "in vestura pauperum puerorum"; and when Thomas Eglesfield is promoted in 1416 from Leylonde Hall, where the College had paid 1*s.* 4*d.* for a term's schooling for him to Mr. John Leylande and 5*d.* for his batells, the first expenditure on his account as a poor boy of the College is "pro factura togae & tabard. ejusd. xii d." Those who are wise in such matters may be able to calculate the size of the tabard from the datum that eight yards of cloth, at a cost of 14*s.* 8*d.*, were provided in 1437 "pro duobus pueris domus, pro tabard. suis." In 1503, 37*s.* 4*d.* is paid "pro liberatura iiij puerorum domus"; and in 1519, 56*s.* for the same for six boys.

The College had probably its pattern for the tabard, but no trace of a description of it has yet been discovered. The word seems, from Ducange, to have been used for almost every sort of upper garment, from the long tabard worn by the Priests of the Hospital of Elsingspittal with tunic, supertunic and hood, to the round mantles or tabards of moderate length permitted by the council of Buda to be worn by Prelates, and the "renones," or capes coming down to the reins, which the French call "tabart." It seems now to be only applied to the herald's coat.

The four orders in their latest manifestation previous to the legislation of 1858 were—1, Fellows; 2, Masters of Arts on the Foundation; 3, Taberdars or Bachelors of Arts on the Foundation; 4, Probationary Scholars, who were undergraduates. Under the subsequent arrangements the name Taberdar has been reserved for the eight senior open scholars.

The Provost was required by Eglesfield to be of mature character, in Holy Orders, a good manager, and he was to be elected for life. He was to be elected by the Fellows, and admit Fellows who had been elected; to devote himself to the rule and care of the College, and to the administration of its property. He was to see to the collection of the debts of the College, going to law if necessary on behalf of its rights and privileges, and to study in all respects to promote the advantage and enlargement of the Hall by obtaining such influence over Royal and other persons as he might be able to secure.

The provision that the Provost should be in Holy Orders seems only once to have been violated. Roger Whelpdale (1404), indeed, seems only to have received priest's orders after his election; but in the person of Thomas Francis all precedents were violated. He was a Doctor of Medicine, of Christ Church, a native of Chester, and Regius Professor of Medicine; and was in 1561, it would seem by Royal influence, intruded into the Provostship. Serious disturbances seem to have taken place at his inauguration,[139] and in two years he had had enough of it. The irregularity prevailing at the time is evidenced by his offering in an extant letter to nominate Bernard Gilpin, the Apostle of the North, as his successor.[140] The Tudor sovereigns seem in this, as in other matters, to have found it difficult to set limits to their prerogative. Later in Elizabeth's reign, on Henry Robinson's promotion from the Provostship to the Bishopric of Carlisle, his chancellor had to write to the College, 8th Oct., 1598, signifying the Queen's pleasure that the election of a Provost in his room "be respited till her Majesty be informed whether it belongs to her by prerogative, or to the Fellows, to chuse a successor."

No fault can be found with the Provosts of the College, as a rule, for want of care of its interests. The names of six occur in the Thanksgiving for the Founder and Benefactors of the College; and others could prefer a claim to the same distinction.

Thomas Langton (1487), the first of the six, who was also Fellow of Pembroke Hall, Cambridge, where his "Anathema" cup is still to be seen, died Bishop of Winchester, having been nominated just before his death to the Archbishopric of Canterbury.

He left memorial legacies both directly to the College, and indirectly to it through a benefaction to God's House at Southampton. Christopher Bainbridge (1506), the next of the Benefactor Provosts, was Cardinal and Archbishop of York, poisoned at Rome by his steward, and buried under a magnificent renaissance monument which now adorns the Church of St. Thomas à Becket in that city.

A chantry priest was till the Reformation paid £5 6s. 8d. for celebrating for the souls of these two benefactors in the Church of St. Michael in Bongate near Appleby, the capital of the county in which they were both born.

Henry Robinson (1581), the third on the list, had been Principal of St. Edmund Hall, and died Bishop of Carlisle. His brass in Carlisle Cathedral, of which the College possesses a duplicate, says of his relations with the College, "invenit destructum, reliquit exstructum et instructum." The College spent, 15th July, 1615, £23 3s. 3d. in celebrating his obsequies, and provided Chr. Potter with a funeral gown and hood to preach his funeral sermon; £10 was paid in 1617 for engraving his monument on copper, and 31s. 6d. for some impressions from the plate.

Henry Airay (1598), who succeeds Robinson as Provost and Benefactor, the Elisha to Robinson's Elijah, as his brass with much variety of symbolic illustration describes him, in spite of his being "a zealous Calvinist," commends himself to Wood "for his holiness, integrity, learning, grauity, and indefatigable pains in the discharge of his ministerial functions." The College proved his will at a cost of 41*s*. 8*d*., and spent £19 16*s*. 8*d*. on his funeral, 9th July, 1616.

Timothy Halton (1677), the fifth of the Provosts commemorated in the Thanksgiving, built the present spacious library of the College mainly at his own expense.

William Lancaster (1704), who is sixth, had the chief hand in building the present College. He incurred Hearne's wrath on private grounds and as a "Whigg," and is abused by him through many volumes of his Collections; but he commended himself to others of his contemporaries, and the favour in which he was held by the Corporation of Oxford was of great service to the College. In the Mayoralty of Thomas Sellar, Esq., 14th Jan., 1709, it was "agreed that the Provost and Scholars of Queen's College shall have a lease of so much ground in the high street leading to East Gate as shall be requisite for making their intended new building there strait and uniform from Michaelmas last for one thousand years at a pepper corn rent, gratis and without fine, in respect of the many civilities and kindnesses from time to time showed unto and conferred upon this city and the principal members thereof by Dr. Lancaster."

It was by thus obtaining influence over Royal and other persons, in conformity with the injunctions of the founder, that Provosts and other members of the

College were enabled to benefit it. The monument to Joseph Smith (1730) which faces one who comes out of the College chapel, seems to preserve the memory of an ideal Provost from Eglesfield's point of view and that which continued to be maintained in the College. "Distinguished for his Learning, Eloquence, Politeness of Manners, Piety and Charity, he with great Prudence and judicious Moderation presided over his College to its general Happiness. Its Interests were the constant Object of his Attention. He was himself a good Benefactor to it, and was blest with the Success of obtaining for it by his respectable Influence, several ample Donations to the very great and perpetual Increase of its Establishment."

Among the "ample donations" obtained by Provost Smith's "respectable influence," the first place belongs to the Hastings foundation. The Lady Elizabeth Hastings, daughter of Theophilus, seventh Earl of Huntingdon, of whom Steele says in the *Tatler*, "To love her is a liberal education," bequeathed to the College in 1739 her Manors, Lands, and Hereditaments in Wheldale in the West Riding of Yorkshire, to found five Exhibitions for five poor scholars that had been educated for two years at one or other of twelve schools in Cumberland, Westmorland, and Yorkshire. Each school was to send a candidate, and the candidates were first to be examined at Abberforth or Aberford in Yorkshire by seven neighbouring clergymen, and the ten best exercises were to be sent to the Provost and Fellows, who were to "choose out of them eight of the best performances which appear the best, which done, the names subscribed to those eight shall be fairly written, each in a distinct paper, and the papers rolled up and put into an Urn or Vase, … and after being shaken well together in the Urn shall be drawn out of the same.… And those five whose names are first drawn shall to all Intents and Purposes be held duly elected.… And though this Method of choosing by Lot may be called by some Superstition or Enthusiasm, yet … the advice was given me by an Orthodox and Pious Prelate of the Church of England as leaving something to Providence." This method of election was observed as late as 1859, the Urn or Vase then employed being the Provost's man-servant's hat. In 1769 the lot not drawn was that of Edward Tatham of Heversham School, afterwards Rector of Lincoln College, probably the most notable person who was ever a candidate for a place on this foundation. A more reasonable provision, that if of the original schools any should so far come to decay as to have no scholar returned by the examiners at Aberford in four successive elections, the College should appoint another school from the same county in its stead, has been of great benefit to the Foundation and to education in the counties. The estate devised has increased in value, coals having been got, which were supposed in Lady Betty's time to be in the estate. Fourteen schools now enjoy the benefits of the Foundation, and nearly thirty Exhibitioners of £90 a year each now take the place of the original five Exhibitioners of £28 a year.

Elaborate regulations were laid down for the election of the Provost, and on one occasion at least the whole course of proceeding had to be gone through.[141] In the oath, which was to precede this as almost all other important ceremonies in the College, the Fellows swear that they will elect the most fit and sufficient of the Fellows to the vacancy.

Disputes have from time to time taken place as to whether a "promoted[142] Fellow" during his year of grace is to be regarded as a Fellow for this purpose. At the time of Wm. Lancaster's election (1704) a pamphlet was published in opposition to his claims, but it would seem without any effect on the election. The pamphleteer has to allow that several earlier Provosts, among them Henry Boost, who was also Provost of Eton, and Bishop Langton, had never been Fellows at all.

The Provost was to receive five marks in addition to the portion assigned to each of the Fellows, and this was to be increased gradually to forty pounds in case the augmentation of the revenues of the College allowed the number of Fellows prescribed in the statutes to increase. He was to receive this for his ordinary expenses and necessities. The community was to defray any expenses incurred in absence on business, or in the entertainment of visitors who might repair to the College in connection with its affairs.—In 1359-60, Adam, the Provost's servant, has his expenses paid for a visit to Southampton to see the condition of God's House while the foreigners were at Winchester. In 1363-4 Henry

Whitfield, the Provost, brings in a bill for his expenses on a voyage to the Court of Rome at Avignon on College business connected with the living of Sparsholt in Berks. A century later the Provost is allowed 5*s.* 10*d.* for his expenses to London in May 1519 to get money for the building of the chapel. In 1600-1 18*d.* is paid for a horse sent to fetch the Provost for the election of a principal at St. Edmund Hall.

The rights of the College in the matter of the appointment of a Principal of that Hall have always been vigorously asserted against the Chancellor of the University, who nominates the Principals of all other public Halls. In 1636, when the Heads of Colleges and Halls were called upon to give their formal submission to Laud's new statutes, Chr. Potter, Coll. Reginæ Præpositus, adds his name "Salvo jure Collegii prædicti ad Aulam St. Edmundi." The record of the proceedings on the occasion of each election of a Principal has been preserved with a care not usually extended to any but the most solemn of the proceedings of the College. On the 18th December, 1614, Mr. French is paid 3*s.* for writing out the agreement made between the University and the College about the election of a Principal of St. Edmund Hall. The agreement, securing the appointment to the College, was made in 1559. Lord Buckhurst (Chancellor from 1591 to 1608) was advised by Lord Chief Justice Walmsley that it was void, but the law officers of the Crown at the time maintained its validity.[143]

The common seal, the jewels, treasure, bulls, charters, writings, statutes, privileges and muniments of the College were to be kept in a chest with three locks, the keys whereof were to be kept by the Provost, the Treasurer, and the "Camerarius." The two last were the technical names for the senior and junior Bursars respectively, and were retained in the Long Rolls to a very recent time.

The Foundation was to be in theory open. Like the University, the College was not to close the bosom of its protection to any race or deserving nation; and the Fellows at the time of election swore not only to put away all hatred, fear, and partiality, and to listen to no requests, but also to act without accepting person or country. The conditions of eligibility were distinguished character, poverty and fitness for studying theology with profit. A preference, however, was to be given to suitable persons who were natives of Cumberland and Westmorland, to which this preference was given on account of their waste state, their uninhabited condition, and the scarcity of letters in them. Within these limits too there was to be a preference for founders' kin. After these a *cæteris paribus* preference was given to those places wherein the College derived benefit either from ecclesiastical benefices, manors, lands or tenements. These limitations soon practically resulted in confining the Foundation to natives of the two counties. They supplied a steady flow of capable persons; and curiously enough, though so unequal in size and population, in about equal numbers.

Pressure was from time to time applied to the College to admit into the society persons not duly qualified. In the reign of James I., Robert Murray, a Scot, was thus recommended by a Royal letter; and, though the College declined to elect him, it was thought politic to pay him £20 "ne in iniquam pecuniarum erogationem traheretur collegium." During the time of the usurpation, as a note in the Entrance Book calls it, four Fellows were intruded, who were promptly got rid of at the Restoration of Charles II. Thomas Cartwright, who was afterwards "Tabiter," and eventually Bishop of Chester, and one of the Commissioners for ejecting the President and Fellows of Magdalen College, is said to have been put into the College by the Parliamentary Visitors during the same period.

The claim to preference as founder's kin does not seem to have been often advanced. The Thomas Eglesfield, to the purchase of whose tabard reference is made above,[144] seems to have been grandson of the founder's brother John. At the time of his admission to the College, his father, also called John, seems to have visited the College and taken away with him a son William, who, like Thomas, had been for a term under the instruction of Mr. John Leylonde. This is probably the William who, with his wife, brother, and sister-in-law, receives from the College gloves in 1459 to the value of 12½d. Leylonde seems to have continued to act as private tutor to Thomas after he joined the College, as x s. is paid in 1418, "Magistro Joh. Leylonde pro scolagio Tho. Egylsfelde." A Christopher Eglesfield was on the Foundation about the same time. Thomas went through all the stages of promotion. He was "puer," "serviens," Fellow, and eventually Provost, besides holding the University offices of Proctor and Commissary (or Vice-Chancellor). An Anthony Eglesfield was Fellow of the College in 1577. A James Eglesfield belonged to it in 1615, and a George Eglesfield in 1670. A Gawin Eglesfield, who had been taberdar, and was passed over at an election to Fellows in 1632, claimed election as founder's kin, and was backed by the Archbishop of York as visitor. The College successfully resisted the claim; but on Gawin's acknowledgment that the claim was unfounded, to please the visitor, presented him to the living of Weston in Oxfordshire.

The College, however, in another way, has from the beginning "opened the bosom of its protection" to students whom it was unwilling out of regard to the preferences of the founder to admit to the pecuniary benefits of the Foundation. Whether it was that the buildings contained more rooms than the slowly growing Foundation was able to fill with its own members, or for some other cause, the receipts of the College have always included "pensiones" for "cameræ" occupied by non-foundationers. The very first Long Roll which has been preserved, that of 1347-8, contains the names of Roger Swynbrok, John Herte, and John Schipton as thus occupying chambers. The word used for the payment has survived in "pensioners," the name given at Cambridge to those whom we call "commoners." The pensioners of the fourteenth century probably differed in many respects from the commoners of the nineteenth. The founder was in one sense the first commoner of the College. The Black Prince was perhaps one of the earliest. Dominus Nicholas monachus, the monachus Eboracensis who paid two marks "pro magna camera," the monachus de Evesham, Robertus canonicus, The Prior of Derbich, Magister John Wicliff, Canonicus Randulphus, the Scriptor Slake, Bewforth, if not Bewforth's more celebrated pupil, afterwards Henry V., Raymund, Rector of Hisley, the treasurer of Chichester, and numerous other Magistri whose names appear in this relation were probably rather researchers or advanced students than anything more resembling the modern undergraduate. It was not unusual for those who had been Fellows to return to the College after some period of absence from Oxford and from the Foundation. But it is doubtless in this element that we find the first traces in the College of those who now occupy so prominent a place in any view of modern Oxford. By the time the first lists occur of residents in the Colleges, and before the regularly-kept register of entrances begins, the present system seems to have been in full swing. In course of time it became profitable for the College even to extend its buildings for the accommodation of this kind of student, and the "musaea" or "studies" in the "*novum cubiculum*" and in the "*novum aedificium*" became a regular source of revenue.

It was not only through these and other payments that these "commoners" contributed to the well-being of the College. Among its most liberal benefactors some of the foremost have been non-foundationers. So John Michel, in some sense the second founder of the College, like his father and his uncle, who, as he records, "in saeculo rebellionis nunquam satis deflendae sedem quietam per 14 annos hic invenerunt," a commoner of the College, besides other benefactions, left an endowment for eight Fellows, four scholars, and four exhibitioners, merged by the Commissioners of 1858 with the smaller Foundation of Sir Orlando Bridgman, another commoner, in the original Foundation of Eglesfield. During the hundred years which this Foundation lasted (the first Fellow was elected in 1764, the last in 1861) more than a hundred Fellows elected to enjoy Michel's liberality contributed an independent element which somewhat modified the monotony of the old north-country corporation. The Michel Fellows were not members of the governing body, and some amusing stories are told of the differences insisted on by some of the less genial of the older order. Yet the "Michels" (*mali catuli*, as the jesting etymology had it) contributed their full share to the glories of the College. A Lord Chief Baron of the Exchequer, a Chief Justice of Ceylon, a Bishop of St. David's, three Bampton Lecturers, a Bishop of Newfoundland, a Bishop of Ballarat, a Professor of Arabic,[145]were only the most prominent among a large number of distinguished men who owed something to Michel's liberality. The value of the Fellowships was small, and the length of tenure limited, and so richer Foundations carried off some of those who had for a while been on this

Foundation. So among others Dornford passed in this way through Queen's from Wadham to Oriel, so Basil Jones from Trinity to University, so Tyler and Garbett back again to Oriel and Brasenose from which they came. The College has not been willing to let Michel's name be altogether forgot, and the four junior Fellows in the list are still called Michel Fellows.

In quite recent times the College has had to thank a commoner for its latest considerable benefaction, and five scholars will always have occasion to bless the memory of Sir Edward Repps Jodrell.

Some of the most characteristic of Eglesfield's injunctions were concerned with the Common Table. In the midst of the table was to sit the Provost or his *locum tenens*. No one was to sit on the opposite side in any seat or chair, nor to eat on that side either kneeling or standing. If necessary, room was to be found at a side table.

They were to meet twice in the day for meals at regular hours. They were to be summoned by a "clarion" blown so as to be heard by all the members of the foundation. Among the charges in the accounts for 1452-3 is 2*s.* 4*d.* for the repair of the trumpet. In 1595-7, either for repair or a new one, there was paid 8*s.* "pro tuba"; and in 1604-5 "pro tuba et vectura a Lond. et emendatione," 28*s.* In 1666 a magnificent silver trumpet was presented by Sir Joseph Williamson, one of the most liberal of the benefactors as he was one of the most loyal of the sons of the College, to which he was never weary of expressing his obligations and his affection. By a curious accident his extensive private correspondence has become incorporated with the Domestic State Papers of the period, and those who are searching for the more secret springs of the public policy of his age have their attention arrested by the details of his familiar relations with his College friends. So too at an earlier time among the State Papers of the reign of James I. are included the Latin verses and orations, the sermon-notes and other occasional papers of a Queen's undergraduate, who was afterwards to be Mr. Secretary Nicholas. And along with these are letters to him from a sister, promising stockings, and asking sympathy for toothache and the mumps; and this three hundred years ago.

As they sat at table, before them was to be read the Bible by a Chaplain. They were to pay attention to him, and not prevent his being heard by loquacity or shouting. They were to speak at table "modeste," and in French or Latin unless in obedience to the law of politeness to converse with a visitor in his own language, or for some other reasonable cause. Unseemly talk or jesting was to be avoided, and punished if necessary by the Provost. Up to the beginning of the present century it was the practice for the porter to bring at the beginning of dinner a Greek Testament to the Fellow presiding at the High Table who returned it to him indicating a verse, and saying, "Legat (so and so)," naming the scholar of the week. The porter then took the book to the scholar and gave it him, saying, "Legat," and the book after the verse had been read was carried away by the porter. When this custom was abolished does not appear, but Provost Jackson remembered that it prevailed when he came into residence (1808).

At both meals, at all times of the year, that their garments might conform to the colour of the blood of the Lord, all the Fellows were to wear purple robes, and if Doctors of Theology or of Decrees, the robes were to be furred with black budge. The Chaplains were to wear white robes, and the Provost was to see that those of each grade wore robes of uniform colour.

The Students in Arts[146] among the poor boys were to dispute a sophism among themselves once or twice a week, under the guidance of an "artist,"[147] who was to look after them, superintend their disputations, and otherwise supervise their instruction. The "grammarians"[148] were to have "collationes" before their instructor every day except Sundays and "double feasts." The Clerks of the Chapel were to instruct the poor boys in singing. All the instructors, artists, grammarians and musicians were to be diligent in watching the progress of the students and in instructing them, and were to swear to be so.

The Students in Theology[149] were to hold theological disputations every week on Saturday, Friday, or some other convenient day, which were to be superintended by the Provost or his *locum tenens*, or the senior present at the disputation; and at these all the theologians except the Provost, who would be very much busied about the affairs of "the Hall," *i. e.* of the College, were bound to be present unless prevented by some lawful cause.

The number of scholars was to be increased as the means of the College allowed. A Provost or anybody else who opposed such increase was to be expelled.

For the maintenance of each scholar a sum of ten marks annually was to be set aside. Of this, at least 1*s.* 6*d.*, and not more than 2*s.*, was to be appropriated to his weekly commons. Anything saved under this head out of 2*s.* in the week was to be devoted to alms and no other purpose. The remainder of the ten marks was to go to the scholars to provide them with clothes and other necessaries. The Provost was to look to the character of the clothes. If they went far in country or town, they were not to wear simple or double "hoods," but long "collobia" (frocks, sleeveless or with short sleeves), or other suitable garments; and they were not to go alone.

An absent Fellow was to forfeit his commons in the long vacation, and the rest of his allowance also at other times, unless he were absent on the business of the Hall. Additional reasons for the enjoyment of commons in absence were subsequently approved. Pestilence in Oxford was a common excuse. In 1400-1, 1*s.* 6*d.* is allowed for the commons of William Warton and Peter de la Mare in time of pestilence. Similarly in 1625-6, £7 4*s.* is allowed to the Fellows dispersed in time of pestilence. Equally urgent reasons commended themselves during the reign of Charles I. In 1642 payments are made to Fellows, Chaplains, boys and servants in place of commons, when the College was for seven weeks dissolved owing to the advance of the enemy; and this in the same "computus," with seven payments for bonfires on the occasion of seven Royalist victories. A Fellow received for each week 5s., a Chaplain and a boy 2s. 6d., a servant 2s. Three Fellows away in the North got smaller payments during eleven months.

In order that there might be plenty to give away, the Scholars and Chaplains were to have two courses at meals on ordinary days, and on the five great feasts—Christmas, Easter, Whitsuntide, the Assumption, and All Saints Day—an extra course with a suitable quantity of wine. Court manners were to be observed at meals and other times.

How soon the custom of bringing in a boar's head at Christmas began does not appear, nor is the date of the carol sung on the occasion ascertained. Wynkin de Worde's version, which differs in some particulars from that used in the College, was printed as early as 1521. On the 24th December, 1660, £1 10s. is paid "pictori Hawkins caput apri in festo nativitatis adornanti." This suggests that the head was then, as now, "adorned" with banners bearing coats of arms: Richard Hawkins was a heraldic painter resident in Oxford, an intimate of Anthony Wood.

The expenses of any Fellows sent out of Oxford on College business were to be defrayed by the

Community. They were to bring an account of their expenses at the end of the journey, which was to be audited by the Provost, Treasurer, and Camerarius, who were to disallow them if in their judgment excessive; and if the three auditors could not agree on this point, the judgment of the Provost was to decide. Thus, in 1386-7, Mr. Richard Brown the Camerarius and Senior Fellow is repaid 12s.4d., his expenses for a journey to Devonshire to get the books bequeathed to the College by Mr. Henry Whitfield, as well as 20d. for the carriage of the said books. Ten years later two and a half marks are paid for Mr. Thomas Burton's expenses in going to the Archbishop of York. In 1411-12 the same Fellow pays a visit on College business to the Roman court.

If the revenues of the College allowed, thrice in the year, at the end of each term, a portion beyond the commons was to be divided among the Fellows fairly, according to the amount of their residence. On the day of this division the statutes of the College were to be read among themselves by the Provost and scholars, and a solemn mass of the Holy Trinity to be said in the College Chapel, or Parochial Church, "if they got one," for the King, Queen Philippa, the other benefactors of the Hall, and other persons specified in the statutes, and for all the faithful living and dead. After the solemn mass the Provost was to inquire separately of each of the Fellows as to the behaviour of the rest in the matters of obedience to the statutes, honesty of deportment, and progress in study. Special regulations were laid down for the conduct of this inquiry. These regularly recurring inquiries might be supplemented by special inquiries whenever the Provost thought it necessary; and at the peril of his soul he was to see that the boys, the chaplains, and the other "*ministri*" conducted themselves properly. All accused persons were to be allowed to purge themselves privately, peacefully, and honestly, but not scandalously or contentiously. No scholar or poor boy was to be expelled except with consent of a majority of the College. The Provost inflicted other punishments after taking counsel with one or two of the scholars.

The Provost was allowed to keep a servant or clerk, to whose maintenance he was to contribute. The other Masters or scholars were prohibited from burdening the community by the introduction of strangers or relatives, and especially of poor clerks of their own or private servants. This was not to prevent hospitality being shown at the expense of the entertainer, in the hall or in his own chamber, to friends, of any rank, from the city or outside, who might come to see one of the community. A visitor on business of the community was to be properly entertained in the hall or Provost's lodging at the common expense.

Nor did this in later times prevent such services as were rendered by a "fag" at a public school some fifty years ago from being rendered in College for a salary by the poorer students to the richer. So George Fothergill, in 1723, writes home—"My Tutor has given me a gentleman commoner last night, wch I call'd up this morning. So that for calling up I have about 5 pounds per year, viz. 5*s.* a quarter of each of the 3 com̄oners wch I had before, wch comes to 3 pounds a year, & 10*s.* a quarter for this Gent: Com: wch makes up 5 pounds."

Harriers, hounds, hawks, and other such animals were not to be kept in the Hall or its precincts by any of the scholars. It was not thought fitting that poor men living mainly on alms should give the bread of the sons of men for the dogs to eat, and woe to those who play among the birds of the air. The "*extructio pullophylacii*" in 1590 would probably not be regarded as a violation of the statute, nor "*le henhouse,*" probably the same building which is referred to a few years later. A caged eagle also seems from time to time to have been kept in the College, in connection with the founder's name and the arms of the College. In 1661, 5*s.* 3*d.* is paid, "*operculum fabricanti ad concludendam aquilam domini praepositi.*"

The use of musical instruments was prohibited within the College except during the hours of general refreshment, as likely to produce levity and insolence, and to afford occasion of distraction from study. This of course did not apply to the musical instruments employed in the chapel service. There was an organ in chapel from very early times. In 1436-7 4*d.* is paid among the expenses of the chapel "pro emendatione organorum"; and in 1490-1 "organa reparantur." In 1676-7 £1 12*s.* is paid "famulis domini episcopi Londinensis organum musicum afferentibus." This was Bishop Compton, who crowned William III., and who had been a gentleman commoner of the College. The present organ, perhaps the largest in Oxford, is mainly due to the skill and liberality of Leighton George Hayne, D.Mus., and sometime Coryphæus of the University, who, with the support of the late Archbishop of York, revived the musical service which had for many years been interrupted.

All sorts of games of dice, chess, and others giving opportunity of losing money, were prohibited, especially dice and other similar games which give occasion for strife and often beggary to the player. An exception was made for such games occasionally played, not in the hall, for recreation only, when it did not interfere with study or divine service. All Chaplains, poor clerks, servants, and other inhabitants of the Hall were bound by this prohibition, and the Provost or his *locum tenens* were bound on pain of perjury to inflict the penalties which might be necessary to stop these or other infractions of the statutes. When stage plays came into vogue the College followed the fashion. In the accounts of 1572-3, 3*s.* 8*d.* is paid "pro fabricatione scenae in aula ad tragicam comoediam narrandam," and 7*s.* 5*d.* "in expensis tragicae comediae in natal. Xti."

The chambers and studies were to be assigned to the scholars by the Provost, who was to assign, except for special reasons, according to seniority. There were to be at least two in each chamber unless the status or pre-eminence of the quality of any of the scholars should require otherwise. The arrangement of rooms adopted in the front quadrangle when the College was rebuilt seems to retain a trace of the old regulations. A large "chamber" with two "studies" recalls the days when John Boast and Henry Ewbank were chamber-fellows or "chums" in their youth, before the dark time when the younger man was the cause of the elder being butchered alive for exercising his priestly functions in England.[150] Nowadays in the rare case of two brothers or intimate friends living together in a set of rooms, the old disposition is reversed, the chamber becomes the joint study, and the two studies the separate bed-chambers.

Except for urgent cause, or by leave of the Provost or his *locum tenens*, the scholars were not to have meals except in the hall, and they were to avoid, in accordance with the laws of temperance, expensive and luxurious meals of all kinds, suppers and other eatings and drinkings. The Provost or his *locum tenens* was to restrain all such excess.

The scholars were not to pass the night outside the College in the town or its suburbs unless leave had been previously obtained from the Provost, his *locum tenens*, or the senior in hall; and the application for leave must specify the cause for which such leave is asked.

A Fellow, poor cleric, or Chaplain expelled was not to have any remedy against the College by law or otherwise, and was to renounce any right to such remedy under the obligation of an oath at the time of his admission to the Hall. The College sometimes showed compassion to former Fellows who fell into misfortune: 28th September, 1625, 50s. is paid to Mr. Lancaster formerly a Fellow, now reduced to the depths of misery, and in following years a similar payment is made, the amount being raised later to £4.

A scholar was to forfeit his emolument by entering religion, by transferring himself to anybody's obedience, by being absent except on College business or by special leave of the Provost for more than the greater half of a full term, or for wilfully neglecting to take the prescribed steps of advancement in study.

Offences generally were to be tried by the Provost and two assessors, and punished by the Provost with the consent of the scholars.

The College was to bake its own bread and brew its own beer within the College, by its own servants acting under the supervision of the steward of the week and of the treasurer's clerk. Every loaf before it was baked was to weigh 46s. 8d. sterling, from whatever market the corn came, and of whatever kind the bread was; and this weight was not to be changed whatever was the price of corn.

A sum of £40 specially given for this purpose by the founder was always to remain in hand, to be set apart at the beginning of each year, and accounted for at the end as ready-money or floating balance, to be used for buying stores of victuals and fuel, and not to be employed in part or whole for any other purpose.

The Scholars were to have a horse-mill of their own to grind their wheat, barley, and other corn within the College, or at least very near thereto, to save the excessive tolls and payments to millers which might otherwise fall upon them.

With these and similar injunctions the founder launched the College on its voyage across the centuries. Into the details of that voyage there is no further room to go. Whatever affected the history of the country affected the history of the University, and whatever affected the history of the University affected the history of the College. Wycliff stayed within the College, and Nicholas of Hereford, who translated for him the Old Testament, was a Fellow. Henry Whitfield, Provost, and three Fellows, one of them John of Trevisa, all four west-countrymen, were expelled for Wycliffism. The phases of the Reformation in England are accurately reflected in the College accounts. A Royal Commission visits the College in 1545, and Rudd, one of the Fellows, is expelled. Eightpence is paid, "pro vino & orengis commissionariis." Three years later 6*s.* 2*d.* is paid, "dolantibus meremium & diripientibus imagines in sacello." The wheel comes round, and in 1555, 9*s.* is paid, "pro ligatione et coopertura unius portiphorii, duorum processionalium, unius missalis, unius gradalis, unius antiphonarii & unius hymnarii." But the reaction is only temporary, and in 1560 appears 4*s.* 8*d.*, "pro destruendo altaria."

The College contributes others besides the Wycliffites and Rudd as victims to the struggles of the times. John Bost is a martyr for Roman Catholicism; as Michael Hudson later, for the King against the Parliament. Thomas Smith's case is the hardest of all; as, having been turned out of his Fellowship at Magdalen for refusing to elect Bishop Parker as President, he is turned out again later on for refusing to take the oath of allegiance to William III.

The College shared the fortunes of the University in the days of the Stuarts. His Majesty desires the College, 5th Jan., 1642-3, to lend him all plate of what kind soever belonging to the College, and promises to see the same repaid after the rate of 5*s.* per ounce for white, and 5*s.* 6*d.* for gilt plate; and nine days later Mr. Stannix, thesaurarius, delivers to Sir William Parkhurst for his Majesty's use such a collection of tankards, two-eared potts, white large bowles and lesser bowles, salts and gilt bowles, and spoones and gobletts, as the College shall never see again, 2319 oz. of both sorts, worth in all £591 1*s.* 9*d.* And then the Provost and scholars, as things grow worse, petition Sir Thomas Glemham that— whereas parcel of the works on the west side of Northgate had been assigned to Magdalen and Queen's College jointly, and Queen's College had already performed more than in a due proportion would have come to their share, most of them labouring in their own persons by the space of twelve days at the least, while those of Magdalen assisted, some very slenderly and some not at all—

that a proportionable part of the work yet unfinish'd may be set forth to themselves in particular apart from Magdalen; and this is ordered to be done. And then the king goes down, and the parliamentary visitors appear; and "This is the answer of mee, Jo. Fisher (Master of Arts and Chaplaine of Queenes Colledge), and which I shall acknowledge is myne: That I cannot without perjury submitt to this visitation, and therefore I will not submitt. *Ita est*: Jo. Fisher." And John Fisher and others are reported to the Committee of Lords and Commons and lose their places. And George Phillip and James Bedford and William Barksdale and Moses Foxcraft appear in the Register of Fellows as "Intrusi tempore usurpationis, exclusi ad Restaurationem Caroli Secundi."

And in all these crises, and those which have followed, "sons of Eglesfield" have been called to play their part. Thomas Barlow, Bishop of Lincoln; Henry Compton, Bishop of London; Thomas Cartwright, Bishop of Chester; Thomas Lamplugh, Archbishop of York; Edmund Gibson, Bishop of London; William Nicholson, Archbishop of Cashel; Thomas Tanner, Bishop of St. Asaph; William Van Mildert, Bishop of Durham; William Thomson, Archbishop of York, among Prelates: John Owen, Dean of Christ Church; John Mill and Richard Cecil, among Divines: Sir John Davies, Sir Thomas Overbury, William Wycherly, Joseph Addison, Thomas Tickell, William Collins, William Mitford, Jeremy Bentham, Francis Jeffrey, among men of letters: Gerard Langbaine, Thomas Hyde, Thomas Hudson, Edward Thwaites, Christopher Rawlinson,

Edward Rowe Mores, Thomas Tyrwhitt, among scholars; Edmund Halley and Henry Highton, among men of science; Sir Edward Nicholas, Sir John Banks, and Sir Joseph Williamson, among lawyers and statesmen—are but a selection of the more distinguished of those to whose equipment the College has contributed in a greater or less degree. May those who now and shall hereafter occupy their places avoid their errors and emulate their virtues.

VII.
NEW COLLEGE.

BY THE REV. HASTINGS RASHDALL, M.A., LATE
SCHOLAR OF NEW COLLEGE, FELLOW OF HERTFORD
COLLEGE.

[A MS. life of Wykeham ascribed to Warden Chaundler, but probably only corrected by him, remains in the possession of the College. The *Historica Descriptio complectens vitam ac res gestas Wicami*, Londini 1597, is the work of Martyn. There are two scholarly lives of the Founder by Lowth (edit. 2, London 1759) and G. H. Moberly (Winchester 1887), but they give little information about the College. Walcott's *William of Wykeham and his Colleges* (Winchester 1852) is the fullest College history that we possess, but it leaves something to be desired. I have to thank the Warden of New College, the Rev. W. A. Spooner, and the Rev. H. B. George for several valuable suggestions or corrections.]

More has been written about the lives of the Oxford College founders than about the institutions which they founded. In some cases the life of a founder properly belongs to the history of his College; the life of William of Wykeham is part of the history of England. For our present purpose, therefore, it is unnecessary to trace his public and political career; but we cannot appreciate the aim of such an institution as New College without understanding the kind of man in whose brain the scheme originated.

William of Wykeham was an ecclesiastic; but in the Middle Ages that meant something very different from what it means now. "The Church" was a synonym for "the professions." In Northern Europe the Church supplied almost the only opportunity of a civil career to the cadet of a noble house, the sole opportunity of rising to the ambitious plebeian. The servants of the Crown, the diplomatists, the secretaries, advisers, or "clerks" of great nobles, the host of ecclesiastical judges and lawyers, many even of the secular lawyers, the physicians, the architects, sometimes even the astrologers, were ecclesiastics. William of Wykeham rose to eminence as a civil servant of the Crown, and was rewarded in the usual way by ecclesiastical preferment, culminating in a bishopric. Such men had usually taken a degree in Canon or Civil Law at the Universities. William of Wykeham is not known to have been a University man; he rose to eminence in the King's Office of Works, and became surveyor at Windsor Castle, which was half rebuilt under his direction. He was the greatest architect of his day. Afterwards he held a series of political appointments—eventually the Chancellorship. As a politician, he was the champion of the old order of things rudely shaken by the Wycliffite heresy and the political movements with which it was associated; the leader of the Church, or Conservative, party; a moderate and far-sighted man withal, but still a sturdy opponent of reform; a pious man in the conventional fourteenth-century way, but still a devoted supporter of all the abuses against which Wyclif had declaimed, as became one who was himself the greatest pluralist of his day.

New College was intended to be another stronghold of the old system in Church and State. It was to increase the supply of clergy, which the statutes declare to have been thinned by "pestilences, wars, and the other miseries of the world." Some have seen in these words a special allusion to the Black Death of 1348; but it was more probably a mere flourish of mediæval rhetoric, or possibly a fashion which had survived from 1348. The general idea of the College was not fundamentally different from that of its predecessors. William of Wykeham, once raised to the splendid See of Winchester, was anxious to do something for the Church; and the general opinion of the day was that monks were out of date, that the Church herself was rich enough, and that to send capable men to the Universities was the best way to fight heresy, to strengthen the Church system, and to save the donor's soul.

Wykeham's ultimate purpose in founding his College was conventional enough; in the manner of carrying it out there was much that was original. It was, however, rather the greater scale of the whole design than any one original feature that gives an historical appropriateness to the name "New" which has accidentally cleaved to "St. Marie Colledge of Wynchester" in Oxford. In the number of the scholars, in the liberality of their allowances, in the architectural splendour of the buildings of his College, Wykeham eclipsed all previous Oxford College-founders. In many respects the founder of Queen's had, indeed, aimed as high as Wykeham; but he had begun to build and was not able to finish; his Provost and apostolic twelve never grew to the seventy which he contemplated. What Eglesfield designed, Wykeham accomplished.

The most original feature of Wykeham's design was the connection of his College at Oxford with a grammar-school at a distance. The fundamental vice of mediæval education was the prevalent neglect of grammatical discipline and the absurdly early age at which boys were plunged into the subtleties of Logic and the mysteries of the Latin Aristotle, the very language of which, unclassical as it was, they could hardly understand. Wykeham had no thought of a Renaissance, or of any fundamental change in the educational system of the day; he was only anxious to remedy a defect which all practical men acknowledged. Boys were still to be taught Latin chiefly that they might read Aristotle, and Peter the Lombard or the Corpus Juris; but they were to learn to walk before they were encouraged to run.

Hard by his own cathedral, the Bishop erected a College for a Warden, Sub-Warden, ten Fellows, a Head Master, Usher, and seventy scholars, with a proper staff of chaplains and choristers. From this College exclusively were to be selected the seventy scholars of St. Marie Colledge of Wynchester in Oxford; and no one could be elected before fifteen or after nineteen, except in the case of "Founder's-kin" scholars, who were eligible up to thirty. This implies that the usual age of Wykehamists upon entering the University would be much above the average, since it was quite common for boys to begin their course in Arts at fourteen or earlier. By the erection of his College at Winchester, Wykeham became the founder of the English public-school system.

The Oxford College consisted of a Warden and seventy "poor clerical scholars," together with ten "stipendiary priests" or chaplains, three stipendiary clerks, and sixteen boy-choristers for the service of the chapel. It entered on a definite existence not later than 1375, the scholars being temporarily lodged in Hart Hall (now Hertford College) and other adjoining houses while the buildings were being completed. The foundation charters were granted in 1379; the foundation-stone laid at 8 a.m. on March 5th, 1379-80; on April 14th, 1387, at 9 a.m. the society, "with cross erect, and singing a solemn litany," marched processionally into the splendid habitation which their Founder had been preparing for them in an unoccupied corner within the walls of the town.

New College is the first, and still almost the only, College whose extant buildings substantially represent a complete and harmonious design as it presented itself to the founder's eye. The quadrangle of New College may indeed have been the first completed quadrangle in Oxford. In that case we might attribute to the architect Bishop the origination of the type to which later English Colleges have so tenaciously adhered. At any rate completeness is the characteristic feature of Wykeham's buildings; every want of his scholars was provided for from their academical birth, if need be to the grave.

Previous Colleges had for the most part occupied the choir of some existing parish church for the solemn services of Sunday and Holy-day; at most they had a little "oratory" in which a priest or two said mass. With Wykeham the chapel formed an integral part of the original design. In spite of the ravages of Puritan iconoclasm, the chapel has always retained the perfect proportion which it received from its founder's hands. It is now regaining, under the touch of modern restoration, so much of its ancient beauty as the cold taste of the present day will tolerate; but we shall never see again the blaze of colour on windows and walls, on groined roof and on sculptured image which it presented to its founder's eye. Wykeham's design provided not merely for things needful, but for ornament. Not only was the chapel a choir of cathedral magnitude, with transepts, though without a nave—henceforth the typical form of the College chapel; there was outside the wall (nowhere else could it have stood so conveniently), the great Bell-tower. There was an ample hall or refectory, the oldest now remaining in Oxford. There were cloisters, round which every Sunday the whole College, in copes and surplices, were to go in procession, "according to the use of Sarum," and within which members of the College might be buried, by special papal bull, without leave of parish-priest or bishop. There was a tower specially provided over the hall staircase with massive doors of many locks to serve as a muniment-room and treasury. There was a library, stored with books by the founder; and an audit-room on the north side of the east gate. Just outside the main entrance were the brewery and the bake-house. A spacious garden supplied the College with vegetables, and perhaps the scholars with room for such exercise as was permitted by the high standard of "clerical" behaviour demanded of Wykeham's tonsured undergraduates. And all remains now substantially as the founder designed it, marred only by the addition (in 1675) of a third story to the front quadrangle, and by the modernization of the windows.

The religious aim of College-founders is often exaggerated, or at least misapprehended. It is true that all Oxford Colleges, like the University itself, were intended for ecclesiastics. But in the earlier Colleges not even the Head is required to be in Holy, or even in minor, Orders; nor are students of any rank required to go to church or chapel except on Sundays and holy-days. As time went on, the ecclesiastical character of Colleges is more and more emphasized; but even then, more is thought of providing for the repose of the founder's soul than of the moral or religious training of his scholars, or the spiritual wants of those to whom they were to minister. Colleges, like monasteries, were largely endowed out of the "impropriated" tithes properly belonging to the parochial churches. But if College Fellows are required to become priests at a certain stage of their career, it is that they may say masses for the founder. If the chapels are provided with a staff of chaplains, it is with the same object. In William of Wykeham's College the ecclesiastical character is at its maximum: Wykeham aimed in fact at erecting a great Collegiate Church and an Academical College in one. The ecclesiastical duties—the masses and canonical hours—were chiefly performed by the hired chaplains. But even the studious part of the community was required to make some return for the founder's liberality by saying certain prayers for him and his royal "benefactors" immediately after rising and before going to bed. They are further required to go to mass daily—it is the first Oxford College where daily chapel is required—and while there (or at some other time) every scholar is to say sixty *Paters* and fifty *Aves* in honour of the Virgin.

Wykeham was indeed the first College-founder, at Oxford at all events, who conceived the idea of making his College not a mere eleemosynary institution, but a great ecclesiastical corporation, which should vie both in the splendour of its architecture and the dignity of its corporate life with the Cathedral chapters and the monastic houses. The earlier Heads had been raised above the scholars or Fellows by the luxury of a single private room: they dined in the common hall with the rest. The Warden of New College was to live, like an abbot, in a house of his own, within the College walls, but with a separate hall, kitchen, and establishment. His salary of £40 was princely by comparison with the 40*s.*, with commons, assigned to the Master of Balliol, or even the forty marks allotted to the Warden of Merton. Instead of the jealous provisions against burdening the College with the entertainment of guests which we meet with in the Paris College-statutes, ample provision is made for the hospitable reception of important strangers by the Warden in his own Hall, or (in his absence) by the Sub-Warden and Fellows in the Great Hall, as they would have been entertained in a Benedictine abbey by the abbot or the prior (the Sub-Warden being evidently intended to hold a position analogous to the latter). The Master of Peterhouse in Cambridge was allowed to have a single horse, on the ground that it would be "indecent for him to go afoot, nor could he, without scandal to the College, hire a hack" (*conducere hakenys*): the Warden of New College is to have *six* horses at his disposal, for himself and the "discreet, apt, and circumspect Fellow," with four servants, who attended upon the annual "progress" over the College estates—more than some provincial canons allowed to a cathedral dean. In chapel the Warden was placed on a level with cathedral canons by the permission to wear an amice *de grisio* (vair or ermine).

The "commons," or weekly allowance of a Fellow, was to be a shilling in times of plenty, which might rise in times of scarcity to 16*d.*, or when the bushel of corn should be at 2*s.*, to 18*d.* But though the College allowances were equal, the money was expended by the officers for the Fellows, and not by the Fellows themselves; and it was expressly provided that the quality of the victuals supplied should vary with "degree, merit and labour." The Sub-Warden and Doctors of superior Faculties sat at the High Table, to which also might be admitted Bachelors of Theology in defect of sufficient Doctors; their plates or courses (*fercula*) might not exceed four. But when the Warden dined in Hall (which he was only privileged to do on certain great festivals), he was to sit in the middle of the table and to be "served alone," *i. e.* to have luxuries provided for him in which his neighbours were not to participate. At the side-tables sat the Graduate-Fellows and chaplains; in the middle of the Hall, the probationers and other juniors. During meals the Bible was read, and silence required. As to the hours of meals it may be observed (though the statutes are silent on this head) that the usual hour for dinner was 10 a.m., and supper was at 5 p.m. There is no trace of breakfast in any mediæval College till near the beginning of the sixteenth century, when it became usual for men to go to the buttery for a hunk of bread and a pot of beer, which were either consumed at the buttery or taken away—the first meal taken in rooms, and the origin of that tradition of breakfast-parties which is still characteristic of University life. But when it is remembered that the day began at five or six, it were a pious opinion that some kind of "hasty snack" at an early hour (such as the *jentaculum* of a later day) was winked at in the case of weaker brethren.

Besides the commons every Fellow received an annual "livery," or suit of clothes, suitable to his University rank, but also of uniform cut and colour; and the rooms were no doubt rudely furnished at the expense of the College.

A Fellow received no other allowance, unless he was of Founder's-kin and poor, or a priest, or an officer, or a tutor, the latter receiving 5*s.* a year for each pupil. A Fellow in need of such assistance might also have the heavy expenses of graduation, especially of banqueting the Regents, defrayed by the College.

In the lower rooms, each of which had four windows and four studies (*studiorum loca*), four scholars were quartered; in the upper rooms, three. The chaplains and clerks slept in rooms under the Hall, which are now appropriated to the College stores. A senior was placed in each room who was responsible for the diligence and good conduct of the juniors, and was bound to report irregularities to the Warden, Sub-Warden, or Dean, "so that such manner of Fellows and scholars suffering defect in their morals, negligent, or slothful in their studies, may receive competent castigation, correction, and punition." Whether the last terrors of scholastic law are contemplated under the head of "castigation" is not quite clear; but Fellows of all ranks were liable to "subtraction of commons"; and were in that case, perhaps, not able to live upon their neighbours in the convenient manner practised by modern New College men "crossed at the buttery."

Only a Doctor might have a separate servant; but all were required to have separate beds, a luxury not altogether a matter of course in the Middle Ages. At Magdalen, for instance, the younger Demies slept two in a bed.

All kinds of service were to be performed by males; though a washerwoman might be tolerated ("in defect of a male washer"), provided she were of such "age and condition" as to be above "sinister suspicions." One of the servants was to be specially entrusted with the task of carrying the scholars' books to the public schools.

The statutes of New College are extraordinarily minute and detailed in their disciplinary regulations, being more than three times as long as those of Merton. In their ample prohibitory code we may probably see a fair picture of undergraduate life in the Middle Ages, as it was outside the Colleges. It was the Colleges which gradually broke down the ancient liberty of the boy-undergraduate; and at last, by the sixteenth century, succeeded in making him a mere school-boy *sub virga et ferula*.

One piece of rough mediæval horse-play which incurs the founder's especial wrath is that "most vile and horrid sport of shaving beards, which is wont to take place on the night preceding the inception of Masters of Arts." Among the more ordinary pastimes forbidden by the founder are the haunting of taverns and "spectacles," the keeping of dogs, hawks, or ferrets; the games of chess, hazard, or ball; and other "noxious, inordinate, or illicit" games, "especially those played for money"; shooting with "arrows, stones, earth, or other missiles" to the danger of windows and buildings; the "effusion of wine, beer, or other liquor" (some unpleasant details are added under this head) upon the floor of upper chambers; "dancing or wrestling or other incautious or inordinate games" in the hall or "perchance in the chapel itself," the reason alleged for this last prohibition being that danger might be done to the sculptured "image of the Holy and Undivided Trinity," and other ornaments on the wall between the chapel and the hall. After this comprehensive list of unlawful amusements, the reader may be inclined to ask, "What recreations did the good bishop allow his scholars?" Only one seems contemplated by the statutes: the founder's experience of human nature told him that "after bodily refection by the taking of meat and drink, men are made more inclined to scurrilities, base talk, and (what is worse) detraction and strife"; he accordingly provides that on ordinary days after the loving cup has gone round, there is to be no lingering in hall after dinner or supper (except for the usual "potation" at curfew), but on festivals and other winter-nights, "on which, in honour of God and his Mother, or some other saint," there is a fire in the hall, the Fellows are allowed to indulge in singing or reading "poems, chronicles of the realm, and wonders of the world."

Such were the modest amusements of the first Wykehamists. How was the bulk of their time passed or meant to be passed? It must be remembered that Colleges were, in the first instance, not intended for teaching-institutions at all; their members resorted for lectures to the public schools. Wykeham is the first Oxford founder who contemplates any instruction being given to his scholars in College.[151] By his provisions on this head he became the founder of the Oxford tutorial system. Both at Paris and in Oxford, College teaching was destined, in process of time, practically to destroy University teaching in the Faculty of Arts. But the process took place in totally different ways. The form which College-teaching has assumed in Oxford was inaugurated by Wykeham. He, or his academical advisers, saw the unsuitableness of formal lectures in the public schools as a means of teaching mere boys. Hence he provides that for the first three years of residence, the scholar was to be placed under the instruction of a tutor ("Informator"), selected from the senior Fellows. By about 1408 the system had so far spread, that the lectures of the public schools were attended mainly by Bachelors.

Let us briefly trace the career of a young Wykehamist newly arrived from Winchester.

For two years he is a probationary "scholar"; after that he becomes a full member or "Fellow" of the College. It may be noticed that the New College statutes are the earliest in which the term "Socius," originally applied to the students who live in the same house or hall, begins to be used in a technical way to distinguish the full member of the society ("verus et perpetuus socius") from the mere probationer or chaplain or chorister: it is not till a still later date that the term "scholar" is confined to a Foundation-student who is not a Fellow.

At the end of the two years, the Fellow, though still an undergraduate, takes his share in the government of the house on such occasions as the election of a Warden. The ordinary administration, however, is in the hands of a certain number of Seniors (varying in different cases). The discipline was mainly in the hands of the Sub-Warden and the five deans—two Artists, a Canonist, a Civilian, and a Theologian—who presided over the disputations of their respective Faculties. But every one was compelled to act as a check upon every one else by means of the three yearly "chapters" or "scrutinies," at which every Fellow was invited and required to reveal anything which he might have observed amiss in the conduct of his brethren since the last "Chapter." Thus, the discipline of the mediæval Colleges, or at least that which their founders desired to introduce, was modelled on that of the monastery.

The lectures which our undergraduate had to attend before his B.A. degree were as follows[152]:—

In College: (1) In Grammar, the *Barbarismus* of Donatus; (2) in Arithmetic, the *Computus*, *i. e.* the method of finding Easter, with the *Tractatus de Sphaera* of Joannes de Sacrobosco; (3) in Logic, the *Isagoge* of Porphyry, and Aristotle's *Sophistici Elenchi*.

In the Public Schools: The whole *Organon* of Aristotle, the *Sex Principia* of Gilbert de la Poirée, and the logical writings of Boethius (except *Topics*, Book IV.).

Thus during the first four years of his course our undergraduate was occupied mainly with Logic, at first in College, afterwards at the more formal lectures of the Regents in the public schools of the University. This programme would represent a very dry and severe course of study to the modern

Honour-man, while it would be simply appalling to the modern Pass-man. The latter will, however, learn with relief that in Oxford (unlike other mediæval Universities) it would appear doubtful whether there was any actual examination for the B.A. degree. Then as now, indeed, the student had to "respond *de quaestione*"; but in the course of his fourth year he would be admitted, as a matter of course, "to lecture upon a book of Aristotle."

After this he was commonly styled a Bachelor, though he did not become one in strictness till he had gone through a disputation called "Determination." This ordeal had to be passed to the satisfaction of the other Bachelors. How glad would be the modern examinee to throw himself upon the mercy of his fellows! Before being admitted to determine, the student had indeed to appear before the examiners of Determinants, but it is not certain that these examiners did more than satisfy themselves by the oaths and certificates of the candidates that they had heard the required books: and it is quite clear that when once Determination was passed, no further examination stood between him and the M.A. degree.

The mediæval student was not, however, supposed to have completed his education when he had become a Bachelor. To the four years of residence required for a B.A., three more must be added for the Mastership. During this time he attended lectures in "the Seven Arts" and "the three Philosophies." In the Arts his text-books were[153]:—In Grammar, Priscian;

in Rhetoric, Aristotle or Boethius[154]; in Logic, Aristotle; in Arithmetic, Boethius; in Music, Boethius; in Geometry, Euclid; and in Astronomy, Ptolemy. Most of the Arts were however very quickly and perfunctorily disposed of. His real work as a Bachelor lay with the three philosophies, studied exclusively in the Latin translation of Aristotle, the following being the "necessary books":—In Natural Philosophy, the *Physics*, or *De Anima*, or some other of the Physical treatises; in Moral Philosophy, the *Ethics*; and in Metaphysical Philosophy, the *Metaphysics*.

Time would fail me to tell of the various disputations in which our student had to figure at various stages of his career; but disputations, though to the nervous student their terrors must have exceeded those of modern *viva*, had this advantage, that there was no "plucking" or "ploughing" in the question. A candidate who had done very badly might fail to get the required number of Masters to testify to his competency when he applied for the degree; and very incapable students, if poor and humbly-born, were probably choked off in this way. It is certain that a large number never took even the B.A. degree. But there is no record of anybody having been formally refused a degree in Arts. And yet the Master's degree in the Middle Ages was in reality what it still is in theory—a license to teach. For a year after admission to his degree, the new M.A. was *necessario regens*, and was obliged to give "ordinary lectures" in the public schools. After that he was free to enter upon the study of one of the higher Faculties.

Those who took Theology spent the rest of their academical career in the study of the Bible and "the Sentences" of Peter the Lombard—much more of the Sentences than of the Bible. It took eleven years' study to become a D.D.; naturally most got livings and "went down" before that.

Those who obtained leave to study Law would usually take a degree in Civil Law first, and then proceed to the study of Canon Law, that is to say the *Decretum* of Gratian and the Papal *Decretals*. There were always to be twenty Canonists and Civilians in the House.

Two scholars alone might take up Medicine, and two Astronomy or Astrology. Wykeham is the only College-founder who treats Astronomy as a recognized Faculty; but belief in Astrology was on the increase in fourteenth-century England, and reached its maximum amid the enlightenment of the sixteenth century.

It is time to allude to the curious "privilege" which exercised so disastrous an effect upon the New College of two generations ago, the privilege of taking degrees without examination. William of Wykeham is not responsible for this *damnosa hereditas*. Nothing is heard of it till the beginning of the seventeenth century; and then the University recognized it as having been enjoyed since the earliest days of the College.[155] But its origin seems to be as follows.—So far from wishing his scholars to be exempt from the ordinary tests, the Founder peremptorily forbids them to sue for "graces" or dispensations from the residence or other statutable conditions of taking a degree. The grace of congregation was then required only when some of these conditions had not been complied with; if they had been, the degree was a matter of right. Even in Wykeham's time these graces were scandalously common. In course of time the full statutable conditions were so seldom complied with that the grace of congregation came to be asked for as a matter of course: Wykehamists alone, mindful of their founder's injunction, sought no graces. Hence what had been intended as an exceptional disability came to be regarded as an exceptional privilege; and when regular examinations were at length introduced, it was understood that the mysterious privilege carried with it exemption from this requirement also. Since a fair level of scholarship was secured by the fact that the places in New College were competed for by the boys of a first-rate classical school (although corrupt elections were not unknown), the privilege was not particularly ruinous so long as the examinations continued on the basis of the Laudian statutes. It was only when the Honour Schools were instituted at the beginning of this century that the exclusion of New College men from the Examination-schools shut out the College from the rapid improvement in industry and intellectual vitality which that measure brought with it for the best Oxford Colleges.

The character of the College during the earlier part of its history was exactly of the kind which the founder designed. In Wykeham's day the Scholastic Philosophy and Theology were already in their decadence. The history of mediæval thought, so far as Oxford is concerned, ends with that suppression of Wycliffism in 1411, which both Wykeham and his College (though not quite free from the prevalent Lollardism) had contributed to bring about. New College produced not schoolmen and theologians like Merton, but respectable and successful ecclesiastics in abundance—foremost among them, Henry Chicheley, Archbishop of Canterbury, the founder of All Souls. It is a characteristic circumstance that a New College man, John Wytenham, was at the head of the Delegacy for condemning Wycliffe's books in 1411, all the other Doctors being monks or friars.

On the other hand, the one piece of reform which Wykeham did seek to introduce into Oxford bore fruit in due season. New College, the one College which was recruited exclusively from a great classical school, became the home of what may be called the first phase of the Renaissance movement which showed itself in Oxford. It is during the latter part of Thomas Chaundler's Wardenship (1454-1475) that traces of this movement become apparent. Chaundler's own style, as is shown by his published letters to Bishop Bekynton of Wells (himself a Wykehamist and benefactor of the College), was more correct than the ordinary "Oxford Latin" of his day; and some time before his death he brought into the College as "Prælector" the first Oxford teacher of Greek, the Italian scholar Vitelli, who remained till 1488 or 1489.[156]The movement made little progress for the next two decades; but it must have been Vitelli who imparted at least the rudiments of Greek and the desire for further knowledge to William Grocyn, the great Wykehamist with whose name the "Oxford Renaissance" is indissolubly associated. Stanbridge, the Head Master of Magdalen College School, and author of the reformed system of teaching grammar imitated by Lily at St. Paul's and at other schools, and Archbishop Warham, the patron of Erasmus, deserve mention among New College Humanists. To Warham we owe the panelling which imparts to our Hall much of its peculiar charm.

But if New College welcomed and fanned the first faint breath of the Renaissance air in Oxford, wherever religion and politics were concerned, she retained that character of rigid and immobile Conservatism which the founder had sought to give it. John London (Warden 1526-1542) was foremost in the persecution of Protestant heretics in Oxford, though afterwards employed in the dirty work of collecting evidence against the Monasteries. One of his victims was Quinley, a Fellow of his own College, whom he starved to death in the College "Steeple." When asked by a friend what he would like to eat, he pathetically exclaimed, "A Warden-pie." His unnatural hunger might have been appeased could he have seen his persecutor doing public penance for adultery, and ending his days a prisoner in the Fleet. The stoutest and most learned opponents of the Reformation were bred in Wykeham's Colleges—the men who were ejected or fled under Edward VI., rose to high preferment under Mary, and became victims again under Elizabeth—men like Harpesfield the ecclesiastical historian, Pits the bibliographer, and Nicholas Saunders, the Papal Legate, who organized the Irish Insurrection of 1579.

Ecclesiastically and politically the Great Rebellion found the College again on the Conservative side. In 1642 the then Warden, Dr. Robert Pincke, as Pro-Vice-Chancellor, took the lead in preparing Oxford to resist the Parliamentary forces. The University train-bands were wont to drill "under his eyes" in the front quadrangle. Dons and undergraduates alike joined the ranks; among them is especially mentioned the New College D.C.L., Dr. Thomas Read, who trailed a pike. The cloisters were converted into a magazine; and the New College school-boys, being thus turned out of their usual school, were removed "to the choristers' chamber at the east end of the common hall of the said College: it was then a dark, nasty room, and very unfit for such a purpose, which made the scholars often complaine, but in vaine." These are the words of Anthony à Wood, then a little boy of eleven, and a pupil in the school.

While the school-boys were with difficulty restrained from the novel excitement of watching the drills in the quadrangle, the Warden's severer studies had been no less interrupted. He had been sent by the University to treat with the old New College-man, Lord Say, who was supposed to be in command of the Parliamentary forces at Aylesbury. Unfortunately for Pincke, Lord Say was not there, and the Parliamentary commander, being without Wykehamical sympathies, sent the Doctor a prisoner to the Gate-house at Westminster. Meanwhile Lord Say had entered Oxford, and immediately proceeded to New College "to search for plate and arms" (no doubt he knew where to look), and even overhauled the papers in the Warden's study. "One of his men broke down the King's picture of alabaster gilt, which stood there; at which his lordship seemed to be much displeased." It is not very clear how Warden Pincke found his way back to Oxford; but soon after the Parliamentary triumph, he came to an untimely end by falling down the steps of his own lodgings.

Pincke was evidently a learned as well as an active man, and published a curious collection of *Quaestiones in Logica, Ethica, Physica, et Metaphysica* (Oxon. 1640); this is a list of problems with a formidable array of references to authorities, classical, patristic, and scholastic. He found time, even in the busy days of his Vice-Chancellorship, to write a narrative of his proceedings in that office, which was still extant in MS. after the Restoration. The only other Wardens who have left any considerable literary remains are Pincke's predecessor, Lake, afterwards Bishop of Bath and Wells, and Shuttleworth (Warden 1822-1840), afterwards Bishop of Chichester, a sturdy opponent of the Tractarian movement.

While speaking of New College learning of the early seventeenth century, we must not pass over Dr. Thomas James, the first Bodley's Librarian, who, besides being a really learned writer on theological subjects, catalogued the MSS. in the libraries of the Colleges of both Universities as well as those under his own charge.

On the arrival of the Puritan Visitors in 1647, no College gave so much trouble as New College. All but unanimously the members of the foundation declared that it was contrary to their oaths to submit to any Visitor who was an actual (*i. e.* resident) member of the University, which was the case with the most active Visitors. Only two unconditional, and one qualified submission, are recorded. Forty-nine out of the fifty-three members of the foundation (choir included) then in residence were sentenced to expulsion on March 15th, 1647-8. But it was not till June 6th that four of the worst offenders were ordered to move; on July 7th the order was extended to seventeen more. On August 1st, 1648, Dr. Stringer, the Warden whom the Fellows had elected in defiance of the Visitors, was removed by Parliament, and in 1649 nineteen more foundationers were "outed."

It must not be assumed that the Fellows left by the Visitors, or even those put in the place of the ejected Fellows, conformed heartily to the Puritan *régime*. The bursars appointed by the Commission found the buttery and muniment-room shut against them. George Marshall, the Parliamentarian Warden appointed in 1649, had to complain to the Visitors that the College persisted in remitting the "sconces" imposed by him upon Fellows for absence from the no doubt lengthy Puritan prayers. Moreover, the Visitors, with scrupulous desire to minimize the breach of continuity, elected only Wykehamists into the vacant places, with, indeed, the notable exception of the intruded Warden; and these new Fellows were most of them no doubt either Royalists and Churchmen, or at least men whose Puritan republicanism was of no very bigoted type. Hence we find that Woodward, the Warden freely elected by the College on Marshall's death in 1658, retained his place after the Restoration. Even in 1654 Evelyn found the chapel "in its ancient garb, notwithstanding the scrupulosity of the times." After the Restoration we are not surprised to find that the Royalist majority was strong enough to turn out many of the "godly" minority before the King's Commissioners arrived in Oxford, and to reinstate "the Common Prayer before it was read in other churches."

Two of "the Seven Bishops" were New College men, the saintly Ken, Bishop of Bath and Wells, and Turner, Bishop of Ely. One of their Judges, Richard Holloway, the only one who charged boldly in their favour, had been Fellow of the College till ejected by the Parliamentary Visitors.

The annals of our University in the eighteenth century are of an inglorious order; and New College exhibits in an intensified form the characteristic tendencies of Oxford at large. The building of the "new common chamber" (one of the first in Oxford) and of the garden quadrangle, at the end of the seventeenth century (finished 1684), seem to herald the age in which the increase of ease, comfort, and luxury kept pace with the decay of study, education, and learning. The *Vimen Quadrifidum* of Winchester still indeed kept alive a tradition of classical scholarship which even the possession of an Academic sinecure at eighteen, with total exemption from University examinations and exercises, could not quite extinguish; but there was a significant proverb about New College men which ran, "golden Scholars, silver Bachelors, leaden Masters." One of the last men of learning whom New College produced was John Ayliffe, D.C.L., the author of the *Past and Present State of the University of Oxford* (1714), who was expelled the University, deprived of his degree, and compelled to resign his Fellowship for certain "bold and necessary truths" contained in that book, partly of a personal, partly of a political (*i. e.* Whiggish) character. Perhaps the most respectable and yet characteristic product of New College during the *ferrea aetas* which succeeded were Robert Lowth, the scholarly antagonist of the slipshod Warburton, and author of the famous lectures *On the Poetry of the Hebrews*, successively Bishop of St. David's, Oxford and London.

Towards the close of the century New College harboured a staunch defender of the Church (including some of its abuses), but a staunch assailant of much else in that old *régime* to which it belonged. Sydney Smith came up from Winchester in 1789, having been Prefect of Hall and third on the roll; but though in the College, he was little of it. It is curious that the most brilliant talker of the century does not seem to have left much reputation behind him in College society. Perhaps his extreme poverty may have something to do with it.

The other most notable Fellow of New College in the first half of the nineteenth century, Augustus Hare (joint-author of *Guesses at Truth*), was also an assailant of the abuses among which he was brought up. When acting as "Poser" in the Winchester election of 1829, he had the spirit to resist the claims of certain candidates to be admitted to one or other of the two Colleges without examination, as "Founder's-kin." At the time there were already twenty-four "Founders" at New College, and fourteen or fifteen at Winchester. His appeal was heard by the Bishop of Winchester as Visitor, with Mr. Justice Patteson and Dr. Lushington as Assessors; a New College man, Mr. Erle (afterwards Lord Chief Justice), was one of the petitioner's counsel. The case was argued not upon the ground that the claimants' demand was based on fictitious pedigrees (which was probably the fact), but upon the precarious contention that by the Civil and Canon Law the term "consanguineus" applies at most only to persons within the tenth generation of descent from a common ancestor, and the appeal was naturally dismissed.

The era of reform may be said to begin with the voluntary renunciation by New College, in 1834, of its exemption from University examinations. The College still retains, indeed, the right to obtain for its Fellows degrees without "supplication" in congregation; and when a Fellow of New College takes his M.A., the Proctor still says, "Postulat A.B., e Collegio Novo," instead of the ordinary "Supplicat, etc.," or (more correctly) omits the name altogether. In spite of the vehement opposition of the College, a more extensive reform was carried out on truly Conservative lines by an Ordinance of the University Commissioners in 1857. The Fellowships were reduced to forty (in 1870 to thirty); but the mystic seventy of the original foundation is maintained by the addition in 1866 of ten open scholarships to the thirty which were still reserved for Winchester men. Further, commoners[157] were made eligible for Fellowships as well as scholars. Half the Fellowships are still reserved for Wykehamists, that is, men educated either at Winchester or at New College. The chaplaincies are now reduced to three, and the number of lay choir-men increased.

Since that beneficent reform, ever since loyally accepted and vigorously carried forward by the Warden and Fellows, the history of the College has been one of continuous material expansion, numerical growth, and academic progress. In 1854 the society voluntarily opened its doors to non-

Wykehamist commoners, whose increasing numbers soon called for the new buildings, the first block of which was opened in 1873.

We take our leave of the College with a glance at one or two of the quaint customs which have unfortunately, if inevitably, disappeared in the course of the process of modernization.

Down to 1830, or a little later, the College was summoned to dinner by two choir-boys[158] who, at a stated minute, started from the College gateway, shouting in unison and in lengthened syllables— "Tem-pus est vo-can-di à-manger, O Seigneurs." It was their business to make this sentence *last out* till they reached with their final note the College kitchen.

On Ascension Day the College and choir used to go in procession to St. Bartholomew's Hospital (the remains of which may still be seen on the Cowley road a little beyond the new church) where a short service was held, after which they proceeded to the adjoining well (Strowell), heard an Epistle and Gospel, and sang certain songs.

At the beginning of the present century the College was still waked by the porter striking the door at the bottom of each staircase with a "wakening mallet." Fellows are still summoned to the quarterly College-meetings in this antique fashion.

VIII.
LINCOLN COLLEGE.

BY THE REV. ANDREW CLARK, M.A., FELLOW OF LINCOLN COLLEGE.

Lincoln College, or, in its full and official title, "The College of the Blessed Mary and All Saints, Lincoln, in the University of Oxford," was founded by Richard Fleming, Bishop of Lincoln, in the year 1429, in the eleventh year of his episcopate and one year and one month before his death.

The founder, a native of Yorkshire, was educated in Oxford, and held the office of Northern (or Junior) Proctor in 1407. He was promoted to a prebendship in York Cathedral in 1415; and was raised to the see of Lincoln in 1419. In 1424 Pope Martin V., who held him in great esteem, advanced him to the Archbishopric of York; but the king (Henry VI.) refused to sanction the nomination; and Fleming, ejected from York, had some difficulty in getting "translated" back to Lincoln.

Richard Fleming, as a graduate resident in Oxford, had been noted for his sympathy with the tenets of the Wycliffists; but in his later years he had come to regard the movement with alarm, foreboding (as his preface to the statutes for his college says) that it was one of those troubles of the latter days which were to vex the Church towards the end of the world. The Wycliffists professed to accept the authority of the

Scriptures and to find in them the warrant for their attacks on accepted Church doctrines and institutions. In these same Scriptures, rightly understood and expounded, Fleming believed that the authority of the Church was laid down beyond contradiction. And so, in the bitterness of his repulse from York, which he perhaps attributed to the growing spirit of rebelliousness against the Church, he determined to found (to use his own words) "collegiolum quoddam theologorum"—"a little college of true students in theology who would defend the mysteries of the sacred page against those ignorant laics who profaned with swinish snouts its most holy pearls."

It is instructive to note the means by which he carried out his purpose. There is a common impression that these pre-Reformation prelates were possessed of great wealth. In some few instances, this was the case, namely, where the prelate had held in plurality several wealthy benefices, or had occupied a rich see for a great number of years, or had inherited a large private fortune; but in the majority of cases, the bishops were not wealthy men, and from year to year spent the revenues of their sees in works of public munificence or private charity. Every bishop, however, had partially under his control several of the Church endowments of his diocese, and could divert them, even in perpetuity, to the use of any institution he favoured, so long as they were not alienated from the Church. Accordingly, Fleming proposed, as it seems, to build the College out of his own moneys; but to provide for its endowment by attaching to it existing ecclesiastical revenues. He therefore obtained the sanction of the king (Henry VI.'s charter is dated 13th Oct., 1427) and Parliament, the Archbishop of Canterbury, the mother-church of Lincoln, the Archdeacon of Oxford, the parishioners of all three parishes, and the Mayor and Corporation of Oxford, to dissolve the three contiguous parish churches of All Saints, St. Mildred, and St. Michael,—all three being in the patronage of the Bishop of Lincoln,—as also the chantry of St. Anne in the church of All Saints, which was in the patronage of the city of Oxford; and to unite them into a collegiate church or college, which was to be "Lincoln College."

St. Mildred's was a small parish occupying the present site of Exeter College, and about half of the site of Jesus College; its church was sadly out of repair, and had no funds for its maintenance; and the ordinary parish population had given place to Academical students with their Halls and Schools. Fleming therefore planned to build his college on the site of this church and its churchyard, increasing the area by the purchase, on 4th April, 1430, of Craunford Hall, which stood south of the churchyard, and, on the 20th June, 1430, by the purchase of Little Deep Hall, which stood on the east of the churchyard. The ground-plot so formed is represented by the present outer quadrangle of the College.

The two churches of All Saints and St. Michael were to provide the endowment of the College. The lands and houses originally belonging to them had already been taken away when they had been reduced from rectories to vicarages, before they came to the patronage of the bishops of Lincoln. Their only revenues now were therefore the offerings in church, the fees at burials, etc., and the petty tithe (called "Sunday pence," being a penny per week from every house of over twenty shillings annual value in the parish, doubled at the four great festivals, viz. Christmas, Easter, Ascension, Whitsuntide).[159] These revenues, together with the income of the chantry of St. Anne, seem to have amounted to about £30; and out of them, when the College was founded, £12 was to be paid for the maintenance of divine service in the two churches and the chantry.

With these revenues Fleming proposed to endow a college consisting of a Warden and seven Fellows, who should, (1) study Theology, the queen and empress of all the faculties (*omnium imperatrix et domina facultatum*); (2) pray for the welfare of the founder during his life and for the health of his soul after his death, as also for the souls of his kindred and of his benefactors and of all faithful deceased.

Fleming's charter, uniting the churches and erecting the College, is dated 19th Dec., 1429. He did not live to see his project accomplished, for he died suddenly on 25th January, 1430-1.

In what condition was the College when the founder died? The following points may be noted:—

(1) The College was founded, and had received its charter of incorporation, together with certain "ordinances" for its government, which Rotheram says he imitated in framing the 1480 statutes;

(2) The buildings of the College had been begun, namely, the present tower, with the rooms over the gateway, in which, according to usual custom, the Head of the College was to reside, and control the comings in and goings out of its members;

(3) MSS. had been given to the library;[160] the Catalogue of 1474 specifying twenty-five "books" as given by the founder, chiefly theological (among these, *Walden against Wycliffe*), but one or two historical;

(4) A small annual revenue had been provided for, but this would probably not become available till the deaths, or cessions, of the vicars of All Saints' and St. Michael's, and the chaplain of St. Anne;

(5) A rector (William Chamberleyn) had been named by the founder, but no Fellows; so that when Chamberleyn died (7th March, 1433-4) Fleming's successor, Bishop William Grey, finding it impossible to supply the vacancy by election, according to Fleming's ordinances, himself nominated (on 7th May, 1434) Dr. John Beke.

In Beke's rectorship (1434-1460) the orphan College found good patrons to carry out the intentions of its deceased founder.

Before 1437 John Forest, Dean of Wells, built the Hall, the Kitchen, the Library (now the Subrector's room), the Chapel (now the Senior Library), with living rooms above and below the Library and below the Chapel, so that he deservedly was recognized by the College as its "co-founder."

In 1444 William Finderne, of Childrey, gave a large sum of money towards the buildings, and his estate of Seacourt, a farm at Botley near Oxford; in return the College was to appoint an additional Fellow ("*sacerdos et collega*") to pray for Finderne.

In 1436, we have evidence of a Rector, seven Fellows, and two Chaplains of Lincoln College. An account-book of 1456 has been preserved, showing the Rector and five Fellows in residence and in receipt of commons.

Beke resigned in 1460, and was succeeded in Jan. 1460-1 by the third Rector, John Tristrop, who had been resident in College as a Commoner in 1455, and had probably at one time been Fellow.

In the first year of Tristrop's rectorship the dissolution of the College was threatened. The charter of incorporation had been obtained from Henry VI.; and now that he had been deposed (on 4th March, 1460-1) by Edward IV., some powerful person seems to have coveted the possessions of the College, and suggested that Edward IV. should not grant it a charter, but seize it into his own hands. The College besought the protection of George Nevill, Bishop of Exeter, Lord High Chancellor, himself a graduate of Oxford. By Nevill's influence the College secured from Edward IV., on 23rd Jan.,

1461-2, pardon of all offences and release of all amercements incurred by them, and on 9th Feb., 1461-2, a charter confirming the College and extending its right to hold lands in mortmain. The reality of the danger and the gratitude of the College for preservation are sufficiently apparent by the way in which the Rector and Fellows tendered their thanks to Bishop Nevill: although he had given nothing to the College, yet by a solemn instrument, dated 20th Aug., 1462, they assigned him the same place in their prayers as the founder himself, "because he had delivered the College from being torn to pieces by dogs and plunderers."

This danger averted, and confidence in the legal position of the College restored, the stream of benefactions again began to flow.

In 1463 the College purchased from University College three halls lying next to it in St. Mildred's (now Brasenose) Lane and in Turl Street, thus doubling its original ground-plot.

In 1464 Bishop Thomas Beckington's executors, out of the monies he had left to be applied by them to charitable uses, gave £200 to build a house for the Rector at the south end of the hall, consisting of a large room on the ground-floor and another on the first floor (the dining-room and drawing-room of the present Rector's Lodgings), with cellar and attic. On the west front of this building was carved Beckington's rebus[161]—a flourished T, followed by a beacon set in a barrel (*i. e.*"beacon"—"tun") for

"T. Beckington"—and his coat of arms, with the rebus, on the east front.

In 1465 the founder's nephew, Robert Fleming, Dean of Lincoln, gave the library thirty-eight MSS., chiefly of classical Latin authors, comprising Cæsar, Cicero, Aulus Gellius, Horace, Juvenal, Livy, Plautus, Quintilian, Sallust, Suetonius, Terence, Virgil. Most of these, along with the old plate of the College, were embezzled by Edward VI.'s commissioners, under pretence of purging the library of Romanist books.

Some years afterwards the very existence of the College was a second time brought into danger. The scribe who wrote out the charter of 1461-2 (1 Edward IV.), had done his work in a most slovenly manner, dropping here and there words required by the grammatical structure. Unfortunately for the College, in one important place the words "*et successoribus*" were omitted; and some one in authority, fastening on this omission, suggested that the grant was only to the Rector and Fellows for the time being, and on their death or removal would lapse to the Crown. The College appealed, in 1474, for protection to Thomas Rotheram, Bishop of Lincoln and therefore Visitor of the College, and (from May 1474 to April 1475, and again from Sept. 1475) Lord High Chancellor of England.

The manner of this appeal, as recounted by Subrector Robert Parkinson about 1570, in the College register, is sufficiently dramatic. When Rotheram, in the visitation of his diocese, was at

Oxford, the Rector or one of the Fellows of Lincoln College preached before him from the text, Ps. lxxx. (lxxxi.), vers. 14, 15, "Behold and visit this vine, and complete it which thy right hand hath planted." The preacher described the desolate condition of the College, founded by Rotheram's predecessor, unprotected from the enemies who sought to destroy it; and his words so moved the bishop that he at once rose up and told the preacher that he would perform his desire.[162]

Rotheram was not slow in fulfilling his promise. To relieve the present necessities of the College he gave, in July 1475, a grant of £4 per annum during his life. Thereafter he completed the front quadrangle by building its southern side;[163] and he very greatly increased the endowments by impropriating[164] the rectories of Long Combe in Oxfordshire and Twyford in Bucks. He increased the number of Fellowships by five; but at least three of these had been provided for by earlier benefactors, one by Finderne, one by Forest and Beckington's executors, and one (for the study of Canon Law) by John Crosby, Treasurer of Lincoln Cathedral.

To secure the legal position of the College, he obtained from Edward IV., 16th June, 1478, a larger charter. In this the king recites his former charter; mentions the doubt which had arisen by reason of its omitting the words "*et successoribus*"; and then sets the position of the College as a *perpetua persona* for ever at rest. In the same charter the king still further increased the amount of lands which the College might hold in mortmain.

On 11th Feb., 1479-80, Rotheram provided for the internal government of the College by the giving of a full body of statutes. Rotheram therefore is justly regarded as our restorer and second founder.

The later years of the fifteenth and the earlier years of the sixteenth centuries increased the estates of the College by four great benefactions. By an agreement with Margaret Parker, widow of William Dagville, a parishioner of All Saints parish, the College in 1488 (5 Henry VIII.) came into possession of considerable property in Oxford,[165] which had been bequeathed by Dagville, subject to his widow's life interest, by his will dated 2nd June, 1474, and proved 9th Nov., 1476. In 1508 William Smith, Bishop of Lincoln, gave his manors of Senclers in Chalgrove in Oxfordshire, and of Elston (or Bushbury) in Staffordshire. In 1518 Edmund Audley, Bishop of Sarum, gave £400, with which lands in Buckinghamshire were bought. And in 1537 Edward Darby, Fellow in 1493, and now Archdeacon of Stowe, gave a large sum of money, with which lands in Yorkshire were bought. Darby directed that the number of Fellowships should be increased by three, to be nominated by himself in his lifetime (one of the first three whom he nominated as Fellows was Richard Bruarne, afterwards Regius Professor of Hebrew); and afterwards, one to be nominated by the Bishop of Lincoln, the other two to be elected by the College.

In connection with Bishop Smith's benefaction, we may note here the singular fatality which has led the College in successive ages to quarrel with its benefactors. Writing in 1570, Subrector Robert Parkinson says, "Bishop Smith would have given to our College all that he afterwards gave to Brasenose (founded by him in 1509) had he agreed with the Rector and Fellows that then were." With Smith's change of plans, part of Darby's benefaction went, for he also founded a Fellowship in Brasenose. Sir Nathaniel Lloyd was a chief benefactor in the early eighteenth century to All Souls in Oxford, and to Trinity Hall in Cambridge: in three successive drafts of his will he takes the trouble to write, "I gave £500 to Lincoln College, which was not applied as I directed: so no more from me!" Lord Crewe, our greatest benefactor of modern times, well deserving the title of "our third founder," was almost provoked[166] to recalling his benefaction. A quarrel with John Radcliffe diverted from Lincoln College the munificence which doubled the buildings of University College and provided for the erection of the Radcliffe Library, the Infirmary, and the Observatory. Other instances, both remote and recent, might also be cited.

Having now brought the history of the endowments of the College to that point where their application within its walls can be conveniently described, it is necessary to leave the annals of the College for a time and consider its organization, as it was arranged for by Rotheram's statutes, modified slightly by subsequent benefactions.

The College was to consist of (I) the Rector; (II) Fellows; (III) Chaplains; (IV) Commoners; (V) and Servants.

(I) To the Rector was, of course, in general terms committed the government of the College and its members. But he was allowed large limits of absence from College; and he was to be capable of holding any ecclesiastical benefice in conjunction with his rectorship. In the founder's intention, therefore, the headship of the College was to be an office of dignity, and the holder set free from the ordinary routine of college work. It was also to be a reward of past services to the College, because only a Fellow, or ex-Fellow, was eligible for the office.

(II) The Fellows were to be thirteen in number, counting the Rector as holding a Fellowship; and consequently, when augmented by Darby, sixteen. Provision was made for the increase of their number if the revenues of the College could bear it; but this provision seems never to have been acted on. The corresponding provision for diminution of the number of Fellowships to eleven, to seven, to five, and even to three, was, however, from time to time had recourse to; and as a rule, the circumstances of the College have not permitted of the extreme number of Fellowships being filled up.[167]

The Fellows were to be elected from graduates of Oxford or Cambridge, born within the counties or dioceses described below; and if not already in priest's orders were to take them immediately they were of age for them. A Bachelor of Arts was not to be elected unless there was no Master of Arts possessed of the proper county or diocese qualification. When, however, Darby in 1537 gave his three additional Fellowships, he recognized the fact that there might be no graduate in the University eligible, and provided that they might be filled up by the election of an undergraduate Fellow[168] either from undergraduates in Oxford, or by taking a boy from some grammar school in Lincoln diocese; but the person so elected was to have no voice in College business until he had taken his degree.

Taking the full number of Rector, twelve Foundation Fellows, and three Darby Fellows, the sixteen places on the foundation of Lincoln College were assigned as follows—

One Fellowship was to be filled up from the diocese of Wells (*i. e.* county of Somerset), in memory of the benefactions of John Forest, dean, and Thomas Beckington, bishop, of Wells; but this Fellow was specially excluded from election to the Rectorship or Subrectorship. All the other places were to be apportioned between the dioceses of York and Lincoln. It is not known whether Fleming, himself a native of Yorkshire and bishop of Lincoln, had made any such limitations; but Rotheram, possessed of the same twofold interest, draws particular attention to the fact that his College is designed to make provision for natives of these two dioceses which had hitherto been neglected by the founders of colleges. Four places were assigned for natives of the county of Lincoln, with a preference to natives of the archdeaconry of Lincoln; four places were open to natives of the diocese of Lincoln; two places were assigned for natives of the county of York, with a preference to natives of the Archdeaconry of York, and within that with a more particular preference to the parish of Rotherham, in which the second founder was born; two places were to be open to natives of the diocese of York. Of the Darby Fellowships, one was to be for a native of the Archdeaconry of Stowe, one for a native of Leicestershire or Northamptonshire (with a preference to the former), and one for a native of Oxfordshire.[169]

The next point which we may consider is the duties of the Fellows. These may be classified as follows:—

(1) They were to be "theologi" (students of theology), with the single exception of the holder of the Fellowship founded by John Crosby for the study of Canon Law. Their orthodoxy was ensured by a very stringent clause directed against heretical opinions:—"if it be proved by two trustworthy witnesses that any Fellow, *in public or in private*, has favoured heretical tenets, and in particular that pestilent sect, lately sprung up, which assails the sacraments, divers orders and dignities, and property of the Church," the College is to compel him to immediate submission and correction, or else to expel him.

(2) They were to pray for the souls of founders and benefactors, at the celebration of mass, in bidding-

prayers, in the graces in hall, after disputations, and on the anniversaries of their death. This was the chief duty contemplated by all pre-Reformation benefactors.

(3) They had considerable duties to perform with regard to their four Churches which may be classified thus:—

(*a*) As regards spiritualities. Although the ordinary services of the Churches throughout the year were to be discharged by four salaried Chaplains, yet, during Lent, a Fellow of the College was to assist the Chaplain of All Saints in hearing confessions and in other ministerial functions; another, similarly, to assist the Chaplain of St. Michael's; another, to assist the Chaplain at Combe; and the Rector, or a Fellow appointed by him, to assist the Chaplain at Twyford. On all greater festival days, the Rector or his representative (in an amice, if he had one, and if not, in surplice, and the hood of his degree), accompanied by all the Fellows (except one who was to attend as representative of the College at St. Michael's), was to go to service at All Saints.[170] St. Mildred's Church was to be commemorated on her day (13th July) by a celebration in the College chapel; and the benefaction of John Bucktot by a Fellow going to Ashendon to say mass on St. Matthias day, and that of William Finderne by a similar service in Childrey parish church.[171] Sermons in English were to be preached at All Saints on Easter Day and on All Saints Day,[172] by the Rector, and on the dedication day of that Church, by one of the Fellows; and at St. Michael's on Michaelmas Day, by one of the Fellows.[173]

(*b*) As regards temporalities. On the 6th of May a "Rector chori" was to be appointed for All Saints and a "Rector chori" for St. Michael's; their duties were to occupy the Rector's stall in the chancel, and to collect all alms, fees, etc., for the bursar of the College. These duties at Twyford belonged to the Rector of the College, and at Combe were supervised by him.

(4) As regards the ordinary academical curriculum, the founder's requirements were by no means exacting.

(*a*) The College disputations were to be weekly during Term, in Logic and Philosophy on Wednesdays, for those members who had taken B.A. and not yet proceeded to M.A. (there being no undergraduates, according to the founder's scheme); and in Theology on Fridays, for all members of M.A. standing. Both sets of disputations were to cease during Lent, when the Fellows were engaged in their ministerial duties.

(*b*) Fellows, elected as B.A., were to proceed to M.A. as soon as possible; Fellows were to take B.D. (or B. Can. L. in case of the Canonist Fellow) within nine years from M.A.; and, unless the College approved of an excuse, to proceed to D.D. (or D. Can. L.) within six years later. The last of these provisions, however, was practically a dead letter, for the College never forced any Fellow to the expensive dignity of the Doctorate.

(5) Study, however, as distinct from formal academical exercises, was inculcated as a virtue both by persuasions and punishments. The Subrector was charged to rebuke Fellows not merely for offences against morality and decorum, but for being neglectful of books; and unless the Fellows so admonished submitted and mended their ways, they were to be expelled.

The founder and later benefactors, as has been from time to time noted, made gifts of "books" (*i. e.* MSS.) for the use of the Fellows; and John Forest built a library for their reception. According to Rotheram's statutes, two classes of books were to be recognized—

(*a*) Those which were to be chained in the library, and which the reader had therefore to consult there. According to the Catalogue of 1474, this library then contained 135 MSS., arranged on seven desks.

(*b*) Those which were to be considered as "in the common choice" of the Rector and Fellows. On each 6th November a list of these was to be made out; the Rector was to choose one, and after him the Fellows one each, according to their seniority,[174] and so on till the books were all taken out; thereafter, the Fellows were to take the books to their own rooms, depositing a bond for their safe custody and return. In 1476 there were 35 books in this "lending library," different from the 135 above-mentioned. A record is also found of the books (18 in number) thus borrowed by the Fellows in 1595 and (17 in number) in 1596; among them are two copies of Augustine *De civitate Dei*, and one of Servius *In Virgilium*.

(6) The Fellows had to take their share in the ordinary routine of College business, especially in the two chief meetings on 6th May and 6th November, called "chapters" (*capitula*), and to serve when called upon in the College offices. These were three in number, all held for one year only.

(*a*) The Subrector was charged with the general management of the College during the Rector's absence, the supervision of the conduct of the Fellows and commoners, the presiding over disputations, and the writing of all letters on College business. The emblem of his office was a whip, which, with his alternative title (Subrector *sive* Corrector[175]), is eloquent as to his original duty of correcting faults of conduct by corporal punishment. This scourge of four tails, made of plaited cord after the old fashion, is still extant and perfect, is solemnly laid down by the Subrector at the conclusion of his term of office, and restored to him next day on his re-election. It has been coveted for the Pitt-Rivers anthropological museum, as a genuine example of the "flagellum" of mediæval discipline.

(*b*) The Bursar (*thesaurarius*) was charged with the duties of paying bills, collecting rents, and keeping accounts; of seeing that commons were duly and sufficiently supplied; and of governing the

College servants (over whom he had the power, with the consent of the Rector, of appointment and dismissal).

(*c*) The Key-keeper (*claviger*) was to keep one of the three keys with which the Treasury was locked, and one of the three keys of the chest in the Treasury which contained the College money, the other keys of these sets being in the charge of the Rector and Subrector. This "chest of three keys" corresponds to the balance to the credit of the College at its bankers and its investments in the public stocks; in it were placed any surplus money or donations to meet sudden calls for payment or to wait investment; and the idea of appointing a key-keeper was that the chest might never be approached by any person at random or singly, but always by responsible officers, protected against themselves by the presence of others.

(7) The Fellows were strictly required to reside in Oxford and within College. During the Long Vacation they might be absent from College for six weeks; at other times not for more than two days, without special leave: the Rector and Subrector had, however, general directions given them in the statutes not to be niggardly in granting leave in cases where the presence of the applicant was required by no College duties.

On several occasions of the visitation of the city by the plague, this requirement of residence was relaxed; and the Fellows were permitted to have all their allowances if they lived in common at some place near Oxford. Thus, in the pestilence of 1535, commons were allowed to the Rector, Subrector, and five Fellows in residence at Launton, for a fortnight in some cases, for a month in others; and in that of 1538, commons were allowed to the Rector, Subrector, and twelve Fellows in residence at Gosford (near Kidlington), during a period of no less than fifteen weeks.

During Elizabeth's reign, leaves of absence become frequent and continuous, and are practically equivalent to non-residence. The Fellows in this reign, and later, developed a bad habit of asking for leave when their turn for disputing, or other duties, came round; and several Visitors' Injunctions are directed against granting leaves unless a substitute has been provided to perform all duties.

From this statement of the duties of the Fellows, we pass on to discuss their emoluments. These can best be understood if we group them together under separate heads.

(*a.*) Commons (*communiæ*), the weekly allowance for food at the common table in the hall of the College, and at the regular time of meals. Rotheram provided that in each week there should be allowed for each Fellow in residence (counting the Rector as a Fellow), the sum of sixteen-pence; fixing the allowance at that amount, and not more, because, as he says, "clerks" should avoid luxury.

Several festivals of the Church's year were to be honoured by an addition to the ordinary table-allowance. In the weeks in which the following Holy-days occurred, the allowance for commons for each Fellow was to be increased by the sum named:—Epiphany (6th Jan.), 4*d.*; Purification of Mary (Feb. 2nd), 2*d.*; *Carnis privium* (Septuagesima Sunday), 2*d.*; Annunciation of Mary (25th Mar.), 2*d.*; Easter, 8*d.*; Ascension, 4*d.*; Whitsun day, 8*d.*; Corpus Christi, 4*d.*; St. Mildred (13th July), 2*d.*; Assumption of Mary (15th Aug.), 2*d.*; Nativity of Mary (8th Sept.), 2*d.*; Michaelmas (29th Sept.), 2*d.*; dedication of St. Michael's Church (in Oct.), 2*d.*; All Saints' Day (1st Nov.), 4*d.*; dedication of All Saints' Church (in Nov.), 4*d.*; Conception of Mary (8th Dec.), 2*d.*; Christmas, 8*d.*

An incidental, and therefore very striking, indication of the plagues which then infected the country is the care the statutes take to provide for cases of leprosy or other noisome disease. The Fellow so afflicted is to live away from the College, and to receive yearly forty shillings in lieu of all allowances.

(*b.*) Salary (*salarium*), payments in money. Rotheram made no grants for these, except to the Rector and the College officers; but he gave liberty to other benefactors to make them. The first distinct mention of such grants is in 1537, when Edmund Darby directs that 3*s.* 4*d.* shall be paid annually to each Fellow, and 6*s.* 8*d.* to the Rector. The dividends of the College rents, after payment of all charges, known as "provision," date no doubt from a very early period, but their history cannot now be traced.

(*c.*) Livery (*vestura*), allowance for clothing. For this also Rotheram made no provision, except to permit it if given by later benefactors. Edmund Audley, Bishop of Sarum, in giving his benefaction in 1518, directed that forty shillings per annum should be allowed *pro robis* to the Rector, and to each of the four senior Fellows.

(*d.*) The Fellows in common were entitled to the services of the common servants; for which see below.

(*e.*) The Fellows were entitled to have rooms (*cameræ*) rent-free. These were to be chosen, according to seniority, on the May chapter. About 1600 we find that along with his room, the Fellow received also the attic ("loft," or "cock-loft") over it, into which he might put a tenant from whom he might receive rent. How far this custom had come down from antiquity we have no means of saying.

(*f.*) Obits (*obitus*), allowances for being present at Mass on the anniversary-day of a benefactor. A considerable benefactor invariably made a bargain with the College, that his name should be kept in remembrance, and his soul's health prayed for in a special Mass, yearly on the anniversary of his death, or, if that should clash with some very solemn season of the Church's year, on the nearest convenient day. To insure the presence of the Rector and Fellows, he generally ordered that each Fellow present at the Commemoration Service should receive a stipulated sum, which was called by the same name as the day itself, an "obit."

The following are the dates of the obits in Lincoln College, and the amount paid to each Fellow; the Rector as celebrant, receiving in each case double the amount which a Fellow received:—Jan. 10th, Edward Darby, 1*s.*; Jan. 16th, Bishop Beckington, 6*d.*; Feb. 23rd, Archdeacon Southam, 1*s.*; March 21st, John Crosby, 8*d.*; March 26th, Dean Forest, 1*s.*; April 11th, Cardinal Beaufort, 8*d.*; May 29th, Rotheram, the second founder, 1*s.*; Aug. 23rd, Bishop Audley, 1*s.*; Oct. 10th, Bishop William Smith, 1*s.*; Oct. 29th, William Dagvill, 1*s.*; Nov. 16th, William Bate, 6*d.*—all of them early benefactors. The obit of the first founder, Fleming, was fixed for Jan. 25th; but no allowances made for it, gratitude alone being strong enough to ensure the attendance of all the Fellows.

At the Reformation, the celebration of Mass and, consequently, the observance of these anniversary services in the form directed by the statutes, became illegal, and the chapel services ceased. The allowances still continued to be paid to each Fellow who was present in College on the particular day, the test of "presence" being now dining in hall at the ordinary hour of dinner.

(*g.*) Pittances (*pietantia*). Besides the sum given to the Rector and each Fellow on a benefactor's anniversary day, it is sometimes directed that a sum shall be paid to them in common for "a pittance," *i. e.* as I suppose, to provide a better dinner on that day. Thus Cardinal Beaufort gave a pittance of 3*s.*

4*d.*; Rotheram, one of 2*s.*; Edward Darby, one of 3*s.* 4*d.*

(III) The Chaplains were four in number. Two were to serve the churches of All Saints and St. Michael in Oxford, one of whom must be of the diocese of York, the other of the diocese of Lincoln. They were to be appointed by the Rector, and to be removed by him when he chose; and each to receive from the College a stipend of £5 per annum. A third Chaplain was to serve the church of Twyford under the same conditions, except that his stipend was to be paid by the Rector; a fourth was to serve the church of Combe Longa.

It was clearly no part of the founder's intention that the chaplaincies should be served by the Fellows: and we find, down to the Civil War and the Commonwealth, instances of Chaplains who were not Fellows. But after the Restoration, when £5 per annum no longer represented a reasonable year's income, there was a growing feeling that it was for the honour of the College that the duties of Chaplain of All Saints, St. Michael's, and Combe should be undertaken by Fellows. And so long as there were Fellows in orders enough for the duties, this was done. In the last half century, recognizing the changed circumstances of the times, the College has provided a more adequate endowment for each of its four chaplaincies.

(IV) The Servants. Rotheram's statutes provided that the Rector and each Fellow should have free of charge his share of the services of the "common" servants (*i. e.* of the College servants). These were (1) the maniple, whose duty it was to buy in provisions and distribute them in College; (2) the cook; (3) the barber;[176] (4) the laundress. From an account-book of 1591, it appears that the salary of the maniple and of the cook was £1 6*s.* 8*d.* per annum; of the barber, 10*s.*; and of the laundress £2.

There was also the bible-clerk (*bibliotista*, contracted *bita*), who was to be the Rector's servant when he was in residence. At dinner in hall he was to read, from the Bible, or some expositor, or some other instructive book, a portion appointed by the Rector or Subrector; and at dinner and supper he was to wait at the Fellows' table. For these services he was to receive food and drink; a room; and washing and shaving (the latter referring to the tonsure probably, and not suggesting that he was old enough to grow a beard). Different benefactors made additions to his emoluments; and at last, until divided by the 1855 statutes into two "Rector's Scholarships," the Bible-clerkship was the best paid office in College, being worth three times the Subrectorship, twice the Bursarship, or once and a half a Tutorship.

(V) The Commoners, or Sojourners (*commensales seu sojornantes*). Almost from the first there had been graduates resident in College, attracted by its quiet and by its social life, but not on the foundation, and therefore receiving no allowances from the College. Rotheram's statutes provided for their discipline, directing that they must take part in the disputations of the Fellows, and so on. Undergraduates are by implication excluded; and this presumption is increased to a certainty by the fact that no provision is made in the statutes for tuition.

In its beginnings, therefore, Lincoln College differs from our modern conceptions of a College alike in its aims and in its constitution. In all external features, and partially also in its domestic arrangements, it resembles a monastic house; but it differs from a convent in two important, though not obvious, points; first, that its inmates are not bound by a rule, and are free to depart from the College into the wider service of the Church; secondly, that the duty of prayer for benefactors and the Christian dead is co-ordinate with two other duties, the duty of serving certain churches, and the duty of studying for study's sake and for the truth. We have next to inquire how the College changed its original character, and was made, like other Oxford Colleges, a place of residence for undergraduates, with a body of Fellows engaged in tuition. This was one of the indirect results of the Reformation.

Under Henry VIII., Edward VI., and Elizabeth, the old freedom of the University was taken away, lest, if the immunities of the place continued, Oxford should become an asylum for disaffected persons.[177] No undergraduate was to be allowed in the University, unless he had the protection of a graduate tutor; and residence was to be restricted to residence within the walls of a College or Hall.

There was thus an external pressure forcing undergraduates to enter Colleges. There was also a readiness from within the College to receive them. The proceedings of the Reformers had been a violent shock to the adherents of the old faith in Lincoln College; and now that the routine of chapel services, masses, anniversaries, obits, could no longer be pursued, these adherents devoted themselves to training up young students in opposition to the new movement. And when, under John Underhill (Rector 1577-1590), the College was purged of the old leaven, the pressure of poverty (which then began to be felt in the University) made the Fellows glad to have undergraduates resident in College to keep up the establishment and pay tuition fees.

Unfortunately, there are no statistics of the stages of this change: the intervals between the years in which statements of the numbers in College occur being too great. In 1552 there were in College, the Rector, eleven Fellows, one B.A. Commoner, and thirteen persons not graduates, of whom some were certainly servitors, and some probably servants. In 1575 the Rector and the greater part of the Fellows have undergraduate pupils assigned to them in grammar and logic. In 1588 there were in College, the Rector and twelve Fellows, sixteen undergraduate Commoners, and nine servitors. In 1746, there were the Rector and twelve Fellows, eight Gentlemen-commoners, eighteen Commoners, and eight Servitors.

What provision was made for their instruction?

From about 1592 the College appointed annually these instructors for its undergraduates: (*a*) two "Moderators," to preside over the disputations in "Philosophy" and in "Logic" (occasionally when the College was full, an additional "Moderator" was appointed in Logic); (*b*) a Catechist, or theological instructor. Also, from 1615, a lecturer in Greek, annually appointed, was added. Of these the catechetical lecture disappears after 1642; the others continued to be annually filled up till 1856, but for many years these had been merely nominal appointments, the work of tuition devolving on regularly appointed Tutors, as in other Colleges. But at what date these last had been introduced into Lincoln College, is nowhere stated. In some few years, exceptional appointments are made; as, for example, in 1624 a Fellow is appointed to teach Hebrew; in 1708, £6 per annum is paid to Philip Levi, the Hebrew master.

Among these lecturers two may be noted. In 1607, and again in 1609 and 1610, Robert Sanderson was Logic lecturer; and began that vigorous course of Logic, which was published in 1615, and long dominated the Schools of Oxford: indeed, its indirect influence survived into the present half century, if, as Rector Tatham wrote to Dean Cyril Jackson, "Aldrich's logic is cribbed from Sanderson's." In 1615 Sanderson was Catechist, and perhaps at that time turned his attention to those questions of casuistry, in which he was to gain enduring fame. John Wesley was appointed to give the Logic and Greek lectures in 1727, 1728, 1730; and the

Philosophy and Greek lectures in 1731, 1732, and 1733.

What provision was made for the maintenance of undergraduates in the College?

In 1568, Mrs. Joan Traps, widow of Robert Traps, goldsmith of London, bequeathed to the College lands at Whitstable in Kent for the maintenance of four poor scholars. One scholar was to be nominated from Sandwich School by the Mayor and Jurats of that town, but not to be admitted unless the College thought him fit; in defect of such nomination, Lincoln College was to fill this place up (as it did the other three) from any grammar school in England. Each of these four scholars was to receive fifty-three shillings and fourpence half-yearly. Mrs. Traps was also, in her husband's name, a benefactor to Caius College, Cambridge, in which College their portraits hang. Descendants of R. Traps' brother are still found in Lancashire, Catholics; and one of them has told me his belief that the Traps had bought Church lands at the dissolution of the monasteries, intending to return them to the Church when the nation was again settled on its old lines; but this hope failing, devoted them to education,[178] as so many other conscientious purchasers of Church lands did. If this be so, it is fitting that the first recorded Traps' Scholar, William Harte (elected 25th May, 1571), should have been one of those sufferers for the old faith, whose cruel and barbarous murders are so dark a stain on the "spacious times" of Elizabeth. Mrs. Joyce Frankland, daughter of the Traps, augmented the stipend of these "scholars." She was afterwards a considerable benefactress to Brasenose College, and a most munificent donor to Caius College, Cambridge. Is she also to be numbered among those "offended benefactors" who have been mentioned above? Or had Lincoln College in her time been "reformed"? These four Traps' scholars,[179] commonly called the "Scholars of the House" (being distinguished, as I suppose, by that name from the servitors maintained privately by any Fellow), were for a century the only undergraduates in Lincoln College in receipt of any endowment.

In 1640, Thomas Hayne left £6 per annum in trust to the corporation of Leicester for the maintenance of two scholars in Lincoln College to be elected by the Mayor, Recorder, and Aldermen of that city. The corporation received this benefaction, but never sent any scholar to the College. Numerous educational benefactions throughout England were lost, like this, in the anarchy of the Civil War.

In 1655, a Chancery suit was begun against Anthony Foxcrofte, who had destroyed a codicil of Charles Greenwood, Rector of Thornhill and Wakefield, by which two Fellowships (or perhaps Scholarships) were bestowed on Lincoln College. What the issue of the suit was, I cannot say; nothing, certainly, came to the College.

About 1670, Edmund Parboe left a rent-charge of £10 per annum issuing out of the Pelican Inn in Sandwich, of which £4 was to be paid to the master of the grammar-school there, £1 to the Mayor and

Juratts for wine "when they keep their ordinary there," £5 to Lincoln College for the increase of the scholarship from Sandwich school; if no scholar is in College, it is to be funded till one is sent, and the arrears paid to him. From that date the corporation of Sandwich never nominated a scholar. I suspect the Mayor and Juratts treated the £5, like the £1, as a *pour boire*.

May the College still hope that the towns of Leicester and Sandwich, or some one for them, will remember the long arrears of these endowments, thus diverted from education? Even at simple interest, they would be now a great benefaction; and at compound interest, how great!

Later Scholarships and Exhibitions were founded by Rectors Marshall (four, in 1688), Crewe (twelve, 1717), Hutchins (several, 1781), Radford (several, 1851); also by Mrs. Tatham, widow of Rector Tatham (one, 1847). In 1857, Henry Usher Matthews, formerly Commoner of the College, founded a Scholarship in Lincoln College, and an Exhibition in Shrewsbury School to be held in Lincoln College: but the Public Schools Commissioners unjustly took the latter from the College. Since that date no Scholarship benefaction has come to the College; but Scholarships and Exhibitions have been created from time to time, under the provisions of the Statutes of 1855, out of suspended Fellowships.

The consideration of this change in the aims of the College has led us beyond the point to which we had come in its annals; it is therefore necessary to go back, and pass rapidly in review its post-Reformation history.

John Cottisford, the eighth Rector of the College (elected in March 1518-19), resigned on 7th Jan., 1538-9, probably[180] in dismay at the course of events in the nation. His successor, Hugh Weston, elected on 8th Jan., was possibly supposed to be on the reforming side; for he was undisturbed by Edward VI.'s Commissioners; but had to resign in 1555 to the Visitors appointed by Cardinal Pole. Christopher Hargreaves, elected on 24th Aug., 1555, and confirmed in his place by Cardinal Pole's Visitors, died on 15th Oct., 1558. His successor, Henry Henshaw or Heronshaw, was hardly elected on 24th Oct., when the hopes of the Romanist party were shattered. The College register, in the greatness of its anxiety, breaks, on this one occasion, the silence it observes as to affairs outside the College.[181] "In the year of our Lord 1558, in November, died the lady of most holy memory, Mary, Queen of England, and Reginald Poole, Cardinal and Archbishop of Canterbury; the body of the former was buried in Westminster, the body of the latter in his cathedral church of Canterbury, both on the same day, namely 14th December. At this date the following were Rector and Fellows of Lincoln College," and then follows a list of them. Clearly the writer of this note did not look forward to remaining long in College. Nor did he; within two years Henshaw had to resign to Queen Elizabeth's Visitors. Francis Babington, who had just been made

Master of Balliol by these Visitors, was transferred to the Rectorship of Lincoln. In this appointment we can detect the sinister influence which was to direct elections at Lincoln for some time to come; Babington was chaplain to Robert Dudley, Earl of Leicester, Chancellor of the University after 1564. The election was in flagrant violation of the Statutes which required that the Rector should be chosen from the Fellows or ex-Fellows of the College. But it was the policy of the Court to break College traditions, by thrusting outsiders into the chief government: the same thing was done in other Colleges, the case of Lincoln being peculiar only in the frequency of the intrusion. Doubts began to be cast on Babington's sincerity; he was accused of secretly favouring Romanism; and in 1563 he found it advisable to betake himself beyond sea.[182] Leicester was ready with another of his chaplains, John Bridgwater, who had been Fellow of Brasenose, and was not statutably eligible for the Rectorship of Lincoln. Again the Court was mistaken in its man. Under Bridgwater the College became a Romanist seminary, and continued so for eleven years; and then Bridgwater had to follow his predecessor across the seas, retiring to Douay, where, Latinising his name into "Aquapontanus," he became famous as a theologian. He is still held in honour among his co-religionists, and I remember several visits paid to the College in recent years by admirers of his, in hopes of seeing a portrait of him (but the College has none) or his handwriting (which we have). Still another of his chaplains was thrust into Lincoln College by the over-powerful Leicester; this time John Tatham, Fellow of Merton. But Tatham's Rectorship was destined to be a brief one: elected in July 1574, he was buried in All Saints' Church on 20th Nov., 1576.

Then there took place a very remarkable contest, six candidates seeking the Rectorship. Only one, John Gibson, Fellow since 1571, was statutably qualified; although of only six years' standing as a Fellow he was still senior Fellow, a fact eloquent as to the removal of the older Fellows from the College. Edmund Lilly, of Magd. Coll., another candidate, relied apparently on his popularity in the University. The other four candidates relied on compulsion from outside, William Wilson, of Mert. Coll., being recommended by the Archbishop of Canterbury, while the Chancellor (Lord Leicester) and the Bishops of Lincoln and Rochester tried to secure the election of their respective Chaplains. Leicester's candidate, John Underhill, was specially unacceptable to the College, having been removed from his Fellowship at New College by the Bishop of Winchester (the Visitor there), because of some malpractices with the College moneys. The Fellows elected John Gibson; the Bishop of Lincoln refused to admit him. Leicester wrote threatening letters to the College; summoned several of the Fellows to London, and browbeat them there. Then, thinking he had now gained his point, he proceeded to frighten off the other candidates, in order to leave a clear field for Underhill. The Fellows again elected Gibson; and the Bishop of Lincoln again refused to admit him. Then the Fellows elected Wilson; but the Bishop refused to admit him. So that, there being no help for it, they met again on 22nd June, 1577, and elected Underhill.

These proceedings caused great indignation in the University; and a petition was drawn up, worded in very strong terms, entreating the Archbishop of Canterbury to undertake the defence of the University against the "iniquity, wrong, and violence" which had been done. This was signed by resident B.D.'s and M.A.'s, and presented to his Grace, who passed it on to Leicester. Leicester thereupon wrote a long letter to Convocation, trying to justify his action, and threatening to resign his Chancellorship of the University if further attacked in this matter.

Underhill's first step after his election was to begin a new register, and to tear out of the old register all records of the proceedings since the death of Tatham; so that the only entry in the College books concerning this controversy is that Underhill was "unanimously elected." Leicester visited the College in 1585, and the Latin congratulatory verses on that occasion are among the earliest printed of Oxford contributions to that particularly dull form of literature. Underhill remained rector till 1590. By that time the see of Oxford had been vacant twenty years; and, as the leases of the episcopal estates were running out, Sir Francis Walsingham required a bishop who would make new leases and give him a share of the fines. He selected Underhill for this purpose, who was consecrated Bishop of Oxford in December 1589, and resigned the Rectorship of the College in 1590. His patron, having no further use for him after the renewal of the leases, neglected him; and Underhill died in poverty and disgrace in May 1592.

Leicester being now dead, the College at this vacancy was left to choose its own head; and Richard Kilby, Fellow since 1578, was elected sixteenth rector on 10th December, 1590. Kilby's Rectorship proved one continuous domestic struggle, which has left its mark in the College register in scored-out pages and blotted entries, as plainly as an actual battle leaves its mark in fields of grain trampled down by contending armies. The question was about the number of Fellows. In Underhill's Rectorship the College appears to have been impoverished, and unable to pay the full body of Fellows their allowances. Kilby's policy was to leave the Fellowships vacant, in order to keep up the income of the present holders; the opposition in College desired to fill up the Fellowships and to submit to a reduction of stipend all round.

In April 1592 the number of Fellows had fallen to nine. On 24th April three Fellows were elected; this election was quashed by the Visitor on 8th December of the same year. But the Fellows returned to the charge, and elected three Fellows on 15th December, and five others on 16th December, 1592; so that in 1593 the College consists of the Rector and the full number of Fellows (*i. e.* fifteen).

Vacancies occur rapidly, the Fellowships being so small in value. In 1596, and again in 1599, elections of one Fellow are made, are appealed against, but confirmed by the Visitor. In 1600 the number of Fellows had again fallen as low as ten, and the Fellows wished to proceed to an election; but the Rector (Kilby) tried to prevent their doing so by retiring to the country. The Subrector, (Edmund Underhill) called a meeting, and on 3rd November, 1600, the Fellows, in the Rector's absence, elected into two vacancies. Kilby induced the Visitor to quash these elections; Edmund Underhill appealed to the Archbishop of Canterbury as primate of the southern province. This was against the statutes, which directed that no Fellow should invoke any other judge than the Visitor; and on this ground, on 4th May, 1602, Kilby procured Underhill's expulsion. At the end of 1605 there were only five Fellows remaining; by 2nd May, 1606, two more had resigned. On the next day the Rector and the three Fellows remaining elected eight new Fellows, the last of the eight being certainly not the least, but the most illustrious Lincoln name of the century, Robert Sanderson, the prince of casuists.

The years which follow, from this election to the breaking out of the Civil War, present two aspects. Externally tokens of prosperity are not wanting. The buildings were considerably increased. In 1610 Sir Thomas Rotheram, probably the same who had been Fellow from 1586 to 1593 and Bursar[183] in 1592, and apparently of kin to the second Founder,[184] built the west side of the chapel quadrangle. The chapel itself, with its beautiful glass (said to be the work of an artist Abbott, brother of the Archbishop), was the gift of John Williams, Bishop of Lincoln and Visitor of the College. Bishop Williams at the same time (1628-1631) built the east side of the chapel quadrangle. The work cost more than he had promised to give, and the College had to complete it at its own charges; £90 being spent on this work in 1629, "as being all the sum that my lord our benefactor did require or the College could spare." It is curious to find[185] the same benefactor doing exactly the same thing in the fixed sum he gave (and would not increase) for building the library at St. John's College in Cambridge. If we turn, however, to the domestic annals of the College during this period we find an unlovely picture of turbulence and disorder. Fellows and Commoners alike are accused of boorish insolence, of swinish intemperance, of quarrelling and fighting. Bursars mismanage their trust and fail to render account of the College moneys they have received. Fellows try to defraud the College by marrying in secret and retaining their Fellowships. Two or three of the less scandalous scenes will be sufficient to indicate the violence of the times. On 20th November, 1634, Thomas Goldsmith, B.A., had to read a public apology in chapel for "a most cruel and barbarous assault" on William Carminow, an undergraduate. In December 1634 Thomas Smith, an M.A. commoner, made "a desperate and barbarous assault" on Nicholas North, another M.A. commoner, in the room of the latter. The same Thomas Smith a month before had been ordered by the Rector "to take his dogs[186] out of the College," which order he had treated with contempt. In October 1636 Richard Kilby and John Webberley, two Fellows, fell out and fought; and "Mr. Kilbye's face was sore bruised and beaten." The College ordered Webberley "to pay the charge of the surgeon for healing of Mr. Kilbye's face."

We must pass very hastily over the period from 1641 to the Restoration, not because the annals of Lincoln are lacking in interest during these years, but because space presses and the chief incidents have been noted in Wood's *History of the University* and in Burrows' *Register of the Parliamentary Visitation*. Paul Hood, the Rector, being a Puritan, kept his place under the Commonwealth, and having been constitutionally elected before the Civil War, retained it at the Restoration. Ten Fellows were ejected by the Parliamentary Visitors, and ten put into their place, at least six of them being persons of unsatisfactory character. At the Restoration Hood got the King's Commissioners to eject those of the ten who remained, and seven Fellows were elected in their place, the only name of interest among these being that of Henry Foulis, famous in his own age for his violent and bulky invectives against Presbyterianism and Romanism.

Lincoln College was singularly fortunate during the latter half of the seventeenth and for the greater part of the eighteenth centuries. Hood, at the Restoration, was in extreme old age, and left the whole management of the College to Nathaniel

Crewe (Subrector 1664-1668), so that it fairly escaped the break-down in manners, morals, and studies which the Restoration brought to many Colleges. Crewe, after a short Rectorship of four years (1668-1672), was raised to the Episcopal Bench; and at the close of his long life proved our greatest benefactor. When he resigned Crewe used his influence to get Thomas Marshall elected Rector, a good scholar and a good governor; who, on his death in 1685, left his estate to the College. His successor, Fitz-herbert Adams, was also a considerable benefactor. Of John Morley and Euseby Isham, who followed, John Wesley speaks in the highest terms. Richard Hutchins, twenty-third Rector (1755-1781), was a model disciplinarian and an excellent man of business; and, following Marshall's example, left his estate for the endowment of scholarships.

During this happy period much was done to improve the College, which can only be touched on in the briefest outline here. In 1662 John Lord Crewe of Steane (father of Nathaniel) converted the old chapel—which since the consecration of the new chapel on 15th September, 1631, had lain empty— into a library, which it still remains, and changed the library into a set of rooms. In 1662 the room under the library westwards was set aside as a room where the Fellows might have their common fires and hold their College meetings;[187] it is still the Fellows' morning-room. In 1684 the common-room was wainscotted at a cost of £90, Dr. John Radcliffe subscribing £10, and George Hickes and John

Kettlewell each £5. In 1686 Fitz-herbert Adams spent £470 on repairing and beautifying the chapel. In 1697-1700 the hall was wainscotted at a cost of £270, to which Lord Crewe gave £100. Rector Hutchins bought from Magdalen College some of the houses between the College and All Saints' Church, and left money to purchase the others, so as to form the present College garden.

During this period also the roll of the Fellows received some of its more famous names. The two eminent non-jurors, George Hickes and John Kettlewell; the celebrated physician, John Radcliffe; John Potter, whose Greek scholarship promoted him to the see of Canterbury; and John Wesley,[188] by and by to win a name only less famous than that of Wycliffe in the history of religion in England, may be cited.

The long period of prosperity which Lincoln College had enjoyed during the later part of the seventeenth and the earlier part of the eighteenth centuries was followed in the end of the eighteenth and the beginning of the nineteenth centuries by a period of decline, during which the College had its full share in the general stagnation of the University, and was chiefly notable for the grotesque eccentricities of its rector, Edward Tatham (Rector 1792-1834). Tatham, an M.A. of Queen's College, had been elected into a Yorkshire Fellowship at Lincoln in 1782. Shortly after his election he came into conflict with the Rector (John Horner) over a number of points in the interpretation of the statutes;

and after several appeals to the Visitor, was successful in his contention. In 1790 he distinguished himself by the ponderous learning, and the vigorous, if coarse, style of his Bampton Lectures, *The Chart and Scale of Truth by which to find the cause of Error* (published in 1790 in two volumes; a copy in the College library has additional MS. notes by the author). In March 1792 he was elected Rector, and one of his first achievements was the use he made of his old practice in controversy over the statutes to obtain from the Visitor an unstatutable augmentation of the stipend of the Rector. In the old obits, the Rector, being celebrant, had been assigned double the allowance of any Fellow; and in elections, according to an almost universal custom in Oxford Colleges, his vote counted for two. By emphasizing these points and suppressing contradictory evidence, Tatham persuaded the Visitor to decree that for the future the Rector's Fellowship should receive double of *all* the allowances of an ordinary Fellowship. Tatham was known as a forcible but most unconventional preacher; and one phrase of his, used in the University pulpit,[189] has become almost proverbial, that namely in which he wished that "all the Jarman[190] philosophers were at the bottom of the Jarman ocean," forgetting in the heat of his rhetoric to make it plain to his audience whether he meant the writers or their writings. In University business Tatham was at war with the Hebdomadal Board, and used to brow-beat its members, accusing them of "intrigues, cabals, and subterfuges." He was therefore well-hated by many of his contemporaries, and a great subject of those pasquils and lampoons which, orally and in writing, circulated freely in the University. In several of these Tatham had been compared in features and disposition to the "devil," who, after the fashion of the similar grotesque at Lincoln Cathedral, "looked over Lincoln" from his niche on the quadrangle-side of the gate-tower. Irritated at this, Tatham ordered the leaden figure to be taken down.[191] Then came out a lampoon, longer and more bitter than any before, in which the wit consists in making the word "devil" occur as often as possible in every quatrain, and the point is to suggest that when Tatham was returning from dining out ("full of politics, learning, and port was his pate") the devil, tired of standing so long inactive, had flown off with him into space; where leaving him, the devil returned to establish himself in person in the Rectorship and to govern the College with the help of "two imps, called tutors." During the later years of his life Tatham availed himself of the large liberty of non-residence allowed the Rector by the then statutes, and lived chiefly in the rectory-house at Combe. There he enjoyed the pleasures of a rough country life, farming the glebe, and devoting himself with marked success to the rearing of his special breed of pigs. He rarely visited Oxford; and when he did, always brought with him in his dog-cart a pair of his pigs to be exposed for sale in the pig-market, which was then held in High Street beside All Saints Church. On these occasions his dress is described by a contemporary to have been so strictly in keeping with his favourite pursuit that he ran no risk of being mistaken for a Doctor of Divinity or the head of a College. There was, however, one occasion on which Tatham came out in his "scarlet," with great effect. The College had some rights in the naming of the master of Skipton Grammar School, Yorkshire. On occasion of a vacancy the local governors were disposed to dispute the claim. Tatham went north, at the previous stage put on his Doctor's robes, drove into Skipton attired in their splendour, and dazzled the opposition into acknowledging the College claim. He died on 24th April, 1834, aged 84.

As might be expected, Lincoln College did not prosper during Tatham's rectorship. A scholarship was lost. Sir George Wheler, a Commoner of the College, had left in 1719 a yearly rent-charge of £10 on a house in St. Margaret's parish, Westminster, to certain trustees "to pay to a poor scholar in Lincoln College that shall have been bred up in the grammar school at Wye." From 1735 to 1759 no payment was made; and then the Rev. Granville Wheler, in recognition of arrears, increased the rent-charge to £20, and directed that if no boy was sent from Wye, the scholarship should be open to any grammar school in England. In Horner's and Tatham's time the matter was neglected; and the benefaction is now for ever lost to the College. Again, part of the money received from the city in payment for the grand old College garden, which by Act of Parliament was taken to form the present Market, was invested in Government securities; but the books were so carelessly kept that the exact details required by the

Exchequer could not afterwards be collected from them: so that part of the property of Lincoln College is amongst those "unclaimed" dividends out of which the new Law Courts were built. It is surely unjust that the nation should thus make a College suffer for the negligence of one generation of its officers. There was also great degeneracy in the *personnel* of the College. Oxford was then passing through that phase of hard-drinking which within living memory still afflicted society in country places; and from this vice Lincoln College was not exempt. Several of the Fellows had curacies or small livings in the neighbourhood of Oxford, to which they rode out, as represented in a well-known cartoon of the time, on Saturday morning, returning to the College on Monday. On Monday evening, therefore, they were all met together, and preparations were made for a "wet night." When the Fellows entered Common-room after Hall, a bottle of port was standing on the side-board for each of their number. These finished there would be a second (and as liberal) supply, and very probably after that several of them would slip out to bring an extra bottle from their private stores. Two instances of the *corruptio optimi* of the times—the degradation of men who had received a University education—may be cited. A Fellow of Lincoln College got into debt, and his Fellowship was sequestrated by his creditors, who allowed him a small pittance out of its proceeds, and applied the rest to the liquidation of his debts; he became an ordinary tramp, and died in the casual ward at Northampton, after holding his

Fellowship for twenty-five years. An ex-Fellow, incumbent of one of the more distant and valuable College livings, got, by his own extravagance, into the clutches of the money-lenders, who sequestrated his living and confined him in Oxford Debtors' prison, where he remained year after year till his death. When, in 1854, the new incumbent went to the living, he found that the parishioners, unable to get anything out of their Rector, had helped themselves from the Rectory-house; windows, doors, staircases, floors, slates, stones had been taken away, and the ruins, sold at auction, fetched less than £10.

The tuition in College became of the meanest and poorest stamp. The public lectures consisted in the lecturer hearing the men translate without comment a few lines of Virgil or Homer in the morning; and the informal instruction was equally paltry. One story of a Lincoln tutor of the time may be set down here, though it is probably exceptional and not typical. The narrator, an Archdeacon, "Venerable" not only by title but by years, said—"I was pupil to Mr. ——, and I did not altogether approve of his method of tuition. His method, sir, was this: I read through with him the greater part of the second extant decade of Livy, in which, as you are aware, the name of Hannibal not infrequently occurs. There was a bottle of port on the table; and whenever we came to the name of that Carthaginian general, my tutor would replenish his glass, saying, 'Here's that old fellow again; we must drink his health,' never failing to suit the action to the word."

An odd incident has to be told in connection with Tatham's death. An examination previous to an election to a Lincoln county Fellowship had been duly announced, and on 24th April, 1834, the candidates were assembled in Hall waiting for the first paper. The opinion of his contemporaries had singled out Henry Robert Harrison of Lincoln as the favourite candidate, and it was, therefore, with some satisfaction that the other candidates learned from one of their own number, that the coach coming from Leicester had been overturned the day before, and that Harrison, who was an outside passenger by it, had had his leg broken, and would be unable to appear. The paper was now given out, and they set to it with zest; but before they had finished it a Fellow came in with a grave face, told them that a messenger had brought word that the Rector had died that morning at Combe, and that, as the College could not proceed to an election till after a new Rector had been elected, the Fellows had decided to postpone the examination. After Radford's election the usual notice was given of the Fellowship examination; Harrison was now able to come to it; and on 5th July, 1834, he was elected.

Mention may also be made of an undergraduate of Lincoln College at this time who was famous beyond any undergraduate of his own or subsequent years. Robert Montgomery, then in the full enjoyment of the reputation of being the great poet of the century, a reputation evinced by the sale of thousands of copies of his poems, and unassailed as yet by any whisper of adverse criticism, entered the College as

Commoner on 18th Feb., 1830. Although he put himself down in the Bible-Clerk's book as son of "Robert Montgomery, esquire," he was really of very poor parentage, and was able to come to the University only by the profits of his pen. His undergraduate contemporaries, whether because they believed it or not, used to assert that he was the son of Gomerie, a well-known clown of the day. He was mercilessly persecuted in College. Some of the forms of this persecution were little creditable to the persecutors, and had best be left unrecorded; but one instance of a practical joke on the victim's egregious vanity may be noted. When about to enter for "Smalls" in his first term, he was persuaded to go to the Vice-Chancellor and request that a special decree should be proposed putting off his *vivâ-voce* till late in the vacation, "to avoid the inconveniences likely to be caused by the crowds which might be expected to attend the examination of that distinguished poet." Montgomery took a fourth class in "Literæ Humaniores" in 1834, and was afterwards minister of Percy Chapel in London, which members of the College used occasionally to attend to listen to his florid but not ineffective preaching.

John Radford, who had succeeded Tatham as Rector in 1834, was succeeded in 1851 by James Thompson, and Thompson by Mark Pattison in 1861. Both these elections were keenly, not to say bitterly, contested, with a partizan spirit which has found its way into several pamphlets and memoirs; but when the present Rector, W. W. Merry, the thirtieth who has ruled over the College, was elected in 1884, the College Register once more recorded an election made *"unanimi consensu omnium suffragantium."* He had been Fellow and Lecturer since 1859; and by his editions of Homer and Aristophanes, had charmed wider circles of pupils than that of the College lecture-room.

It will be the duty of the future historian of Lincoln College to mention with all honour the persons by whom, in these later Rectorships, the College has reasserted its good name, which in the beginning of the century had been somewhat tarnished; but for the present the gratitude of members of the Society to these must remain unexpressed in words; most of them are still alive, and we must not praise them to their face. Of Radford, however, this much may be said, that though not a strong governor, his care for the College, and his munificence to it, well earned his portrait its place among the benefactors in the College hall, and the inscription on his stone in All Saints Church, which says that he "dearly loved his College."

One effect of Radford's bounty must, however, be regretted. Under his will the sum of £300 was expended in putting battlements on the outer (and the earliest) quadrangle of the College, so destroying its monastic appearance, and giving to it a castellated air foreign to the time of its building and alien to its traditions. This was the last step in a process of injudicious repair, which beginning about 1819 had robbed the buildings of their quaintness and individuality. Recent work has been more reverent for the past. In 1889 the College removed the lath-and-plaster wagon-roof in the hall and restored to view the fine chestnut timbers of the original building. The liberality of resident and non-resident members of the College has in the present year provided a fund to complete this restoration of the hall, and to recover in 1891 something of the grace which it possessed in 1435, but lost in 1699.

IX.
ALL SOULS COLLEGE.[192]

BY C. W. C. OMAN, M.A., FELLOW OF ALL SOULS.

Henry Chichele, the son of a merchant of Higham Ferrars, was one of the first roll of scholars whom William of Wykeham nominated at the opening of his great foundation of New College. He left Oxford with the degree of Doctor of Laws, and soon found both ecclesiastical preferment and a lucrative legal practice. He attached himself to the House of Lancaster, and served Henry IV. so well that he was made Bishop of St. Davids, and sent to represent England at the Council of Pisa. In such favour did he stand at Court, that when Thomas Arundel, Archbishop of Canterbury, died in the first year of Henry V., the young king appointed Chichele to succeed him.

For the long term of thirty years Henry Chichele held the Primacy of all England, and played no small part in the governance of the realm. The two main characteristics of his policy, whatever may be urged in his defence, were most unfortunate: he was a stout supporter of the unhappy war with France, and he was a weak defender of the liberties of the Church of England against Papal aggression. History remembers him as the ambassador who urged so hotly the preposterous claims of Henry V. on the French throne, and as the first Primate who refused to accept the Archbishopric from the King and the

Chapter, till he had obtained a dispensation and a Bull of Provision from the Pope.

However great may have been his faults as a statesman, Chichele (like his successor Laud) was throughout his life a liberal and consistent patron of the University. He presented it with money and books, and, mindful of what he owed to his training at New College, resolved to copy his old master Wykeham in erecting one more well-ordered and well-endowed house of learning, among the obscure and ill-managed halls which still harboured the majority of the members of the University. He first began to build a small College in St. Giles'; but this institution—St. Bernard's as it was called—he handed over unfinished to the Cistercian monks, in whose possession it remained till the Reformation, when it became the nucleus round which Sir Thomas White built up his new foundation of St. John's.

Chichele's later and more serious scheme for establishing a College was not taken up till 1437, when he had occupied the Archiepiscopal see for twenty-three years, and was already past the age of seventy. It was one of the darkest moments of the wretched French war; the great Duke of Bedford had died two years before, and Paris had been for twelve months in the hands of the French. The old Archbishop, all whose heart had been in the struggle, and who knew that he himself was more responsible for its commencement than any other subject of the Crown, must have spent his last years in unceasing regrets. Perhaps he may have felt some personal remorse when he reflected on his own part in the furthering of the war, but certainly—whether he felt his responsibility or not—the waste of English lives during the last twenty years lay heavy on his soul. Hence it came that his new college became a chantry as well as a place of education—the inmates were to be devoted as well *ad orandum* as *ad studendum*— hence also, we can hardly doubt, came its name. For, as its charter drawn by Henry VI. proceeds to recite—the prayers of the community were to be devoted, "not only for our welfare and that of our godfather the Archbishop, while alive, and for our souls when we shall have gone from this light, but also for the souls of the most illustrious Prince Henry, late King of England, of Thomas late Duke of Clarence our uncle, of the Dukes, Earls, Barons, Knights, Esquires, and other noble subjects of our father and ourself who fell in the wars for the Crown of France, as also for the souls of all the faithful departed." Not unwisely therefore has the piety of the present generation filled the niches of Chichele's magnificent reredos with the statues of Clarence and York, Salisbury and Talbot, Suffolk and Bedford, and others who struck their last stroke on the fatal plains of France. Nor can we doubt that the Archbishop's meaning was well expressed in the name that he gave to his foundation, which, copying the last words in the above-cited foundation-charter, became known as the "Collegium Omnium Animarum Fidelium Defunctorum in Oxonia."

To found his College, Chichele purchased a large block of small tenements, among them several halls, forming the angle between Catte Street and the High Street. The longer face was toward the former street, the frontage to "the High" being less than half that which lay along the narrower thoroughfare. The ground lay for the most part within the parish of St. Mary's, with a small corner projecting into that of St. Peter in the East. The buildings which Chichele proceeded to erect were very simple in plan. They consisted of a single quadrangle with a cloister behind it, and did not occupy more than half the ground which had been purchased: the rest, where Hawkesmore's twin towers and Codrington's library now stand, formed, in the founder's time, and for 250 years after, a small orchard and garden. Chichele's main building, the present "front quadrangle," remains more entirely as the founder left it than does any similar quadrangle in Oxford. Except that some seventeenth century hand has cut square the cusped tops of its windows, it still bears its original aspect unchanged. The north side is formed by the chapel; the south contains the gate-tower with its muniment-room above, and had the Warden's lodgings in its eastern angle; the west side was devoted entirely to the Fellows' rooms, as was also the whole of the east side, save the central part of its first floor, where the original library was situate. Into space which now furnishes seventeen small sets of rooms, the forty Fellows of the original foundation were packed, together with their two chaplains, their porter, and their small establishment of servants.

To the north of this quadrangle lay the cloister, a small square, two of whose sides were formed by an arcade with open perpendicular windows, much like New College cloister; the third by the chapel; while the fourth was occupied by the College hall, an unpretentious building standing exactly at right angles to the site of the modern hall. The cloister-quadrangle's size may be judged from the fact that the chapel formed one entire side of it. It took up not more than a quarter of the present back-quadrangle, and was surrounded to north and east by the garden and orchard of which we have already spoken. For many generations it formed the burial-ground of the Fellows, and on several occasions of late years, when trenches have been dug across the turf of the new quadrangle, the bones of fifteenth and sixteenth century members of the College have been found lying there undisturbed. To conclude the account of Chichele's buildings, it must be added that on the east side of the hall the kitchen and storehouses of the College made a small irregular excrescence into the garden; their situation is now occupied by that part of the present hall which lies nearest the door.

All Chichele's work was on a small scale save his chapel, on which he lavished special care. His reredos, preserved for two centuries behind a coat of plaster, still remains to witness to his good taste; but its original aspect, blazing with scarlet, gold, and blue, must have been strangely different from that which the nineteenth century knows. Of the figures which adorned it a part only can be identified: at the top was the Last Judgment, of which a considerable fragment was found *in situ* when the plaster was cleared away, with its inscription, "Surgite mortui, venite ad judicium" still plainly legible. Immediately above the altar was the Crucifixion; the cross and the wings of the small ministering angels of the modern reproduction being actually parts of the old sculpture. The carver, Richard Tillott, who executed the work, mentions, in his account of expenses sent in for payment to Chichele, "two great stone images over the altar"; these may very probably have been the founder and King Henry VI.; and the restorers of our own generation ventured to fill the two largest niches with their representations. How the central and side portions of the reredos were occupied is unknown; but it would seem that the founder did not leave every niche full, as fifty years after his death, Robert Este, a Fellow of the College, left £21 18s. 4d. for the completing of the images over the high altar.

In addition to the high altar, the chapel contained no less than seven side altars; where they were placed it is a little difficult to see, as the stalls bear every mark of being contemporary with the founder, and extend all along the sides of the chapel from the altar-steps to the screen. Probably then the smaller altars—of which we know that one was dedicated to the four Latin Fathers—must have been all, or nearly all, placed in the ante-chapel. The windows, both in the chapel and ante-chapel, were filled with excellent glass; all that of the chapel has disappeared, but in the ante-chapel there is much good work remaining. The most interesting window contains an admirable set of historical figures; the founder, his masters Henry V. and Henry VI., John of Gaunt, and several more being in excellent preservation; but this was not originally placed in the chapel, and seems to have belonged to the old library. The other windows are filled with saints.

The total cost of the foundation of the College to Chichele was about £10,000; that sum covered not only the erection and fitting up of the buildings, but the purchase of some of the lands for its endowment. The two largest pieces of property which the Archbishop devoted to his new institution were situated respectively in Middlesex and Kent. The first estate lay around Edgeware, of which the College became lord of the manor, and extended in the direction of Hendon and Willesden. It was mainly under wood in the founder's day, and formed part of the tract of forest which covered so much of Middlesex down to the last century. The second property consisted of a large stretch of land in Romney Marsh, already noted as a great grazing district in the fifteenth century. Many lesser estates lay scattered about the Midlands; they consisted in no small part of land belonging to the alien priories, which Chichele had assisted Henry V. to abolish, and included at least one of the suppressed houses— Black Abbey in Shropshire. For these confiscated estates the Archbishop paid £1000 to the Crown.

The College as designed by Chichele contained forty Fellows; he nominated twenty himself, and these with their Warden, Richard Andrew, chose twenty more. By the Charter sixteen of the forty were to be jurists—the founder remembered that he himself had taken his degree in Laws—and twenty-four artists. As Wykeham had done before him, Chichele took pains to obtain a Bull from the Pope to sanction and confirm his new foundation: in this document, dated from Florence in 1439, Eugenius IV. grants numerous spiritual privileges to the *pauperes scholares* of All Souls. They are excused certain fasts, freed from any parochial control of the Vicar of St. Mary's, permitted to bury their dead in the precincts of the College, and even granted leave to celebrate the Mass in their chapel in time of interdict, "but with hushed bells and closed doors." Chichele was such a confirmed Papalist that he took the unusual step of sending the first Warden to Italy in person, to receive the Bull from the Pope's own hands.

Nor was it only his spiritual superior that Chichele resolved to interest in the College. When all was complete he went through the form of handing over the foundation to his young god-son Henry VI., and of receiving it back from the King's hands as co-founder. Hence comes the constant juxtaposition of their names in the prayers of the College.

Chichele lived to see his College completely finished; in 1442 he presided at the solemn entry of the Fellows into their new abode, and formally delivered the statutes to Warden Andrew. Next year he died, at the end of his eightieth year, an age almost unparalleled among the short-lived men of the fifteenth century. His successor, Archbishop Stafford, on taking up the office of Visitor, was pleased to grant an indulgence of forty days to any Christian of the province of Canterbury who should visit the chapel and there say a *Pater* and an *Ave* for the souls of the faithful departed. This grant made the College a place of not unfrequent resort for pilgrims. If a passage cited by Professor Burrows[193] is correct, as many as 9000 wafers were consumed in the chapel on one day in 1557.

For the first century of the College's existence the succession of Wardens and Fellows was very rapid. Richard Andrew, the first head of the foundation, resigned his post in the same year that the new buildings were opened, on receiving ecclesiastical preferment outside Oxford. He became Dean of York, and survived his resignation for many years. His successor, Warden Keyes, had been the architect of the College; he presided for three years only, and then gave place to William Kele. Altogether in the first century of its existence 1437-1537 the College knew no less than eleven Wardens, of whom seven resigned and only four died in harness. The Fellows were as rapid in their succession; not unfrequently seven or eight—a full fifth of the whole number— vacated their Fellowships in a single year; the average annual election was about five. The shortness of their tenure of office is easily explained; a Fellowship was not a very valuable possession, for beyond food and lodging it only supplied its holder with the "livery" decreed by the founder, an actual provision of cloth for his raiment. A Fellow's commons were fixed on the modest scale of "one shilling a week when wheat is cheap, and sixteenpence when it is dear." The annual surplus from the estates was not divided up, but placed in the College strong-box within the entrance-tower, against the day of need. Moreover, as the Fellows were lodged two, or even in some cases three, in each room, the accommodation can hardly have been such as to tempt to long residence. The acceptance of preferment outside Oxford, or even an absence of more than six months without the express leave of the College, sufficed to vacate the Fellowship; and since every member of the foundation was in orders, it naturally resulted that the "jurists" drifted up to London to practice, while the "artists" accepted country livings. Only those Fellows who were actually studying or teaching in the University held their places for any length of time.

There is little to tell about the first fifty years of the history of All Souls; but it is worthy of notice that its connection—merely nominal though it was—with its co-founder, Henry VI., brought on trouble when the House of York came to the throne. Edward IV. pretended to regard the endowments of the College as wrongly-alienated royal property, and had to be appeased, not only by the insertion of his name and that of his mother Cecily in the prayers of the College, but by payment of a considerable fine. However, the College might congratulate itself on an easy escape, and its pardon was ratified when, some years later, its head, Warden Poteman, was made envoy to Scotland, and afterwards promoted to be Archdeacon of Cleveland.

In the reign of Henry VII., when the Renaissance began to make itself felt in Oxford, All Souls had the good fortune to produce two of the first English Greek scholars, Linacre and Latimer. The name of the latter is forgotten—the present age remembers no Latimer save the martyr-bishop; but Linacre's memory is yet green. With Grocyn and Colet he stands at the head of the roll of Oxford scholars, but in his medical fame he is unrivalled. His contemporaries "questioned whether he was a better Latinist or Grecian, a better grammarian or physician"; but it is in the last capacity that he is now remembered. He was elected to his Fellowship at All Souls in 1484, resided four or five years, and then went to Italy, where he tarried long, taught medicine at Padua, and then returned to England to found and preside over the College of Physicians. The two Linacre professorships were both endowed by him. The example of his career was not soon forgotten, and for two centuries All Souls continued to produce men of mark in the realm of medicine. To this day it excites the surprise of the visitor to the College library to see the large proportion of books on medical subjects contained in its shelves. Among the manuscripts there are many such, which Linacre's own hands must have thumbed; while throughout the sixteenth and seventeenth centuries the purchases of medical books are only exceeded by those of works on theology. But with the incoming of the reign of the Founder's-kin Fellows in the early eighteenth century the physicians ceased out of the land, and at last, "holding a physic place" became a convenient fiction by which lay members of the College succeeded in excusing themselves from taking orders, though they might be in reality anything rather than medical men.

The reign of Henry VII. saw the beginning of two sources of trouble to All Souls, which were not to cease for many generations. The first was the interference of the Archbishop as Visitor, to determine the conditions of the tenure of Fellowships. William of Warham is found writing to the College to denounce a growing practice of endeavouring to keep a Fellowship in conjunction with a benefice outside Oxford. He strictly forbade it, and his commands seem to have been more effectual than Visitor's injunctions have usually proved. The other interference with the College from without, was an attempt made by Arthur Prince of Wales to influence the annual elections of Fellows. He writes from Sunninghill in 1500 to recommend the election of a young lawyer named Pickering to a Fellowship, "because that his father is in the right tender favour of our dearest mother the Queen." Pickering's name does not appear in the register of Fellows, so it is evident that the College found some excuse for evading compliance with the Prince's request.

All Souls seems to have passed through the storms of the Reformation with singularly little friction from within or without. One single Warden, John

Warner—the first Regius professor of Medicine in the University—continued to steer the course of the College from 1536 to 1556, complying with all the various commands of Henry VIII., making himself acceptable both to Somerset and Northumberland, and even holding on for two years into Mary's reactionary time. It is true that he then resigned his post, but he was evidently no less complying under the Papalist Queen than under her Protestant predecessor, as no harm came to him though he continued to reside in Oxford. Warden Pope, his successor, having died in the first year of Elizabeth, Warner was immediately restored to his old post, and held it till he was made Dean of Winchester in 1565.

It was during Warner's wardenship that we have the first mention of an evil custom in the College, which was to form for a hundred years a subject of dispute between the Fellows and their Visitor the Archbishop. This was the habit of "corrupt resignation." A member of the College, when about to vacate his Fellowship, not unfrequently had some friend or relation whom he wished to succeed him. This candidate he naturally pushed and supported at the annual election on All Souls' Day. It came to be the tacit custom of the College to elect candidates so supported; for each Fellow, when voting for an outgoing colleague's nominee, remembered that he himself would some day wish to recommend a *protégé* for election in a similar manner. This right of nomination being once grown customary, soon grew into a monstrous abuse, for unscrupulous

Fellows, when about to vacate their places, began to hawk their nominations about Oxford. Actual payments in hard cash were made by equally unscrupulous Bachelors of Arts or Scholars of Civil Law, to secure one of these all-powerful recommendations. Hence there began to appear in the College not the poor but promising scholars for whom Chichele had designed the foundation, but men of some means, who had practically bought their places. Cranmer was the first Visitor who discovered and endeavoured to crush this noxious system. In 1541 we find him declaring that he will impose an oath on every Fellow to obey his injunction against the practice, and that every Fellowship obtained by a corrupt resignation shall be summarily forfeited. At the same time we find him touching on other minor offences in the place— misdoings which seem ludicrously small compared to the huge abuse with which he couples them. Fellows have been seen clad not in the plain livery which the pious founder devised, but in gowns gathered round the collar and arms and quilted with silk; they have been keeping dogs in College; some of them have hired private servants; others of them have engaged in "compotationibus, ingurgitationibus, crapulis et ebrietatibus." All these customs are to cease at once. It is to be feared that the good Archbishop was as unsuccessful in suppressing these smaller sins and vanities, as he most certainly was in dealing with the evil of corrupt resignations.

It was in the reign of the same compliant Warden Warner, under whom Cranmer's visitation took place, that All Souls was robbed of its greatest ornament—the decorations of its chapel. In 1549, by order of the Royal Commissioners appointed by Protector Somerset, havoc was made with the whole interior of the building. The organ was removed, the windows broken, the high-altar and seven side-altars taken down, and, worst of all, the whole reredos gutted; its fifty statues and eighty-five statuettes were destroyed, and so it remained, vacant but graceful, though much chipped about in the course of ages, till in the reign of Charles II. the Fellows in their wisdom concluded to plane down its projections, stuff its niches with plaster, and paint a sprawling fresco upon it! The church vestments of the College were probably destroyed at the same time that the chapel was made desolate, but its church plate was not defaced, but merely removed to the muniment-room and put in safe keeping. There it remained till 1554, when it came down again, and was again employed in Queen Mary's time. In 1560 it was once more put into store in the strong-room, and there it remained till in 1570 Archbishop Parker had it brought forth and bade it be melted down, "except six silver basons together with their crewets, the gilt tabernacle, two silver bells, and a silver rod." After a stout resistance lasting three years, the College was obliged to comply. Charles I. received nearly all that Parker spared, and of the old communion-plate of All Souls there now survives nought but two of the crewets preserved in 1573.

They are splendid pieces of the work of about 1500, eighteen inches high, shaped like pilgrim's bottles, and ornamented with swans' heads. The founder's silver-gilt and crystal salt-cellar, the only other piece of antique silver which All Souls now owns, was most fortunately not in the hands of the College in Charles's time, or it would have shared the fate of the rest of its ancient plate.

One more incident of Warner's tenure of office needs mention. He erected with subscriptions raised from all quarters as a residence for himself, the building which faces the High Street in continuation of the front quadrangle to the east. For the future, Wardens had six rooms instead of two to live in, and there is splendour as well as comfort in the magnificent panelled room on the first floor which forms the chief apartment in the new building. Here dwelt Warner's successors, till in the reign of Anne the present Warden's lodgings were erected still further eastward.

Warden Hoveden, whose long rule of forty-three years covered most of the reign of Elizabeth and half that of James I. (1571-1614) was a man of mark. He adorned the old library, now the "great lecture-room," in the front quadrangle, with the beautiful barrel-roof and panelling which make it the best Elizabethan room in Oxford. He bought and added to the grounds of the College a large house and garden called "the Rose," where the Warden's lodgings now stand. He arranged and codified the College books and muniments. He caused to be constructed a splendid and elaborate set of maps of the College estates, ten years before any other College in the University thought of doing such a thing (1596). These maps are worked out on a most minute scale: every tree and house is inserted; and as a proof of how English common-fields were still worked in minutely subdivided slips, only a few yards broad, they are invaluable. One map gives a bird's-eye view of All Souls, with its two quadrangles as then existing, and is the first good representation of the College that remains. But Hoveden's greatest achievements were his two victories in struggles with Queen Elizabeth. The first contest concerned the parsonage and tithes of the parish of Stanton Harcourt; the Crown and the College litigated about them for just forty years, 1558-98; but Hoveden had his way, and in the latter year they came back into the hands of the College. In the regrant of the disputed property, the Queen's reasons are stated to be the poverty of the College and the want of a convenient house near Oxford to which the Fellows might retire in times of pestilence in the University. Epidemical disorders had been very common at the date: in 1570-1 the plague carried off 600 persons, and in 1577 a fearful distemper in consequence of the "Black Assize" was no less fatal. Such a house as Stanton Harcourt parsonage was then of infinite utility, and for more than 200 years the College used to compel its tenants by a covenant in their lease, to "find four chambers in the house, furnished with bedding linen, and woollen for so many of the fellows as shall be sent to lodge there whenever any pestilence or other contagious disorder shall happen in the University." The second struggle resulted from an attempt of Elizabeth to induce All Souls to grant a lease of all their woods to Lady Stafford, at the ridiculously small rent of twenty pounds per annum. Hoveden resisted stoutly, and his refusal drew down a most disgraceful letter of threats from Sir Walter Raleigh. Sir Walter intimates that the Queen is highly incensed that "subjects of your quality" should presume to chaffer with her, and hints at evils to come if compliance is still refused. The Warden replied that the terms offered were so bad that if they were taken the Fellows would be compelled to give up housekeeping and take to the fields. To this it was answered that "their state was so plentiful by her Majesty's statute, that they seemed rather as fat monks in a rich abbey than students in a poor College." Hoveden stood his ground and enlisted Whitgift, the Visitor, to work with Lord Burleigh in the defence of the College. Burleigh moved Elizabeth to relax her pressure, and Lady Stafford never obtained her cheap lease.

By the end of Hoveden's time a new subject of interest comes to the front in the management of the College. The rise in wealth and in prices which characterized the Tudor epoch resulted in the development of the annual surplus from the College estates into unexpected proportions. When all outgoings were paid there were often £500 or £600 left to be transferred to the strong-box in the gate-tower. It naturally occurred to the Fellows that some of this money might reasonably come their way.

Archbishop Whitgift allowed them to augment their daily commons from it, and afterwards bade them commute their "livery" in cloth for a reasonable equivalent in cash. This was done, but still the annual surplus cash grew. Archbishop Bancroft directed it "to amendment of diet and other necessary uses of common charge." He soon found that this merely led to luxurious living. "It is astonishing," he wrote, "this kind of beer which heretofore you have had in your College, and I do strictly charge you, that from henceforth there be no other received into your buttery but small-and middle-beer, beer of higher rates being fitter for tippling-houses." Yet the College strong ale still survives! Nor was it only in its drinking that the College offended: its eating corresponded: the gaudés, and the annual Bursar's dinner became huge banquets, costing some £40; guests were invited in scores, and the festivities prolonged to the third day. Such things were only natural when the Fellows had the disposal of a large revenue, yet were not allowed to draw from it more than food and clothing. At last, Archbishop Abbott, in 1620 bethought him of a less demoralizing way of disposing of the surplus: he boldly doubled the livery-money. Then for the first time a Fellowship became worth some definite value in hard cash. The next step was easy enough; instead of a fixed double livery, there was distributed annually so many times the original livery as the surplus could safely furnish. The seniors drew more than the juniors, and the jurists more then the artists. This arrangement, after working in practice for many years, was sanctioned in theory also by Archbishop Sheldon in 1666.

It is in a letter of Archbishop Abbott's, dealing with one of the riotous feasts to which the College had grown addicted, that we have our first mention of that celebrated bird, the All Souls Mallard. The Visitor writes—"The feast of Christmas drawing now to an end, doth put me in mind of the great outrage which, as I am informed, was the last year committed in your College, where although matters had formerly been conducted with some distemper, yet men did never before break forth into such intolerable liberty as to tear down doors and gates, and disquiet their neighbours as if it had been a camp or a town in war. Civil men should never so far forget themselves under pretence of a foolish mallard, as to do things barbarously unbecoming." Evidently the gaudé had developed into one of those outbreaks, which a modern Oxford College knows well enough when its boat has gone head of the river. Furniture had been smashed, perhaps a bonfire lighted; certainly the noise had been long and loud. But what of the Mallard? Pamphlets have been written on him, and College tradition tells that when the first stone of the College was laid a mallard was started out of a drain on the spot. In commemoration of the event, the Fellows annually went round the College after the gaudé, pretending to search for the tutelary bird. The song concerning him was written to be sung by "Lord Mallard," a Fellow chosen as the official songster of the College. It bears every appearance of being of Jacobean date—

"Griffin, Turkey, Bustard, Capon,
Let other hungry mortals gape on,
And on their bones with stomachs fall hard,
But let All Souls' men have their Mallard.

Chorus—O by the blood of King Edward,
It was a swapping, swapping Mallard!

"The Romans once admired a gander
More than they did their chief Commander,
Because he saved, if some don't fool us,
The place that's named from the scull of Tolus.[194]

Chorus, etc.

"The poets feign Jove turned a swan,
But let them prove it if they can,
As for our proof it's not at all hard—
He was a swapping, swapping Mallard.

Chorus, etc.

"Then let us drink and dance a Galliard
Unto the memory of the Mallard,
And as the Mallard dives in pool,
Let's dabble, duck, and dive in bowl."

Chorus, etc.

So for three hundred years, if not for four, has Lord Mallard annually chanted. But the last time that we have proof of a procession having gone round the College with torches, pursuing the mock search for the bird, is in 1801, when Bishop Heber, then a scholar of Brazenose, mentions in a letter home that he had witnessed the scene from his windows across the Radcliffe Square.

Professor Burrows in a most ingenious passage of his *Worthies* makes a plausible suggestion as to the real origin of the Mallard. He found in Alderman Fletcher's copy of Anthony à Wood, now in the Bodleian, the impression of a seal bearing a griffin, inscribed *"Sigillum Guilielmi Mallardi Clerici."* This seal of one Mallard was actually dug up in making a drain on the site of All Souls, to the east of the Warden's lodgings. Can the exhuming of Mallard's seal have been turned by oral tradition into the finding of an actual mallard?

Down to the time of the great Civil War the College, though always more or less tainted with the evil of corrupt resignations, continued to produce a great number of able men. Since the Reformation laymen are found among them as well as clerics. We may name Lord Chancellor Weston, Mason and Petre, both Privy Councillors of note, and the Persian traveller Sir Anthony Sherley, under Elizabeth; while in the early seventeenth century we meet Archbishop Sheldon—long Warden of the College—Bishop Duppa, and Jeremy Taylor. The election of the last-named illustrates in the most striking way the manner in which corrupt resignations had come to be looked upon as matters of routine. Osborne, a Fellow about to vacate his place, instead of putting his nomination up for sale, made a present of it to Archbishop Laud. Laud, taking the procedure as the most natural thing in the world, bade him nominate Taylor, who was therefore elected, but with great murmurs from the College, for he was a Cambridge man, and of nine years standing since his degree.

Those who know only the modern constitution of All Souls, will find it startling to learn that down to the Great Rebellion the College was not without its fair share of undergraduates. There was no provision for them in the statutes, but a number of "poor scholars" (*servientes*) were allowed to matriculate. In 1612 there were as many as thirty-one of them on the books at once. In going through a list of All Souls men who became Fellows of Wadham between 1615 and 1660, I found that about one in three were *servientes*, so their number must have been not inconsiderable. The College narrowly escaped having a regular provision of scholars, for Archbishop Parker had planned the endowment of a considerable number of scholarships from Canterbury Grammar School when he died. After the Restoration the *servientes* are no more heard of, or at least the four Bible-clerks then appear as their sole successors.

Few Colleges suffered more from the Civil Wars than All Souls. Its head, Sheldon, was one of the King's chaplains, and all, save a very small minority of the Fellows, were enthusiastic Royalists. One of them, William St. John, was slain in battle in the King's cause, and others of them bore arms for him. It is most pitiful to read the account of the College plate which went to the melting-pot in New Inn Hall, to come forth as the ugly Oxford shillings of Charles I. All Souls contributed 253 lbs. 1 oz. 19 dwts. in all, more than any other house save Magdalen, besides a large sum in ready money. Its treasury was swept clean of the founder's gifts, of Warden Keyes' "great cupp double gilt with the image of St. Michael on its cover," of all the church-plate that had escaped Parker, of tankards, flagons, and goblets innumerable. Worse was to follow: the bulk of the

College estates lay in Kent and Middlesex, counties in the hands of the Parliament, and their rents could not be raised. At the end of the first year the tenants were £600 in arrears, and the evil went on growing, while at the same time the demands on the purse of the College were increasing. In June 1643 the College was directed by the King to maintain 102 soldiers for a month, at the rate of four shillings a week per man. It had to contribute towards the fortifications, towards stores for the siege, and towards the relief of the poor of the city. Altogether it would seem that the finances of the College went to pieces, and that the greater part of the Fellows dispersed. When the Parliamentary Visitors got to work on the University, as much as two years after the fall of Oxford, they found only eleven members of the College in residence. Warden Sheldon was summoned before them to ask whether he acknowledged their authority, and replied with frankness, "I cannot satisfy myself that I ought to submit to this visitation." Next day a notice of ejectment was served upon him, and the day following the Chancellor Pembroke went with the Visitors to expel him. They found Sheldon walking in his little garden, read their decree to him, and then sent for the College buttery-book, out of which they struck his name, inserting instead of it that of Dr. Palmer, whom they had designated as his successor. Next they bade him give over his keys, and when he refused broke open his lodgings, installed Palmer in them, and sent the rightful owner away under a guard of musketeers, "followed as he went by a great company of scholars, and blessed by the people as he passed down the street."

Of the Fellows, only five made their peace with the Visitors, and avoided expulsion; even five of the College servants were deprived of their places. The Commissioners proceeded for five years to nominate to the Fellowships, and intruded in all forty-three new members on to the foundation between 1648 and 1653. It is only fair to say that if some of them were abnormal personages—such as Jerome Sanchy, who combined the functions of Proctor and Colonel of Horse—others were men of conspicuous merit. The most noteworthy of them was Sydenham, the greatest medical name except Linacre that the College—perhaps that England—can boast.

In 1653, free elections recommenced, and as the first-fruits of their labours the new Fellows co-opted Christopher Wren. This greatest of all the Fellows of All Souls was in residence for eight years, working from the very first year of his election at architecture, though astronomy and mathematics were also taking up part of his time. Ere he had been many months a Fellow, he erected the large sundial, with the motto *pereunt et imputantur*, which now adorns the Library. In 1661 he resigned his Fellowship on becoming Professor of Astronomy, and shortly after departed for London. Almost the only note of his All Souls life that survives is the fact that he was a great frequenter of the newly-established coffee-house, next door to University

College. His famous architectural drawings were left to the College, and are still preserved in the Library.

The troubles of the Restoration passed over with very little friction at All Souls. Palmer, the intruding Warden, died in the very month of King Charles' return, and Sheldon peaceably took possession of his old place. But within two years he was called off, to become Archbishop of Canterbury, and John Meredith reigned in his stead. This Warden's short tenure of office is marked by the horrible mutilation of the reredos to which we have already alluded. The College must needs have a "restoration" of its chapel, and in the true spirit of the "restorer," broke away much of what was characteristic in it, plastered up the rest, and hired Streater, painter to the king, to daub a "Last Judgment" on the flat space thus obtained. Having accomplished this feat Meredith died.

Meredith's successor, Jeames, prompted and supported by Archbishop Sancroft, succeeded in finally putting down the evil of corrupt resignations, which had survived the Parliamentary Visitation, and blossomed out into all its old luxuriance in the easy times of the Restoration. The fight came to a head in 1680-1, when Jeames, for two years running, used his veto to prevent the election of all candidates nominated by resigners. The veto frustrating any election, the Visitor was by the statutes allowed to fill up the vacant places, and did so. The threat that the same procedure should again be carried out in the next year brought the majority of the College to reason, though for the whole twelve months, Nov. 1680-Nov. 1681, twenty-four discontented Fellows, whom Jeames called "the Faction," were moving heaven and earth to get the Warden's right of veto rescinded. From 1682 onwards, the type of Fellow improved, and some of the most distinguished members of the College date from the years 1680-1700. It is in this period, however, that the complaint begins to be heard that All Souls looked to birth quite as much as to learning in choosing its candidates. "They generally," says Hearne—a great enemy of the College—"pick out those that have no need of a Fellowship, persons of great fortunes and good birth, and often of no morals and less learning." For the former part of this statement, the names in the College register give some justification: concerning the latter, we can only say that the average of men who came to great things in the list of Fellows is higher in Hearne's time than at any other. To this period belong Dr. Clarke, Secretary of War under William III., Christopher Codrington—of whom more hereafter—Bishop Tanner the antiquary, Sir Nathaniel Lloyd, and many more.

The reign of James II. was fraught with as much danger to All Souls as to the other Colleges of the University. Warden Jeames died in 1686, and every one expected and dreaded an attempt to force a Papist head on the College. What happened was almost as bad. There was in the foundation a very junior Fellow—only elected in 1682—named Leopold Finch, son of the Earl of Winchelsea, whose riotous outbreaks and habitual fits of inebriety had done much to embitter Jeames' last years of rule. Finch was a hot Tory, and when, on the outbreak of Monmouth's rebellion, the University proposed to raise a regiment of trained-bands for the King, was one of the leaders in the movement. He enlisted a company of musketeers from members of All Souls and Merton, and this company was the only part of the University battalion that actually took the field. Its not very glorious record of service consisted in occupying Islip for ten days, to secure the London road, and stop all transit of suspicious persons. When the news of Sedgmoor came, Lord Abingdon bade the company dine with him at Rycot, and they came home "well fuzzed with his ale," insomuch that their very drum was stove in, and remains so to this day, stored, with one of the muskets borne by the volunteers, in All Souls Bursary.

Finch had nothing to recommend him save this military exploit, his good birth, and his notorious looseness of life and conscience. He was thought by the King capable of anything in the way of submission—perhaps even of conversion to Papacy—and on the death of Jeames the College, to its horror, learned that Finch had been nominated as Warden. Less courageous than the Fellows of Magdalen, the All Souls men, though they refused to elect Finch in due form, refrained from choosing any other head, and allowed the intruder to take possession of the Warden's house and prerogatives. Finch, though a man of some learning, made as disreputable a head of the College as might have been expected: he jobbed, he drank, he ran into debt, and finally he was found to have embezzled College money. But when William of Orange landed, his Toryism disappeared, and he saved his place by suddenly becoming a hot Whig. All the punishment that he ever got for his usurpation, was that he was compelled to acknowledge himself as only "pseudo-custos," and to submit to be re-appointed to his Wardenship in a more legal way. He presided for sixteen years over the College with much disrepute, and died in 1702—with the bailiffs in his house.

Finch was succeeded by Bernard Gardiner, a very different character. Gardiner was a good scholar and a good man, but decidedly testy and choleric; in politics he was that somewhat abnormal creature, a Hanoverian Tory, and succeeded in earning the dislike of both parties. He was the Vice-Chancellor who deprived Hearne of his place in the Bodleian for Jacobitism, yet he also fought a furious battle with Wake, the Whig Archbishop, who was his Visitor. With a large faction of the Fellows he had equally numerous passages of arms, yet still the College flourished under him. It was in his time that the great back quadrangle, the new Hall, and the new Warden's lodgings, were built.

These spacious buildings were erected not with College money, but by generous and long-continued benefactions from the Fellows. Dr. Clarke, the Secretary of War, was the chief donor: "God send us many such ample benefactors" wrote his grateful Warden in the College book. He built the Warden's lodgings out of his own pocket, besides paying for the "restoration" of the east end of the chapel. This consisted in painting over Streater's bad fresco[195] a much better production by Sir James Thornhill—the somewhat heathenish but spirited Apotheosis of Chichele—which was taken down in our own generation. Below the fresco were placed two marble pillars, supporting an entablature, which framed Raphael Mengs' pleasing "*Noli me tangere*," the picture which now adorns the ante-chapel. After Clarke the most generous donors were Sir Nathaniel Lloyd, who gave £1350 in all; Mr. Greville, who built the new cloister; and General Stuart. Hawkesmoor, Wren's favourite pupil, was their architect; it is to him that we owe the strange but not ineffective twin-towers, the classic cloister, the vaulted buttery, and the lofty hall with its bare mullionless windows.

But there was one Fellow in the reign of Anne who was even a greater benefactor than Clarke and Lloyd. It was to Christopher Codrington that the College owes the magnificent library, which so far surpasses all its rivals in the University, save the Bodleian alone. Codrington was a kind of Admirable Creighton, poet and soldier, bibliophile and statesman. In the same year he gained military promotion for his gallantry at the siege of Namur, welcomed William III. to Oxford in a speech whose elegant Latinity softened even Jacobite critics, and undertook the government of the English West India Islands. He died at Barbadoes in 1710, and left to his well-loved College 12,000 books, valued at £6000, with a legacy of £10,000 to build a fit edifice to hold them, and a fund to maintain it. The Codrington Library, commenced in 1716, took many years to build, but at last stood completed, a far more successful work than the hall which faces it across the quadrangle. It is 200 feet long, and holds with ease the 70,000 books to which the College library has now swollen. A public reading-room was added to it in 1867, and it is for students of law and history as much of an institution as the Bodleian itself.

The eighteenth century gave All Souls many brilliant Fellows, but it destroyed the original purpose of the foundation, and ended by making it an abuse and a byword. It is only necessary to mention the names of a few of its members, to show how large a share of the great men of the time passed through the College. It claims the great Blackstone—for many years an indefatigable bursar—the second name to Wren among the list of Fellows. Two Lord Chancellors came from it, Lord Talbot of Hensoll, and Lord Northington; Young the poet was a resident for many years; one Archbishop, Vernon Harcourt of York, and eight Bishops had been Fellows. With them, though elected in the opening years of the present century, must be mentioned Reginald Heber, the first and greatest of our missionary prelates.

But in spite of these great names, the College—like the whole University—was in a bad way. Two abuses destroyed its usefulness. The first was the introduction of non-residence. Down to the reign of Anne, a Fellow who left Oxford without the *animus revertendi*, forfeited his Fellowship. Every one quitting the College, even for a few months, had to obtain a temporary leave of absence, and to state his intention to return. Gradually Fellows began to devise ingenious excuses for prolonged non-residence; the favourite ones were that they were about to study physic, and must therefore travel; or that they were in the service of the Crown, and must be excused on public grounds. The test case on which the battle was finally fought out was that of Blencowe, a Fellow who had become "Decypherer to the Queen" (interpreter of the cyphers so much used in despatches at that time). Warden Gardiner strove to make him resign, but Blencowe moved Sunderland, the Secretary of State, to interfere in his behalf with the Visitor, and it was formally ruled that his service with the Crown excused him from residence, as well as from his obligation under the statutes to take orders. For the future the Fellows all found some excuse—taking out a commission in the militia was the favourite one—for saying that they were in the royal service, and thereby excused from residence. From about 1720 the number of residents goes down gradually from twenty or thirty to six or seven. The remainder of the Fellows, like Gibbon's enemies at Magdalen, remembered to draw their emoluments, but forgot their statutory obligations.

Almost as injurious as the exemption from residence was the introduction of a new theory that Founder's-kin candidates had an absolute preference over all others. Archbishop Wake is responsible for its recognition: a certain Robert Wood, in 1718, claimed to be elected simply on account of his birth, and the Visitor ruled that he must be admitted, in spite of the custom of the College, which had never before taken account of such a right. At first the Founder's-kin appeared in small numbers—there are only twelve between 1700 and 1750—but about the middle of the century they appear to have suddenly woken up to the advantages of obtaining a Fellowship without condition or examination. Between 1757 and 1777 thirty-nine Fellows out of fifty-eight elected are set down as *cons. fund.* in the College books. Archbishop Cornwallis in 1777 ruled that it was not obligatory upon the College that more than ten of the Fellows should be of Founder's kin, and from this time forth the claim of Founder's kin had no direct influence upon the elections. But the doctrine had done its work. It brought the Fellowships within a charmed circle of county families, outside of which the College rarely looked when the morrow of All Souls Day came round.

The effect of this was to create a society of an abnormal sort in the midst of a group of Colleges which, whatever their shortcomings may have been, continued to make a profession of study and teaching. The Fellows were men of good birth, and usually of good private means. Hence came the well-known joke that they were required to be "bene nati, bene vestiti, et moderate docti," a saying formed, as Professor Burrows has pointed out, by ingeniously twisting the three clauses in the statutes which bade them be "de legitimo matrimonio nati," "vestiti sicut eorum honestati convenit clericali," and "in plano cantu competenter docti."

The Fellows had no educational duties or emoluments, and consequently no inducement to reside except for purposes of study: and for the most part they were not studious, nor resident. The Fellowships were poor, and so were only attractive to men of means. Hence the management of the College property was a matter of indifference, and it was neglected. Other Colleges no doubt neglected their duties and mismanaged their properties, but All Souls men took a pride in having no duties and in being indifferent to the income arising from their estates. Gradually the College drew more and more apart from its neighbours, until the Fellows made it a point to know nothing and to care nothing about the teaching, the study, or the business that was going on just outside their walls.

Yet a period during which Blackstone, Heber, and the present Prime Minister were numbered among the Fellows, cannot be said to be undistinguished in the history of the College; and this system, indefensible in itself, has handed down some things which the present generation would not be willing to lose. This College, which had become somewhat of a family party, was animated by a peculiarly strong feeling of corporate loyalty. And throughout the change and stir of the last forty years, and in the new and many-sided development of the College, the close tie which binds the Fellow, wherever he may be, to the College has never been weakened. And as the College has come back to an intimate connection with the life of the University, its non-resident element is not without value. The lawyer, the member of Parliament, the diplomatist, and the civil servant, no longer disregarding the University and its pursuits, are an element of great value in a society which is too apt to be engrossed in the details of teaching and of examinations.

The University Commission of 1854 swept away the rights of Founder's kin together with many other provisions of the Statutes of Chichele, appropriated ten Fellowships to the endowment of Chairs of Modern History and International Law, and threw open the rest to competition in the subjects of Law and Modern History. The Commission of 1877 threatened graver changes, and for a while it was doubtful whether All Souls might not become an undergraduate College of the ordinary type. But in the end the College was allowed to retain, by means of non-resident Fellowships, its old connection with the world outside, while in other ways its endowments were utilized for study and teaching. On the whole it cannot be said to have suffered more than others from the want of constructive genius in the Commissioners. It is and will be a College of many Fellows and several Professors, with liabilities to contribute annual sums to Bodley's Library and to undergraduate education. The Fellowships are terminable in seven years, but may be renewed in limited numbers and on a reduced emolument.

Under these new conditions All Souls—though still somewhat scantily inhabited—is no longer given over during a great part of each year to the bats and owls. It now plays a useful and important part in the University. Its Hall and lecture-rooms are crowded with undergraduates, its reading-room is full of students of law and history, and its Warden and Fellows have produced in the last ten years about twice as many books as any two other Colleges in the University put together. Last, but not least, it has continued most loyally to fulfil its obligation of providing prize Fellowships; no other foundation can say, though several are far richer than All Souls, that it has regularly offered Fellowships for competition for twenty consecutive years.

X.
MAGDALEN COLLEGE.

BY THE REV. H. A. WILSON, M.A., FELLOW OF
MAGDALEN COLLEGE.

In the cloisters of Magdalen College, over one of the arches of the "Founder's Tower," there is to be seen a heraldic rose surmounting the armorial bearings common to the kings of the rival Houses of York and Lancaster. The rose itself, apparently once red and afterwards painted white, is a curiously significant memorial of the civil strife which affected the early fortunes of the College, and of animosities which were perhaps still too keen, when Waynflete's tower was built, to allow the Red Rose to appear even as a witness to the fact that his foundation had its beginning under a Lancastrian king.

It was in the reign and under the patronage of Henry VI. that the founder himself rose to his greatness. Of his early life little is known with any certainty. His father, Richard Patten or Barbour, was apparently a man of good descent and position.[196] His mother Margery was a daughter of Sir William Brereton, a Cheshire gentleman who had received knighthood for his military services in France. His change of surname was probably made at the time of his ordination as sub-deacon in 1421. That which he adopted was derived from his birthplace, a town on the coast of Lincolnshire. He is sometimes said to have received his education at one or both of the "two St. Mary Winton Colleges," but of this there is no evidence, and we know nothing of his University career except the fact that he proceeded to the degree of Master of Arts. He must have been still a young man when he was appointed in 1428 to the mastership of the school at Winchester, where he also received, from Cardinal Beaufort, the mastership of a Hospital dedicated to St. Mary Magdalen. To his connection with this foundation we may perhaps trace his especial devotion to its patron Saint, and the consequent dedication of St. Mary Magdalen College. In 1440, Henry VI. visited Winchester to gather hints for his scheme for Eton College, and invited Waynflete to become the first master of the school which formed part of his new foundation. He also made him one of the original body of Fellows of Eton, and a few years later promoted him to be Provost. It was most probably at this time, and to commemorate his connection with Eton, that Waynflete augmented his family arms by the addition of the three lilies which appear, with a difference of arrangement, on the arms of Eton College, and on those which Magdalen College derives from its founder.

In 1447, the See of Winchester became vacant by the death of Cardinal Beaufort, and the King at once recommended William Waynflete for election. He was elected within a few days, and was consecrated at Eton on the 13th July of the same year. Immediately after his elevation to the Episcopate, he seems to have set himself to promote the interests of learning, and to provide for a need which his experience as a schoolmaster had impressed upon his mind, by a foundation in the University of Oxford. Early in 1448, before his enthronement at Winchester, he obtained from the King a license to found a Hall for a President and fifty scholars, to be called St. Mary Magdalen Hall.[197] At the same time he obtained, for a term of years, a site and buildings which occupied the ground now covered by the new Examination Schools, and in two or more of the halls included in this property he placed his new society, of which he chose John Hornley to be the first President. In 1456 Waynflete became Chancellor, and on his elevation to that position he at once conceived the idea of improving his foundation at Oxford, by converting it from a Hall into a College, and by providing it with a better habitation and more ample endowments. For this purpose, having obtained the necessary permission from the King, he acquired for the Hall the buildings, site, and property belonging to the ancient Hospital of St. John Baptist. The property of the Hospital included the tenements which the members of the Hall had until this time inhabited. The Hospital itself was a non-academical institution, having for its purpose the care of pilgrims and the relief of the poor.[198] It had been in existence before the reign of John, from whom, while he was still known as Count of Mortain, its Master and Brethren had received benefactions; and it had been endowed, and perhaps refounded, by Henry III. The existing Master and Brethren retired upon pensions, the poor inmates of the Hospital were duly provided for, and the Hospital was united to the College, which Waynflete founded by a charter of June 12th, 1458. The members of the Hall, with the exception of Hornley, who retired to make way for William Tybarde, the first President of the College, were transferred to the new foundation, and the Hall ceased to exist.

The members of the College appear to have continued to occupy the buildings formerly leased to the Hall, which had now become their own property, until the Founder should carry out his intention of providing new buildings on the site of the Hospital, and the land adjoining it. The fulfilment of this intention was long deferred, as were some of the plans upon which Waynflete now entered for the increased endowment of his foundation. The troubles in which the country was now for some years involved, and the change in Waynflete's own position, probably account for the delay. In 1460, a few days before the battle of Northampton, Waynflete resigned the Chancellorship, an act which seems to have brought him into discredit with the Lancastrian party, though not with Henry himself. He does not seem to have taken any active part in the events which followed, on either side; but his sympathies appear to have been with the House of Lancaster. We are told by one authority that he "was in great dedignation with King Edward, and fled for fere of him into secrete corners, but at last was restored to his goodes and the kinges favour." In 1469, when Edward's power was fully established, a full pardon for all offences, probable and improbable, was granted to Waynflete: but some years earlier Edward had confirmed to him the charters and privileges of his See, from which we may reasonably infer that his period of hiding had not been very long. It was not, however, till after the death of Henry VI. that the College began to resume its prosperity, and the work of building was actually begun. The foundation-stone of the chapel was laid in 1474; and in 1480, before the building was actually finished, the President and scholars removed from their temporary quarters, and occupied the College, using the oratory of the Hospital for their place of worship until the chapel was completed. The Vicar of St. Peter's in the East, in which parish the College was situated, gave up all claims to tithes and dues within its precincts in consideration of a fixed annual payment, and the College was transferred by the Bishop of Lincoln, with consent of the Dean and Chapter, to the jurisdiction of the Bishops of Winchester, who were to be also its Visitors.

The society had until this time possessed no body of statutes. Such a code was now given by the founder, and a new President was also appointed by him as successor to Tybarde, who was old and in failing health. The person chosen for this office was Richard Mayew, of New College, who took possession on August 23rd, 1480, and at once proceeded to administer to the members of the College the oath of obedience to the statutes. Ten of the thirty-six members, it appears, at first refused compliance, and were for a time suspended, by the founder's command, from the benefits of the society. In the following year Waynflete himself came to visit the College, and there received the King, who came from Woodstock to Oxford to inspect the new foundation, and passed the night within its walls. Some further statutes, chiefly concerning elections and admissions, were issued by the founder in 1482, in which year a large number of Fellows and Demies[199] were formally admitted, and the society regularly organized, though its numbers were not yet fixed. In 1483, Richard III. visited the College, being received, as Edward had been, by the founder, and disputations were held before him, at his desire, in the College Hall, in one of which William Grocyn took part. At this time the founder delivered to the College the whole body of the statutes which he had framed, reserving to himself, however, the right to add to them or revise them as he should see fit.

The regulations thus made for the government of the society, provided that it should consist of a President, forty Fellows, thirty Demies, four chaplains, eight clerks, sixteen choristers, a schoolmaster, and an usher. The Fellows were to be chosen from certain counties and dioceses; the Demies, in the first instance, from places where the College had property bestowed by the founder or acquired in his lifetime. The Demies were not to be less than twelve years of age at the time of their election, and were not to retain their places after reaching the age of twenty-five years. The system by which Demies succeeded to vacant Fellowships was the growth of later custom, and was not provided for by the statutes. The schoolmaster and usher were to give instruction in grammar to the junior Demies, and to all others who should resort to them. Provision was made for the teaching of moral and of natural philosophy, and of theology, by the appointment of readers in these subjects, whose lectures were to be open to all students, whether members of the College or not. Besides the foundation members of the College, the statutes allowed the admission of commoners of noble family, whose numbers were not to exceed twenty, and who might be allowed to live in the College at the charge of their relations. The regulations as to the dress, conduct, and discipline of the College were based upon those laid down in the statutes given by William of Wykeham to New College, from which society a Fellow, or former Fellow, might be chosen as President. Save for this exception, no one who had not been a Fellow of Magdalen College was to be accounted eligible for that office.

The endowments of the College, besides the property which was derived from the Hospital of St. John Baptist, and that which had been originally settled upon the Hall, consisted partly of lands acquired by Waynflete for the purpose, partly of the endowments of other foundations which were united or annexed to the College at different times as the Hospital of St. John had been. These were the Hospital of SS. John and James at Brackley in Northamptonshire, the Priory of Sele in Sussex,[200]the Hospital of Aynho, a hospital or chantry at Romney, the Chapel of St. Katharine at

Wanborough, and the Priory of Selborne in Hampshire.[201] An intended foundation at Caister in Norfolk, for which Sir John Fastolf had provided by his will, was by Waynflete's influence diverted to augment the foundation of the College. The Fellowships to be held by persons born in the dioceses of York and Durham, or in the county of York, were partly provided for by special benefactions from Thomas Ingledew, one of Waynflete's chaplains, and by John Forman, one of the Fellows of St. Mary Magdalen Hall.

Besides the endowments which Waynflete bestowed on his College during his lifetime, he bequeathed to it by will all his manors, lands, and tenements, with one exception; and he further recommended it to the special care of his executors, directing that they should bestow upon it a share of the residue of his estate.

The royal favour which had been shown towards the College during Waynflete's life was continued after his decease (which took place on August 11th, 1486), by Henry VII., who visited the College in 1487 or 1488, and is still annually commemorated on May 1st as a benefactor, on account, as it would seem, of his having secured to the College the advowsons of Findon in Sussex, and Slymbridge in Gloucestershire, and having directed that the latter benefice should be charged with an annual payment for the benefit of the College.[202] Henry also extended his patronage to the President, Richard Mayew, whom he employed in many matters of state business, appointing him to be his almoner, and also to be his Procurator-general at the Court of Rome. Mayew also held during his Presidentship several ecclesiastical offices. In 1501 he was sent to Spain to conduct the Infanta Katharine, about to be married to Arthur, Prince of Wales, to England. This marriage forms one of the subjects depicted in some pieces of tapestry still preserved in the President's lodgings, which are believed to have been a gift bestowed upon Mayew by Prince Arthur, who twice at least took up his abode in the College, and was entertained by the President on his visits. Mayew's non-academical employments must have necessitated his repeated absence from his duties as President; and at last, after his election to the See of Hereford, a dispute seems to have arisen as to the compatibility of his episcopal and academical functions. A party among the Fellows, headed by Stokesley, afterwards Bishop of London, who was then Vice-President, declared that by the fact of Mayew's consecration the office of President had become vacant, and at last obtained from Bishop Fox of Winchester, the Visitor of the College, a decision in favour of their own view. Mayew, in the meantime, had attempted to assert his authority as President in a manner not altogether in accordance with the statutes, and it became necessary for the Bishop of Winchester to hold a formal visitation of the College. This he did by a Commissary, and the records of the Visitation contain many extraordinary charges made by the partizans on each side. Stokesley himself was accused, among other things, of having taken part in some magical incantations, including the baptizing of a cat, in order to discover hidden treasure. The cat, it may be remarked, is sometimes described as *cattus*, sometimes with more elegant Latinity as *murilegus*. These proceedings were alleged to have taken place in Yorkshire; concerning the more immediate affairs of the College, it appears that the strife between the parties had run so high, that some of the Fellows went about the cloisters with armour offensive and defensive. The general result of the Visitation was the acquittal of Stokesley, who cleared himself from all charges to the satisfaction of the Commissary. Bishop Mayew retired from the Presidentship, and was succeeded early in 1507 by John Claymond, formerly Fellow, one of the many distinguished men who were members of the College during the quarter of a century over which Mayew's term of office had extended. Among other members of the College under Mayew's rule may be mentioned the celebrated Grocyn, who was Praelector in Divinity, Richard Fox (already referred to as Bishop of Winchester), John Colet, afterwards Dean of St. Paul's, and Thomas Wolsey—the last, perhaps, the most celebrated man whom the College has produced. It was during Mayew's Presidentship that the Tower, sometimes attributed to Wolsey,[203] was built, and that the cloister on the south side of the quadrangle was added.

The rise of Wolsey in the King's favour secured the College a friend at Court whose influence was for a time more powerful than that of either

Waynflete or Mayew had been. He was appointed one of the King's chaplains, and employed by Henry VII. in some important missions. Soon after the accession of Henry VIII. he became almoner, and "ruled all under the King." Throughout the time of his prosperity he kept up friendly relations with the College, and frequent exchanges of presents took place between him and its members. The first Dean of his College in Oxford was John Hygden, who had succeeded Claymond as President of Magdalen; and several members of Magdalen College were among the first Canons of Cardinal College.

Another new foundation closely connected with Magdalen College was the College of Corpus Christi, founded by Richard Fox, Bishop of Winchester, who not only induced Claymond to become the first President of his new society, but closely imitated Waynflete's statutes in those which he gave to Corpus Christi College. These statutes provided that the students of Theology and Bachelors of Arts of Corpus Christi College should attend lectures at Magdalen—the lectures intended being no doubt those of the Praelectors or readers established by Waynflete, who occupied a position not unlike that of the University Professors of a later time. It was perhaps with a view to the advantages afforded by these lectures that a further direction enjoined the members of Corpus Christi College, if compelled by a visitation of the plague to move from Oxford, to take up their quarters near the place where the members of Magdalen College had settled for the time. The second President of Corpus Christi

College, Robert Morwent, had been Vice-President of Magdalen, and had migrated with Claymond to take charge of Fox's infant foundation. These two Presidents of Corpus, with John Hygden, first Dean of Cardinal College and of Christ Church, joined together in a benefaction to their former society. They made provision for the yearly distribution to its members of a sum of money, which was to be, and still is, distributed by the bursar in the chapel during the singing of Benedictus on the first Monday of every Lent.

The "revolution under the forms of law," effected in the reign of Henry VIII., of which Wolsey's fall was the beginning, had no great direct effect upon the College. Indirectly, however, the suppression of the religious houses was a cause of considerable expense. The College had permitted the Carmelites of Shoreham, whose house was much decayed, to occupy their annexed Priory of Sele; and it was perhaps only in accordance with the justice of the King's proceedings that the Priory was in consequence treated as a Carmelite house, and the College compelled to buy back its own property from the persons to whom Henry had granted it. A less important expenditure involved by the King's proceedings was incurred by the provision of new painted glass, no doubt to replace portions of the chapel windows which had been defaced by the King's commissioners as containing emblems derogatory of his Majesty's supremacy. The "linen-fold" panelling of the hall appears to have been placed in its present position in the year 1541; it is said to have come from Reading Abbey, but the groups of figures, the heraldic ornaments, and the not too flattering effigy of Henry VIII., which are now inserted in it, were probably designed for the decoration of the Hall. Except for the acquisition of this wood-work, the College seems to have received nothing from the spoil of the religious orders.

The accession of Edward VI., and the visitation of the University, brought serious trouble upon the College. The President, Owen Oglethorpe, was apparently prepared to accept the earlier stages of the Reformation movement, but he was not prepared to go so far as the party in power required. Some members of the College were of the more advanced school of the Reformers; and much irreverence, with a good deal of wanton destruction, was committed by them, encouraged by letters from the Protector inciting the College to the "redress of religion." Oglethorpe was removed from the office of President, into which Walter Haddon, a person not eligible according to the statutes, was intruded, in spite of a petition from the Fellows, and the work of reformation proceeded according to the desire of the Council. Haddon is said to have sold many of the effects of the chapel, valued at about £1000, for about a twentieth part of that sum, and to have "consumed on alterations" not only the sum so received, but a larger sum of the "public money" of the College. It was fortunate for the society that the scheme of the Council for the total suppression of the choir, and the alienation of a corresponding part of the College revenue, had been promulgated while

Oglethorpe was still President. Under his guidance, with considerable difficulty, the College managed to preserve this part of its foundation unimpaired.

Immediately on the accession of Queen Mary, Walter Haddon received, as appears from the Vice-President's register, leave of absence on urgent private affairs, and his example was soon followed by those of the Fellows who had been especially notable for their zeal in the "redress of religion." Laurence Humphrey, one of this party, obtained leave for the express purpose of conveying himself *in transmarinas partes*; and this leave of absence was continued to him at a later time provided that he did not resort to those towns which were known to be the refuge of heretics. He took up his abode forthwith at Zürich. As he was absent from the College during the whole of Mary's reign, he is perhaps not a sufficient witness of the events of that time. He asserts that the Roman party had great difficulty in re-establishing the old order of things in College, and that the younger members of the society suffered many things at their hands. Of all this, however, there is no evidence in the Vice-President's register, where most of the offences and almost all the penalties recorded during this period are of an ordinary kind.[204] Oglethorpe was restored to his Presidency, and was succeeded on his elevation to the See of Carlisle, by Arthur Cole, a Canon of Windsor.[205] During the tenure of Cole, and of his successor Thomas Coveney (whom the College chose in preference to three persons recommended by the Queen), there appear to have been differences of opinion on religious matters within the College, and some difficulties in enforcing the due attendance of its members at the chapel services; but there is no sign of what might be called a tendency to persecution on the part of the authorities. The most recalcitrant members of the society seem to have been the Bachelor Demies and Probationer Fellows. Coveney remained President for some time after Queen Elizabeth's coronation by Oglethorpe; and in the interval between that event and the consecration of Archbishop Parker there are some indications in the register of religious strife within the College. The end of Coveney's term of office was marked by a contest between himself and some of the Fellows, concerning matters of College business, in which he seems to have exceeded his power as President. He was deprived by Bishop Horn at a Visitation in 1561, on the ground, it is said, that he was a layman; but it might be at least doubtful whether the founder's statutes strictly required the President to be in Holy Orders; and it is probable that the real reason for his deprivation lay in the fact that Horn regarded him as being too much "addicted to the Popish superstition."

This fault at all events could not be laid to the charge of Laurence Humphrey, who succeeded him. Horn himself had reported that the members of the College, whom he expected to find of the same school as their President, were willing to accept the tests he proposed to them—to acknowledge the Queen's supremacy, and to accept the Book of Common Prayer, and the Advertisements. Before

Humphrey had been long President the College had ceased to be "conformable," but its non-conformity was of the Puritan, not of the Romanizing, type. Humphrey himself had a strong objection to wearing a surplice, or using his proper academical dress, and many of his Fellows followed his example in this matter. It required more than one Visitation to induce compliance on such matters. Abuses of another kind, however, were left uncorrected, and even encouraged, by the Visitors. Many Fellowships were filled up by nominations from the Queen, or from the Bishop of Winchester, and it may be added that the persons nominated were not always model members of a College. There were many contentions between the Fellows, and between the President and the Fellows. The general impression given by reading the register of the time of Humphrey and his immediate successors is, that the College was becoming a home of disorder rather than of learning. Nicolas Bond, Humphrey's successor, seems, however, in 1589 to have made some rather ineffectual efforts to provide for more regular and systematic study among its members. During his tenure of office the society received a visit from King James I., accompanied by his son Henry, then Prince of Wales, who was matriculated as a member of the College. The King was much impressed by the buildings, and greatly enjoyed his visit. The grotesque figures or "hieroglyphics" in the Cloister Quadrangle were painted, as it would seem, in honour of his coming, Moses in particular being adorned *toga coerulea.*

The College, which was Puritan under Humphrey, was even more Puritan under Bond, Harding, and Langton; with Langton's successor, however, in 1626, the tide set in the contrary direction. Accepted Frewen, if, as his name suggests, he was of Puritan descent, was himself a supporter of Laud's ecclesiastical policy, and acted with vigour both as President in his own College and as Vice-Chancellor in the University, for the restoration of discipline and good order. The numbers of the College had been increased during his predecessor's time by the influx of a number of so-called "poor scholars," whose connection with the College was very slight, and who seem to have in many cases been entered as members of the society by the mere authority of the person to whom they had attached themselves. Frewen made regulations on this subject, and these seem to have been re-inforced a few years later by a letter from the Visitor. Other matters he also took in hand with good effect, especially the restoration of the chapel, on which he seems to have spent large sums of his own, in addition to the corporate expenditure of the College. The windows of the ante-chapel (except the great west window) were part of Frewen's work, the only part which has been left by the later restoration of 1832.

The outbreak of the Great Rebellion found the College converted from a nest of Puritans into a nest of Royalists and High Churchmen. The King's demand for loans of money and plate was met with some difficulty, but without hesitation, by a loan of £1000 in money and by the delivery of plate to the value of about £1000 more. When the Parliamentary forces entered Oxford in September 1642 they found at Magdalen "certain Cavaliers in scholars' habits," who had "feathers and buff-coats" in their chambers. Some of the scholars, being malignant persons, "scoffed" at the invaders and "at the honourable Houses of Parliament," and were accordingly made prisoners. Other members of the College had left Oxford a few days before with Byron's horse, to join the King: among them was John Nourse, Fellow and Doctor of Civil Law, who fell at Edgehill. After that action the King entered Oxford, and Prince Rupert took up his quarters at Magdalen. The King's artillery was placed in Magdalen College Grove, which served as a drill-ground for the regiment of scholars and strangers which was raised in 1644; batteries were erected in the Walks, and gunners exercised in the College meadows. The timber in the Grove was probably felled for use in the defensive works.[206] A curious contrast to this military preparation was furnished by the imposing ceremonial of Frewen's consecration as Bishop of Lichfield, which took place in the chapel of the College in April 1644.[207]

Some members of the College were as active on the side of the Parliament as those who remained in Oxford were on the side of the King. A Demy named Lidcott was deprived of his place for having been in arms against the King, serving in Essex's army as an "antient" of a foot company. A far more celebrated member of the Parliamentary party, John Hampden, had formerly been a member of the College which was the head-quarters of the commander of the troops against whom he fought at Chalgrove.

After the surrender of Oxford, considerable havoc was wrought in the chapel of the College by the Parliamentary troops, who destroyed, among other things, the glass of many of the windows. The organ was appropriated by Cromwell to his own use, and removed by him to Hampton Court, whence it was brought again after the Restoration.[208] The Parliamentary Visitors of the University found few members of the College willing to submit to their authority. The President, Dr. John Oliver, and the greater part of the members were ejected, and the bursar, who obstinately refused to give up keys or papers, was imprisoned. The tenants of the College, however, persisted in paying their rents to him, and special injunctions had to be given to prevent them from doing so. The places in College rendered vacant by expulsions were filled up by the importation of Independents and Presbyterians, Dr. John Wilkinson, a former Fellow, being made President. He was succeeded two years later by Goodwin, a gloomy person, whose examination of a candidate for a Demyship has been recounted by Addison in the *Spectator*.[209] The records of the events in College during the Commonwealth are very scanty. One of the most remarkable proceedings of the intruders was the appropriation and division among themselves of a sum of money which they found in the muniment-room; this was the fund provided by the Founder for special necessities, which had remained untouched since 1585, and the existence of which had perhaps been forgotten. It was for the most part in ancient coinage, the pieces being of the kind known as "spur royals." Of these a hundred fell to the share of Wilkinson, who seems to have been the instigator of the division; nine hundred more were divided among the thirty Fellows, and the Demies and others, including the servants, received portions of the spoil. Before the Restoration, however, some of the recipients restored the pieces they had obtained, and the greater part of the money was actually repaid in course of time. The fund, under more modern financial arrangements, no longer remains in the muniment-room, but some of the old coins are still preserved there.

On the Restoration the ejected members of the College, or those who were left, were restored to their home. They included the President, seventeen Fellows and eight Demies.[210] Dr. Oliver, however, did not long survive his return; and upon his death began a time of trouble. Charles II. recommended as his successor Dr. Thomas Pierce, a divine who had done much service in the defence of the Church against her assailants, but whom the Fellows, who perhaps knew him better than the King were unwilling, as it seems, to elect. Charles however enforced obedience by a letter as peremptory as any communication which the College afterwards received from his brother, and Dr. Pierce became President. The result was a long warfare between Pierce, the Fellows, and the Visitor, Bishop Morley, whose intentions seem to have been better than his judgment. At last the King interfered, and the difficulty was solved by the promotion of Dr. Pierce to the Deanery of Salisbury, where he found scope for his energies in a controversy with his Bishop. Dr. Henry Clerk was now recommended by the King, and elected by the Fellows, and the society was at peace for some years. That peace was again disturbed, on Dr. Clerk's death, by the action of James II., who attempted to force upon the College as its President a man unqualified by statute and disqualified by notorious immorality. The history of the struggle which followed is too well known to need repetition here.[211] The Fellows almost unanimously chose one of their own number, and supported him, when duly elected, against the King's second nominee. In the end, after a year's exile, they were restored to their College, under Dr. John Hough, the President of their own choice, by the Bishop of Winchester, acting on instructions from the King.

The Revolution brought with it new causes of disquiet, and some members of the College were again ejected as Nonjurors. The great majority, however, of those who had contended against the usurpation of James were content to submit themselves to the new Sovereigns, and retained their places. The most notable member who was thus lost to the College was Dr. Thomas Smith, a man of much learning and ability, and a steady and uncompromising Royalist. In 1689 occurred what was afterwards known as the "Golden Election" of Demies, which included, besides others less known, Hugh Boulter, afterwards Archbishop of Armagh,

Smallbrook, afterwards Bishop of St. David's and later of Lichfield, the notorious Henry Sacheverell, and Joseph Addison, the most celebrated member of the College since the Revolution. The residence of Addison in College was not prolonged beyond his year of probation as Fellow; but he has left a memory of himself in the fact that his name has been attached to a portion of the Walks. These it would seem in his time did not extend beyond what is now called Addison's Walk, but was formerly known as "Dover Pier."

The members of the College who remained seem to have maintained friendly relations with those who had withdrawn from it as Nonjurors, and even at this time, and certainly after the accession of George I., the sympathy of many among the Fellows was with the exiled rather than with the reigning branch of the Royal House. During the first half of the eighteenth century, indeed, politics flourished in the society more than learning; and although Gibbon's picture of the condition of the College during his brief residence is rather highly coloured, it cannot be doubted that the general decline of academic activity which affected many of the Colleges in Oxford during the last century, affected Magdalen in no slight degree. A large part of the attention of the society seems to have been given to plans for the rearrangement or the destruction of the College buildings, and for the re-construction of the College on the pattern adopted in what are known as the "New Buildings," erected in 1735. Some amazing designs for "College improvements" remain in the library, as a memorial of the architectural ambitions of this period. Among the Presidents of the eighteenth century, if we except Dr. Routh, whose lengthened tenure extended over the last years of that century and the first half of the nineteenth, there is but one name of mark—that of George Horne, afterwards Bishop of Norwich, once widely-known by his Commentary on the Psalms. Nor are there many names of mark among the other members of the College in the same century. The learning of Dr. Routh does not seem to have been shared in any conspicuous degree by more than a small proportion of those who passed through the College in his long Presidentship—though towards the end of that period Magdalen numbered among its members several men of note in different ways—James Mozley and William Palmer among theologians, Ferrier among philosophers, Roundell Palmer, now Lord Selborne, among lawyers, Conington among scholars, Charles Reade among novelists, Goldwin Smith among essayists, Charles Daubeny among those who laboured to advance the study of natural science.

Of the changes which have been brought about in the College since the days of Routh, of its transformation from a small society of Fellows and Demies into one of the larger among the Colleges in Oxford, it is hardly possible to speak as of history. They are changes of the present day. But it is a matter of history, which ought not to be forgotten, that the College, which has owed much to its Presidents in the past, owes much in this matter to its last President, who governed it during the trying times of two University Commissions, and of the changes which resulted from them. By his own example of the loyal acceptance of what was necessary, even when it was uncongenial to his tastes, and by the kindly sympathy which enabled him to reconcile conflicting interests, he did more to preserve the peace of his College, and to promote its progress, than he would himself have thought possible, or than those to whom he was less well known than to the members of his own College would have been inclined to imagine.

XI.
BRASENOSE COLLEGE.
(*Aula Regia et Collegium de Brasenose, Collegium Aenei Nasi.*)

BY FALCONER MADAN, M.A., FELLOW OF BRASENOSE.

I. THE KING'S HALL OF BRAZEN-NOSE.
(*Aula Regia de Brasinnose.*)

Professor Holland has given a clear account[212] of the three stages through which a University passes, first as *scholae*, where there is "a more or less fortuitous gathering of teachers and students"; next as a *studium generale*, when the teachers become "a sort of guild of masters or doctors," with control over the admission by a degree to their own body; and lastly as a *Universitas*, when the society "acquires a corporate existence," with a well-defined constitution and privileges. The first and second of these stages were attained by Oxford in the twelfth century, and the third early in the thirteenth century. It is early in this latter century that we also find the earliest associations of students among themselves. The system of Halls was due to the desire of the poorer class of students to live for economy's sake in a common house with common meals, under the charge of a Principal whose duty was quite as much to manage household affairs as to superintend the studies of his scholars.[213]

The existence of the house which became Brasenose Hall may be carried back with certainty to the second quarter of the thirteenth century, the earliest facts at present known being that it belonged, in or before A. D. 1239,[214] to one Jeffry Jussell, and that it passed into the hands of Simon de Balindon, who sold it in about 1261 to the Chancellor and Masters of the University, for the use of the scholars enjoying the benefaction of William of Durham. Soon after this purchase the occupier, Andrew the son of Andrew of Durham, was forcibly ejected by Adam Bilet and his scholars, and no doubt at this time, if not earlier, the tenement acquired the name of Brasenose, and was used as schools, for in 1278 an Inquisition[215] says, "Item eadem Universitas [Oxon.] habet quandam aliam domum que vocatur Brasenose cum quatuor Scholis … et taxantur ad octo marcas, et fuit illa domus aliquo tempore Galfridi Jussell." The transition from these Scholae or lecture-rooms to a Hall cannot now be traced, but no doubt took place within the same century.

In the early part of 1334 a striking incident occurred in the history of the Hall. Under stress of internal faction, and not on this occasion, it would seem, from excesses on the part of the citizens, there was a migration of a large number of the students of the University from Oxford to Stamford, fulfilling the (later!) prophecy of Merlin—

"Doctrinae studium quae nunc viget ad Vada Boum
Tempore venturo celebrabitur ad Vada Saxi."

But of all the emigrants the only men who kept together were the students of Brasenose Hall, as is evidenced by the existence at Stamford to this day of a fourteenth century archway, belonging to an ancient hall called for centuries "Brasenose Hall in Stamford," the refectory of which was standing till A.D. 1688,[216] and still more by a brass knocker which is assigned by antiquaries to the early part of the twelfth century, and which from time immemorial hung on the doors of the Stamford gateway. It is reasonable to suppose that the knocker had originally given a name to the Oxford Hall, and had been carried as a visible sign of unity to the distant Lincolnshire town.[217] The King used all his power to force the students to return to Oxford, and in a final commission in July, 1335, the name of "Philippus obsonator Eneanasensis" occurs among the thirty-seven who resisted to the last the mandates of the King.[218]

The list of Principals of Brasenose is preserved from 1435 onwards (see p. 271), but little or nothing is recorded of the life of the Hall. Its flourishing state may be inferred from its vigorous annexation of the surrounding buildings, as Little St. Edmund Hall, Little University Hall, and St. Thomas Hall. An inventory of the furniture belonging to Master Thomas Cooper of Brasenose Hall, who died in 1438, is printed in Anstey's *Munimenta Academica*, ii. 515. The Vice-Chancellor in 1480-82 was William Sutton, Principal of Brasenose Hall, and Proctors in 1458 (John Molineux) and 1502 (Hugh Hawarden) were Brasenose men.

The new College, founded in 1509, was in several special ways a continuation of, and not merely a substitute for, the old Hall. The site of the Hall was exactly at the principal gateway of the College; it had already annexed many of the adjacent buildings required for the new erection, and the last Principal of the Hall was the first Principal of the College. It may fairly be claimed therefore that there is a real succession, both of name and fame, from the one to the other.

II. THE FOUNDERS OF BRASENOSE COLLEGE.

William Smyth, the chief founder of Brasenose, was the fourth son of Robert Smyth, of Peel House, in Widnes (Lancashire), and belonged to a Cuerdley family. Of the date of his birth, early education, and career at Oxford nothing whatever is certainly known. In 1492 when he was instituted to the Rectory of Cheshunt, he was a Bachelor of Law. Through the influence of the Stanley family, and of Margaret, Countess of Richmond, Smyth obtained promotion both in civil and ecclesiastical lines, until in 1491 he was elected Bishop of Coventry and Lichfield. In the closing years of the fifteenth century he presided over the Prince of Wales's Council in the Marches of Wales, and was President of Wales in 1501 or 1502. In Lichfield he founded, in 1495, a Hospital of St. John, which has preserved a portrait of him almost identical with the one owned by the College. In the same year he was translated to

Lincoln. The Bishop's connection with Oxford was renewed in 1500, at the end of which year he was elected Chancellor, retaining the office till August, 1503. This link with the University had great results, for in 1507 the Bishop established a new Fellowship in Oriel, endowed Lincoln College with two estates, and formed his plans with a view to the foundation of Brasenose. After that event there is little of importance to notice in his public life before his death on 2nd January, 1513/4.

Sir Richard Sutton, Knight, the co-Founder of Brasenose, and the first lay founder of any College, was of the family of Sutton, of Sutton near Macclesfield, and probably a kinsman of William Sutton, Principal of Brasenose Hall in and after 1469; but no connection can be traced between this family and the wealthy Thomas Sutton who founded the Charterhouse a century later. Of his birth and education there is no record, but he was a Barrister of the Inner Temple and was made a Privy Councillor in 1497. In 1513 he was Steward of the Monastery of Sion at Isleworth, a house of Brigittine nuns. At his expense Pynson printed the *Orcharde of Syon*, a devotional book, in 1519. In 1522 or 1523 he received the honour of knighthood, and died in 1524.

III. THE FOUNDATION AND EARLY STATUTES OF THE COLLEGE.

The first record of the proposal to found Brasenose is contained in the will of Edmund Croston, dated (four days before his death) on Jan. 23, 1507/8, where are bequeathed £6 13*s*. 4*d*. to "the building of Brasynnose in Oxford, if such works as the Bishop of Lyncoln and Master Sotton intended there went on during their life or within twelve years after." It is probable that the Bishop at one time intended that Lincoln College should enjoy his benefactions, for Robert Parkinson, Sub-rector of Lincoln, wrote about 1566-69, "Proposuerat enim [episcopus], ut ferunt, omnia nostro collegio praestitisse quae postea in Brasinnos egit, si voluissent R[ector] et S[cholares] qui tum fuerunt ab eo propositas conditiones recipere."

The actual foundation can be best shown in the form of annals, it being understood that the disposition of the halls mentioned was nearly as follows—

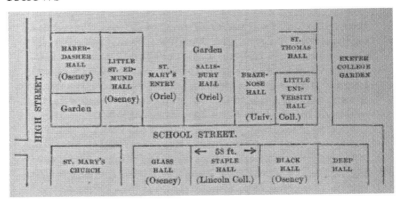

1508, Oct. 20, Brazen Nose and Little University Halls are leased by University College to Richard Sutton, Esq., and eight others (four of whom were among the first Fellows) for ninety-two years at an annual rent of £3, on condition that the lessees should spend £40 on the tenements within a year.

The College agreed to renew the lease and to give over all their rights, as soon as property of the annual value of £3 should be given them. In 1514 Sutton assigned this lease to trustees to carry out his purposes.

1509, summer. Edward Moseley's stone quarry at Headington is let to the founders and Roland Messenger for their lives.

1509, June 1. The foundation stone of the College is laid, as recorded on a modern copy of the original inscription, now and probably always placed over the doorway of Staircase No. 1, which used to lead to the first chapel of the College:—

"Anno Christi 1509 et Regis Henrici octavi primo | Nomine diuino lincoln | presul quoque sutton. Hanc posu | ere petram regis ad imperium | primo die Iunii."

1509/10, Feb. 20. Oriel College lets Salisbury Hall and St. Mary's Entry (Introitus S. Mariae) to Sutton and others for ever in consideration of an annual rent of 13s.4d.

1511/2, Jan. 15. A Charter of Foundation granted to Smyth and Sutton.

1523, May 6. Sutton transfers the property acquired from University College in 1508, to the Principal and Fellows of Brazenose.

1530, May 12. Haberdasher, Little St. Edmund, Glass and Black Halls are granted to the College on a lease of ninety-six years by Oseney Abbey, the first being at once converted by payment into the property of the College, but the others not till March 6, 1655/6.

1556, Nov. 2. Staple Hall, which had once belonged to the Abbey of Eynsham, is leased by Lincoln College to Brasenose for ever at a rent of 20*s.* per annum.

"Rome was not built in a day," and it is curious to note how the old and new foundations overlap each other. The College building clearly began at the south-west corner of the present front quadrangle, and Brasenose Hall was no doubt left until the building naturally reached it. Thus John Formby was Principal of the Hall till Aug. 24, 1510, when Matthew Smyth succeeded him, and in Smyth's name on Sept. 9, 1511 Roland Messenger still became surety for the dues payable by the Hall to the University, for the ensuing year; and even on Sept. 9, 1512, Smyth himself "cautioned," as it was called, for the moribund hall. Moreover, a scholar of the Hall was locked up in August 1512 for interfering with the workmen who were building Corpus. The first occasion on which the College appears in the University Registers is in Sept. 1514, when Matthew Smyth, "Principal of the College or Hall of Brasen Nose" is mentioned; but there is evidence that the corporate action of the College dates from at least as early as Nov. 1512. We thus have before us the successive steps by which a College gradually grew, and literally piece by piece took the place of the precedent Halls.

It is now time to turn to the statutes, the buildings being reserved for a later section.

The Charter of Foundation is dated Jan. 15, 1511/2, and the original statutes were no doubt shortly after drawn up and ratified by the two founders, but no copy of them remains. Bishop Smyth's executors in about 1514 revised and signed a modification of the code, which still exists, and finally at the request of the College Sir Richard Sutton once more revised them, on Feb. 1, 1521/2.

As in conception and in form of buildings, so in respect of their statutes also, Merton and New College are the two cardinal foundations. From the latter were derived the statutes of Magdalen, founded in 1458, and from these latter the earliest statutes of Brasenose. The general sense of the Code of 1514 with Sutton's changes in 1522, can be well gathered from the Churton's abstract in his *Lives of ... (the) Founders of Brazen Nose College* (Oxf. 1800), pp. 315-40. The preamble is as follows, the original being in Latin—

"In the name of the Holy and undivided Trinity, Father, Son, and Holy Spirit, and of the most blessed Mother of God, Mary the glorious Virgin, and of Saints Hugh and Chad confessors, and also of St. Michael the archangel: We, William Smyth, bishop of Lincoln, and Richard Sutton, esquire, confiding in the aid of the supreme Creator, who knows, directs and disposes the wills of all that trust in him, do out of the goods which in this life, not by our merits, but by the grace of His fulness, we have received abundantly, by royal authority and charter found, institute and establish in the University of Oxford, a perpetual College of poor and indigent scholars, who shall study and make progress in philosophy and sacred theology; commonly called *The King's Haule and Colledge of Brasennose in Oxford*; to the praise, glory, and honour of Almighty God, of the glorious Virgin Mary, Saints Hugh and Chad confessors, St. Michael the Archangel and All Saints; for the support and exaltation of the Christian Faith, for the advancement of holy church, and for the furtherance of divine worship."

The College is to consist of a Principal and twelve Fellows, all of them born within the diocese of Coventry and Lichfield; with preference to the natives of the counties of Lancaster and Chester; and especially to the natives of the parish of Prescot in Lancashire, and of Prestbury in Cheshire. One of the senior Fellows is annually to be elected Vice-Principal; and two others Bursars. The only language tolerated for public use, unless when strangers are present, is Latin. The Bishop of Lincoln has always been the Visitor.

Thus Brasenose started fairly on its course, equipped with statutes, with property from its founders and benefactors, and with students drawn, as ever since until recently, chiefly from good families of Cheshire and Lancashire, Leighs and Watsons, Lathams and Brookes and Egertons. But the history of a College which has not been at any time predominant in the University is both difficult and unnecessary to trace; difficult from the paucity of records of its internal social life, and unnecessary from the lack of general interest in the domestic affairs of one particular College among so many. It will be the task of one who deals with the social life of Oxford to seize on those features of College history which from time to time best represent the character of successive periods: in this place it will suffice to give a few scenes or facts which being themselves of interest have also sufficient illustration from existing records.

IV. FROM THE REFORMATION TO THE RESTORATION.

In the Bodleian (MS. Rawl. D. 985) there is a volume of copies of Latin letters written by Robert Batt of Brasenose, chiefly to a brother, in which among much of the usual rhetoric there is also curious information about the life of the College. They range from 1581 to 1585, and we read of his complaints to the Principal because a junior man is put into his study (*musæum*), of an archery meeting at Oxford, which much distracts the young Batt, and of the visit of the Prince Alaskie to Oxford. He asks his Cambridge brother to come up for Commem, and with Yorkshire bluntness writes letters to the Master and a Fellow of University College, asking for a Fellowship!

So too in 1609-11 we find ten letters from Richard Taylor as tutor to Sir Peter Legh's son (Hist. Manuscripts Commission, *Report 3*, 1872, p. 268), which throw light on College affairs and expenses of that time.

In the Register of the Parliamentary Visitors of the University from 1647 to 1658 we obtain an insight into the condition of the College, which shows it to have been in a creditable state. At first the College is as Royalist as any, the proportion of submitters to those who were willing to endure actual expulsion rather than acknowledge the Visitors' rights, being probably only twelve to twenty-three, in May 1648. Their Principal, Dr. Samuel Radcliffe, had already, on Jan. 6, been deprived of his office, and Daniel Greenwood, a submitter, had been on April 13, put in his place. But the spirit of the College is abundantly shown by the proceedings which ensued on Dr. Radcliffe's death. Three days after that event, on June 29, the Society, to use Wood's words, "(taking no notice that the Visitors had entred Mr. Greenwood Principal) put up a citation on the Chappel door (as by Statute they were required) to summon the Fellows to election. The Visitors thereupon send for Mr. Thom. Sixsmith and two more Fellows of that House to command them to surcease and submit to their new Principal Mr. Greenwood; but they gave them fair words, went home, and within four days after [July 13] chose among themselves, in a Fellow's Chamber, at the West end of the old Library, Mr. Thom. Yate, one of their Society." The Visitors immediately deposed him, in favour of Greenwood; but at the Restoration Dr. Yate's claims were at once recognized, and he long enjoyed the headship. This resistance by the

Fellows was proved to be not lawlessness but loyalty, for when resistance was of no avail, they "speedily[219] recovered their working order, and gave but little trouble to the Visitors," a contrast to the general example of other Colleges.

The more eminent Brasenose men who belong to this period are: Alexander Nowell, Fellow and Principal, Dean of St. Paul's (matr. 1521); John Foxe, the Martyrologist (*c.* 1533); Sampson Erdeswick, the historian of Staffordshire (1553); Thomas Egerton, afterwards Lord Chancellor Ellesmere (*c.* 1556); Sir Henry Savile, afterwards Warden of Merton (1561); John Guillim, the herald (*c.* 1585); Robert Burton, the author of the *Anatomy of Melancholy* (1593); Sir John Spelman, the antiquary (1642); Elias Ashmole, the herald, founder of the Ashmolean Museum (1644); and Sir William Petty (1649).

V. BRASENOSE IN MODERN TIMES.

The period from the Restoration to 1800 was in Oxford as elsewhere marked rather by the excellence of individuals than by a high standard of general culture. In the first part of the period Brasenose is not especially distinguished, except by an undue prominence in the records of the Vice-Chancellor's Court; but as we approach the close of the eighteenth century there are signs of a period of great prosperity, which distinguished the headships of Cleaver, Hodson and Gilbert, the first and last of whom were Bishops of Chester (then of Bangor, and finally of St. Asaph) and Chichester respectively. The signs of this are unmistakable. The numbers show an unusual increase, and the College is in the front both in the class-lists and in outdoor sports. The high-water mark was perhaps reached when the story could be told of Dr. Hodson (in about 1808), which is related in Mark Pattison's *Memoirs*. "Returning to College, after one Long Vacation, Hodson drove the last stage into Oxford, with post-horses. The reason he gave for this piece of ostentation was, 'That it should not be said that the first tutor of the first College of the first University of the world entered it with a pair.' ... The story is symbolical of the high place B.N.C. held in the University at the time, in which however, intellectual eminence entered far less than the fact that it numbered among its members many gentlemen commoners of wealthy and noble families."

But intellectual eminence there certainly was at this time, for in the class-lists of Mich. 1808 to Mich. 1810, out of thirty-seven first-classes Brasenose claimed seven, monopolizing one list altogether; and out of seventy-five second-classes it held twelve. This was the period of what has been called the "famous Brasenose breakfast." Reginald Heber won the Newdigate in 1803 with a poem which will never be forgotten—his *Palestine*. His rooms were on Staircase 6, one pair left, under the great chestnut in Exeter Garden called Heber's Tree. In 1803 Sir Walter Scott went to Oxford with Richard Heber, Reginald's brother. The story may be told in Lockhart's[220] words: Heber "had just been declared the successful competitor for that year's poetical prize, and read to Scott at breakfast in Brazen Nose College the MS. of his *Palestine*. Scott observed that in the verses on Solomon's Temple one striking circumstance had escaped him, namely that no tools were used in its erection. Reginald retired for a few minutes to the corner of the room, and returned with the beautiful lines—

> 'No hammer fell, no ponderous axes rung;
> Like some tall palm the mystic fabric sprung,
> Majestic silence!'"[221]

In connection with this literary and social side of the College may be mentioned the Phœnix Common-room or Club, the only social Club in the University which is more than a century old. It was started in 1781 or 1782 by Joseph Alderson, an undergraduate of Brasenose, afterwards Fellow of Trinity College, Cambridge, and received a full constitution with officers and rules in 1786. It has always nominally consisted of twelve members, generally dining together once a week. The records of the Club are singularly complete, even to the caricatures on the blotting-paper of the dinner-books. Of the twelve original members five were soon elected to Fellowships, and such names as Frodsham Hodson (afterwards Principal), Viscount Valentia (*d.* 1844), Earl Fortescue (*d.* 1861), Reginald Heber (Bishop of Calcutta), Lord George Grenville (*d.* 1850), the Earl of Delawarr, the friend of Byron, Richard Harington (afterwards Principal), Lord Sidney Godolphin Osborne ("S. G. O."), and the present Deans of Rochester and Worcester, have raised it to no ordinary level. Its contemporary from 1828 to 1834, the Hell-fire Club, was of a very different character; but from one or two dubious incidents in its career has found its way into literature.[222] The incident which produced from the pen of Reginald Heber the humorous poem entitled the *Whippiad* [223] was connected with members of the Phœnix, though not with a meeting of the Club. The Senior Tutor had incautiously endeavoured to wrest a whip from Bernard Port, who had been loudly cracking it in the quadrangle; but alas, the representative of constitutional authority soon measured his length on the grass, being, not for the first time (as Heber maliciously notes) "floored by Port."

The Ale Verses were an ancient social custom, probably at least as old as the Restoration. On Shrove Tuesday the butler presented a copy of English verses on Brasenose Ale to the Principal, written by some undergraduate, and received thereupon a certain sum of money. The earliest extant poem is of about the year 1700; but there is a long gap from that year till 1806, and they are not continuously preserved till from 1826, having been printed first in about 1811. They supply all kinds of contemporary information, collegiate, academical and political, chiefly of course by way of allusion. At last in 1886 the College Brew-house was removed to make room for new buildings, and with it went the Ale Verses, except that in 1889 one more set was issued. In 1888 a Fellow of the College printed a Latin dirge over the sad surcease; but soon the Verses will be forgotten, and the Brew-house.

On the river Brasenose has always been prominent: never once in the Eights or Torpids has it sunk below the ninth place. In the first inter-collegiate races, in 1815, Brasenose is at the head, and when the records begin again, in 1822, again takes the lead. At the present time (June 1891) B.N.C. has started head in the Eights on 110 days.[224]

The only clubs which had cricket grounds of their own in about 1835 were the Brasenose and the Bullingdon (Ch. Ch.), and even in 1847 the Magdalen, *i. e.* the University Club, was the only additional one. Early cricketing records are difficult to find; but in recent times no College has been able to show such a record as B.N.C. in 1871, when it had eight men in the University eleven, and when sixteen of the College beat an All-England eleven. In 1873 sixteen of B.N.C. also beat the United North of England eleven. The Inter-University high-jump of 1876, when M. J. Brooks of B.N.C. cleared 6 feet 2½ inches, was an extraordinary performance.

The characteristics of the College at all times have been remarkably similar and persistent, if the present writer can trust his judgment. They may be described as, first and foremost, a marked but not exclusive predilection for the exercises and amusements of out-door life, the result of sound bodies and minds, and in part, no doubt, of a long connection with old county families of a high type. And next a certain pertinacity, perseverance, power of endurance, doggedness, patriotism, solidarity, or by whatever other name the spirit may be called which leads men to do what they are doing with all their might, to undergo training and discipline for the sake of the College, and hang together like a cluster of bees in view of a common object. The Headship of the River for any length of time cannot possibly be obtained by fitful effort, or the unsustained enthusiasm of a single leader; but rather (and herein consists its value) by a continuous, often unconsciously continuous, effort of several years, backed up by the general support of the College. Lastly, Brasenose seems to be singularly central, intermediate, and in a good sense average and mediocre. Its position and buildings, its history, its achievements, the roll of Brasenose authors, all give evidence that the College is a good sample of the best sort of academical foundation. A writer who might wish to select a single College for study as a specimen of the kind, would find the history of Brasenose neither startling nor commonplace, neither eccentric nor uninteresting, neither full of strong contrasts nor deficient in the signs of healthy corporate life.

Among the *alumni* of Brasenose in this period, to omit the names of living persons, are the following: Thomas Carte the historian (1699); John Napleton (matr. 1755), an academical reformer; Dr. John Latham, president of the College of Physicians (1778); Bishop Reginald Heber (1800); Richard Harris Barham, author of the *Ingoldsby Legends*, after whom a College club is named the Ingoldsby (1807); Henry Hart Milman, Dean of St. Paul's (1810); and the Rev. Frederick William Robertson, of Brighton, the preacher (1837). Mr. Buckley has compiled a list of more than four hundred Brasenose authors, and twenty-seven bishops or archbishops.

VI. THE BUILDINGS, PROPERTY, ETC., OF THE COLLEGE.

The front quadrangle of the College is as it stood when the College was first built, except that as usual an extra story was added in about the time of James I., and that for the old mullioned windows have been unhappily substituted in a few places modern square ones. The Principal's lodgings were at first, as always in Colleges, above and about the gateway.

The *Chapel* was originally the room now used for the Common Room, namely, on the first floor of No. 1 staircase, and the foundation stone was no doubt placed there as leading to the chapel. The shape of the old chapel windows may still be seen on the outside of the south side of the room. The present chapel was built between 26th June, 1656, and the day of consecration (to St. Hugh and St. Chad) 17th Nov., 1666. There is a persistent tradition that the design of the chapel was due to Sir Christopher Wren, and that the roof at least came from the chapel of St. Mary's College (now Frewen Hall). In support of this latter belief are the two facts that the roof does not appear precisely to fit the window spaces of the building, and that the principal rafters of the chapel and of the western part of the hall are numbered consecutively, as if they once belonged to a single building. The architecture of the chapel is interesting as a genuine effort to combine classical and Gothic styles. The ceiling, with its beautiful and ingeniously constructed fan-tracery, and the windows are Gothic, but the internal buttresses and altar decoration are Grecian. The East window[225] is by Hardman (1855), the West (by Pearson) was given by Principal Cawley in 1776. Among the other painted glass is one on the north side to F. W. Robertson. The brass eagle was given in 1731 by T. L. Dummer; the two candelabra were replaced within the last few years, having been formerly presented to Coleshill Church, in Buckinghamshire, by the College. The pair of pre-Reformation chalices with pattens form a unique possession.

The first *Library* was the room now known as No. 4 one pair right, and still retains a fine panelled ceiling with red and gold colouring. The present library is of the same date as the chapel, having been finished in 1663, and is no doubt by the same architect. The internal fittings date from 1780, and not till then were the chains removed from the books. Among the few MSS. are a tenth century Terence (once in the possession of Cardinal Bembo, and therefore periodically raising unfulfilled hopes in foreign students that it might exhibit the unique recension of the other "Bembine Terence") and the only MS. of Bishop Pearson's minor works. A large folio printed Missal of 1520 bears a miniature of Sir Richard Sutton, with other fine illuminations. Among the printed books are several given by the founder, Bishop Smith, and by John Longland, Bishop of Lincoln. There is a copy on vellum of Alexander de Ales's commentary on the *De Animâ* of Aristotle, printed at Oxford in 1481; a copy of Cranmer's Litany (1544), and of Day's Psalter (1563) for four-part singing. In general the library has a large number of controversial theological pieces and pamphlets, both of the latter part of Elizabeth's reign and of the period succeeding the Restoration. For the former the College is indebted to a large and (at the time) extremely valuable donation from Dr. Henry Mason, who died in 1647. There is also a very large quantity of the theological literature of the eighteenth century, partly bequeathed by Principal Yarborough, who also presented the library of Christopher Wasse; many county histories; and many pamphlets on Oxford Reform up to and including the time of the first Commission. In all there are about 15,000 volumes, and there is an adequate endowment from the legacy of Dr. Grimbaldson. Mr. Willis Clark has remarked in his *Architectural History of Cambridge* that College libraries before the sixteenth century usually, in both Universities, had their sides facing east and west, the early morning light being so important; that from that time to the Restoration, when more luxurious habits had come in, they face north and south, and afterwards again east and west. It is singular that of each change Brasenose Library is the earliest example.

The *Hall* has remained almost untouched from the first. The open fireplace in the centre under a louvre was retained until 1760 (when the Hon. Ashton Curzon gave the present chimney-piece), and the louvre itself is still intact but hidden above the ceiling.

The north-west corner of the quadrangle affords a striking view of the dome of the Radcliffe and the spire of St. Mary's, which has been often painted and engraved. The present grass-plot was once a formal maze or Italian garden, which is to be seen in Loggan's view, and was removed in October 1727, much to Hearne's disgust, to allow of a "silly statue" of Cain and Abel, the gift of Dr. George Clarke, who bought it in London, being erected in the centre. This well-known statue was for a long time believed to be an original by Giovanni da Bologna; and its removal in 1881 and subsequent destruction excited the wrath of the writer of the article on "Sculpture" in the ninth edition of the *Encyclopædia Britannica*. But the external evidence points to it being only a copy of the valuable original presented to Charles I. at Madrid, and by George III. to the great-grandfather of the present possessor, Sir William Worsley, of Hovingham Hall, Yorkshire.

The *Kitchen*, which forms the western part of the second quadrangle is (as at Christ Church) as old as any part of the College. The eastern side was till about 1840 an open cloister beneath the library, and in it and in front of it many former members of the College were buried.

Early in the last century the College purchased the houses between St. Mary's and All Saints, and the idea of a front to the High Street soon forced itself on the mind. Some very heavy classical designs are preserved, by Nicholas Hawksmoor (about 1720), who erected the High Street front of Queen's College; by Sir John Soane (1807); and by Philip Hardwick (1810); until at last a pure Gothic design by Mr. T. G. Jackson was accepted; and by the end of 1887 a gateway and tower, a Principal's house, and some undergraduates' rooms were erected, forming on the inside a large third quadrangle, and by its front a notable addition to the glories of the High Street. A drawing of a more ambitious design by the same architect is framed and hung in the College library.

The chief benefactors and property of the College are the following—Bp. William Smith, founder, gave Basset's Fee near Oxford, and the entire property of the suppressed Priory of Cold Norton, lying chiefly in Oxfordshire. Sir Richard Sutton gave lands in Burgh or Erdborowe in Leicestershire; the White Hart in the Strand, London; and lands in Cropredy, North Ockington, Garsington, and Cowley. The earliest gift of all was from Mrs. Elizabeth Morley, who in 1515 gave the manor of Pinchpoll, in Faringdon, coupled with conditions of undertaking certain services in St. Margaret's, Westminster. Joyce Frankland in 1586 gave the Red Lion in Kensington, &c., and money. Queen Elizabeth, 1572 and 1579, founds Middleton School in Lancashire, and connects it with the College by scholarships, and by giving the manor of Upberry and rectory of Gillingham. Sarah Duchess of Somerset in 1679 gave Somerset Iver and Somerset Thornhill scholarships, and alternate presentation to Wootton Rivers. William Hulme, 1691, land producing £40 a year for four exhibitions, tenable at Brasenose, from Lancashire; the property increased enormously in value, being in the Hulme district of Manchester, and now provides, besides High Schools for boys and girls at Manchester, and a Hulme Hall connected with the Victoria University, eight Senior and twelve Junior Exhibitions, of the value of £120 and £80 respectively. Sir Francis Bridgeman in 1701 gave money for an annual speech, originally in praise of James II.

Pictures, busts, &c.

In the Hall are pictures of King Alfred[226] (modern), Bp. William Smith (founder), Sir Richard Sutton (founder), Joyce Frankland (benefactress, with a sixteenth century watch in her hand), Alexander Nowell (Principal), Bp. Frodsham Hodson (Principal), William Cleaver (Principal), Thomas baron Ellesmere, Dr. John Latham, John Lord Mordaunt (benefactor), Samuel

Radcliffe (Principal, two), Sarah Duchess of Somerset (benefactress), Robert Burton, Thomas Yate (Principal), Francis Yarborough (Principal), Bp. Ashurst Turner Gilbert (Principal), Edward Hartopp Cradock (Principal). The Brazen Nose is fixed in a frame beneath the picture of King Alfred. A picture of the first Marquis of Buckingham once here is now in the possession of the representatives of the family.

In the north window at the east end of the Hall are portraits of the two founders, and a face with a grotesque nose, in painted glass. The glass of the south window is modern.

In the *Library* are busts of Lord Grenville by Nollekens, and of Pitt.

In the *Bursary* is a second picture of Joyce Frankland.

In the *Chapel* are an old copy of Spagnoletto's Entombment of Christ, a copy of Poussin's Assumption of St. Paul, and busts of the two founders, formerly in niches in the middle of the north side of the Hall outside and engraved in Spelman's *Ælfredi Magni Vita* (Oxon. 1678).

On the gateway outside is a metal gilt Nose of a grotesque type, probably derived from the painted glass in the hall.

On the entrance to the hall are two worn busts of Johannes Scotus Erigena and King Alfred.

In the *Buttery* are pictures of the Child of Hale (John Middleton, *d.* 1623, a Lancashire man distinguished for size and strength, after whom the Brasenose boat is always named), of Joyce Frankland, and of the Brasenose Boat in about 1825.

In the Principal's lodgings are pictures of Lord Mordaunt, Bp. Cleaver, and Joyce Frankland.

The *title* of the College is "the King's Hall and College of Brasenose in Oxford" (Aula Regia et Collegium de Brasenose in Oxonia), the spelling of the chief word being in chronological sequence, omitting minor variations, Brasinnose, Brazen Nose (eighteenth century), Brasenose; but the latest spelling is also found early in the seventeenth century, probably showing that it was at all times pronounced as a disyllable. The phrases *King's College* and *Collegium Regale* are also found at an early date, the latter occurring on the College seal, which consists of three Gothic niches or compartments, with St. Hugh and St. Chad on either side and the Trinity in the centre: underneath is a small shield with Smyth's arms, and round is the legend, "Sigillum commune colegii regalis de brasinnose in oxonia."

The *Arms* of the College are: The escutcheon divided into three parts paleways, the centre or, thereon an escutcheon charged with the arms of the See of *Lincoln* (gules, two lions passant gardant in pale or, on a chief azure Our Lady crowned, sitting on a tombstone issuant from the chief, in her dexter arm the Infant Jesus, in her sinister a sceptre, all or), ensigned with a mitre, all proper: the dexter side argent, a chevron sable between three roses gules seeded or barbed vert, being the arms of the founder William *Smyth*: on the sinister side the arms of Sir Richard *Sutton* of Prestbury, knight, viz. quarterly first and fourth, argent a chevron between three bugle-horns stringed sable, for *Sutton*, second and third, argent a chevron between three crosses crosslet sable, for *Southworth*.

A coat of arms tripartite paleways is a very rare phenomenon, but is found among Oxford Colleges at Lincoln and Corpus. The cause at Brasenose was no doubt an attempt to combine symmetrically on one shield the arms of the founders, the see of Lincoln being given a disproportionate amount and a central position, from the honour brought by connection with it as both the Founder's and the Visitor's see. For the sake of appearance also the arms of Lincoln are placed within the field, the mitre with which they are ensigned being included in the pale. The only variations are that (1) in some old examples the arms of Lincoln cover the whole central pale, the entire College arms being ensigned with a mitre or stringed, and sometimes with a crosier and key in saltire; (2) the crosses crosslet are found as crosses crosslet fitchy or crosses patoncé. The nearest approach to an early official declaration of the arms is to be found in Richard Lee's report from the best evidence he could obtain, made at the same time as his Visitation in 1574, and to be found in MS. H 6 of the College of Arms.

The College seems never to have had a motto, but Bishop William Smyth's ("Dominus exaltatio mea") has been occasionally and unofficially used, as in the new Principal's house.

VII. STATISTICS.

1. Principals of Brasenose Hall.

MENTIONED IN	
1435	William Long, B.A.
1436	R. Marcham or Markham, M.A.
1438	Roger Grey.
1444	R. Marcham, again.
1451	William Curth or Church, M.A., *d.* 1461.
1461	William Braggys, M.A.
1461	William Wryxham, M.A.

1462	William Braggys, again.
1462	John Molineux, again.
	In 1468 the Hall was repaired by
1469	William Sutton, M.A., who occurs also as late as 1483.
1501 1503	Edmund Croston, M.A., who died 27th Jan., 1507/8; his brass in St. Mary's church is engraved in Churton's *Lives of the Founders*.
1502 1505 1508-10	John Formby, M.A., resigned 24th Aug., 1510.
1510-12	Matthew Smyth, B.D.

2. Principals of the College.

ELECTED		
1512		Matthew Smyth.
		(*Original Fellows*: John Haster, probably first Vice-Principal, John Formby, Roland Messenger, John Legh. Shortly after: Richard Shirwood, Richard Gunston, Simon Starkey, Richard Ridge, Hugh Charnock, Ralph Bostock).
154	Fe	John Hawarden.

Date		Name
7/8	b. 27	
1564/5	Feb.	Thomas Blanchard.
1573/4	Feb. 16	Richard Harrys.
1595	Sept. 6	Alexander Nowell (Head-master of Westminster School 1543-55, Dean of St. Paul's 1560-1602).
1595	Dec. 29	Thomas Singleton.
1614	Dec. 14	Samuel Radcliffe (ejected by the Oxford Commissioners 6th Jan., 1647. Died 26 June, 1648).
1648	July 13	Thomas Yate (ejected, but reinstated 10th Aug., 1660).
1648	April 13	Daniel Greenwood (ejected Aug. 1660).
1681	May 7	John Meare.
1710	June 2	Robert Shippen (Professor of Music in Gresham College, London, 1705-11?).
1745	Dec. 10	Francis Yarborough.
1770	May 10	William Gwyn.

1770	Sept. 4	Ralph Cawley.
1777	Sept. 14	Thomas Barker.
1785	Sept. 10	William Cleaver (Bishop of Chester 1788, Bangor 1800, St. Asaph 1806-15).
1809	June 21	Frodsham Hodson.
1822	Feb. 2	Ashurst Turner Gilbert (Bishop of Chichester, 1842-70).
1842	June 9	Richard Harington.
1853	Dec. 27	Edward Hartopp Cradock.
1886	Feb. 26	Albert Watson.
1889	Oct. 1	Charles Buller Heberden.

VIII. NOTANDA.

Proverb: *Testons are gone to Oxford to study in Brazen Nose*, when Henry VIII. debased the coinage.

Census in Aug. 1552: Principal, 8 M.A.'s, 12 B.A.'s, 49 who had not taken a degree, including the steward and cook; in all 70 in residence.

Census in 1565/6: Principal, 31 graduates, 57 undergraduate scholars and commoners, 8 poor scholars, 5 matriculated servants: in all 102 names on the books.

Census in 1612: Principal, 21 Fellows, 29 scholars, 145 commoners, 17 poor scholars, 14 batellers and matriculated servants: in all 227 members in residence. Revenue £600 a year. (Principalship £80.)

Plate presented to the King, January 1642/3, by the College, 121*lb. 2oz. 15d.*

A scheme of amalgamation with Lincoln College was proposed in Oct. 1877, and on March 22, 1878, there was a meeting of both governing bodies in Brasenose Common Room; but by the end of that year the plan had come to nothing, partly owing to a vigorous pamphlet by H. E. P. Platt, Fellow of Lincoln.

XII.
CORPUS CHRISTI COLLEGE.

By T. Fowler, D.D., F.S.A., President of Corpus.

This College was founded by Richard Foxe, Bishop of Winchester and Lord Privy Seal to Kings Henry VII. and VIII., in the year 1516. For the life of Foxe, which is full of interest, and thoroughly typical of the career of a statesman-ecclesiastic of those times, I must refer the reader to my article on Richard Foxe in the *Dictionary of National Biography*.[227] Foxe had, in early life, linked his fortunes with those of Henry VII., then Earl of Richmond, while in exile in France; and, after the battle of Bosworth Field (22nd August, 1485), he became, in rapid succession, Principal Secretary of State, Lord Privy Seal, and Bishop of Exeter. He was subsequently translated to Bath and Wells (1491-2), Durham (1494), and Winchester (1501), then the wealthiest See in England. The principal event in his life (at least in its far-reaching consequences) was his negotiation, while Bishop of Durham, of the marriage between James IV. of Scotland and the Princess Margaret, eldest daughter of Henry VII., which resulted, a century later, in the permanent union of the English and Scottish crowns under James VI.

It is probable that Foxe, who, as we learn from his woodwork in the banqueting-hall of Durham Castle, had, so early as 1499, adopted, as his device, the pelican feeding her young, was early inspired with the idea of founding some important educational institution for the benefit of the Church. This idea, shortly before the foundation of his present College, had taken the shape of a house in Oxford for the reception of young monks from St. Swithin's Priory in Winchester while attending academical lectures and disputations in Oxford. There were other such houses in Oxford, such as Canterbury College, Durham College,[228] and the picturesque staircases, connected with various Benedictine monasteries, still standing in Worcester College. But his friend, Hugh Oldham, Bishop of Exeter, more prescient than himself, already foresaw the fall of the monasteries and, with them, of their academical dependencies in Oxford. "What, my Lord," Oldham is represented as saying by John Hooker, *alias* Vowell (see *Holinshed's Chronicles*), "shall we build houses and provide livelihoods for a company of bussing[229] monks, whose end and fall we ourselves may live to see; no, no, it is more meet a great deal that we should have care to provide for the increase of learning, and for such as who by their learning shall do good in the Church and commonwealth." Thus Foxe's benefaction (to which Oldham himself liberally contributed, as did also the founder's steward, William Frost, and other of his friends) took the more common form of a College for the education of the secular clergy. A site was purchased between Merton and St. Frideswide's (the monastery subsequently converted into, first, Cardinal College, and then Christ Church), the land being acquired mainly from Merton and St. Frideswide's, though a small portion was also bought from the nuns of Godstow. It has been suggested that the sale by Merton (comprising about two-thirds of the site on which Corpus now stands) was a forced one, a supposition which derives some plausibility from the fact that the alienation effectually prevented the extension of the ante-chapel of Merton College as well as from Foxe's powerful position at Court. But against this theory we may place the fact that the then Warden of Merton (Richard Rawlyns), when subsequently accused, amongst other charges, before the Visitor, of having alienated part of the homestead of the College, does not appear to have pleaded, in extenuation, any external pressure from high quarters.

Foxe induced his friend John Claymond, who, like himself, was a Lincolnshire man, to transfer himself from the Presidentship of Magdalen to that of the newly-founded College, the difference in income being made up by his presentation to the valuable Rectory of Cleeve in Gloucestershire. Robert Morwent, another Magdalen man, was made perpetual Vice-President, to which exceptional privilege was subsequently (1527-8) added that of the right of succession to the Presidency. Several of the original Fellows and scholars were also brought from Magdalen, so that Corpus was, in a certain sense, a colony from what has usually been supposed, and on strong grounds of probability, to have been Foxe's own College.

The statutes were given by the founder in the year 1517, and supplemented in 1527, the revised version being signed by him, in an extremely trembling hand, on the 13th of February, 1527-8, within eight months of his death, which occurred on the 5th of October, 1528, probably at his Castle of Wolvesey in Winchester. These statutes are of peculiar interest, both on account of the vivid picture which they bring before us of the domestic life of a mediæval college, and the provision made for instruction in the new learning introduced by the Renaissance.

The greatest novelty of the Corpus statutes is the institution of a public lecturer in Greek, who was to lecture to the entire University, and was evidently designed to be one of the principal officers of the College. This readership appears to have been the first permanent office created in either University for the purpose of giving instruction in the Greek language; though, for some years before the close of the fifteenth century, Grocyn, Linacre, and others, had taught Greek at Oxford, in a private or semi-official capacity. On Mondays, Wednesdays, and Fridays, throughout the year, the Greek reader was to give instruction in some portion of the Grammar of Theodorus or other approved Greek grammarian, together with some part of Lucian, Philostratus, or the orations of Isocrates. On Tuesdays, Thursdays, and Saturdays, throughout the year, he was to lecture in Aristophanes, Theocritus, Euripides, Sophocles, Pindar, or Hesiod, or some other of the more ancient Greek poets, with some part of Demosthenes, Thucydides, Aristotle, Theophrastus, or Plutarch. It will be noticed that there is no express mention in this list of Homer, Aeschylus, Herodotus, or Plato. Thrice a week, moreover, in vacations, he was to give private instruction in Greek grammar or rhetoric, or some Greek author, to all members of the College below the degree of Master of Arts. Lastly, all Fellows and scholars below the degree of Bachelor in Divinity, including even Masters of Arts, were bound, on pain of loss of commons, to attend the public lectures of both the Greek and Latin reader; and not only so, but to pass a satisfactory examination in them to be conducted three evenings in the week.

Similar regulations as to teaching are laid down with regard to the Professor of Humanity or Latin, whose special province it is carefully to extirpate all "barbarism" from our "bee-hive," the name by which, throughout these statutes, Foxe fondly calls his College.[230] The lectures were to begin at eight in the morning, and to be given all through the year, either in the Hall of the College, or in some public place within the University. The authors specified are Cicero, Sallust, Valerius Maximus, Suetonius, Pliny's *Natural History*, Livy, Quintilian, Virgil, Ovid, Lucan, Juvenal, Terence, and Plautus. It will be noticed that Horace and Tacitus are absent from the list.[231] Moreover, in vacations, the Professor is to lecture, three times a week, to all inmates of the College below the degree of Master of Arts, on the *Elegantiae* of Laurentius Valla, the *Attic Nights* of Aulus Gellius, the *Miscellanea* of Politian, or something of the like kind according to the discretion of the President and Seniors.

The third reader was to be a Lecturer in Theology, "the science which we have always so highly esteemed, that this our bee-hive has been constructed solely or mainly for its sake." But, even here, the spirit of the Renaissance is predominant. The Professor is to lecture every working-day throughout the year (excepting ten weeks), year by year in turn, on some portion of the Old or New Testament. The authorities for their interpretation, however, are no longer to be such mediæval authors as Nicolas de Lyra or Hugh of Vienne (more commonly called Hugo de Sancto Charo or Hugh of St. Cher), far posterior in time and inferior in learning,[232] but the holy and ancient Greek and Latin doctors, especially Jerome, Augustine, Ambrose, Origen, Hilary, Chrysostom, John of Damascus, and others of that kind. These theological lectures were to be attended by all Fellows of the College who had been assigned to the study of theology, except Doctors. No special provision seems to be made in the statutes for the theological instruction of the junior members of the College, such as the scholars, clerks, etc.; but the services in chapel would furnish a constant reminder of the principal events in Christian history and the essential doctrines of the Christian Church. The Doctors, though exempt from attendance at lectures, were, like all the other "theologians," bound to take part in the weekly theological disputations. Absence, in their case as in that of the others, was punishable by deprivation of commons, and, if persisted in, it is curious to find that the ultimate penalty was an injunction to preach a sermon, during the next Lent, at St. Peter's in the East.

In addition to attendance at the theological lectures of the public reader of their own College, "theologians," not being Doctors, were required to attend two other lectures daily: one, beginning at seven in the morning, in the School of Divinity; the other, at Magdalen, at nine. Bachelors of Arts, so far as was consistent with attendance at the public lectures in their own College, were to attend two lectures a day "in philosophy" (meaning probably, metaphysics, morals, and natural philosophy), at Magdalen, going and returning in a body; one of these courses of lectures, it may be noticed, appears from the Magdalen statutes to have been delivered at six in the morning. Undergraduates (described as "sophistae et logici") were to be lectured in logic, and assiduously practised in arguments and the solution of sophisms by one or two of the Fellows or probationers assigned for that purpose. These lecturers in logic were diligently to explain Porphyry and Aristotle, at first in Latin, afterwards in Greek. Moreover, all undergraduates, who had devoted at least six months and not more than thirty to the study of logic, were to frequent the argumentative contest in the schools ("illud gloriosum in Parviso certamen"), as often as it seemed good to the President. Even on festivals and during holiday times, they were not to be idle, but to compose verses and letters on literary subjects, to be shown up to the Professor of Humanity. They were, however, to be permitted occasional recreation in the afternoon hours, both on festival and work days, provided they had the consent of the Lecturer and Dean, and the President (or, in his absence, the Vice-President) raised no objection. Equal care was taken to prevent the Bachelors from falling into slothful habits during the vacations. Three times a week at least, during the Long Vacation, they were, each of them, to expound some astronomical or mathematical work to be assigned, from time to time, by the Dean of Philosophy, in the hall or chapel, and all Fellows and probationers of the College, not being graduates in theology, were bound to be present at the exercises. In the shorter vacations, one of them, selected by the Dean of Arts as often as he chose to enjoin the task, was to explain some poet, orator, or historian, to his fellow-bachelors and undergraduates.

Nor was attendance at the University and College lectures, together with the private instruction, examinations, and exercises connected with them, the only occupation of these hard-worked students. They were also bound, according to their various standings and faculties, to take part in or be present at frequent disputations in logic, natural philosophy, metaphysics, morals, and theology. The theological disputations, with the penalties attached to failure to take part in them, have already been noticed. The Bachelors of Arts, and, in certain cases, the "necessary regents" among the Masters (that is, those Masters of Arts who had not yet completed two years from the date of that degree), were also bound to dispute in the subjects of their faculty, namely, logic, natural philosophy, metaphysics, and morals, for at least two hours twice a week. Nor could any Fellow or scholar take his Bachelor's degree, till he had read and explained some work or portion of a work of some Latin poet, orator, or historian; or his Master's degree, till he had explained some book, or at least volume, of Greek logic or philosophy. When we add to these requirements of the College the disputations also imposed by the University, and the numerous religious offices in the chapel, we may easily perceive that, in this busy hive of literary industry, there was little leisure for the amusements which now absorb so large a portion of the student's time and thoughts. Though, when absent from the University, they were not forbidden to spend a moderate amount of time in hunting or fowling, yet, when actually in Oxford, they were restricted to games of ball in the College garden. Nor had they, like the modern student, prolonged vacations. Vacation to them was mainly a respite from University exercises; the College work, though varied in subject-matter, going on, in point of quantity, much as usual. They were allowed indeed, for a reasonable cause, to spend a portion of the vacation away from Oxford, but the whole time of absence, in the case of a Fellow, was not, in the aggregate, to exceed forty days in the year, nor in the case of a probationer or scholar, twenty days; nor were more than six members of the foundation ever to be absent at a time, except at certain periods, which we might call the depths of the vacations, when the number might reach ten. The liberal ideas of the founder are, however, shown in the provision that one Fellow or scholar at a time might have leave of absence for three years, in order to settle in Italy, or some other country, for the purposes of study. He was to retain his full allowance during absence, and, when he returned, he was to be available for the office of a Reader, when next vacant.

This society of students would consist of between fifty and sixty persons, all of whom, we must recollect, were normally bound to residence, and to take their part, each in his several degree, in the literary activity of the College, or, according to the language of the founder, "to make honey." Besides the President, there were twenty Fellows, twenty scholars (called "disciples"), two chaplains, and two clerks, who might be called the constant elements of the College. In addition to these, there might be some or even all of the three Readers, in case they were not included among the Fellows; four, or at the most six, sons of nobles or lawyers (*juris-consulti*), a kind of boarder afterwards called "gentlemen-commoners"; and some even of the servants. The last class consisted of two servants for the President (one a groom, the other a body-servant), the manciple, the butler, two cooks, the porter (who was also barber), and the clerk of accompt. It would appear from the statutes that these servants, or rather servitors, might or might not[233] pursue the studies of the College, according to their discretion; if they chose to do so, they probably proceeded to their degrees.[234] Lastly, there were two inmates of the College, who were too young to attend the lectures and disputations, but who were to be taught grammar and instructed in good authors, either within the College or at Magdalen School. These were the choristers, who were to dine and sup with the servants, and to minister in the hall and chapel; but, as they grew older, were to have a preference in the election to scholarships.

Passing to the domestic arrangements, the Fellows and scholars—there are curiously no directions with regard to the other members of the College—were to sleep two and two in a room, a Fellow and scholar together, the Fellow in a high bed, and the scholar in a truckle-bed. The Fellow was to have the supervision of the scholar who shared his room, to set him a good example, to instruct him, to admonish or punish him if he did wrong, and (if need were) to report him to the disciplinal officers of the College. The limitation of two to a room was a distinct advance on the existing practice. At the most recently founded Colleges, Magdalen and Brasenose, the number prescribed in the statutes was three or four. As no provision is made in the statutes for bed-makers, or attendants on the rooms, there can be little doubt that the beds were made and the rooms kept in order by the junior occupant, an office which, in those days when the sons of men of quality served as pages in great houses, implied no degradation.

In the hall there were two meals in the day, dinner and supper, the former probably about eleven a.m. or noon, the latter probably about five or six p.m. At what we should now call the High Table, there were to sit the President, Vice-President, and Reader in Theology, together with the Doctors and Bachelors in that faculty; but even amongst them there was a distinction, as there was an extra allowance for the dish of which the three persons highest in dignity partook, providing one of the above three officers were present. The Vice-President and Reader in Theology, one or both of them, might be displaced, at the President's discretion, by distinguished strangers. At the upper side-table, on the right, were to sit the Masters of Arts and Readers in Greek and Latin, in no prescribed order; at that on the left, the remaining Fellows, the probationers, and the chaplains. The scholars and the two clerks were to occupy the remaining tables, except the table nearest the buttery, which was to be occupied by the two bursars, the steward, and the clerk of accompt, for the purpose, probably, of superintending the service. The steward was one of the graduate-fellows appointed, from week to week, to assist the bursars in the commissariat and internal expenditure of the College. It was also his duty to superintend the waiting at the upper tables, and, indeed, it would seem as if he himself took part in it. The ordinary waiters at these tables were the President's and other College servants, the choristers, and, if necessary, the clerks; but the steward had also the power of supplementing their service from amongst the scholars. At the scholars' tables, the waiters were to be taken from amongst the scholars and clerks themselves, two a week in turn. What has been said above with regard to the absence, at that time, of any idea of degradation in rendering services in the chambers would equally apply here. Such services would then be no more regarded as degrading than is fagging in a public school now.[235] During dinner, a portion of the Bible was to be read by one of the Fellows or Scholars under the degree of Master of Arts; and, when dinner was finished, it was to be expounded by the President or by one of the Fellows (being a theologian) who was to be selected for the purpose by the President or Vice-President, under pain of a month's deprivation of commons, if he refused. While the Bible was not being read, the students were to be allowed to converse at dinner, but only in Greek or Latin, which languages were also to be employed exclusively, except to those ignorant of them or for the purposes of the College accounts, not only in the chapel and hall but in the chambers and all other places of the College. As soon as dinner or supper was over, at least after grace and the loving-cup, all the students, senior and junior, were to leave the hall. The same rule was to apply to the *bibesia*, or *biberia*, then customary in the University; which were slight refections of bread and beer,[236] in addition to the two regular meals. Exception, however, was made in favour of those festivals of Our Lord, the Blessed Virgin, and the Saints, on which it was customary to keep up the hall fire. For, on the latter occasions, after refection and potation, the Fellows and probationers might remain in the hall to sing or employ themselves in any other innocent recreations such as became clerics, or to recite and discuss poems, histories, the marvels of the world, and other such like subjects.

The services in the chapel, especially on Sundays and festivals, it need hardly be said, were numerous, and the penalties for absence severe. On non-festival days the first mass was at five in the morning, and all scholars of the College and bachelor Fellows were bound to be present from the beginning to the end, under pain of heavy punishments for absence, lateness, or inattention. There were other masses which were not equally obligatory, but the inmates of the College were, of course, obliged to keep the canonical hours. They were also charged, in conscience, to say certain private prayers on getting up in the morning or going to bed at night; as well as, once during the day, to pray for the founder and other his or their benefactors.

I have already spoken of the lectures, disputations, examinations, and private instruction, as well as of the scanty amusements, as compared with those of our own day, which were then permitted. Something, however, still remains to be said of the mode of life prescribed by the founder, and of the punishments inflicted for breach of rules. We have seen that, when the Bachelors of Arts attended the lectures at Magdalen, they were obliged to go and return in a body. Even on ordinary occasions, the Fellows, scholars, chaplains and clerks were forbidden to go outside the College, unless it were to the schools, the library, or some other College or hall, unaccompanied by some other member of the College as a "witness of their honest conversation." Undergraduates required, moreover, special leave from the Dean or Reader of Logic, the only exemption in their case being the schools. If they went into the country, for a walk or other relaxation, they must go in a company of not less than three, keep together all the time, and return together. The only weapons they were allowed to carry, except when away for their short vacations, were the bow and arrow. Whether within the University or away from it, they were strictly prohibited from wearing any but the clerical dress. Once a year, they were all to be provided, at the expense of the College, with gowns (to be worn outside their other habits) of the same colour, though of different sizes and prices according to their position in College. It may be noticed that these gowns were to be provided for the *famuli* or servants no less than for the other members of the foundation; and that, for this purpose, the servants are divided into two classes, one corresponding with the chaplains and probationary Fellows, the other with the scholars, clerks, and choristers.

Besides being subjected to the supervision of the various officers of the College, each scholar was to be assigned by the President to a tutor, namely, the same Fellow whose chamber he shared. The tutor was to have the general charge of him; expend, on his behalf, the pension which he received from the College, or any sums which came to him from other sources; watch his progress, and correct his defects.

If he were neither a graduate nor above twenty years of age, he was to be punished with stripes; otherwise, in some other manner. Corporal punishment might also be inflicted, in the case of the juniors, for various other offences, such as absence from chapel, inattention at lectures, speaking English instead of Latin or Greek; and it was probably, for the ordinary faults of undergraduates, the most common form of punishment. Other punishments—short of expulsion, which was the last resort—were confinement to the library with the task of writing out or composing something in the way of an imposition; sitting alone in the middle of hall, while the rest were dining, at a meal of dry bread and beer, or even bread and water; and lastly, the punishment, so frequently mentioned in the statutes, deprivation of commons. This punishment operated practically as a pecuniary fine, the offender having to pay for his own commons instead of receiving them free from the College. The payment had to be made to the bursars immediately, or, at latest, at the end of term. All members of the College, except the President and probably the Vice-President, were subject to this penalty, though, in case of the seniors, it was simply a fine, whereas undergraduates and Bachelors of Arts were obliged to take their commons either alone or with others similarly punished. The offenders, moreover, were compelled to write their names in a register, stating their offence and the number of days for which they were "put out of commons." Such registers still exist; but, as the names are almost exclusively those of

Bachelors and undergraduates, it is probable that the seniors, by immediate payment or otherwise, escaped this more ignominious part of the punishment. It will be noticed that rustication and gating, words so familiar to the undergraduates of the present generation, do not occur in this enumeration. Rustication, in those days, when many of the students came from such distant homes and the exercises in College were so severe, would generally have been either too heavy or too light a penalty. Gating, in our sense, could hardly exist, as the undergraduates, at least, were not free to go outside the walls, except for scholastic purposes, without special leave, and that would, doubtless, have been refused in case of any recent misconduct. Here it may be noticed that the College gates were closed in the winter months at eight, and in the summer months at nine, the keys being taken to the President to prevent further ingress or egress.

Such were the studies, and such was the discipline, of an Oxford College at the beginning of the sixteenth century; nor is there any reason to suppose that, till the troubled times of the Reformation, these stringent rules were not rigorously enforced. They admirably served the purpose to which they were adapted, the education of a learned clergy, trained to habits of study, regularity, and piety, apt at dialectical fence, and competent to press all the secular learning of the time into the service of the Church. Never since that time probably have the Universities or the Colleges so completely secured the objects at which they aimed. But first, the

Reformation; then, the Civil Wars; then, the Restoration of Charles II.; then, the Revolution of 1688; and lastly, the silent changes gradually brought about by the increasing age of the students, the increasing proportion of those destined for secular pursuits, and the growth of luxurious habits in the country at large, have left little surviving of this cunningly devised system. The aims of modern times, and the materials with which we have to deal, have necessarily become different; but we may well envy the zeal for religion and learning which animated the ancient founders, the skill with which they adapted their means to their end, and the system of instruction and discipline which converted a body of raw youths, gathered probably, to a large extent, from the College estates, into studious and accomplished ecclesiastics, combining the new learning with the ancient traditions of the ecclesiastical life.

The first President and Fellows were settled in their buildings, and put in possession of the College and its appurtenances, by the Warden of New College and the President of Magdalen, acting on behalf of the Founder, on the 4th of March, 1516-17. There were as many witnesses as filled two tables in the hall; among them being Reginald Pole (afterwards Cardinal and Archbishop of Canterbury), then a B.A. of Magdalen, and subsequently (February 14th, 1523-4) admitted, by special appointment of the Founder, Fellow of Corpus. Of the first President and Vice-President, and the large proportion of Magdalen men in the original society, mention has already been made. The first Professor of Humanity was Ludovicus Vivès, the celebrated Spanish humanist, who had previously been lecturing in the South of Italy; the first Professor of Greek expressly mentioned in the Register (not definitely appointed, however, till Jan. 2nd, 1520-21), was Edward Wotton, then a young Magdalen man, subsequently Physician to Henry VIII., and author of a once well-known book, *De Differentiis Animalium*.[237] The Professorship of Theology does not seem to have been filled up either on the original constitution of the College or at any subsequent time. It is possible that the functions of the Professor may have been performed by the Vice-President, who was *ex officio* Dean of Theology. In the very first list of admissions, however, to the new society, we find the names of Nicholas Crutcher (*i. e.* Kratzer) a Bavarian, a native of Munich, who was probably introduced into the College for the purpose of teaching Mathematics. He was astronomer to Henry VIII.; left memorials of himself in Oxford, in the shape of dials, in St. Mary's churchyard and in Corpus Garden;[238] and still survives in the fine portraits of him by Holbein. The sagacity of Foxe is singularly exemplified by his free admission of foreigners to his Readerships. While the Fellowships and scholarships were confined to certain dioceses and counties, and the only regular access to a Fellowship was through a Scholarship, the Readers might be natives of any part of England, or of Greece or Italy beyond the Po. It would seem, however, as if even this specification of countries was rather by way of exemplification than restriction, as the two first appointments, made by the founder himself, were of a Spaniard and a Bavarian.

Erasmus, writing, shortly after the settlement of the society, to John Claymond, the first President, in 1519, speaks (*Epist.*, lib. 4) of the great interest which had been taken in Foxe's foundation by Wolsey, Campeggio, and Henry VIII. himself, and predicts that the College will be ranked "inter praecipua decora Britanniae," and that its "trilinguis bibliotheca" will attract more scholars to Oxford than were formerly attracted to Rome. This language, though somewhat exaggerated, shows the great expectations formed by the promoters of the new learning of this new departure in academical institutions.

Of the subsequent history of the College, the space at my command only allows me to afford very brief glimpses.

In 1539, John Jewel (subsequently the celebrated Bishop of Salisbury) was elected from a Postmastership at Merton to a scholarship at Corpus. From the interesting life of Jewel by Laurence Humfrey (published in 1573), we gather that at the time when Jewel entered it, and for some years subsequently, Corpus was still the "bee-hive" which its founder had designed it to be. His Merton tutors, we learn, were very anxious to place him at Corpus, not only for his pecuniary, but also for his educational, advancement. The lectures, disputations, exercises, and examinations prescribed by the founder seem still to have been retained in their full vigour, though it is curious to find that the author with whom young Jewel was most familiar was Horace, whose works, as we have seen, were strangely omitted from the list of Latin books recommended in the original statutes. But that the College shared in the general decay of learning, which accompanied the religious troubles of Edward VI.'s reign, is apparent from two orations delivered by Jewel: one in 1552, in commemoration of the founder; the other probably a little earlier, a sort of declamation against Rhetoric, in his capacity of Praelector of Latin. In the latter oration, he contrasts unfavourably the present with the former state of the University, referring its degeneracy, its diminished influence, and its waning numbers, to the excessive cultivation of rhetoric, and especially of the works of Cicero, "who has extinguished the light and glory of the whole University." In the former, and apparently later, oration, he deals more specifically with the College, and admonishes its members to wash out, by their industry and application to study, the stain on their once fair name, to throw off their lethargy, to recover their ancient dignity, and to take for their watchword "Studeamus."

Jewel's words of warning and incentive to study would seem to have borne good fruit in the days of Elizabeth, though they were speedily followed by his flight, during the Marian persecution, first to Broadgates Hall (now Pembroke College), and subsequently to Germany and Switzerland, never more to return to Oxford, except in the capacity of a visitor. But, at the time of his death (1571), he was represented at his old College by one who was to be a still greater ornament of the Church of England even than himself. In the year 1567, in the fifteenth year of his age, according to Izaac Walton's account, Richard Hooker, through Jewel's kindness and with some assistance from his uncle, John Hooker of Exeter, was enabled to go up to Oxford, there to receive, on the good bishop's recommendation, a clerk's place in the gift of the President of Corpus.[239] It would be futile to extract, and presumptuous to recast, the graphic account of young Hooker's College life as delineated by his quaint and venerable biographer. From his clerkship he was elected to a scholarship, when nearly twenty years of age, and from that he passed in due course to a Fellowship, which he vacated on marriage and presentation to a living in 1584. Thus Hooker resided in Corpus about seventeen years, and must there have laid in that varied and extensive stock of knowledge and formed that sound judgment and stately style which raised him to the highest rank, not only amongst English divines, but amongst English writers. "From that garden of piety, of pleasure, of peace, and a sweet conversation," he passed "into the thorny wilderness of a busy world, into those corroding cares that attend a married priest and a country parsonage"; and, most bitter and least tolerable of all the elements in his lot, into the exacting and uncongenial society of his termagant wife. Corpus, at that time, is described by Walton as "noted for an eminent library, strict students, and remarkable scholars." Indeed, a College which, within a period of sixty years, admitted and educated John Jewel, John Reynolds, Richard Hooker, and Thomas Jackson, four of the greatest divines and most distinguished writers who have ever adorned the Church of England, might, especially in an age when theology was the most absorbing interest of the day, vie, small as it was in numbers, with the largest and most illustrious Colleges in either University.

There is another picture of college life at Corpus, during the reign of Elizabeth, less pleasing than that on which we have just been dwelling. It seems that during the reign of Edward VI. and the early part of Elizabeth's reign, possibly even to a much later period, several members of the foundation were secretly inclined to the Roman Catholic religion, or, to speak with more precision of the earlier cases, had not yet embraced the doctrines of Protestantism. It was probably with a view to accelerate the reception of the reformed faith, that, on the vacancy of the Presidentship in 1567 or 1568, Elizabeth was advised to recommend William Cole, a former Fellow of the society, who had been a refugee in Switzerland, and had there suffered considerable hardships, which do not seem to have improved his temper. The Fellows, notwithstanding the royal recommendation, elected one Robert Harrison, who had been recently removed from the College by the Visitor on account of his Romanist proclivities, "not at all taking notice," says Anthony Wood, "of the said Cole; being very unwilling to have him, his wife and children, and his Zurichian discipline introduced among them." The Queen annulled the election, but the Fellows still would not yield. Hereupon the aid of the Visitor was invoked; but, when the Bishop of Winchester came down with his retinue, he found the gate closed against him. "At length, after he had made his way in, he repaired to the chapel," where, after expelling those Fellows who were recalcitrant, he obtained the consent of the remainder. A Royal Commission was also sent down to the College the same year, which, "after a strict inquiry and examination of several persons, expelled some as Roman Catholics, curbed those that were suspected to incline that way, and gave encouragement to the Protestants. Mr. Cole," Wood[240] proceeds, "who was the first married President that Corp. Chr. Coll. ever had, being settled in his place, acted so foully by defrauding the College and bringing it into debt, that divers complaints were put up against him to the Bishop of Winchester, Visitor of that College. At length the said Bishop, in one of his quinquennial visitations, took Mr. Cole to task, and, after long discourses on both sides, the Bishop plainly told him, 'Well, well, Mr. President, seeing it is so, you and the College must part without any more ado, and therefore see that you provide for yourself.' Mr. Cole therefore, being not able to say any more, fetcht a deep sigh and said, 'What, my good Lord, must I then eat mice at Zurich again?' At which words the Bishop, being much terrified, for they worked with him more than all his former oratory had done, said no more, but bid him be at rest and deal honestly with the College." The sensible advice of the Bishop, however, was not acted on; and, whether the fault lay with the President or with the Fellows, or, as is most likely, with both, the bickerings, dissensions, and mutual recriminations between the President, and, at least, one section of the Fellows, continued during the whole of Cole's presidency, which lasted thirty years. There are some MS. letters in the British Museum, by one Simon Tripp, which give a painful idea of the bitterness of the quarrel. And Mrs. Cole seems to have added to the embroilment: "nimirum Paris cum nescio qua Italica Helena perdite omnia perturbavit" (Tripp's letter to Jewel). In 1580 there appear to have been hopes of Cole's resigning; but his Presidency did not come to an end, nor peace return to the College, till 1598, when an arrangement, much to the advantage of the College, was made, by which Dr. John Reynolds, who had been recently appointed to the Deanery of Lincoln, resigned that office, on the understanding that Cole would be appointed his successor, and that, on Cole's resignation of the Presidency, he would himself be elected by the Fellows. Cole died two years afterwards, and is buried in Lincoln cathedral. Reynolds, the most learned and distinguished President the College ever had, famous for his share in the translation of the Bible and in the Hampton Court controversy, rests in Corpus chapel.

I will now shift the scene to the year 1648, the second year of the Parliamentary Visitation. On the 22nd of May, in this year, two orders were issued by the "Committee of Lords and Commons for the

Reformation of the University of Oxford," one depriving Dr. Robert Newlyn of the Presidentship of Corpus as "guilty of high contempt and denyall of authority of parliament," the other constituting Dr. Edmund Staunton President in his stead. On the 27th of May, we read, in Anthony Wood's *Annals*, that the Visitors (who sat in Oxford, and must be distinguished from the Committee mentioned above, who sat in London) "caused a paper to be stuck on Corp. Ch. College gate to depose Dr. Newlin from being President, but the paper was soon after torn down with indignation and scorn." And again, on the 11th of July, they "went to C. C. Coll., dashed out Dr. Newlin's name from the Buttery-book, and put in that of Dr. Stanton formerly voted into the place; but their backs were no sooner turned but his name was blotted out with a pen by Will. Fulman and then torn out by Tim. Parker, scholars of that House. At the same time (if I mistake not) they[241] brake open the Treasury, but found nothing." After this audacious feat we can hardly wonder that Will. Fulman and Tim. Parker were expelled by the Visitors on the 22nd of July. Fulman (the famous and industrious antiquary, many volumes of whose researches are still preserved in the Corpus library) was restored in 1660. Corpus being one of the specially Royalist Colleges, it is not surprising to find that almost a clean sweep was made of the existing foundation, including the five principal servants.[242] Dr. Staunton, who was himself one of the Visitors, seems to have ruled the College vigorously and wisely, though, very early in his

Presidentship, there are signs of dissensions among the Fellows, due, possibly, to differences between the rival factions of Presbyterians and Independents. Any way, he knew how to maintain his authority. In the record of punishments, made in the handwriting of the culprits themselves, we find that, in 1651, four of the scholars were put out of commons "usque ad dignam emendationem," "till they had learnt to mend their ways," for sitting in the President's presence with their caps on. The discipline appears to have been almost exceptionally stringent at this time. Amongst other curious entries, we find that Edward Fowler, one of the clerks (subsequently Bishop of Gloucester), was similarly deprived of his commons for throwing bread at the opposite windows of the students of Ch. Ch. ("eo quod alumnos Aedis Christi pane projecto in tumultum provocavit"). Two scholars who had been found walking in the town, without their gowns, about ten o'clock at night, were put out of commons for a week, and ordered one to write out, in Greek, all the more notable parts of Aristotle's Ethics, the other to write out, and commit to memory, all the definitions and divisions of Burgersdyk's Logic. Another scholar, for having in his room some out-college men without leave and then joining with them in creating a disturbance, was sentenced to be kept hard at work in the library, from morning to evening prayers, for a month, a severe form of punishment which seems not to have been uncommon at this time. Under the Puritan *régime* there was certainly no danger of the retrogression of discipline.

Dr. Newlyn, with some of the ejected Fellows and scholars, returned to the College, after the Restoration, in 1660. The old President lived to be over 90, dying within a few months of the Revolution of 1688, and having been President, including the years of his expulsion, over 47 years. He is finely described in the monument to his memory, which still exists in the College Chapel, as "ob fidem regi, ecclesiae, collegio servatam annis fere XII. expulsus." But the College does not seem to have gained in learning, discipline, or quiet, by the change of government. The constant appeals to, or intervention of, the Visitor (George Morley) revealing to us, as they do, the internal dissensions of the Society itself, recall the troubled days of Cole's presidency. Nor does Newlyn himself seem to have been free from blame. His government appears to have been lax, and his nepotism, even for those days, was remarkable. During the first fourteen years after his return, no less than four Newlyns are found in the list of scholars, while, in the list of clerks and choristers (places exclusively in the gift of the President), the name Newlyn, for many years after his return, occurs more frequently than all other names taken together. It would appear as if there had been a perennial supply of sons, nephews, or grandsons, to stop the avenues of preferment to less favoured students.

It is pleasing to turn from these unsatisfactory relations among the seniors to a contemporary account[243] of his studies and his intercourse with his tutor, left by one of the scholars of this period, John

Potenger, elected to a Hampshire Scholarship in 1664. From the account of his candidature, it appears that, even then, there was an effective examination for the scholarships, though it only lasted a day and seems to have been entirely *vivâ voce*. It is curious to find Potenger largely attributing his success to his age, "being some years younger" than his rivals,[244] "a circumstance much considered by the electors." Can the well-known preference of the Corpus electors for boyish candidates in the days of Arnold and Keble, and even to a date within the memory of living members of the College, have been a tradition from the seventeenth century? It appears that the tutor was then selected by the student's friends. "I had the good fortune," says Potenger, "to be put to Mr. John Roswell" (afterwards Head Master of Eton and a great benefactor of the Corpus library), "a man eminent for learning and piety, whose care and diligence ought gratefully to be remembered by me as long as I live. I think he preserved me from ruin at my first setting out into the world. He did not only endeavour to make his pupils good scholars, but good men. He narrowly watched my conversation" (*i. e.* behaviour), "knowing I had too many acquaintance in the University that I was fond of, though they were not fit for me. Those he disliked he would not let me converse with, which I regretted much, thinking that, now I was come from school, I was to manage myself as I pleased, which occasioned many differences between us for the first two years, which ended in an entire friendship on both sides." Potenger "did not immediately enter upon logick and philosophy, but was kept for a full year to the reading of classical authors, and making of theams in prose and verse." The students still spoke Latin at dinner and supper; and consequently, at first, his "words were few." There were still disputations in the hall, requiring a knowledge of logic and philosophy; but Potenger's taste was mainly for the composition of Latin and English verse and for declamations. His poetical efforts were so successful, that his tutor gave him several books "for an encouragement." For his Bachelor's degree he had to perform not only public exercises in the schools, but private exercises in the College, a custom which survived long after this time. One of these was a reading in the College Hall upon Horace. "I opened my lectures with a speech which I thought pleased the auditors as well as myself." After taking his degree he fell into vicious habits which, though commenced in Oxford, were completed by his frequent visits to London. "Though I was so highly criminal, yet I was not so notorious as to incur the censure of the Governors of the College or the University, but for sleeping out morning prayer, for which I was frequently punished." "The two last years I stayed in the University, I was Bachelour of Arts, and I spent most of my time in reading books which were not very common, as Milton's works, Hobbs his Leviathan; but they never had the power to subvert the principles which I had received of a good Christian and a good subject." The exercises for his Master of Arts' degree he speaks of as if they were difficult and laborious.

The century which elapsed from the Restoration to the accession of George III. was, perhaps, the least distinguished and the least profitable in the history of the University. In this lack of life and distinction Corpus seems fully to have shared. With the exceptions of General Oglethorpe, the friend of Dr. Johnson, and the founder of Georgia (who matriculated as a gentleman-commoner, in 1714), and John Whitaker (the author of a History of Manchester, &c.), not a single entry of any person who subsequently attained to distinction occurs in the registers from the Restoration down to the election, as a scholar, of William Scott (afterwards Lord Stowell, the celebrated Admiralty Judge) in 1761. It may be noted too, as illustrating the moral level of these times, that the punishments, of which a record is still preserved, are no longer inflicted for the faults of boys, but for the vices of men.

At the period, however, which we have now reached, the College seems to have been recovering its pristine efficiency and reputation. Richard Lovell Edgeworth, the father of Miss Edgeworth, entered Corpus as a gentleman-commoner in 1761, his father having "prudently removed him from Dublin." "Having entered C. C. C., Oxford," he says,[245] "I applied assiduously not only to my studies under my excellent tutor, Mr. Russell" (father of Dr. Russell, the Head-master of Charterhouse), "both in prose and verse. Scarcely a day passed without my having added to my stock of knowledge some new fact or idea; and I remember with satisfaction the pleasure I then felt from the consciousness of intellectual improvement." "I had the good fortune to make acquaintance with the young men, the most distinguished at C. C. for application, abilities, and good conduct. ... I remember with gratitude that I was liked by my fellow-students, and I recollect with pleasure the delightful and profitable hours I passed at that University during three years of my life." He tells some characteristic stories of Dr. Randolph, the "indulgent president" of that time, whose "good humour made more salutary impression on the young men he governed than has ever been effected by the morose manners of any unrelenting disciplinarian." It is curious to contrast the account of Mr. Edgeworth's Corpus experiences with that given by Gibbon of his Magdalen experiences some nine or ten years before this time, or with Bentham's account of his undergraduate life at Queen's, which almost coincided with that of Mr. Edgeworth at Corpus. Something, however, may, perhaps, be set down to the difference of character and temper in the men themselves.

From Edgeworth's time to this, the College has maintained its educational efficiency and reputation; and, though with occasional changes of fortune, it has, notwithstanding its smallness, invariably taken a high rank among the educational institutions of the University. Considering the extreme smallness of its numbers at that time, the number of undergraduates varying from about sixteen to twenty, it is truly remarkable to observe the large proportion of distinguished names which occur in the lists between 1761 and 1811. They comprise, taking them in chronological order, William Scott (Lord Stowell), Richard Lovell Edgeworth, Walker King (Bishop of Rochester), Thomas Burgess (Bishop of Salisbury), Richard Laurence (Archbishop of Cashel, author of a famous course of Bampton Lectures), Charles Abbott (Lord Chief Justice of the King's Bench and Lord Tenterden), Edward Copleston (Provost of Oriel, Dean of St. Paul's, and Bishop of Llandaff), Henry Phillpotts (Bishop of Exeter), Charles James Stewart (Bishop of Quebec), Thomas Grimstone Estcourt (Burgess for the University from 1826 to 1847), William Buckland (Dean of Westminster, the famous geologist), John Keble, John Taylor Coleridge (better known as "Mr. Justice Coleridge"), and Thomas Arnold. These names, together with those previously mentioned, namely, John Claymond, Ludovicus Vivès, Edward Wotton, Nicholas Kratzer, Cardinal Pole, Bishop Jewel, John Reynolds, Richard Hooker, Thomas Jackson, William Fulman, General Oglethorpe, John Whitaker, and some others which I will immediately subjoin, may be taken as the list of distinguished men connected with or produced by Corpus, down to the time of Dr. Arnold. More recent names I refrain from adding, partly owing to the invidious nature of such a selection, partly because they can easily be supplied by those acquainted with the recent history of the University. The names already mentioned, belonging to the period from 1516 to 1811, may be supplemented by those of Nicholas Heath, Archbishop of York and Lord Chancellor to Queen Mary; William Cheadsey, third President (1558), who disputed with Peter Martyr in 1549, and with Cranmer in 1554; Robert Pursglove, last Prior of Guisborough, and subsequently Archdeacon of Nottingham and Suffragan Bishop of Hull; Nicholas Udall (or Owdall), Headmaster of Eton; Richard Pates, Bishop of Worcester; James Brookes, Bishop of Gloucester; Richard Pate, founder of the Cheltenham Grammar School; (perhaps) Nicholas Wadham, the founder of Wadham College; Miles Windsor and Brian Twyne, who, like Fulman, were famous Oxford antiquaries; Henry Parry, Bishop successively of Gloucester and Worcester; Miles Smith, Bishop of Gloucester, and one of the translators of the Bible; Sir Edwin Sandys, the pupil of Hooker, and author of the *Europæ Speculum*; the "ever-memorable" John Hales of Eton; Edward Pococke, the celebrated Oriental scholar; Daniel Fertlough, Featley, or Fairclough, a famous theological controversialist, and one of the translators of the Bible; Robert Frampton, and his successor, Edward Fowler, Bishops of Gloucester; Edward Rainbow, Bishop of Carlisle; Basil Kennett; Richard Fiddes; and John Hume, Bishop of Oxford. To these names must be added one which is, perhaps, rather notorious than distinguished, that of the unhappy James, Duke of Monmouth, the eldest natural son of Charles II. Wood tells us, in the *Fasti*, that in the plague year, 1665, when the King and Queen were in Oxford, the Duke's name was entered on the books of C. C. College. But his name does not occur in the buttery-books till the week beginning May 11, 1666, when it is inserted between the names of the President and Vice-President. Whether, after this time,[246] he ever resided in the College, or indeed in Oxford, is uncertain; but the name remains on the books till July 12th, 1683, when it was erased after the discovery of Monmouth's conspiracy and flight. The erasures are carried back as far as the week beginning June 1.

The charming account of Corpus, its studies, and its youthful society, contributed by Mr. Justice Coleridge to Stanley's *Life of Arnold*, is so well known that it hardly requires more than a passing reference; but, to complete my series of glimpses of the College at different periods of its history, it may be well to revive the recollections of the reader by a few brief extracts. "Arnold and I, as you know" (and, as we may add, the two Kebles, John and Thomas), "were undergraduates of Corpus Christi, a College very small in its numbers and humble in its buildings, but to which we and our fellow-students formed an attachment never weakened in the after course of our lives. ... We were then a small society, the members rather under the usual age, and with more than the ordinary proportion of ability and scholarship: our mode of tuition was in harmony with these circumstances; not by private lectures, but in classes of such a size as excited emulation and made us careful in the exact and neat rendering of the original, yet not so numerous as to prevent individual attention on the tutor's part, and familiar knowledge of each pupil's turn and talents. ... We were not entirely set free from the leading-strings of the school; accuracy was cared for; we were accustomed to *vivâ voce* rendering and *vivâ voce* question and answer in our lecture-room, before an audience of fellow-students whom we sufficiently respected. At the same time the additional reading, trusted to ourselves alone, prepared us for accurate private study and for our final exhibition in the schools. One result of all these circumstances was that we lived on the most familiar terms with each other; we might be—indeed we were—somewhat boyish in manner and in the liberties we took with each other: but our interest in literature—ancient and modern—and in all the stirring matters of that stirring time, was not boyish; we debated the classic and romantic question; we discussed poetry and history, logic and philosophy; or we fought over the Peninsular battles and Continental campaigns with the energy of disputants personally concerned in them. Our habits were inexpensive and temperate: one break-up party was held in the junior common-room at the end of each term, in which we indulged our genius more freely, and our merriment, to say the truth, was somewhat exuberant and noisy; but the authorities wisely forbore too strict an inquiry into this."

Soon after Arnold was elected Fellow of Oriel, in the autumn of 1815 a scholar was elected at Corpus, William Phelps, afterwards Archdeacon of Carlisle, whose published letters[247] contain abundant information about the social condition and studies of the College. Phelps did not, like Arnold, possess those intellectual and social charms which captivate undergraduate society, and it is plain that he was in restricted circumstances. But he speaks enthusiastically of the friendliness, tolerance, and good humour which pervaded the small society of undergraduates (only nine members of the foundation at that time, namely, six undergraduate scholars, the remaining scholars being then B.A.'s or M.A.'s, and three exhibitioners; besides the six gentlemen-commoners, who dined at a separate table, and shared with the Bachelors a separate common-room), and he is constantly recurring in terms of respect and appreciation, which bear evident marks of sincerity, to the friendliness, helpfulness, and competence of the two tutors, as well as to the kindly interest shown in their juniors by the other senior members of the College. The relations were those of a large and harmonious family. "There are no parties or divisions here as at other Colleges; each desires to oblige his neighbour. The Fellows are not supercilious, the scholars are respectful. There is only one establishment that rivals ours in literature, which is our neighbour Oriel."

Through the combined action of the Parliamentary Commissions of 1852 and 1877, the constitution of the College has been largely altered. By the reception of commoners, though it still remains a small College, the number of its undergraduate members has risen from about twenty to about seventy. The county restrictions have been removed from the Fellowships and scholarships, all of which are now entirely open. The number of Fellowships (from which the obligation to Holy Orders has been now removed) has been diminished, while that of the scholarships has been increased. And, in the spirit of the original intentions of the founder, a considerable proportion of the revenues has been devoted to the creation or augmentation of University Professorships. If, by the operation of these changes, the College has lost something of its unique character, it may be hoped that it has proportionately extended its sphere of usefulness.

XIII.
CHRIST CHURCH.

BY THE REV. R. ST. JOHN TYRWHITT, M.A.,
FORMERLY RHETORIC READER OF CHRIST CHURCH.

For the purposes of this volume we apprehend that the history of Christ Church, Oxford, means chiefly its academical history, which begins in 1524 with the foundation of Cardinal College by Wolsey, in the ancient Priory of St. Frideswide's. All his buildings and other works were stopped by his fall in 1529; and three years afterwards "bluff Harry broke into the spence" with his usual vigour, and refounded Cardinal College, to which he gave his own name, calling it "King Henry the Eighth his College." Then he suppressed it, and re-constituted the whole foundation, November 4th, 1546; removing the new see of Oxford (erected at Oseney in 1542) to St. Frideswide's, the then church, with the style of "The Cathedral Church of Christ in Oxford." This foundation comprised a Dean and Canons, with other capitular or diocesan officers, besides an academic staff, and probably numerous scholars of different ages. The ancient church has had a twofold character ever since. It is the Cathedral of the diocese, but it is also the College chapel; and as the Dean of Christ Church is always present, and the Bishop of Oxford very seldom, academic uses and appearances rather prevail over the ecclesiastical, in a way which may have been the reverse of satisfactory to more than one occupant of the see of Oxford.

But the connection between the Chapter and the College cannot be severed; and as Christ Church certainly would not be itself without its most ancient buildings, some account of its ecclesiastical foundations (of almost pre-historic antiquity) seems highly advisable before we attempt to chronicle it as a seat of learning.

St. Frideswide's College certainly existed from of old in Wolsey's time. Her story has passed through the hands of Philip, her third Norman prior; through William of Malmesbury's and John of Tynemouth's; and is found in Leland's *Collectanea*. It runs as follows.[248] About A.D. 727 an alderman, or *subregulus*, of the name of Didan is discovered ruling in all honour over the populous city of Mercian Oxford. He and his wife Saffrida have a daughter called Frideswide. She embraces the monastic life with twelve other maidens. Her father, at her mother's death, builds a conventual church in honour of St. Mary and All Saints, and thereof makes her prioress. The munificent kings of Mercia also build inns or halls in the vicinity.[249] This seems to anticipate even Alfred's imagined foundation of University College; and is therefore to be adhered to as dogma for the present by all members of the larger House. But Mr. Boase's remarks on the probabilities of the story are strongly in its favour.

Many days and troubles passed over St. Frideswide's Church, or its site. It was wholly or partially burnt in the massacre of Danes in 1002; also in 1015. It was rebuilt and made a "cell" or dependency of the great monastery of Abingdon. It became a house of Secular Canons, who were dispossessed after the Conquest; when a Norman church was constructed by restoration of the old Saxon one, whose foundations, however, exist and form part of the actual structure still. The present chapter-house, or rather its doorway, may have belonged to this period. It is justly celebrated as a fair specimen of Norman architecture, and is considered by several authorities to be more ancient, not only than the chapter-house itself (which, however, Sir Gilbert Scott places about the middle of the thirteenth century; see *Report*, p. 7), but than the old nave and transept walls, which are generally taken as twelfth century, if we must reject Dr. Ingram's belief in them as Ethelred's,[250] grateful as it must be to all members of the foundation. The doorway certainly bears marks of fire, which may be referred to the conflagration of 1190, when a great part of Oxford was destroyed.[251]

Ten years before, the body of St. Frideswide had been translated from its resting place to the north choir aisle, to be again (but not till one hundred and ten years after, on 10th September, 1289) removed to a new and more costly shrine in the Lady Chapel, which had been added to that aisle early in the thirteenth century, or between that and the north choir aisle.

Her first regular prior, Guimond, had been employed till his death in 1141, in the re-arrangements of monastic buildings which would be necessary on the change, at the Conquest, from Secular Canons to Regular Augustinians. Both he and his successor, Robert of Cricklade, seem to have been wise and well-meaning ecclesiastics; and a school was connected with the convent which really may be considered as the original germ of the historical University.

Robert of Cricklade spent much labour upon the present structure, tower, nave, transepts, and choir; and the works were far enough advanced in 1180, under prior Philip, for St. Frideswide's first translation. Then, we presume, the fire of 1190 gave occasion to some re-constructions, and let in Transitional Architecture, of which something has to be said here. The term "transitional" seems to mean change or progress in a style (as from the round to the pointed arch in Gothic-Romanesque), where principles and rules are adhered to; not attempts to combine incongruous styles. England is full of transitions, through Norman to Early English, to Decorated, and so on; and they seem natural, and not lawless or contradictory. But the Roman way of encrusting their own great vaults and arches with Greek lintels and pediments, constructively useless, is a different and worse thing—just as bad as the Baroque or Fancy Renaissance. Still, a mixture of pure elements is at all events a pure mixture; and in Christ Church the Romanesque, Norman, and Decorated features are all of the best. The north-east walls and turrets might remind one of the Cathedral of Mainz or of Trier; while the Chapter-house door is fine Norman, and the Early-Decorated windows excellent in their way. It was just at this time of the later twelfth and early thirteenth centuries, when Northern builders were eliminating all traces of the Greek or trabeated structure, that the new or pointed arch began to present itself, and be welcomed here and there, just for its beauty's sake. In Christ Church the arches of the nave, and other principal ones, are round, but two of the four which carry the tower are pointed; the greater supporting power of the latter form may have been already observed.

The ancient interior must have been one of considerable beauty from the twelfth to the sixteenth century, when Wolsey destroyed three bays of the west end of the nave, reducing it to one-half its original length; and probably his name must also be associated with the lowering of all the roofs. If he executed the beautiful choir-vaulting, that is no small merit to balance these destructions; but it is questioned. The curious treatment of the side arcades should be noticed; the solid pillars of the twelfth century have been ingeniously divided in their thickness; the halves facing the aisle have been left in their natural proportions, while those which face the central nave have been raised so as to embrace the triforium stage.[252]

The upper stage of the Cathedral tower with its spire, twice since rebuilt, belongs to the thirteenth century, like the chapter-house; and just within that century (1289) is a second northern aisle, built as a Lady Chapel, and containing a new shrine of St. Frideswide. The curious wooden structure at present existing is really the watching-chamber of the shrine erected in the next century, and is placed on the donor's tomb in all probability, instead of the saint's.

The large chapel, now called the Latin, and formerly the Divinity Chapel, was added in the next (fourteenth) century, to the north of the northern choir aisle, by building two more bays eastward to the north-east chapel of the thirteenth century just mentioned. This is called "the dormitory," being the burial-place of several deans and canons; the word is a simple translation of the Greek *cœmeterium*, or sleeping-place, applied to the catacombs of Rome from the second century. Windows were now altered from Norman to Decorated; three of which at the East end of the choir are again restored to their original style. In 1340 the Lady Elizabeth de Montacute gave the convent the present Christ Church meadow in order to maintain a chantry in the Lady Chapel. Her tomb is between that chapel and the other on the north-east, near a prior's (Robert de Ewelme's or Alexander de Sutton's), and near also to that of Sir George Nowers, a companion of the Black Prince.

Important alterations began towards the end of the fifteenth century: the choir clerestory was remodelled, the rich vaulting (probably) added, and various side windows altered to the Perpendicular style, which was then extending its rigid rule over England.

The great north transept window and the wooden roof of the transepts and tower (that of the nave is later) are early sixteenth-century. But at the end of the first quarter of that century (1524) came Wolsey's great scheme for Cardinal College, with its good and evil. The latter may be soon disposed of; he certainly spoilt St. Frideswide's Church by cutting off its three western bays for his great quadrangle. His intended Perpendicular Church on the north side of that quadrangle would hardly have atoned, with all its magnificence, for the destruction of the nave, which (even now, when partially restored) is an affliction to the spectator as he enters the double doors.

But from Wolsey's time the whole society became academic, as he had intended, rather than monastic, and its new architecture is henceforth secular. Unfortunately, it is not quite in that truest collegiate style, or rather scale, which is best represented by the quadrangles of Brasenose and Merton, St. John's and Wadham Colleges; but its hall, gate-tower, and library have been chief sights of Oxford from their foundation. The principal quadrangles are too extensive and public-looking to wear the old Oxford air of slight seclusion and great comfort, of a life just as monastic as you please and no more.

Wolsey's Hall[253] and Tower,[254] then, the stone kitchen, and the east, south and west sides of the great quadrangle belong to the same sixteenth century group of buildings as Magdalen Tower (1505), the Tower of St. Mary Magdalene Church at the end of Broad Street, and Brasenose Gate.

John Hygden was appointed by Wolsey the first Dean of his College. Already before the foundation of his College, and in preparation for it, Wolsey had instituted lectureships and appointed lecturers—the earliest of them in 1518, others at later dates. A few names of these may be added here. Thomas Brynknell, of Lincoln College, presided over Divinity; over Law, probably Ludovicus Vives, a Spaniard; and over Medicine, Thomas Musgrave of Merton College. Philosophy was committed to "one L. B.," apparently Laurence Barber, M.A., Fellow of All Souls. In Mathematics the Lecturer was Kraske, or Kratcher, in fact, the well-known Kratzer, maker of the Corpus sun-dial and of that on the south side of St. Mary's. The Greek lecture was held by Matthew Calphurne, a Greek. "Whether," says Wood, "William Grocyn then taught it also I know not; sure it is that he, after he had been instructed in Italy by those exquisite masters, Demetrius Chalcondila, and Angelus Politianus, read the Greek tongue several years to the Oxonians." The Rhetoric and Humanity Lecturer was John Clements of C. C. C., called "Clemens meus" by Sir Thomas More; his successor in the lecture was Thomas Lupset.

When King Henry VIII. reconstituted Wolsey's College under his own name, he reconstituted also some of these lectures of Wolsey's foundation, calling them "the King's Lectures." The King's

Lecturer in Divinity in 1535 was Richard Smyth of Merton College, who seems to have retired before the prospect of holding a disputation with Peter Martyr, who was made Canon of Christ Church in 1550. He lived to be restored to his chair in 1554; but was soon succeeded by Friar John de Villa Garcina, a young Spanish friar greatly regarded, who seems to have been the friar who tried to convert Cranmer at the last, and disappeared in 1558. Dr. Hygden was reappointed Dean by the King, but died within a few months, and was succeeded by Dr. Richard Oliver. Among the canons secular of the second foundation were Robert Wakefield, a famous Hebraist; John Leland, the learned antiquary; and Sir John Cheke, afterwards tutor to Edward VI.

The new see of Oxford remained at Oseney from 1542 to 1546; and the King transferred it to his College in Oxford by letters patent of November 4th in the latter year. He styles it in his foundation charter, "Ecclesia Christi Cathedralis Oxon ex fundatione Regis Henrici octavi;" combining the form of a Cathedral with that of an academic College. This foundation consisted of a bishop, a dean, eight canons, eight petty canons or chaplains, a gospeller and a postiller (Bible-clerk), eight singing-clerks, eight choristers and their master, a schoolmaster and usher, an organist, sixty scholars or students, and forty "children," corresponding we presume to the junior students of later days. Perhaps the children, as in later days occasionally, proved too childish; at all events the whole scholastic part of the establishment, usher and all, was soon replaced by one hundred students, who, with the one "outcomer" of the Thurston foundation,[255] are still nightly told (or tolled) by a corresponding number of strokes on "the mighty Tom," or great bell. Gates are closed all over Oxford five minutes after it is concluded.

A royal foundation by King or minister, "whose hand searches out all the land," is more likely to come in contact with history than a private one; and Christ Church was soon involved in the early troubles of the Reformation. Wolsey had done more and other things than he knew of in inviting his Cambridge scholars to Cardinal College. One may say that the first Christ Church men had true martyrs among them; certainly that they were early made to face danger and death for the faith that was in them. Anthony Dalaber's description of the scene in "Frideswide," on the arrest of Garrett and discovery of his books, as given in Froude's history, vol. ii. p. 48, *sqq.*, is not to be omitted. He had just sent forth poor Garrett from his Gloucester Hall rooms, in such lay-clothes as he possessed, only to be taken at Bristol; and went himself to Frideswide or Cardinal College (he uses both terms), "to speak with that worthy martyr of God, Master Clark," soon to perish in the hands of the Bishop of Lincoln; with the words "Crede et manducasti," when Communion was refused him at the last. Dalaber takes Corpus on his way, having "faithful brethren" there, as might have been expected in Fox's new foundation. He passes through Peckwater Inn, we presume, and through the half-finished buildings of the new quadrangle, and reaches the half-ruined Church, not yet Cathedral. "Evensong was begun," he says; "the Dean (Hygden) and the Canons were there, in their gray amices; they were almost at Magnificat before I came thither. I stood in the choir door,[256] and heard Master Taverner play, and others of the chapel there sing, with and among whom I myself was wont to sing also; but now my singing and music were turned into sighing and musing. As I there stood, in cometh Dr. Cottisford,[257] the commissary, as fast as ever he could go, bareheaded, as pale as ashes (I knew his grief well enough); and to the dean he goeth into the choir, where he was sitting in his stall, and talked with him very sorrowfully; what, I know not, but whereof I might and did truly guess. I went aside from the choir door to see and hear more. The commissary and dean came out of the choir, wonderfully troubled as it seemed. About the middle of the church met them Dr. London,[258] puffing, blustering, and blowing, like a hungry and greedy lion seeking his prey. They talked together awhile; but the commissary was much blamed by them, insomuch that he wept for sorrow."

Many men and women were to do the same for similar troubles in the years that were to follow; and the failure, as it seemed, of Wolsey's best intentions as to his College must have been one of the griefs which were now beginning to accumulate round him; acting also, as it must have acted, on the perturbed spirit of his dread master.

Christ Church was founded in suffering and danger suited to the name it bears; though as yet, to do them justice, most of the persecutors seemed to have been heartily distressed at their new duties. A generation so wofully afraid of death and privation as our own should not think too harshly of the severities of men who feared neither. The sufferings of those times have certainly left their traces on the features of many of Holbein's sitters. I remember observing this particularly in the lay portraits of his school at the late "Tudor Exhibition" in London. His faces of soldiers and country gentlemen are rather meditative than fierce; though almost always with a turn of recklessness, in reserve, as it were. They frequently express rather dubiety than doubt; as of men of conscience whom conscience might endanger.

Before passing to another crisis of history, it seems best to bring our account of the College buildings to the middle of the present century—for the later nineteenth century has done more than any other period in judicious repair and effective restoration.

In 1630, Brian Duppa being Dean, the choir suffered a sweeping restoration, when many gravestones and monuments were destroyed, and others removed to the aisles, having been duly deprived of their brasses. Some of them bore "Saxon" inscriptions (Gutch's Wood's *Colleges and Halls*, p. 462). There certainly were chapters in those days, with the average disregard for earlier dates than their own, and for the interesting heraldry of the cathedral, which extended, as Dr. Ingram says, "from the blazonry of Montacute, Monthermer, Mountfort, and Courtenay, to the pencase and inkhorn of Zouch in the north aisle of the transept." However, the Parliament would have done it if the capitular body had refrained. They might also have cut away all the tracery of the windows north and south; but they would not have filled the two-light holes thus obtained with Van Linge's queer Dutch glass, some of which was extant in our undergraduate days. Dean Duppa must have been a cultured and well-meaning man of taste in the lower English Renaissance, and he wrote a life of Michael Angelo; but we shall for life retain the impression of an immense yellow pumpkin in one of the north-west windows, illustrative of the history of Jonah, which always caught our eyes in going out of chapel, and while it lasts will preserve Duppa's name from oblivion.

The ruins of Wolsey's unfinished church seem to have been for a while something of an encumbrance to the path from Peckwater to the Cathedral; and the present way under the deanery arch is due to Dean Samuel Fell, father of Bishop (and Dean) John Fell, who made it through his garden. The way up to the Hall was then very incomplete, and he "made it as it is now, by the help of one Smith, an artificer of London;" and built the arch as it now is, besides re-edifying the cloister.

The north side of the great quadrangle was completed by Bishop Fell; and a balustrade was substituted on the roof for the original battlements, possibly for the purpose of lecturing from the housetop, a course which, however, has not been pursued in recent times. Tom Tower was finished by Wren in 1682; Tom himself (the bell) having been recast by Christopher Hodson in 1680. He, or his original metal, was once the old clock bell of Oseney Abbey.[259]

The original grant of Peckwater Inn to St. Frideswide's is as early as Henry III.'s time. Dean Aldrich and Dr. Anthony Radcliffe are answerable for the present structure, which contains seventy-two sets of rooms and a canon's lodgings. Dr. Radcliffe also gave a statue "Mercury" to adorn the central fountain in the great quadrangle, which had originally issued from a sphere, as seen in old prints. Long ago, before the Reformation, there is said to have been a cross in the place now occupied by the fountain, with a pulpit, from which Wycliffe may have frequently preached. The base of this cross is preserved in the gallery at the end of the S. Transept.

The common-room under the hall, was fitted up by Dr. Busby, whose bust in marble long adorned it, but is now transferred to the library. This bust is a work of merit, with a countenance unlikely to spare for anybody's crying. The room is panelled with oak, and contains a Nineveh tablet presented by Hormuzd Rassam, Esq.

What is called the Old Library was once the Refectory of St. Frideswide's convent. A few books remain in charge of the Margaret Professor. The large Library in Peckwater was begun in 1716, but not finally completed till 1761. The original intention was to leave an open piazza beneath it, but the space was required for its books and collections, and its massive columns were accordingly connected by a wall. Its gallery of pictures (or the bulk of the collection) was the gift of Brigadier-General Guise in 1765, and of the Hon. W. F. Fox-Strangeways in 1828.

Canterbury Gate was built by Wyatt in 1778; and we presume that the laws of gravity and attraction will continue to apply to it as to other objects, so that it may reasonably be expected to remain there till it is taken away. QVOD BENE VORTAT, as the Bodleian motto, with pantheistic piety, observes.

It only remains to say, that the present Meadow buildings occupy the position of the Chaplains' quadrangle and Fell's buildings, or "the garden staircase" of other days, up to 1863. Their gate-tower is not admired; otherwise they are a solid and beautiful building in quasi-Italian Gothic. Their quadrangle is bounded on the north by the old library, on the south by the meadow, on the east by the Margaret Professor's garden, and on the west by the vast and venerable kitchen, with its time-honoured gridiron, happily employed in culinary labours only, and never (so far as we know) for purposes of persecution. The kitchen was said to be the first-completed of all Wolsey's buildings, greatly to the amusement of the outer world of Oxford. This recognition of the dependence of the spirit on the body was ingeniously defended by the Rev. M.

Creighton[260] in a well-remembered University sermon.

Christ Church has naturally had from the first its share of pageant and festivity. Henry VIII. took his pastime therein in 1533 with grandeur and jollity. There were public declamations of the whole University here under Edward VI.; and plays were acted in the hall before Queen Elizabeth in 1566 and 1592, and before James I. in 1605 and 1621; and again before Charles I. in 1636. It is a question whether scenery and stage-mechanism were used for the first time in England, says Anthony à Wood, on this occasion, or as early as the festivity of 1605. All are gone by this time who could remember the visit of the allied sovereigns in 1814, and their entertainment in the Hall by the Prince Regent, on whom the title of "the first gentleman in Europe" then sat very gracefully. Old General Blücher, as best regarded of all foreign soldiers present, had to acknowledge his honours in German, and the Prince translated him with freedom and elegance, only omitting his own praises.

Four years after Charles I.'s entertainment, were to develop the full bitterness of evil days already begun. On August 18th, 1642, came the first Cavalier muster; three hundred and fifty and more of "privileged" University men and their servants, and also many scholars. They met at the Schools and marched by High Street to Christ Church, "where in the great quadrangle they were reasonably instructed in the word of command and their postures;" and this mustering and drilling continued more or less till the end of all things by surrender on St. John's Day, 1646. Some considerable part of the corps were bowmen volunteers (about 1200, it is said further on), duly armed with "barbed arrows." By that time, out of the one hundred and one students of Christ Church twenty were officers in the King's army; the rest, almost to a man, were either there, or formed part of the Oxford garrison. And so of commoners in full proportion. All plate and available money were gone, and the House as much damaged, not to say demoralized, as the rest of the University.

Lord Say had at first occupied Oxford with a Parliamentary force for a few days, and carried away much plate from Christ Church, particularly all Dr. Samuel Fell's (the Dean's). Iconoclasm began with his zealous followers, not quite to his satisfaction, as it included a precious statue of the King at New College. This was September 19th. On October 29th, just after Edgehill, the King occupied Oxford, keeping his Court in Christ Church with Prince Charles as long as he remained.

Another ominous vespers in Christ Church Cathedral, besides Anthony Dalaber's, is on record. On Friday, February 3rd, 1643-4, his Majesty appointed a thanksgiving to be made at Evening Prayer at Christ Church for the taking of Cirencester by Prince Rupert the day before. The doctors were in their red robes; and polished breast-plates and laced buff-coats must have had a brilliant effect under the massive white arches. "But there was no new Form of Thanksgiving said, save only that Form for the victory of Edgehill, and a very solemn anthem, with this several times repeated therein—'Thou shalt set a Crown of pure gold upon his Head, and upon his Head shall his Crown flourish.'"

The scarlet gowns appeared again to welcome the Queen at Tom Gate on July 13th, 1644. There was a fair show of state in the way of trumpets, heralds, and the like; and "Garter, coming last, was accompanied by the Mayor of Oxon in his scarlet and mace on his shoulder." But Naseby field ended all pageant and hope alike in July 1645, just after Fairfax's siege of fifteen days on the Headington Hill side without result. The next two years must have been a miserable time.

In April 1648, at the "visitation" by the Parliamentary Visitors, the Dean of Christ Church (Dr. Samuel Fell) being in custody in London, Mrs. Fell and her children, with certain ladies, elected to be carried out of the Deanery rather than walk out, and were deposited in the quadrangle in feminine protest against extrusion. Her husband's name was scored out of the Buttery-Book, with those of seven Canons, the eighth (Dr. Robert Sanderson) being respited during absence; and Dr. Edward Reynolds was substituted, with a new set of Canons. A clean sweep was at the same time made of all "malignant" members, hardly any taking the Parliamentary Oath or the Solemn League and Covenant. In January 1647-8 the Latin version of the Common Prayer, and the Common Prayer itself, ceased in Christ Church.

It was maintained by three Christ Church men—John Fell, Richard Allestree, and John Dolben—till the Restoration, in a house in Merton Street, and seems to have escaped interference.

A less dire debate than the Parliamentary War was the celebrated controversy with Bentley on *The Epistles of Phalaris* in 1695. It deserves notice in a chapter on Christ Church.

The Hon. Charles Boyle, afterwards second Earl of Orrery, is wickedly described by Bentley as "the young gentleman of great hopes, whose name is set to the new edition" of *Phalaris*; and, as Boyle was but nineteen years of age at the time of publication, it may be considered certain that he received very material assistance from Dr. Atterbury, Dr. Friend, and from the admired Dean Aldrich. Perhaps all four had a very different idea of accurate criticism from that style of it which Bentley initiated in England, and which now seems somewhat overpowered by the burden of its research. The celebrated answer to Bentley's *Dissertation*, published under Boyle's name in 1689, was really a joint production of the leading Christ Church men, and Atterbury claimed a principal share. Between them they made a good fight for it; but it is difficult for any set of men, however learned, ingenious, and petulantly witty, to maintain a long controversy at the stress of being wholly wrong. Unquestionably it was premature in Aldrich to set young noblemen in their teens to publish editions of writers believed to have been contemporary with Pythagoras or thereabouts.

Nevertheless such critical work as they could do would probably teach them something more than a dilettante knowledge of language: and this the Dean evidently understood to be a chief want of his time. Boyle was no match for Bentley; but he came to be an accomplished and gallant gentleman who never through a stirring life forsook the love of learning, or of his old abode of learning—perhaps rather, of literature. He could see the vast shapes of the natural sciences advancing with new wonders; and was the benefactor of George Graham, who named his great planetary instrument after his title. His gifts to the Christ Church Library should be commemorated; and he is one instance out of a great number of men who have made Christ Church to themselves a home of friends, and so from their Alma Mater forward have faced the world together.

Aldrich could not work miracles of discipline or reform the manners of the Restoration. He has been blamed for allowing too much license to pupils of high degree, and because he failed to correct the habits of intemperance in which many of them had been educated. It may have been so; and he must suffer with all tutors. The very name connotes a false position, and a most difficult duty; to find means to persuade without any power to control, and to reduce untamed lads to order who have never seen it before. Military service was the only alternative method in that day, where they regulated each other's folly by the duello, or at all events might be referred to the provost-marshal. But Aldrich had to do what he could by the way of letters and culture; to try to awaken the higher instincts, the better ambitions, and natural virtues; since every religious restraint was scouted as Puritanism and every devout aspiration as Popery. He had to contend with a most dissipated and drunken age, whose coarse and direct temptations had already a hold on his charge; nor is it easy to see how he could cure what St. John, Pulteney, Carteret, and the rest had learned in evil homes and schools. The morale of the aristocracy was still that of a beaten army; nor was the public's much better.

Aldrich's many accomplishments have left varied traces behind them. "The merry Christ Church Bells," the celebrated catch, is a living remembrance of him, happier than most men leave; Peckwater Quadrangle would be stately and handsome enough, but for the leprous Headington stone; he must have had the Themistoclean power of doing just what was wanted at the time. But his achievement was after all the Oxford Logic. Till twenty years ago, most tutors found that all its shortcomings led straight to explanations. It was like the noble and kindly conservatism of Mansel, to spend his great learning on the notes and prolegomena which have developed the good old manual into a valuable treatise on Logic and Psychology.

The name of Cyril Jackson marks a period of twenty-six years from 1783-1809, which may be compared to Aldrich's best days with better discipline. His life marks a restoration of order and efficiency in Christ Church which has never been lost, and he chose to have no other monument. He was wedded to his House, and it was enough for one lifetime to make her love and obey him as he did. His statue and picture give the idea of clearness, courage, and benevolence. The straightforward face is unconsciously commanding, and seems made to judge of a man. There is a dignity of presence; but Christ Church never was yet governed by deportment only, and there must have been much more than that about the great Dean who would be nothing more than Dean. *Spartam nactus est, hanc exornabat*: and Jackson's discipline, if not Spartan, was perfectly real. He did not invent new rules; but worked the old ones with a just and determined spirit, using "all the advantages which a capacious mind, an enlarged knowledge of the world, a spirit of command or guidance, and an unconquerable perseverance, could confer." I have heard old country gentlemen speak of Jackson, still seeming to delight in him as a beloved person whom it was natural to obey, and as a leader of men sure to lead right.

Jackson's daily system of work has only of late been changed to suit the needs of continual examinations. The terminal "Collections" or Examinations from his time to the end of Dean Gaisford's, were intended to supply the want of general University Examinations before their regular institution; and many have thought that the pass-work for a Degree had better be done in College, since the College presents the candidate. The weekly themes and Latin verses in the Hall are gone; but the

Bachelors' prizes for Latin prose; the Undergraduates' for hexameters; the public lectures in logic, grammar, and mathematics; the Censor's annual address to the whole House, were in full force thirty years ago.

One more curious tradition remains of his subtle influence—that all the handwriting of the leading Christ Church Dons of the last generation is imitated from their chief's; with great difference of character, but strong relation to his thoroughly-formed letters, to the graceful unhurried hand that everybody can read easily. This has been said of Dean Gaisford and many Censors of earlier days; Osborne Gordon's writing, though, has a freedom of its own.

Perhaps the chief secret of Cyril Jackson's success was that he did his work so much himself; and yet was always Dean. He would have order in College; and he had a regular police to enforce it, and attended to it himself. He entertained his undergraduates daily, seven or eight at a time, all round. He lectured and taught personally in Greek, logic, and composition, sometimes in mathematics. He tried to understand and make the acquaintance of every youth in the House; and like St. Paul, he was all desire to impart any excellent gift. When he felt his strength failing in his work, he gave it up. He had refused bishoprics and an archbishopric; he bade farewell to Christ Church and the world in love unfeigned, and turned his spirit wholly to God whom he desired, and so died full of years and honours; nor can we anywhere find a word about him that is not in his praise. Dr. Parr, who professed a not ill-natured hostility to "the Æde-Christians," forgets it heartily and with handsome language when he speaks of the Dean (see *Notes to Spital Sermon*, published 1800)—"Long have I thought and often have I said that the highest station in an ecclesiastical establishment would not be more than an adequate recompense for the person who presides over this College." It is worthily said; but if the notes are as sonorous as this, what must be the rumble of the text?

Dean Gaisford, as we have said, continued Jackson's educational method ably and faithfully; and his view that pass-work should be done entirely in College, and Colleges be made responsible for it, may well find advocates now. All men respected the stout old scholar, and had in most things to own the shrewdness, and particularly the justice, of his judgment. The piquancy of many anecdotes and sketches of him has departed with the generation who honoured him as the first Greek scholar of England in his time. He too felt his high position sufficient, and had real happiness in efficient discharge of its duties, which were thoroughly well suited to him; and he had perhaps a better understanding of the nature and ways of his undergraduates than many younger and less outwardly formidable seniors.

Two more great names, as of a father and son, so faithfully did the younger reflect the mind and second the purposes of the elder, must of right find mention here;—not due honour, since that would involve the whole history of the Oxford Movement, both earlier and later. It is hoped that the late Dr. Liddon's Life of Dr. Pusey is so far advanced, or its material is so well ordered and prepared, that it may soon appear—as a monument to two great English Doctors. The elder entered at Christ Church in 1819, and returned as Canon in 1828, after having been Fellow of Oriel College; the younger matriculated at the House in 1846. Dr. Barnes, then Sub-Dean, made Henry Parry Liddon Student in 1846. From thenceforth Pusey had one near him like-minded: not in the obsequious mimicry of imitation which has produced so many pseudo-Newmans, but in true following of one Master, in intelligent apprehension of and devotion to the principles of the Catholic Church of England, and in self-denying holiness of life. Many friendships for life date from Christ Church, but this has excelled them all: and these two rest from their labours.

Some brief account of the latest buildings and restorations, on which the fine taste of Dean Liddell has left its mark, seems desirable here. The new buildings, before-mentioned (p. 309), are by Mr. Thomas Deane, son of Sir T. N. Deane. They consist of six staircases, containing forty-three sets of students' chambers of three rooms each, and ten chaplains' or tutors' rooms of four apartments and upwards. The front towards the Meadow is partly masked by the trees of the old Broad Walk (planted by Dean Fell in Feb. 1670) and the other avenue to the river. The roof is continuous on the meadow front, but there are gables towards the quadrangle. The roof-supports rest on corbels, and the beam-ends are free. The whole is 331 feet long and 37 deep. The stone walls are carried through to the roof between the staircases and lined with brickwork. The style is a variety of Italian Gothic, massively built, story upon story, with good pointed arches, but not in any Northern or regularly "arcuated" style. But the ornament is all beautiful flower-work, and by the artist-workmen whom Messrs. Woodward and Dean gathered round them, whom Prof. Ruskin himself educated in the then Working-Man's College. In as far as that teaching has succeeded, a share of the honour is due to Christ Church, through that son of hers who has done her highest and most honour in the literature of the century, and whose name will for ever be a call to all artists who love honour and their work.[261]

A recent Oxford Almanac represents the Interior of the Cathedral as it appeared in 1876, before the new woodwork of the Choir and the Reredos. Both were needed, and both are beautiful in their way; but the reredos has the fault or misfortune of the new one in St. Paul's, London—nothing can make it look like part of the structure. The rich depth of tint and carven gloom are fine. Still the general effect of the Cathedral, with its bright windows and warm stone-tints, is rather one of lightness and pleasant colour, like pages of a Missal, as Ruskin says of St. Mark's. The new glass by Morris and Faulkner, after Burne Jones, is decidedly beyond any praise we have room to give it here: the great North Transept window glows with all the fires which a fervid fancy can bestow on the inwards of the Dragon. Clayton and Bell's windows are beautiful in crimson and white; and all we can say of Jonah's dear old gourd is that we hope its shadow may now never be less.

There are some works of art of considerable interest in the Library, amidst a number of no particular value. On the right of the door, the Nativity of Titian was certainly a part of Charles I.'s collection, and is probably an original, though it reminds one of Bonifazio. There is a portrait of A. Vezale by Tintoret; and a small head attributed to Holbein, of the greatest beauty. We cannot feel sure about the John Bellini Madonna; but the Piero della Francesca Madonna with Angels is beautiful and interesting. There are four very authentic Mantegnas, one of which (No. 59, Christ bearing the Cross) certainly belonged to Charles I. The possible Giorgione of Diana and her Nymphs is worth attention; and there is a genuine-looking Veronese, with his beautiful striped silk drapery, of the Marriage of St. Catherine. Two good portraits and the unfinished man-at-arms by Vandyke, with the admirable brush-work in white on the horse, are in the east room on the other side of the great door, and complete our list of the more modern pictures.

The more ancient Italian schools, from the semi-Byzantine Margheritone to Taddeo Gaddi and the Giotteschi, are well represented at the western end of the lower floor of the Library. Margheritone is said, in the notes to Mrs. Browning's *Casa Guidi*

Windows, to have died of disgust ("infastidito") at the successes of the new, Italian or Cimabue, school; and she remarks that

"Strong Cimabue bore up well
Against Giotto."

It is most satisfactory to have original works by all these three. The Margheritone is a thoroughly Byzantine saint, with a gold background and an expression certainly best characterized by the word "infastidito." Next comes the Cimabue triptych: its central Madonna has some resemblance to the Borgo Allegri picture on a small scale. The Giottos show some such advance of art in his hands as Dante described. There is an apparently genuine Filippo Lippi, which must be of no small value.

The drawings are most beautiful. The small Lionardo head and the large Madonna are unmistakable and beyond praise, and may be contrasted with a singularly beautiful head which displays his taste for "monsters," and the portrait of Ludovico Sforza is excellent. There are two drawings by Masaccio, and the Titian Landscapes are capital. The visitor should not miss the red chalk head attributed to Gentile Bellini, we suppose rightly: it is hard to say who else, except his son, could have done it.

To give an account of the portraits in the Hall would set us adrift on general history. Locke and the Marquis of Wellesley, the two Sir Joshua bishops, Cyril Jackson looking forth at a world he knew the worth of, Wolsey and Henry VIII.—founders, crowned heads, members of the foundation—survey the College dinner like guests departed. They are forgotten, or their remembrance is like his that tarrieth but a day.

Note on the Date of the Cathedral.

Mr. J. Park Harrison has most kindly enabled me to give his conclusions on the dates of the cathedral in his own words. Having inspected the building with him, I entirely adhere to them. I think they are fully borne out by the remains of the old building, and scarcely to be got over when one has seen the joints and ornamentation inside, and the foundations without.

1. "The commonly-assigned date of the cathedral, 1160-1180, is absolutely incorrect.

2. "The late Norman work, attributed with much probability to Prior Robert of Cricklade, is an addition to the old church restored by Guimond in the earlier part of the twelfth century.

3. "There is no document, or anything tending to show that the original fabric, as restored by Ethelred, was ever rebuilt on a new plan.

4. "Several of the choir capitals differ essentially in their ornamentation from any others in the cathedral; but resemble very closely the ornamental work in illuminated MSS. of Ethelred's time. They[262] should consequently belong to the church as enlarged by him in 1004.

5. "The east wall of the 'ecclesiola' built by Didanus in the eighth century still exists, with two arches once communicating with apses, whose foundations have been discovered about two feet below the ground, with a third midway between them."

The junction of the eleventh century, or Ethelred's, work with the twelfth century, or Norman, is clearly visible at the north and south-west corners of the choir, and the abaci though resembling each other are of different thickness. The ashlar work is different, and the courses are not continuous.

XIV.
TRINITY COLLEGE.

BY THE REV. HERBERT E. D. BLAKISTON, M.A.,
FELLOW OF TRINITY.

"The College of the Holy and Undivided Trinity in the University of Oxford of the Foundation of Sir Thomas Pope, Knt., commonly called Trinity College," is one of the first instances of the attempt to endow learning out of the funds thrown into private hands by the suppression of the monasteries. It was founded during the period of reaction, and its statutes may be characterised as transitional. Its numbers and endowments have never entitled it to rank with the larger foundations, but the vigorous character of various members of the College has saved it from obscurity. It has some mediæval associations, through its informal connexion with the older Durham College, on the vacant site of which it was established: for some years Trinity drew on the same counties, still preserves in part the old buildings, and has lately supplied several officers to the modern University of Durham. A short sketch of the history of Durham College should properly precede that of Trinity.

DURHAM COLLEGE was originally a hall for the accommodation of students from Durham Abbey who had come to Oxford to obtain better teaching than they could find in the cloister, even before the Benedictine Constitutions of 1337, which provided that each convent should maintain at some place of higher study one in twenty of their numbers. Monastic authorities did not like the young monks to live in lodgings with the secular students, and they were originally sent in the case of Cistercians to Rewley, and of Augustinians to St. Frideswide's. The Benedictines had houses at Reading and Abingdon, but none at Oxford; and when Walter of Merton invented the collegiate system, the Benedictines of Gloucester imitated him by the foundation of Gloucester College in 1283, which was enlarged by hostels, built after a general chapter at Abingdon, for such influential abbeys as Norwich, Glastonbury, and St. Alban's; but the rich society at Durham, probably from the traditional hostility between North and South, stood aloof; while Canterbury established a separate "nursery" in 1363, and Croyland and others sent their students to Cambridge, and eventually founded Buckingham College, now Magdalene.

The Durham chronicler says that Hugh of Darlington (Prior of Durham 1258-72 and 1285-89) hated Richard of Houghton, who was a young man of grace, and therefore sent the monks to study at Oxford, "et eis satis laute impensas ministrabat." Richard, sometime Prior of Lytham, may have been the "master of the novices"; he became Prior in 1289, and obtained leave to build on a site between Horsemonger Street or Canditch (Broad St.) and the King's Highway of Beaumont (Park St.), already acquired from St. Frideswide's, Godstow, and other grantors. Of the original buildings, presumably unmethodical in plan, some remains may survive in the lower part of the hall, and the adjoining buttery and bursary. A chapel was contemplated in 1326, but not erected till a century later; the present common-room may have been used as an oratory meanwhile.

There was no endowment at first, but the Convent maintained six to ten monks as early as 1300; in 1309 they sent the second of two gifts or loans of books; a John of Beverley is called "Prior Oxoniae" in 1333. In a deed of 1338, Edward III. announces that, in fulfilment of a vow made at Halidon Hill to God and St. Margaret, he surrenders to Richard of Bury, Bishop of Durham, the valuable rectory of Symondburne (the title to which they were then disputing) to endow a prior and twelve monks from Durham on the site in the suburbs of Oxford, with a church and lodgings to be erected at his expense; but this plan of endowment was never carried out.

The Bishop, however, did not forget his project, and left to the College at his death the library, immense for the time, which his position as courtier, prelate, ambassador, and Chancellor had enabled him to amass, till he had more books, in his bedroom and elsewhere, "than all the bishops in England had then in their keeping." His intention is recorded in the famous *Philobiblon*. It has been stated that the collection was sold by the Bishop's executors to pay his debts; but besides indirect evidence, there is the statement of Dr. T. Cay (Master of University 1561) that he saw *in bibliotheca Aungervilliana* a MS. of the treatise, supposed to be the autograph. The

Library retains in its windows the arms of the older society and its benefactors, and effigies of the saints of the Order, etc.; but the books, with Bishop Langley's *Augustine on the Psalms* in three vols., and other additions, disappeared at the Reformation. They cannot be traced to Balliol or Duke Humphrey's library; so perhaps they were among the purchases made by Archbishop Parker from Dr. G. Owen, or they may have been secured for the Durham Chapter by the first Dean and the first senior Canon, previously Prior of Durham and Warden of the College in Oxford respectively.

The next Bishop, Thomas of Hatfield, a secular clerk of good family, great military capacity (he was one of the commanders at Nevill's Cross) and architectural taste, and tutor to the Black Prince, was stimulated by the examples of Islip (Canterbury College) and Wykeham to endow the Durham Hall permanently; his charter still exists in the form of a contract with the prior and convent, executed in 1380. Four trustees (including William Walworth Lord Mayor, and Master Uthred a monk of Durham, who was soon afterwards tried for heresy) will furnish money to purchase property worth two hundred marks a year, to maintain a warden and seven other student monks, under rules closely resembling those of a Benedictine cell, and also (which is a new departure) eight secular students in Grammar and Philosophy at five marks each, from Durham and North Yorkshire, on the nomination of the prior, who are to dine and sleep apart from the monks, and perform any *honesta ministeria* that do not interfere with their studies. These are under no obligation to take orders or vows; but must take an oath to further the interests of the Church of Durham.

No buildings are mentioned, but probably the north and east sides of the original quadrangle containing library, warden's lodging, and rooms, had been built *c.* 1350. Hatfield died in 1381; the convent purchased from John Lord Nevill of Raby and appropriated the churches of Frampton (Linc.), Fishlake and Bossall (Yorks), and Roddington (Notts), giving for them £1080 and two other churches. The revenue was two hundred and sixty marks. Many of the bursarial rolls sent to Durham between 1399 and 1496 are preserved there. But the income soon declined; and even after the convent had added the church of Brantingham, there was generally a deficit.

Little further is known: Bishops Skirlaw and Langley left legacies, as did probably members of the families of Mortimer, Nevill, Kemp, Grey, Arundell, and Vernon. Several Wardens became Priors of Durham: Gilbert Kymer, physician to Duke Humphrey, and ten years Chancellor of the University, lived in the College. The Priors regulated the College from time to time; in a letter of 1467 some strong language is addressed to a fellow who had indulged in riotous living till "vix superest operimentum corporis et grabati."

The College, though in part a secular foundation, fell with the Abbey, surrendered by Hugh Whitehead in 1540. In Henry VIII.'s valuation its income was £115 4*s.*4*d.* (warden £22, fellows £8, scholars 4 marks, each), and it owned a sanatorium at Handborough. Out of the estates confiscated a school was endowed, as well as the Durham Chapter; a larger scheme which provided for branches at Oxford and Cambridge fell through. In 1545 the site of the College reverted to the Crown; the part occupied by the Cistercian Bernard College passed to Christ Church, and is now part of St. John's College garden. In 1553, W. Martyn and George Owen, physician to Henry VIII. and his successors, and the grantee of Godstow nunnery, received the rest of the "backside" with the buildings, which were by that time mere *canilia lustra* (dog-kennels), though they had been used by Dr. W. Wright, Archdeacon of Oxford, Vice-Chancellor 1547-9, as a private hall. The site was then sold to Sir T. Pope, Owen transferring to his own estates a quit-rent of 26*s.* 2*d.* due to the Crown. In 1622, Trinity had to pay some arrears of this, which they recovered from Owen's heirs, and settled the matter by the aid of Sir George Calvert, a Trinity man, then Secretary of State.

SIR THOMAS POPE appears to have belonged to the class of Tudor statesmen of which More, Fisher, and Wolsey are representative, who, while personally attached to the traditional ideas in religious matters, did not oppose all reform; and were anxious that the revival of learning should be assisted by part at least of the funds justly taken from the monasteries, according to the precedent set by Wykeham,

Chichele, and Waynflete. He was born *c.* 1508, at Deddington, and was the eldest son of a small landowner. After being educated at Banbury and Eton, he studied law with success. He held various offices in the Star-Chamber, Chancery, and the Mint, from 1533 to 1536, in which year he became Treasurer of the new and important Court of Augmentations, which dealt with monastic property. After five years he was succeeded by Sir Edward North, in whose family his own was merged in the next century. He obtained a grant of the arms still borne by his College; and was knighted in 1536 with the poet-Earl of Surrey. In 1546 he became Master of the Woods, etc. South of Trent, and was a privy councillor. He did not personally receive the surrender of any religious house except St. Alban's, where he saved the abbey church; but he probably had exceptional opportunities of acquiring abbey lands. The Abbess of Godstow, where his sister was a nun, claims his protection in some letters still extant. Among his intimate friends were Sir Thomas More, Lord Chancellor Audley, Sir Nicholas Bacon, Sir Thomas Whyte, Lord Williams of Thame, Bishop Whyte of Winchester, and many of the moderate party of the Humanists.

Under Edward VI. he withdrew from public life; but Mary recalled him to the Privy Council, and employed him on commissions connected with the Tower, Wyat's rebellion, Gresham's accounts, the suppression of heresy, etc. In 1555 he had to take charge of the Princess Elizabeth at Hatfield, and managed to treat her kindly without incurring suspicion. Elizabeth took an interest in his project; he writes that "the princess Elizabeth her grace, whom I serve here, often askyth me about the course I have devysed for my scollers: and that part of mine estatutes respectinge studies I have shown to her, which she likes well." Again, when two of the junior fellows had broken the statute "de muris noctu non scandendis," he says "they must openly in the hall before all the felowes and scolers of the collegge, confesse their faulte: and besides paye such fyne, as you shall thynke meete, whiche being done, I will the same be recorded yn some boke; wherein I will have mencion mayde that for this faulte they were clene expelled the Coll. and at my ladye Elizabeth her graces desier and at my wiffes request they were receyved into the house agayne." He soon retired from public life, and died probably of a pestilence then epidemic, on January 29th, 1558/9, in the Priory of Clerkenwell, his favourite residence. He was buried at St. Stephen's Walbrook, with his second wife, Margaret (widow of Sir Ralph Dodmer, Lord Mayor 1529) and his only child; in 1567 his third wife Elizabeth Blount (of Blount's Hall, Staffs.), widow of Anthony Beresford, removed the bodies to a vault beneath the fine tomb with alabaster effigies of her husband and herself, which she erected in Trinity chapel. A contemporary writer records the magnificence of the funeral, "and aftyr to the playse to drynke with spyse-brede and wyne. And the morow masse iii songes, with ii pryke songes, and the iii of Requiem, with the clarkes of London. And after, he was beried: and that done, to the playse to dener; for ther was a grett dener, and plenty of all thynges, and a grett doll of money." In a will, dated 1556, besides large sums to the poor, prisoners, and churches, he bequeaths money for specified purposes to Trinity with a quantity of plate, rings and various articles to his friends, *e. g.* his "dragon-whistle," and his "black satten gowne with luserne-spots" (both seen in his portraits) to Sir N. Bacon and "Master Croke, my old master's son," considerable legacies to his relations, and the residue of his goods to his wife. His estates had been already settled; Tyttenhanger (Herts.), the country house of the abbots of St. Alban's, went to the widow for life, afterwards to her nephew Sir Thomas Pope-Blount (whose mother was Frances Love, daughter of Alice Pope), and eventually through an heiress to the Earls of Hardwicke; his brother John Pope received estates in north-west Oxfordshire, but preferred to settle at Wroxton Abbey, which he and his descendants, the Earls of Downe, and their representatives, the Lords North and Earls of Guildford, have since held on long leases from the College; other estates passed to his widow, his uncle John Edmondes, and his nephew Edmund Hutchins. Dame Elizabeth Pope married Sir Hugh Paulet, K.G., of Hinton St. George, a statesman and soldier of some eminence. Lady Paulet usually nominated to the fellowships, scholarships, and advowsons (in one instance after an appeal to the Visitor) till her death in 1593, when she was buried in Trinity chapel with funeral honours from the University.

It is particularly noticeable that Sir Thomas Pope, having been able to provide handsomely for his family as well as for his College, did not saddle the latter with any of the preferences for founder's-kin which proved fertile in litigation elsewhere. Indeed he appears to contemplate that his heirs will resort to the College as Commoners, and sets apart the best room for such uses if required. Accordingly we find the College constantly receiving besides presents of game, etc. substantial assistance from the Popes, Norths, and others, and sending them in return not only the traditional gloves, but money in time of need; while the college books record as undergraduates many generations of the Popes and Pope-Blounts and Norths, and members of families connected with them by descent or marriage, such as Brockett, Perrot, Danvers, Sacheverell, Combe, Greenhill, Poole, Lee (Lichfield), Bertie (Lindsay), Wentworth (Cleveland), Tyrrell, Legge (Dartmouth), Stuart (Bute), and Paulet (Poulett).

On March 1st, 1554/5, Sir Thomas Pope obtained Royal Letters Patent to found TRINITY COLLEGE for a president (a priest), twelve fellows (four priests), and eight scholars, and a free school (Jesus Scolehouse), at Hooknorton; and to endow them from his estates enumerated, viz. eighteen manors in north and west Oxfordshire, and eleven elsewhere (including Bermondsey and Deptford), and fifteen advowsons. On March 28th he gave a "charter of erection," and admitted in the presence of the University authorities fourteen or fifteen members of the foundation. In May, and subsequently, he furnished them with large quantities of plate, MSS. and printed books, and "churche stuffe and playte," inventories of which are printed by Warton. Besides the silver-gilt chalice and paten, once belonging to St. Albans, we find crosses, censers, missals, antiphoners, copes, chasubles, hangings, corporas-cases, canopies, tunicles, paxes, banners, a rood and other images for the Easter sepulchre, etc., bells, and a pair of organs, which it cost £10 to bring from London. By 1556 he had made a selection from his estates, and gave the College the manors, etc., of Wroxton and Balscot near Banbury, the rectorial tithe of Great Waltham and Navestock in Essex, with some farms and rent-charges, all formerly the property of religious houses.

Most of these estates had been already let on lease for long periods; and the income from them, minutely apportioned to various purposes by the statutes, proved sufficient for the requirements of a sixteenth century college, except as regards the buildings, which were in bad repair from the first.

The statutes, dated May 1st, 1556, were drawn up by the Founder and the first president, Thomas Slythurst, in very fair Latin, for which Arthur Yeldard, one of the fellows, was responsible. They provide very detailed rules for the position and conduct of the members of the foundation. The president's duties are mainly disciplinary and bursarial. The twelve fellows are to study philosophy and theology; they are to furnish a vice-president, a dean, two bursars, four chaplains, a logic or philosophy reader, and a rhetoric or grammar reader. The eight (afterwards twelve) scholars are to study polite letters and elementary logic and philosophy; they are to be elected by the five College officers after examination in letter-writing, heroic verse and plain song, being natives of the counties in which College property is situated (Oxford, Essex, Gloucester, and Bedford), or of the Founder's manors, or scholars of Eton or Banbury, or at least Brackley and Reading; and they must be really in need of assistance. They have a prior claim on vacant fellowships. There may be twenty commoners of good family, under the care of the fellows. The salaried servants are the Obsonator, Promus (a poor scholar who is also to act as Janitor), Archimagirus, Hypomagirus, Barbaetonsor, and Lotrix; the last-named is to be above suspicion, but may not enter the quadrangle. A scholar or fellow is to act as organist, with a small extra stipend. There is to be high mass with full services on Sundays and feasts; on week-days mass before six a.m. according to the received forms of the "Ecclesia Anglicana," and the use of Sarum; public and private prayers for the Founder and his family are prescribed. The Bible is to be read aloud in hall during the *prandium* and *cœna*, and afterwards expounded; after dinner, when the "mantilia longa, et lavacra, cum gutturniis et aqua" have been used, and the loving cup passed round, silence is to be observed while the scholars "qui in refectionibus ministrant" have their meal, and a declamation is made. All public conversation, especially among the scholars, is to be in a learned language. Then follow minute regulations about degrees and disputations. Lectures are to be given from six to eight a.m. in arithmetic (from "Gemmephriseus" and Tunstall), geometry (from Euclid), logic (from Porphyry, Aristotle, Rodolphus Agricola, and Johannes Cæsarius), and philosophy (Aristotle and Plato); from three to five p.m. on Latin authors, prose and verse alternately, such as Virgil, Horace, Lucan, Juvenal, Terence, and Plautus, Cicero *de Officiis*, Valerius Maximus, Suetonius, and Florus; and for the more advanced, Pliny's Natural History, Livy, Cicero's oratorical works, Quintilian, "vel aliud hujusmodi excelsum." It is noticeable that Latin has a distinct preference; though Greek is to be taught as far as possible.

In a letter to Slythurst, Pope writes, "My Lord Cardinall's Grace [Pole] has had the overseeinge of my statutes. He much lykes well that I have therein ordered the Latin tongue to be redde to my schollers. But he advyses mee to order the Greeke to be more taught there than I have provyded. This purpose I well lyke; but I feare the tymes will not bear it now. I remember when I was a yonge scholler at Eton, the Greeke tongue was growinge apace; the studie of whiche is now alate much decaid." Lectures in the Long Vacation may be on solid geometry and astronomy, Laurentius Vallensis, Aulus Gellius, Politian, or versification; for the shorter vacations declamations and verse exercises are prescribed. The scholars may not leave the college precincts without permission, nor take country walks in parties of less than three; they may not indulge in "illicitis et noxiis ludis alearum, cartarum pictarum (*chardes* vocant), pilarum ad aedes, muros, tegulas, vel ultra funes jactitarum"; but they may play at "pilæ palmariae" in the grove, and cards in the hall during "the xii daies" at Christmastide for "ligulis, lucernis, carta, et hujusmodi vilioris pretii rebus, at pro nummis nullo modo." No member of the foundation may wear fine clothes, or any suit but a "toga talaris usque ad terram demissa," and the hood of his degree; they are to sleep two or three in a room, some in "trochle-beddes"; and they may not carry arms, though they are afterwards enjoined to keep in their rooms a "fustis vel aliquod aliud armorum genus bonum et firmum," to defend the College and University. Gaudys with extra commons are allowed on twelve festivals; and at Christmas they may make merry with the six good capons and the boar "bene saginatus," provided by two tenants, together with the "cartlode of fewel," "wheate and maulte," due from the president as *ex-officio* rector of Garsington. Founder's-kin are to be preferred as tenants. Three times a year the statutes are to be read, and once the president and one fellow are to hold a scrutiny of the conduct and progress of the rest, during which delation appears to be encouraged. The chief penalties to enforce these rules are impositions and loss of commons, with expulsion on the third repetition of a minor offence; the violation of some statutes involves summary deprivation; scholars under twenty may be birched or caned by the dean. The statutes conclude, and are pervaded with, exhortations to unity and fidelity. When we take into account the fact that except in special cases the limit of absence was forty days in the year for a fellow and twenty for a scholar, it is clear that the life contemplated was one of almost monastic strictness in matters of detail.

A postscript dated 1557 adds to the revenues to increase certain allowances, and provides five obits, one on Jesus-day (Aug. 7th) for the Founder, with doles for the poor and the prisoners in the Castle and Bocardo. A design for building a house at Garsington, as a place of retreat for the College in times of the pestilences then common, is mentioned; a quadrangular building built with five hundred marks left by the Founder, and help from his widow, was finished about 1570. The College removed there bodily in 1577; we find payments for "black bylles" for protection there, food at Abingdon, Woodstock, etc., antidotes for those left behind, carts for the carriage of kitchen utensils, books, and surplices, and the clock. In 1563/4 they had retired to lodgings in Woodstock.

The annual computus commences on Lady Day, 1556. On Trinity Sunday the Founder formally admitted the president, twelve fellows, and seven scholars in the chapel. In July he came again with Bishops Whyte (Winchester) and Thirlby (Ely), and others. The president held his stirrup, the vice-president made an oration "satis longam et officii plenam," and the bursars offered "chirothecas aurifrigiatas." The banquet in the hall and the twelve minstrels cost £12 3s. 9d. The president celebrated "missam vespertinam" in the best cope, and Sir Thomas "obtulit unam bursam plenam angelorum." After service he gave the bursars the whole of their expenses and a silver-gilt cup from which he had drunk to the company in "hypocrasse," and a mark each to the scholars. The accounts record many other visits from him and his wife and their influential friends, gifts of timber and game, and presents of gloves in return.

Dr. Thos. Slythurst was a canon of Windsor, and held several benefices, chiefly by court favour; the original fellows came from other foundations, especially Queen's and Exeter. Yeldard was a fellow of Pembroke, Cambridge, and had been educated in Durham Convent. The scholars were mainly from the Midlands, and afterwards usually natives of the preferred counties, with Bucks and Herts; two or three were elected annually, with one or two fellows; till 1600 the tenure of a fellowship rarely exceeds ten years. In 1564/5 there were already seventeen commoners, and from the caution-books it seems that from fifteen to thirty were admitted annually, and resided for two or three years. There were two or three grades, and some instances are found of private servants or tutors; and of the residence for short periods of persons not *in statu pupillari*. At first several Durham and Yorkshire names occur, as Claxton, Conyers, Lascelles, Blakiston, Shafton, Trentham; and Edward Hindmer (sch. 1561) was probably son of the last warden of Durham College; afterwards the families of the southern Midlands are largely represented, and Fettiplaces, Lenthails,

Chamberlains, Newdigates, Annesleys, Bagots, Fleetwoods, Lucys, Chetwoods, Hobys, etc. abound.

The early years of the College were uneventful except for two visitations in the interests of the reformed religion. In 1560 several of the fellows retired; Slythurst was deprived, and died in the Tower. No objection appears to have been offered by the Foundress to the enforced disregard of many explicit regulations in the statutes: the "sacerdotes missas celebrantes" became "capellani preces celebrantes"; but incense was sometimes bought, and the feasts of the Assumption and St. Thomas à Becket kept as gaudys. It is noticeable that an English Bible and two Latin "Common Prayer" books had been sent with the Founder's service-books. In 1570 Bishop Horne ordered the destruction or secularisation of the Founder's presents as "monuments tending to idolatrie and popish or devill's service, crosses, censars, and such lyke fylthie stuffe"; several of the Romanising fellows retired to Gloucester Hall and Hart Hall (one was executed at York as a popish priest in 1600; another was George Blackwell, the "archpriest"). A table took the place of the three altars, but the paintings and glass remained. "In 1642, the Lord Viscount Say and Seale came to visit the College, to see what of new Popery they could discover. My L.[d] saw that this" (the painting) "was done of old time, and Dr. Kettle told his Lo.[p], 'Truly we regard it no more than a dirty dish-clout,' so it remained untoucht till Harris's time, and then was coloured over with green"; much to the disgust of Aubrey.

Yeldard, a writer of some academic reputation, became president; but the computus, during his thirty-nine years of office, records nothing more exciting than journeys to the estates, and small repairs to the old buildings. In his time the foundation included Thomas Allen, Henry Cuffe, who was expelled for remarking to his host when dining at another college, "A pox *this* is a beggarly college indeed—the plate that our Founder stole would build another as good" (he became fellow of Merton and Regius Professor of Greek, and was executed after Essex's rebellion), Thomas Lodge the dramatist, Richard Blount the Jesuit, Bishops Wright of Lichfield and Coventry, Adams of Limerick, and (according to Wood) Smith of Chalcedon *in partibus*; among commoners were Sir Edward Hoby, John Lord Paulett, and Sir George Calvert, first Lord Baltimore.

Yeldard was succeeded in 1598/9 by Dr. Ralph Kettell, of Kings-Langley, scholar on the nomination of the Foundress in 1579. Though not a man of mark outside Oxford, he seems to have initiated the development of the College in the seventeenth century. He personally supervised every department of college life, and left in his curious sloping handwriting full memoranda of lawsuits and special expenses, lists of members, and copies of deeds. By husbanding the resources of the College, he restored extensively the old Durham quadrangle, superimposing attics or "cock-lofts," rebuilding the hall, and erecting on the site of "Perilous Hall," then leased from Oriel, the handsome house which bears his name. He was a "right Church of England man," and disliked Laud's despotic reforms. When an old man he became very eccentric, if we may believe John Aubrey (commoner 1642), who saw him as he is painted with "a fresh ruddie complexion—a very tall well-grown man. His gowne and surplice and hood being on, he had a terrible gigantique aspect, with his sharp gray eies. The ordinary gowne he wore was a russet cloth gowne—He spake with a squeaking voice—He dragged with his right foot a little, by which he gave warning (like the rattle-snake) of his comeing. Will. Egerton would go so like him that sometimes he would make the whole chapel rise up." "When he observed the scholars' haire longer than ordinary, he would bring a paire of cizers in his muffe (which he commonly wore), and woe be to them that sate on the outside of the table. I remember he cutt Mr. Radford's haire with the knife that chipps the bread on the buttery-hatch, and then he sang, '*And was not Grim the Collier finely trimmed?*'" The whole of Aubrey's remarks on him and other Trinity men is good reading, and we may conclude with an anecdote which is at once suggestive of, and a contrast with, a chapter in *John Inglesant*.

"'Tis probable this venerable Dr. might have lived some yeares longer, and finish't his century, had not the civill warres come on; wch much grieved him, that was absolute in the Colledge, to be affronted and disrespected by rude soldiers. I remember, being at the Rhetorique lecture in the hall, a foot-soldier came in and brake his hower-glasse. The Dr. indeed was just stept out, but Jack Dowch pointed at it. Our grove was the Daphne for the ladies and their gallants to walk in, and many times my Lady Isabella Thynne would make her entrys with a theorbo or lute played before her. ... She was most beautiful, humble, charitable, &c., but she could not subdue one thing. I remember one time this Lady and fine M^ris Fenshawe (she was wont, and my Lady Thynne, to come to our chapell, mornings, halfe dressed like angells) would have a frolick to make a visit to the President. The old Dr. quickly perceived that they came to abuse him; he addressed his discourse to M^ris Fenshawe, saying, 'Madam, your husband and father I bred up here, & I knew your grandfather; I know you to be a gentlewoman, I will not say you are a whore, but gett you gonne for a very woman.' The dissoluteness of the times, as I have sayd, grieving the good old Dr., his days were shortned, & dyed" in July 1643.

About this time Trinity produced among Bishops, Glemham of St. Asaph's, Lucy of St. David's, Ironside of Bristol, Skinner of Bristol, Oxford, and Worcester, Gore of Waterford, Parker of Oxford, Stratford of Chester, and Sheldon of Canterbury; among authors, Sir John Denham, William Chillingworth, Ant. Faringdon, Arthur Wilson, Daniel Whitby, Sir Edw. Byshe, Francis Potter, Henry Gellibrand, George Roberts, M.D., and James Harrington; among Cavalier leaders, Thomas Lord Wentworth, created Earl of Cleveland, Sir Philip Musgrave of Edenhall, and Sir Hervey Bagot; on the other side, Henry Ireton and Edmund Ludlow;

besides the chivalrous William Earl of Craven, and John Lord Craven of Ryton, founder of the Craven scholarships, Cecil Calvert second Lord Baltimore, Sir Henry Blount the traveller, Milton's friend Charles Deodate, Dr. Nathaniel Highmore, and Chief Justice Newdigate.

The next president, Hannibal Potter, was elected during the disorders of the Civil War. The college buildings were occupied during the siege of Oxford by the courtiers and officers; many of the undergraduates enlisted; the register and accounts are defective; the elections were irregular, and the number of commoners admitted dropped from thirty-two in 1633 to four in 1643, none in 1644, and one in 1645, reviving to twenty-one in 1646. The tenants fell behind with their rents, and in 1647 the arrears from estates and battels amounted to £1385; in November 1642 the King "borrowed" £200, and in the following March Sir Wm. Parkhurst gave the College a receipt for 173 pounds of plate, which included everything given by the Founder and others, except the chalice, paten, and two flagons. In 1647 and 1648 the College sent £145 13*s.* 4*d.* and £45 to the Earl of Downe and his uncle Sir Thomas Pope. In 1647 a lessee of College property, Sir Robert Napier of Luton-Hoo, deposited £160 for emergencies.

In 1648 the members of the College were cited before the Puritan Visitors of the University; eventually twenty-six submitted and nineteen were ejected; some of them never appeared, *e. g.* the bursar Josias Howe, who had carried off many of the College documents into the country. Nine persons were intruded by the Visitors at different times. Potter, who, as acting Vice-Chancellor, had for some time baffled the commissioners, was turned out of his house by Lord Pembroke in person, to make room for one of the Visitors, Dr. Robert Harris, of Magdalen Hall. He was an old man, but still vigorous, a good scholar, an orthodox though popular preacher; and was fairly well received by the fellows, some of whom remained without having submitted. Under him things settled down, and the numbers rose again; some scandalous stories were afterwards current of the appropriation of a large sum left behind by Potter, and of the exaction from one of the tenants of an exorbitant fine; but on the whole Harris probably tolerated much of the old *régime, e. g.* he allowed payments to absent fellows and the Founder's kinsmen, and the old saints'-days were still observed as gaudys.

On his death in 1658, William Hawes was elected, and confirmed by a mandate from the Protector. In 1659 he resigned on his death-bed in order that no time might be lost in electing (illegally, since he was not a member of the College), Dr. Seth Ward, a deprived fellow of Sydney Sussex, Cambridge, who had settled at Wadham, where he became Savilian Professor of Astronomy, and one of the founders of the Royal Society. He was "very well acquainted and beloved in the College," and less likely to be objected to by the Government than Dr. Bathurst, who was really the mainstay of the society. In 1660

Ward had to retire on the restoration of Potter (with Howe and perhaps a married fellow, Matthew Skinner), was made Dean and subsequently Bishop of Exeter, on the recommendation of the West country gentlemen in the Restoration Parliament, and died Bishop of Salisbury in 1689.

On Potter's death in 1664 Ralph Bathurst naturally became president. Shortly afterwards "A. Wood and his mother and his eldest brother and his wife went to the lodgings of Dr. R. B., to welcome him to Oxon, who had then very lately brought to Oxon his new-married wife, Mary, the widdow of Dr. Jo. Palmer, late Warden of Alls. Coll. which Mary was of kin to the mother of A. Wood. They had before sent in sack, claret, cake, and sugar. Dr. Bathurst was then about forty-six years of age, so there was need of a wife." He was the fifth son of George Bathurst (commoner 1605) and Elizabeth Villiers, Kettell's step-daughter; many of his family before and after him were at Trinity, and six of his brothers are said to have died in the King's service. He was ordained priest in 1644; but submitted to the Visitors, "neither owning their authority nor concurring in his principles with them, but rather acting separately from them," as he said afterwards; studied medicine (M.D. 1654), and practised in Oxford and as a navy surgeon. During the persecution of the Church he assisted Bishop Skinner as archdeacon at the secret ordinations at Launton and in Trinity chapel. Skinner was the only prelate who ordained regularly, and claimed to have conferred orders on 400 to 500 persons. Bathurst was an original F.R.S., and P.R.S.

in 1688; and also a classical scholar of some ability, as his remains show. In 1670 he became Dean of Wells, but refused the bishopric of Bristol, for which Lord Somers recommended him in 1691.

Bathurst was well known in the best society of his day; and his reputation, together with the traditions of the families mentioned above, attracted to Trinity in his time a large number of gentlemen-commoners of high rank. John Evelyn, for instance, whose elder brother George was a commoner in 1633, took pains to place his eldest son under his care. The University was sinking into the intellectual torpor of the eighteenth century, and we find few men of learning educated at Trinity for 100 years; the best known were Arthur Charlett the antiquarian, and William Derham, an ingenious writer on natural religion. Among the commoners were Lord Chancellor Somers, Wm. Pierrepoint Earl of Kingston, the second Earl of Shaftesbury, Sir Chas. O'Hara Lord Tyrawley, Commander-in-chief in Ireland, Spencer Compton Earl of Wilmington (the Prime Minister *faute de mieux*), Allen Earl Bathurst, Cobbe Archbishop of Dublin, and the heads of the families of Abdy, Broughton, Wallop, Reade, Gresley, Trollope, Shelley, Knollys, Hall, Clopton, Topham, Lennard, Dormer, Napier (of Luton-Hoo), Curzon, Shirley (Ferrers), Herbert (Herbert of Cherbury), Cobb, Bridgeman, Jodrell, Boothby, Jenkinson, and Shaw of Eltham, and many others long connected with Trinity.

In 1685, some undergraduates, under the command of Philip Bertie, volunteered against Monmouth; they drilled in the Grove, and the College paid for the keep of some horses ("Pro avenis in usū Coll. pro equo Mri. Praesidis ad militiā mutuato, 12*s.*" Comp. 1685). In Bathurst's time there appears to have been some connection with the West of England, Guernsey, Wales, and South Ireland, and in the next century a large number of entries from the West Indies are found; but on the whole Trinity continued to draw mainly on the southern Midlands, especially Oxfordshire and Warwickshire.

To receive the increased numbers Bathurst almost rebuilt the college, partly from the revenues increased by the rise in the value of land, partly from contributions skilfully extracted from his old pupils and friends, and partly from his private means, on which he drew with great liberality. His chief works were the north wing of the garden quadrangle (nearly the first Palladian work in Oxford) in 1665; the west side in 1682, both from Wren's designs; the Bathurst building, now replaced by the new president's house; the new kitchens, &c.; and the present chapel, with the tower and gateway, from Aldrich's plans corrected by Wren, in 1691-4. He spent £2000 on the shell, and the fittings with the carving by Gibbons were supplied by subscriptions. In his time a Fellows' Common-room, one of the earliest, was instituted, in the room now the Bursary. Anthony à Wood used to visit it, till his passion for gossip made him objectionable to the fellows.

Bathurst, whose portrait by Kneller represents him as a clever and vigorous-looking man, with an oval face and singularly large eyelids, became in his old age "stark blind, deaf, and memory lost." ("This is a serious alarm to me," Evelyn continues after recording his death; "God grant that I may profit by it.") At last, when walking in his front garden, from which in his dotage he used to throw stones at Balliol chapel windows, he fell and broke his thigh, and refusing to have it set on the ground that "an old man's bones had no marrow in them," died June 14th, 1704, and was buried in the chapel. His will mentions a large number of legacies to Trinity, Wells, the Royal Society, &c.

During the seventeenth century, besides the benefactions by way of subscriptions already mentioned, and small gifts of books and plate, the College received an endowment for the library from Ric. Rands, rector of Hartfield, Sussex; a small farm in Oakley and Brill, purchased with money left by John Whetstone; lands at Thorpe Mandeville from Edward Bathurst, rector of Chipping-Warden; the moiety of the manor lands of Abbot's Langley, Herts, from Francis Combe, great-nephew of the Founder; and a rent-charge from Thomas Unton, all three for exhibitions; the livings of Rotherfield-Greys from Thomas Rowney of Oxford, and Oddington-on-Otmoor from Bathurst; and a reading-desk in the form of the College crest, a two-headed griffin, from Beckford "promus." In the eighteenth century several legacies occur, the most noticeable being the livings of Farnham (Essex), Hill-Farrance, and Barton-on-the-Heath; the Tylney exhibition; several large donations towards various schemes connected with the buildings and grounds; the iron gates on Broad Street from Francis North, first Earl of Guildford; the clock from Henry Marquis of Worcester and his brother; and a quantity of plate from fellows and gentlemen-commoners, including a very fine ewer and basin from Frederick Lord North and his step-brother Lord Lewisham. Unfortunately the general revenues of the College never received any augmentation, and though they rose with the value of agricultural produce, are not likely to develop further.

The next president was Thos. Sykes, Lady Margaret Professor; but he had waited so long for the vacancy that he died in the following year, and was succeeded by Wm. Dobson, after whose death in 1731 George Huddesford governed the College for nearly half a century. He was followed by Jos. Chapman (1776-1808) and Thos. Lee (1808-1824). They all took their doctor's degree, and were all buried in the chapel; but they were not men of any particular distinction, and it is difficult to individualise them. Huddesford, however, had some reputation as a wit and antiquarian, and his brother William, also at Trinity, is known as the editor of some important works. In the eighteenth century the foundation of Trinity did no better in producing learned men than other Colleges. There were, however, at various dates, a few fairly well-known men—Rev. Thomas Warton, M.D., and his better known son and namesake, the Professor of Poetry and Laureate; John Gilbert, Archbishop of York; Mant, Bishop of Down and Connor; Wise, Lethieullier, Dallaway, and Ford, antiquarians; James Merrick and Wm. Lisle Bowles, authors. Among commoners were Frederick Lord North, the Prime Minister, as well as his father and son, his brother Brownlow Bishop of Winchester, and stepbrother William Earl of Dartmouth; the heads of the Beaufort, Donegal, Umberslade, Hereford, De Clifford, Ashbrook, and Winterton families; William Pitt, the great Earl of Chatham; Johnson's friends, Bennet Langton and Topham Beauclerk; the usual number of country baronets, *e. g.* a Northcote, a Cope, a Carew, and several Shaws, together with members of families long connected with Trinity, such as Escott, Borlase, Whorwood, Wheeler, Lingen, Woodgate, Guille, Sheldon, Norris; and Walter Savage Landor, who had to be rusticated for firing a gun into the rooms of another man, whom he hated for his Toryism, when he was entertaining what Landor called a party of "servitors and other raffs of every description."

Trinity seems to have been considered a quieter college than others, if we may believe one G. B., who writes to the *Gentleman's Magazine* in 1798, that "at the small excellent College of Trinity were Lord Lewisham, Lord North, Mr. Edwin Stanhope[?] &c., all as regular as *great Tom*. Of Lord Lewisham and Lord North it was said that they never missed early prayers in their College chapel one morning, nor any evening when not actually out of Oxford, either dining out of town, or on a water-party." In

1728 the south side of the new quadrangle was built on the site of the north side of the Durham buildings; the Lime Walk was planted in 1713, at a cost of £8 19s. 3d.; the hall was cheaply refitted; but on the whole the College must have presented the same homely appearance that it bore up to 1883. The old houses on Broad Street, formerly academic halls, were bought from Oriel, and the ground recently the President's kitchen-garden from Magdalen; but no use was made of the site till late in the present century.

The best known Trinity man in the eighteenth century was Thomas Warton, who was intimate with Dr. Johnson and the chief literary men of the time. Personally he was a man of retiring character, and undignified appearance and manners, though he has a pleasant expression in the portrait by Reynolds. In the Bachelors' Common-room at Trinity he founded the custom of electing annually a Lady-Patroness, and a Poet-Laureate to celebrate her charms. His poetry has considerable merit; he was an indefatigable researcher into English history and literature; his *History of English Poetry* is still reprinted; and Trinity owes him a heavy debt for the Lives of Sir Thomas Pope and Dr. Bathurst. Dr. Johnson often visited him and stayed at Kettell Hall, where he made the acquaintance of his lively friend, Beauclerk, and received the adoration of Langton. "If I come to live at Oxford," he said, "I shall take up my abode at Trinity," and he gave the library in which he preferred to read—("Sir, if a man has a mind to *prance*, he must study at Christchurch and All Souls")—a copy of the Baskerville Virgil.

Some poetical letters, as yet unpublished, by John Skinner, great-great-grandson of the Bishop, contain some particulars of life in Trinity. He matriculated with a friend from home, one Dawson Warren, on November 16th, 1790; dined with Kett, who gave them wine left to him that year by Warton. They lived in Bathurst buildings, had chapel at 8.0; breakfasted together on tea, rolls, and toast at 8.30; read Demosthenes for Kett's lectures, &c., till 1.0. After riding or sailing in a "yacht" called their Hobby-Horse, they had a hasty shaving and powdering from the College barber for dinner at 3.0 in "messes" or "sets." This concluded with a "narrare" declaimed in hall from the Griffin. Then they talked till 5.30, when they had a concert with professionals (*e. g.* Dr. Crotch) from the town, concluding with a "tray" of negus, &c. at 9.30. The less virtuous had a wine; their tray was meat and beer; and eventually those of the party who could helped the rest to bed. President Chapman was considered good-natured; "Horse" Kett (who wrote several treatises used as text-books, and some poems and novels which the undergraduates did not appreciate), was respected but not liked. Kett's equine features and pompous bearing figure in a good caricature of 1807, "A view from Trinity."

But if the fellows of Trinity as a rule contented themselves with the routine well satirised by Warton in the *Rambler*, the ability and energy of some of the tutors, particularly Kett, Ingram, Wilson, and Short, enabled the College to take a leading place in the revival of Oxford as a place of education at the opening of the nineteenth century. The fellow-commoners gradually drop off; among the last were Ar. French first Lord De Freyne, and the late Earl of Erne. But the scholarships, always virtually open owing to the latitude as to counties allowed by the Founder, began to be held by really able men, and the elections to them became an honour keenly competed for. The number of fellowships was small, and the choice subject to some limitations, so that Trinity could not retain all its ablest scholars; but it succeeded in retaining their affection. Cardinal Newman for instance (admitted as a commoner, 1816; scholar, 1818[?]), had time to remember his first college at a critical moment of his life; of his leaving Oxford in 1846 he writes, "I called on Dr. Ogle [the Regius Professor of Medicine], one of my very oldest friends, for he was my private tutor when I was an undergraduate. In him I took leave of my first College, Trinity, which was dear to me, and which held on its foundation so many who had been kind to me both when I was a boy, and all through my Oxford life. Trinity had never been unkind to me. There used to be much snapdragon growing on the walls opposite my freshman's room there, and I had for years taken it as the emblem of my own perpetual residence even unto death in my University." Newman was made an Honorary Fellow in 1878; and in 1885, on sending to the library a set of his works, wrote, "This May the 18th is the anniversary of the Monday on which in 1818 I was elected a member of your foundation. May your yearly festival ever be as happy a day to you all as in 1818 it was to me."

At one time it seemed as if Trinity might take a lead in the Tractarian movement; but the influence possibly of Ingram and Haddan directed the attention of their pupils to historical studies, at first ecclesiastical, but afterwards of a more general character. It is too early at present to estimate the exact place of individuals in the literature of the nineteenth century; but among those who will be said to have "flourished" since 1800, and by whose work the influence of Trinity on the period may be judged, may be mentioned the late Archdeacon Randall, Rev. Isaac Williams the poet and theologian, Rev. W. J. Copeland, J. W. Bowden, Rev. W. H. Guillemard, Sir G. K. Rickards, Rev. A. W. Haddan, the elder Herman Merivale, Mountague Bernard the international jurist, Bishops Claughton of St. Alban's, Stubbs of Oxford, Basil Jones of St. David's, and Davidson of Rochester, Vere (Lord) Hobart Governor of Madras, Roundell Palmer Earl of Selborne, Ralph (Lord) Lingen, Professors Rawlinson, Freeman, Dicey, Sanday, Bryce, Pelham, Ramsay, Rev. Sir G. Cox, Rev. North Pinder, Rev. Isaac Gregory Smith, Bosworth Smith, the travellers William Gifford Palgrave and Sir Richard Burton, to omit more junior present and recent members of the foundation and commoners. Some of those mentioned when scholars were famed for the "Trinity ἦθος," which denoted "considerable classical attainments and certain theological susceptibilities."

The annals of the College during this period can only be glanced at. Dr. James Ingram, president 1824-1850, was well known as one of the first authorities on English antiquities and Anglo-Saxon literature: by the undergraduates he was looked upon as what an old pupil has called a "physical force man." He left to the College a large and valuable collection of topographical and antiquarian books. The next president, Dr. John Wilson, of whose great care for the College estates and archives many striking proofs remain, was one of those Heads of Houses who adopted a *non possumus* attitude towards the first University Commission; he resigned in 1866, and retired to Woodperry House, where he died in 1873. His successor, the Rev. Samuel William Wayte, had been one of the secretaries to the Commissioners; he conferred great benefits on the College by his careful management of the property, and exercised considerable influence in the University. In 1878 he retired to Clifton, where he still lives. In electing in his place the Rev. John Percival, head master of Clifton College, who had never been on the books of Trinity, the fellows took a step unusual but not unprecedented in College history; in 1887 he resigned, on accepting the headmastership of Rugby School. Under Dr. Percival the new statutes of the Commission of 1877-81 came into force; to them is due a slight increase which has taken place in the number of Scholars. The number of commoners had already exceeded the traditional limit of "forty men and forty horses," and partly in consequence of this, it was determined to build; between 1883 and 1887 the large block of rooms and the new president's lodgings in the front quadrangle, both by Mr. T. G. Jackson, were constructed; Kettell Hall was bought from Oriel, and the picturesque cottages on Broad Street and the old president's house converted into college rooms. A large portion of the money necessary for these purposes was contributed by present and past members of the foundation, and other graduates of the College.

We may conclude by mentioning some other important benefactions of the present century. James Ford, B.D., rector of Navestock, left funds for the purchase of advowsons, and for exhibitions appropriated to certain schools; the Millard bequest provides an endowment for natural science. A present of money from a "Member of the College" has been spent on portraits for the hall; an organ for the chapel was given by President Wayte; and seven windows of stained-glass representing Durham College saints, have recently been given by the Rev. Henry George Woods, M.A., the present President, to whom this account of Trinity College may be appropriately inscribed.

NOTE.—It is impossible to form a complete list of the persons educated at Trinity College, since the first general Register of Admissions commences only in 1646, and the entries are not autograph till 1664. But an approximate estimate may be made from various records, such as (1) the Admission

Registers A, B, and C, 1646-1891, (2) the formal admissions before a notary public of the Scholars or Fellows from 1555, contained in the College Registers, (3) the Bursars' annual account from 1579-1646 of Caution-money paid by Commoners, (4) the University Registers, which give some names not contained in the preceding, principally of the "poor scholars" who did not pay Caution-money. The total numbers seem to be not much under 6000, and of this nearly 1000 persons have been members of the foundation.—H. E. D. B.

XV.
S. JOHN BAPTIST COLLEGE.

BY THE REV. W. H. HUTTON, M.A., FELLOW OF S. JOHN'S.

After the dissolution of the religious houses there were in Oxford numbers of deserted buildings, little suited for private residences, but useful only, as they were designed, for corporate life. Some fell into decay, and have now utterly disappeared; others, by the wisdom of men interested in the intellectual revival of the age, were refounded as places of religion, learning, and education. To this latter class belongs the College of S. John Baptist. It occupies the site and some of the buildings of a Bernardine House founded by Archbishop Chichele in 1437, as a place where the Cistercian scholars studying at Oxford "might obtain humane and heavenly knowledge." By Letters Patent of Henry VI. the Archbishop received leave to "erect a College to the honour of the most glorious Virgin Mary and S. Bernard, in the street commonly called North Gate street, in the parish of S. Mary Magdalene, without the North Gate."[263] The buildings consisted only of a single block facing westwards, with one wing behind.[264] The hall was built about 1502, and the chapel consecrated in 1530. All of these remain in use. The monks had also a garden, leased at first part from University College and part from Durham College.

At the dissolution in 1539, the lands, buildings, and revenues of S. Bernard's College were given by Henry VIII. to his newly founded College and Cathedral of Christ Church, in whose possession they remained some sixteen years. In 1555, the deserted buildings were restored to use, and the College refounded under Letters Patent of Philip and Mary, granted at the request of a rich and munificent London trader, Sir Thomas White. He was a Merchant Taylor of renown, who had been Sheriff of London in 1547, and Lord Mayor in the year of Sir Thomas Wyatt's rebellion, when he had rallied the citizens to the cause of Queen Mary. He had, says a College chronicler,[265] poured over England a torrent of munificence, and now among the many things in which he deserved well of the State, this was the worthiest. There is a legend that he was directed in a dream to found a College hard by where three trunks grew from the root of a single elm,[266] and the tree which was said to have decided him to purchase the buildings of S. Bernard's was pointed out as still standing in the garden of Dr. Levinz, President of S. John's College from 1673 to 1697. Beyond the buildings, there was no link between the old Society and the new. The Cistercian tradition had left no trace; Sir Thomas White's foundation was a new creation.

The College thus founded in 1555, was to be set apart[267] for study of the sciences of Sacred Theology, Philosophy, and good Arts; it was dedicated to the praise and honour of God, of the Blessed Virgin Mary His Mother, and S. John

Baptist, and the Society was to consist of a President and thirty graduate or non-graduate scholars. In 1557,[268] both the scope and numbers of the original Foundation were enlarged; Theology, Philosophy, Civil and Canon Law were now declared to be the subjects of study, and the number of Fellows and scholars was raised to fifty, of whom[269] six were to be founder's kin, two from Coventry, Bristol, and Reading schools, one from Tunbridge and the rest from the Merchant Taylors' school in London. Twelve were to study Civil and Canon Law, one Medicine, and the rest Theology. There were also added three priests as chaplains, six clerks not priests yet not married, and six choristers. From the first the College was intimately connected with the country round Oxford, for the founder endowed it with the manors of Long Wittenham, Fyfield, Cumnor, Eaton, Kingston-Bagpuze, Frilford and Garford, in the counties of Berks and Oxon, and with sundry advowsons in the neighbourhood. It was at Handborough that the first President, Alexander Belsire, B.D., who was appointed by the Founder, died. He had been Rector for several years, and had retired there when removed from the headship on account of his maintenance of the papal supremacy. Several of the earlier Presidents held the living of Kingston-Bagpuze. In the manor-house at Fyfield the kinsfolk of the founder continued to live on for many generations, paying a nominal rent to the College, which from its piety thus suffered a considerable pecuniary loss at a time when its finances were at a very low ebb.[270] Nearer home, the manor of Walton, which had formerly belonged to the nunnery of Godstow, gave the College a share in the interests of the citizens of Oxford, which has continued to our own time.

During its earlier years Sir Thomas White watched over the institution which he had founded. The statutes which he gave were substantially those of New College, and this return to the scheme of William of Wykeham, which had been so largely adopted at Cambridge, shows that the alterations made by the founders of Magdalen, Corpus Christi, and Trinity, were not felt to be improvements. He had nominated the first President, his own kinsman John James as Vice-President for life, and the earlier Fellows. By his advice probably the second and third Presidents, and certainly the fourth, were appointed. He drew up also the most minute directions for the election and for the binding of the President to the performance of his duties, and for the government of the College. In all he set himself on behalf of the Society to seek peace and ensue it. If any strife should arise which could not within five days be appeased by the President and Deans, it must—so he ruled—be referred to the Warden of New College, the President of Magdalen, and the Dean of Christ Church, and by their decision all must abide. As he drew towards his end he wrote a touching letter of farewell to the Society which lay so near his heart. It runs thus—"Mr. President, with the fellows and scholars, I have me recommended unto you from the bottom of my heart, desiring the Holy Ghost may be among you until the end of the world, and desiring

Almighty God that every one of you may love one another as brethren, and I shall desire you all to apply your learning, and so doing God shall give you His blessing, both in this world and in the world to come. And furthermore if any strife or variance do arise among you I shall desire you for God's love to pacify it as much as you may, and so doing I put no doubt but God shall bless every one of you. And this shall be the last letter that ever I shall send unto you, and therefore I shall desire every one of you to take a copy of it for my sake.[271]No more to you at this time, but the Lord have you in His keeping until the end of the world. Written the 27th of Jan., 1566. I desire you all to pray to God for me that I may end my life with patience, and that He may take me to His mercies. By me, Sir Thomas White, Knight, Alderman of London, and founder of S. John Baptist College in Oxford."

Within a fortnight from the writing of this letter the founder died. He was buried with solemn ceremonial in the College chapel, where his coffin was found intact when that of Laud was laid beside it nearly a century later. A funeral oration was preached by one of the most brilliant of the junior Fellows, Edmund Campion, soon to win wider notoriety, and eventually to die a shameful death.

The loss of the founder made more evident the weaknesses with which the College had had to struggle from the first. It was wretchedly poor. The munificence of Sir Thomas White himself had more than exhausted his purse. He died a poor man; much of what he had intended for the College never reached it,—it would have been less still but for the scarcely judicial assistance, "partly by pious persuasions and partly by judicious delays," of his executor Sir William Cordell, who was Master of the Rolls,—and some of the estates, like Fyfield, were burdened with encumbrances which he had left behind. Nor was this all. Before the end of the century one of the Bursars seems to have embezzled the College money and fled, becoming a Papist, and getting employment where his antecedents were not known, as paymaster to an Archduke of Austria. As early as 1577 the expenses had to be cut down; the chapel foundation was reduced if not altogether suspended. But the College not only suffered from pecuniary troubles; it seems to have been peculiarly affected by the religious changes of the time. So long as the founder had lived, his tact had smoothed the difficulties of the transition from the Marian to the Elizabethan rule. Two at least of the earlier Presidents were deprived for asserting the Pope's supremacy, yet the change was managed without disturbance. But when the wise counsels of the founder could no longer be heard, and when the Papal Court had declared itself the bitter foe of Elizabeth, Fellow after Fellow retired, or was deprived, and joined the Roman party. For this cause no less than six members of the foundation are recorded within a few years to have been imprisoned. Some, like Gregory Martin, who had been tutor to the Duke of Norfolk's children, and was afterwards the translator of the "Rheims Bible," fled over sea; some died in hiding, some in English gaols. One, Edmund Campion, a brilliant orator and a bold defender of the Papal jurisdiction, became a Jesuit, was mixed up in several political intrigues, and eventually was hanged at Tyburn. It might seem as though the little College, poor and divided, would never weather the storm. That it did so was no doubt due to the patience and devotion of its members. During its darkest years, at the end of the sixteenth century, there were found philosophers and theologians, such as Dr. John Case,[272] and skilful administrators such as Dr. Francis Willis (President, 1577-1590), poets and rhetoricians, and London merchants, who gave their talents and their money to support the fame of the struggling Society.

By the beginning of the sixteenth century the College was on its feet again; before a quarter of the century had passed its influence was the most important in the University. Great men had begun to send their sons there. In 1564 came two sons of the Earl of Shrewsbury; in 1572 two Stanleys and young Lord Strange. At the accession of James I. few Colleges had among their members so many men already distinguished or soon to win distinction. Tobie Matthew, a former President, had risen to be Dean, and then Bishop, of Durham, and died Archbishop of York. Sir William Paddy, a Fellow and notable benefactor, was the King's physician. John Buckeridge (President, 1605-1611) became Bishop first of Rochester and then of Ely. A Fellow of the College had been the Maiden Queen's ambassador to Russia; many others were famous in the law courts. But two men especially were destined to play a part on a wider scene. In 1602 William Juxon, a lad of gentle birth, from Sussex, matriculated at S. John's. William Laud, born at Reading on October 7th, 1573, elected a Fellow of S. John's College at the early age of twenty, was Proctor in the year of the King's accession. From this year the history of the College may be considered to be inseparable from that of the little energetic personage who left so great a mark upon the history of the English Church.

On the 18th of January, 1605, Dr. John Buckeridge was elected President on the death of Ralph Hutchinson. In August of the same year, King James visited the University. At the gate of S. John's "three young youths[273] in habit and attire like nymphs, confronted him, representing England, Scotland, and Ireland, and talking dialogue-wise each to other of their state, at last concluding yielding up themselves to his gracious government. The Scholars stood all on one side of the street; and the strangers of all sorts on the other. The Scholars stood first, then the Bachelors, and last the Masters of Arts." Two days afterwards, at the end of a long day, the King saw a comedy, called *Vertumnuus*, written by Dr. Gwynne, a Fellow of S. John's. "It was acted much better than either of the other that he had seen before, yet the King was so over-wearied that after a while he distasted it and fell asleep. When he awaked he would have been gone, saying, 'I marvel what they think me to be,' with such other like speeches, showing his dislike thereof. Yet he did tarry till they had ended it, which was after one of the clock."

At this time the University was greatly influenced by Calvinist doctrines. It was from S. John's that the first opposition to the prevalent opinions came, and it was thus that William Laud first became famous. Laud was ordained deacon and priest by Dr. Young, Bishop of Rochester, who, "finding his study raised above the systems and opinions of the age, upon the noble foundations of the fathers, councils, and the ecclesiastical historians, early presaged that if he lived he would be an instrument of restoring the Church from the narrow and private principles of modern times to the more enlarged, liberal, and public sentiments of the apostolic and primitive ages." Dr. Young was right in his prophecy, for Laud was soon the leader of the reaction against Calvinism in the University, as he was afterwards successful in asserting more liberal and Catholic sentiments in the Anglican Church at large. By maintaining in theological lectures and sermons before the University the doctrine of baptismal regeneration and the divine institution of Episcopacy, he made himself prominent in opposition to the chief authorities of the day, who were all imbued with Calvinistic views. It was reckoned, so in later years he told Heylin, a heresy to speak to him, and a suspicion of heresy to salute him as he walked in the street. Yet he had no lack of friends; the most eminent members of his own College seem always to have stood by him,—we have Sir William Paddy's approval of an University sermon that had caused much offence,—and before long he found the whole University converted to his views. There were sermons and pamphlets and answers and counterblasts, inquiries by Vice-Chancellor and Doctors, threats of suspension, murmurs of disloyalty to the Church, as there have often been since in Oxford theological tempests; but the misconception and bitter feeling were gradually overcome by the steadfast conscientiousness of Laud. He received a number of preferments outside the University, was especially honoured by Bishop Neile of Rochester, and resigned his Fellowship in 1610 to devote himself entirely to parochial work. At the end of that year, however, Dr. Buckeridge, President of S. John's, was elected Bishop of Rochester in succession to Dr. Neile, and by his advice and support Laud was proposed for the vacant headship of the College. Calvinist influence in the University was set to work to induce the King to prevent the appointment, but without success, and Laud was elected on May 10th, 1611. The election was marked by keen and violent party feeling. When the nomination papers had been laid on the altar (as was the custom in College elections down to within living memory), and the Vice-President was about to announce the result, one of the Fellows, Richard Baylie, snatched the papers from his hands and tore them in pieces. It is characteristic of Laud's freedom from personal animosity, that he passed over this act of irritable partisanship and showed special favour to the culprit. He procured the choice of Baylie as Proctor in 1615, afterwards made him his chaplain, married him to his niece, supported his election in 1632 to the Presidency itself, and in 1636 appointed him Vice-Chancellor of the University. In the same year, 1611, Laud became one of the King's chaplains, and from this time was not without royal influence to assist him in his University contests.

He had still great difficulties to contend with. Dr. Abbot, Regius Professor of Divinity and brother of the Primate, preached against him in S. Mary's, his assertion of anti-Calvinistic doctrine, or Arminianism as it was now called, being the cause of complaint. "Might not Christ say, what art thou? Romish or English, Papist or Protestant?—or what art thou? A mongrel compound of both; a Protestant by ordination, a Papist in point of free will, inherent righteousness, and the like. A Protestant in receiving the Sacrament, a Papist in the doctrine of the Sacrament. What, do you think there be two heavens? If there be, get you to the other and place yourself there, for into this where I am ye shall not come." To such coarse stuff as this was Laud compelled to listen; he "was fain to sit patiently" among the heads of houses, and "hear himself abused almost an hour together, being pointed at." But this was merely the vindictive retort of a vanquished party.

In 1616 the King sent some instructions to the Vice-Chancellor which exercised a powerful effect on the theology and discipline of the University. Care was to be taken that the selected preachers throughout the city should conform to the doctrine of the Church, and that students in Divinity should be "excited to bestow their time on the Fathers and Councils, schoolmen, histories and controversies, … making them the grounds of their studies in divinity." In the same year Laud was made Dean of Gloucester. In 1621 he became Bishop of S. David's, and resigned the headship of the College. During the following years he does not seem to have been much in Oxford, and it was not till 1630, when he was made Chancellor, that he exercised effective control over the University. While he was busied in the affairs of the Church at large, and was rising step by step to the highest ecclesiastical preferment, his College, under the government of Dr. William Juxon, grew in prosperity. Sir William Paddy, always a benefactor, gave a "pneumatick organ of great cost," and by his will endowed an organist with singing men, and left books and money to the Society of which he was, says a College chronicler, a member as munificent as learned. The organ, though its erection was made by Prynne one of the accusations against Laud, escaped destruction during the Rebellion, and was in use till 1768. Bishop Buckeridge left more money to the College, and altar furniture for the chapel. Within the years 1616-1636 large sums of money came in, and gifts of land and advowsons of livings were made by persons more or less connected with the College; the buildings were added to, and by the time when Laud, as Bishop of London and Chancellor of the University, had set himself to "build at S. John's in Oxford, where I was bred up, for the good and safety of that College," the

College, still much less than a century old, was freed from the pecuniary troubles which so much crippled it in its earlier years.

The new quadrangle, which was begun in July 1631, when the King gave two hundred tons of wood from the royal forests of Stow and Shotover to aid in the building, was a magnificent expression of the donor's generosity and love for the College. It was completed in 1636, and Laud, now Archbishop of Canterbury, having assigned by special direction the new rooms to the library, to the President, and for the use of commoners, made elaborate preparations to receive the King and Queen when they "invited themselves" to him. They brought with them the King's nephew, the Elector Palatine and Prince Rupert, who were entered on the books of S. John's. Laud's College and his new library were the centre of the entertainments that marked their stay in Oxford. The Archbishop's own words[274] give the best account of the festivities. On the 30th of August, 1636, he says, "When they were come to S. John's they first viewed the new building, and that done I attended them up to the Library stairs, where as soon as I began to ascend the music began and they had a fine short song fitted for them as they ascended the stairs. In the Library they were welcomed to the College with a short speech made by one of the Fellows (Abraham Wright). And dinner being ready they passed from the old into the new library, built by myself, where the King, the Queen and the Prince Elector dined at one table which stood cross at the upper end. And Prince

Rupert with all the lords and ladies present, which were very many, dined at a long table in the same room. When dinner was ended I attended the King and the Queen together with the nobles into several withdrawing chambers, where they entertained themselves for the space of an hour. And in the meantime I caused the windows of the hall to be shut, the candles lighted, and all things made ready for the play to begin. When these things were fitted, I gave notice to the King and Queen and attended them into the hall. ... The play[275] was very good and the action. It was merry and without offence, and so gave a great deal of content. In the middle of the play I ordered a short banquet for the King, the Queen, and the lords. And the College was at that time so well furnished as that they did not borrow any one actor from any College in town. The play ended, the King and Queen went to Christ Church." A contemporary notes among the quaintnesses of the entertainment that "the baked meats were so contrived by the cook, that there was first the forms of archbishops, then bishops, doctors, etc., seen in order, wherein the King and courtiers took much content." "No man," says Laud, "went out at the gates, courtier or other, but content; which was a happiness quite beyond expectation." The next day, when the royal party had left, the Chancellor entertained the University authorities, "which gave the University a great deal of content, being that which had never been done by any Chancellor before." "I sat with them," he says, "at table; we were merry, and very glad that all things had so passed to the great satisfaction of the King and the honour of that place."

By this time Laud had not only given to his own College a notable position in the University, but had reformed and legislated for the University itself. The statutes had long been in confusion; Convocation in any case of difficulty passed a new rule which frequently conflicted with the old statutes, and the government of the undergraduates seems to have been very lax. The University submitted its laws to the Chancellor, who, with the aid of a learned lawyer of Merton College, revised and codified them. How he desired that the students should be ruled may be seen by his careful direction to the heads of Colleges,[276] that "the youths should conform themselves to the public discipline of the University. ... And particularly see that none, youth or other, be suffered to go in boots or spurs, or to wear their hair undecently long, or with a lock in the present fashion, or with slashed doublets, or in any light or garish colours; and that noblemen's sons may conform in everything, as others do, during the time of their abode there, which will teach them to know the difference of places and order betimes; and when they grow up to be men it will make them look back upon that place with honour to it and reputation to you." So successful was he in impressing the spirit of discipline and self-restraint, that Sir John Coke was able to congratulate the University in 1636 that "scholars are no more found in taverns, nor seen loitering in the streets or other places of idleness or ill-example, but all contain themselves within the walls of their Colleges, and in the schools or public libraries, wherein I confess you have at length gotten the start, and by your virtue and merit have made this University, which before had no paragon in any foreign country, now to go beyond itself and give a glorious example to others not to go behind." In the Register of S. John's College there are curious examples of the discipline maintained. To take an instance from a somewhat later time, under the date of April 4th, 1668, we have "Memorandum, that I, Thomas Tuer, being convented and convicted, *secunda vice*, before the Vice-President and Seniors of the breach of the statutes *de morum honestate* by injuriously striking Sir Waple, was for this my fault according to the statutes on that behalf put out of commons for 15 days. Thomas Tuer."

By his example of conscientious perseverance, by his devotion to learning, and by his munificent building and endowment, Laud had brought both his College and the University to a high standard of culture and research. These were indeed the halcyon days of S. John's, when Laud, its "second founder," was Chancellor of the University and Primate of all England; Juxon his pious and sagacious successor as President was Bishop of London and Lord Treasurer; and Dr. Richard Baylie governed the College, whose annalist says that never was there more diligent scholar, more learned Fellow, or more prudent Head.[277] But the University soon fell on evil days; discipline was dissolved, teaching and learning were alike suspended, and the streets rang with the summons to arms. The city bore for several years the aspect at once of a camp, and of an exiled Court. In these troubles S. John's had its full share. Scholars joined the King's troops, Fellows were driven from their country livings, the College gave up its treasures to the Royal cause. In the College Register of 1642 is inserted the following letter—"Charles R. Trusty and well beloved, we greet you well. We are so well satisfied with your readiness and Affection to our service that we cannot doubt but you will take all occasions to express the same. And as we are ready to sell or engage any of our lands, so we have melted down our Plate for the payment of our Army raised for our defence and the preservation of the Kingdom. And having received several quantities of Plate from divers of our loving subjects we have removed our Mint hither to our City of Oxford for the coining thereof. And we do hereby desire you that you will send unto us all such plate of what kind soever which belongs to your College, promising you to see the same justly repaid unto you after the rate of 5s. the ounce for white, and 5s. 6d. for gilt plate as soon as God shall enable us. For assure yourselves we shall never let persons of whom we have so great a care to suffer for their affection unto us, but shall take special order for the repayment of what you have already lent to us according to our promise. ... And we assure ourselves of the very great willingness to gratify us herein, since besides the more public considerations you cannot but know how much yourselves are concerned in our sufferings. And we shall always remember this particular service to your advantage. Given at our Court at Oxford this 6th day of Jan. 1642 (1643)."

"In answer to his Majesty's letters," says the Register, "it was consented and unanimously agreed by the President and Fellows of the College that the plate of the College should be delivered unto his Majesty's use." It was melted down, and the coin so struck was stamped with the initials of the President, Dr. Richard Baylie.

In June 1643 the King wrote again to the College, asking that some of its members should subscribe 4*s.* a week for a month for the support of soldiers: "we do assure you on the word of a king that this charge shall lie on you but one month." Soon after this Laud resigned his Chancellorship in a touching letter from his prison, and in making his will showed the deepest attachment to the College where he "was bred." Baylie, who was his executor, was not long suffered to remain in his post. The Parliamentary Commission which visited the University in January 1648 ordered that the President of S. John's College, "being adjudged guilty of high contempt by denial of the authority of Parliament, be removed from" his office, "and accordingly the said Dr. Baylie is required forthwith to yield obedience hereunto, and to remove from the said College and quit the said place, and all emoluments, rights and appointments thereunto belonging." They abolished the choral service, appropriating Sir William Paddy's endowment to the increase of the President's salary. These Commissioners, says Dr. Joseph Taylor, were men "in whom there was nothing lacking save religion, virtue, and learning," and the oath which they required of the Fellows, for the sake of ejecting them when they refused it, was "as ridiculous as it was detestable." In the place of the existing foundation they put as President Francis Cheynell, the zealot who had anathematized Chillingworth as he lay dying (a man, says Taylor, "non tantum fanaticus sed et furiosus"), and they filled the Fellowships with men collected anywhere and than the majority of whom "there could be nothing more ignorant or more abject." Cheynell held the Presidency only two years, when he was obliged to make choice between it and a valuable living in Sussex. He was succeeded by one Thankful or Gracious Owen, a Fellow of Lincoln College, under whose rule the College languished in poverty and neglect until the Restoration, its property dissipated and its learning in decay.

The return of the King brought back Head and Fellows. A blank page in the College Register is followed by a lease signed by "R. Baylie," without note or comment on his deprivation or return. The first results of the Restoration were works of piety. Before long the body of the aged Juxon was laid near the founder beneath the altar in the chapel. It was now possible to carry out the last wish of Laud himself, who in his will had desired "to be buried in the chapel of S. John Baptist College, under the altar or communion table there." All was done privately, as he had himself directed. Yet the stillness of night, the torches and the flickering candles, the reverence of the restored foundation to the greatest and most loyal of its sons, must have given a unique solemnity to the scene. "The day then, or rather the night," says Anthony Wood, "being appointed wherein he should come to Oxon, most of the Fellows, about sixteen or twenty in number, went to meet him towards Wheatley, and after they had met him, about seven of the clock on Friday, July 24th, 1663, they came to Oxon at ten at night, with the said number before him, and his corpse lying on a horse litter on four wheels drawn by four horses, following, and a coach after that. In the same way they went up to S. Mary's Church, then up Cat's Street, then to the back-door of S. John's Grove; where, taking his coffin out, they conveyed [it] to the chapel; when Mr. Gisbey, Fellow of that house and Vice-President, had spoke a speech, they laid him inclosed in a wooden coffin in a little vault at the upper end of the chancel between the founder's and Archbishop Juxon's."

The most interesting period of the College history was during the reigns of the Stuarts. The same spirit of devotion to the Church and loyalty to the throne which had animated Laud and Juxon still breathed in their successors. Tobias Rustat, Esquire, Yeoman of the Robes to Charles II., and Under Housekeeper of Hampton Court, left a large sum to endow loyal lectures—two on "the day of the horrid and most execrable murder of that most glorious Prince and Martyr"; one to be read by the Dean of Divinity, and the other by "some one of the most ingenious Scholars or Fellows whom the President shall appoint," setting forth the "barbarous cruelty of that unparalleled parricide"; one by the Dean of Law on October 23rd, "which was the day wherein Rebellion did appear solemnly armed against Majesty"; and a fourth on the 29th of May, "setting forth the glory and happiness of that day," which saw the birth of Charles II. and his "triumphant return." There is in the College library a curious portrait of Charles I., over which in a minute hand several Psalms are written. Tradition has it that when the "merry monarch" visited Oxford he asked for this eccentric piece of work, and that when, on leaving, in recognition of his loyal welcome he offered to give the Fellows anything they should ask, they declared that no gift could be so precious as the restoration to them of the portrait of his father. The story, true or not, could only be told of a College which was famous as the home of devoted loyalty to the Stuarts. It was Dr. Peter Mews (or Meaux), Baylie's successor as President, who lent his carriage horses to draw the royal cannon to Sedgmoor. When Nicholas Amherst (the author of a collection of scurrilous essays which he called after the name of the licensed buffoon at the Encænia, Terræ Filius) was expelled the College for his irregularities, he made up a plausible tale that the reason for his expulsion was that he was the only man loyal to the Hanoverian line in a nest of Jacobites. He lost no opportunity of attacking the College, with no regard for truth or consistency. Dr. Delaune (President 1698-1728) was his most prominent victim. Once, says he, that learned President was affronted in the theatre by Terrae Filius, who called out to him by name as he came in, shaking a box and dice, and crying "*Jacta est alea*, doctor, seven's the main," in allusion to "a scandalous report handed about by the doctor's enemies, that he had lost great sums of other people's money at dice." But Jacobitism was an accusation much more plausible, and we are inclined not altogether to disbelieve him when he says that the Latitudinarian Hoadly was abused in a Latin oration in chapel as "iste malus logicus, pejor politicus, pessimus theologus; a bad logician, a worse statesman, and the worst of all divines." Dr. Richard Rawlinson, who had been a gentleman commoner of the College, and left to it on his death in 1755 the bulk of his estate, was a typical antiquary and worshipper of the exiled House. His collection of letters and MSS., the researches which he made into the early history of the Foundation, are among the most cherished possessions of the College. "Ubi thesaurus ibi cor" is the motto of the urn in chapel which contains his heart. His "treasure" was divided between S. John's and the Bodleian; his heart, which had beaten with an equal affection for the Stuarts and for the College, remained among those who shared his semi-sentimental attachment. It was said of Dr. Holmes (President 1728-48) that he was probably the first Fellow, and certainly the first Head, of the College who was loyal to the Hanoverian Succession. Almost within living memory the Fellows of S. John's in their Common Room, "a large handsome room, the scene of a great deal of learning and a great many puns,"[278] toasted the king "over the water." Up till the middle of the present century, indeed, it was a college of survivals. The old loyal lectures were read, the old "gaudies" held, the old rules maintained. Throughout the eighteenth century the founder's order against absence from College was strictly observed: all permissions to be away from Oxford were carefully recorded in the Register. Leave was at first only granted on the business of the College, or the king, or a bishop; and it is said of one Dr. Sherard that he had to give up his Fellowship when he had exhausted the list of the Episcopal bench. Even Doctors of Divinity were obliged to get license to "go down." Dr. Smith, though Master of Merchant Taylors' School (died 1730), could not teach his boys without the College leave to be absent from Oxford. Only in recent years has iconoclastic modernism destroyed the old progresses round the College estates, formal fishing of the College waters, and festive commemoration of days of ecclesiastical or royalist note. The history of the last and of the present century lies outside the scope of this sketch, and the share that S. John's has had in the important movements of the last seventy years is left untold. Much has undergone change, at the hands of Time and of Parliamentary Commissions; but there still lingers one feature of the old life of the University which elsewhere has passed away. S. John's alone of all the Colleges has (1891) no married Fellows; thus here as it can scarcely be elsewhere, the College life is most closely centered within the College walls.

XVI.
JESUS COLLEGE.

BY THE REV. LL. THOMAS, M.A., VICE-PRINCIPAL
OF JESUS COLLEGE.

Jesus College was the first Protestant Society established in Oxford, and its appearance marks an epoch in the history of the University; for "if Christ Church was the last and grandest effort of expiring Mediævalism, if Trinity and St. John's commemorated the re-action under Philip and Mary, Jesus, by its very name, took its stand as the first Protestant College."[279]

It may seem at first sight that there ought to be little difficulty in tracing the origin and settlement of a College which thus came into being in the latter half of the sixteenth century; but, partly because much is obscure in the history of the institution out of which it was erected, and partly because there are practically no College records for the first sixty years of its own existence, the historian of Jesus College has very scanty materials for his account of its foundation and early annals, and has to put down much which rests rather on inference than on documentary evidence.

About the year 1460, John Rowse, the Warwick antiquary, wrote down a list[280] of Halls and other places of study in Oxford. In this four Halls are mentioned, all for "legists," that is, students of

Canon and of Civil Law, viz. White, Hawk, Laurence, and Elm Halls, which stood on the site now occupied by Jesus College. These represented a once greater number of Halls, for Laurence Hall had absorbed Plomer (or Plummer) Hall; and in White Hall had been merged another White Hall,[281]which stood back to back with it, and apparently (but the evidence is hardly tangible) other Halls. In the next century the number of Halls was still further reduced, and by 1552 we find White Hall alone left,[282] having possibly drawn into its own precincts the buildings of its old neighbours. This White Hall stood on the north side of Cheyney Lane (now called Market Street), a short distance from the corner where it enters the Turl. It was a very old place of study, being mentioned as early as 1262, and having a well-marked succession of Principals from 1436 to 1552.

The point of capital importance in view of its relation to Jesus College is whether, about the time of the Reformation, White Hall became distinctly a Hall for Welsh students; but that point cannot be determined. The occasional and imperfect lists of members of White Hall found up to 1552 exhibit only a few Welsh names, from which it may perhaps be inferred that Welshmen were then in a distinct minority in this Hall. The two graduates of White Hall who are mentioned in 1562[283] are both Welsh, as also are their pupils; but these notices are a mere accident. If, however, Jesus College took over the inmates of White Hall, they must have been mostly Welshmen, because the first College list[284] (1572-3, two years after the foundation) exhibits almost exclusively Welsh names. On the whole, it is best to say that the evidence does not justify the belief that White Hall, which Jesus College superseded, was distinctly a Hall of Welsh students.

At the petition of Hugo Price, or Ap Rice, Doctor of Laws, Treasurer of St. Davids, Queen Elizabeth granted the first Letters Patent, dated the 27th of June, 1571, establishing "quoddam Collegium eruditionis scientiarum, philosophiae, bonarum artium, linguarum cognitionis, Hebraicae, Graecae, et Latinae, ad finalem sacrae Theologiae professionem," and conferring on the new foundation all the lands, buildings, and personalty of White Hall. From these words of the Foundation Charter it appears that the College was primarily intended to be a place of training for theologians; a secondary object is thus summed up, "denique ad Ecclesiae Christi, regni nostri, ac subditorum nostrorum communem utilitatem et felicitatem."

Soon after the issue of the Letters Patent, but it is not known exactly when, the building of the College began, the first portion erected being two stories of the east front and two staircases[285] of the southern side of the outer quadrangle. For many years, probably till 1618, the work was not extended, and the following story is handed down. A stone was inserted in the wall on the south side of the gateway, bearing this inscription—

"Struxit Hugo Prisius tibi clara palatia, Iesu,
Ut Doctor Legum pectora docta daret."

"Nondum," laughed a University wit, one Christopher Rainald,

"Nondum struxit Hugo, vix fundamenta locavit:
Det Deus ut possis dicere 'struxit Hugo'!"

Of the first founder, Hugo Price, very little is known. "He was born," Wood says, "at Brecknock,[286] bred up as 'tis generally thought, in Oseney Abbey, under an uncle of his that was a Canon there;" he did not long survive the foundation of the College, and was buried (August 1574) in the Priory Church at Brecon.

The Letters Patent provide for the constitution of the College to consist of a Principal, eight Fellows, and eight Scholars, nominate persons to fill all these places, and arrange for future appointments.

The Principal nominated was David Powell, Doctor of Laws. Among the Fellows may be noticed Robert Johnson, B.D.,[287] afterwards Archdeacon of Leicester, the founder of Uppingham and Oakham Schools. Among the scholars Thomas Dove, afterwards Bishop of Peterborough, and Lancelot Andrews, Bishop successively of Chichester, Ely, and Winchester. The College is then incorporated, invested with corporate legal powers and a common seal, and united with the University "ut pars, parcella, et membrum." Concession is granted to Hugo Price to endow the College with lands and revenues to the amount of a clear £60 per annum, and to the College to receive further endowments to the extent of £100 a year; and finally an important body of Commissioners is appointed (including Lord

Burghley and other magnates, and the Chancellor or Vice-Chancellor of the University, together with the Principal and two Fellows), to draw up all the necessary statutes for the government of the College. There is also a tradition that leave was given to the College to receive a supply of timber from the royal forests of Stow and Shotover towards the erection of the fabric.

The second Letters Patent of Queen Elizabeth were issued on the 7th day of July, 1589, eighteen years after the first patent. Their object appears to have been to appoint Francis Bevans to the Principalship, to authorize the College to receive further benefactions to the amount of £200 a year, and to nominate a still more important body of Commissioners to draw up the College statutes. These second Commissioners included several ecclesiastical and legal dignitaries, the Chancellor and Vice-Chancellor of the University, the Principal, and apparently three Fellows of the College, and Richard Harrys, Principal of Brasenose College. The presence of the last-mentioned Commissioner probably accounts for the fact that the new statutes were framed upon the model of the Brasenose statutes. There seems to have been some delay in drawing up these statutes, but they were finally completed and ordered to be written "fayre in a Booke." This "Booke" seems to have been sent from one Commissioner to another for approval and correction, and at least once was reported to be lost; but was eventually recovered and deposited in the College.

The third Letters Patent concerning the College are those of King James I., dated June 1st, 1621, in the fiftieth year of the College. After reciting both the Letters Patent of Queen Elizabeth, the King confirms the establishment of the College; arranges for the addition and co-optation of eight additional Fellows and eight additional scholars; and incorporates the College anew to consist of sixteen Fellows and sixteen scholars. Further, Sir Eubule Thelwall, one of the Masters of the Court of Chancery, is nominated to the Principalship; and vacancies in the Fellowships and scholarships are filled up. It is worthy of notice that two of the original Fellows, Robert Johnson and John Higgenson, and two of the original scholars, Lancelot Andrews and Thomas Dove, are still retaining their places.

It is remarkable that in the three documents above-mentioned there is no word or expression which implies any local limitation of the College. There is no direct or indirect allusion to place of birth or education in the Letters Patent or in the statutes. And yet the founder was a Welshman, and probably intended his new foundation to be a Welsh College. The Tudors were always ready to acknowledge their Welsh origin; hence the readiness of Queen Elizabeth to accede to the request of Dr. Hugo Price, and even to contribute something of her royal bounty. Yet no formal means were adopted to secure and continue the connection of the College with Wales. If we review the lists of the Fellows nominated in the two Letters Patent of Elizabeth, we know by the names only (even apart from our actual knowledge from other sources) that they are not all Welshmen. But it is otherwise with the Principals. Every one of these, from the foundation to the end of the eighteenth century, shows by his name[288] his connection with Wales. The times in which Dr. Hugo Price lived were times of somewhat despotic government; the Principal appointed the Foundationers; and it may have seemed a sufficient safeguard to the first founder if it should become a tradition that the Principal must be a Welshman. At any rate, if it was not his intention to secure the connection with Wales by such means, it does not seem possible that he could have selected any which would have been more successful. From the time of the Restoration it is exceedingly rare to find the admission of any one to a Scholarship or Fellowship who was not qualified for the preferment by birth in Wales. It is only important to notice that this exclusiveness grew up by custom and tradition, but was not ordained by statute or authority. In the time of Sir Leoline Jenkins a fixed system was adopted,[289] and certain Fellowships and Scholarships were assigned respectively to North and South Wales; but it was not so at the first.

Of the first six Principals, five were Fellows of All Souls, and only two in Holy Orders. The diversity in the authority by which they were appointed is to be remarked. The first and third were nominated by the Crown in the Letters Patent; of the appointment of the second there is no record; the fourth was "elected Principal, 17th May, 1602, by three Fellows that were then in the College"; the fifth was nominated by the Chancellor of the University, and admitted, under his mandate, by the Vice-Chancellor, 8th September, 1613, no Fellows appearing or claiming the right of election; the sixth Principal was nominated by the Chancellor, and admitted by the Vice-Chancellor, after a contest with the Fellows, which brought about the final settlement of the dispute in favour of the College by the third Letters Patent.

The cause of this uncertainty is not difficult to discover. Had the College been definitely constituted, the statutes would have provided for the filling up of vacancies in the ordinary way of election by the Fellows. But the Royal Commissioners had neglected to settle the College by statutes, and the Chancellor of the University claimed to appoint the Principal of the College as he had enjoyed the right of appointing the Principal of White Hall.

The question between the claims of the Fellows and of the Chancellor was brought to an issue in 1620. On 29th June in that year the Chancellor (Lord Pembroke) nominated Francis Mansell (his kinsman and chaplain) Principal on the death of Griffith Powell; and on 3rd July the Vice-Chancellor (Dr. John Prideaux, Rector of Exeter) admitted him in spite of the protests of the Fellows who claimed the election. On 13th July, Mansell expelled from their Fellowships three of his chief opponents; and on 17th July the Vice-Chancellor interposed in

Mansell's favour the authority of his office against a fourth.[290]

The subsequent stages in the dispute are not upon record; but that Mansell felt his position insecure is obvious from his resignation of the Principalship and his return to his All Souls Fellowship before his year of grace at that College had expired. His successor, Eubule Thelwall, by what authority appointed is not known, obtained within a year the third Letters Patent under which the constitution of the College was finally determined, and the right of election secured to the Fellows.

Griffith Powell, the fifth Principal, had been a considerable benefactor, and was the first to extend the buildings of the College since the foundation. He began to enlarge it by the addition of the buttery, kitchen, and hall; but dying before they could be completed, he left them, together with the south side of the outer quadrangle, to be completed by Sir Eubule Thelwall, "that most bountiful person, who left nothing undone that might conduce to the good of the College." Francis Mansell, his successor, was a Fellow of All Souls, but had been a commoner of the College. He was third son of Sir Francis Mansell, of Muddlescomb, in the county of Carmarthen. Of him we have very full information from the *Life*,[291] by Sir Leoline Jenkins, which presents a most interesting and vivid picture of the troublous times in which he lived. Dr. Francis Mansell performed the unprecedented feat of holding the Principalship three times, being twice appointed, and once restored, to the office. He watched the growth of the buildings under the two great benefactors—Sir Eubule Thelwall and Sir Leoline Jenkins; and he himself aided the work by his advice, gifts, and diligence in collecting contributions.

On Mansell's resignation of the Principalship in 1621 his place was filled by Sir Eubule Thelwall. He was the fifth son of John Thelwall of Bathavarn Park in the county of Denbigh, bred in Trinity College in Cambridge till he was Bachelor of Arts, then coming to Oxford, was incorporated here in the same degree in 1579. Afterwards Master of Arts of this University, Counsellor at Law, Master of the Alienation Office, and one of the Masters in Chancery, he was admitted Principal in the month of May 1621. He procured from King James a new charter (mentioned above), and greatly increased the buildings of the College, not only completing the kitchen, buttery, and hall, but adding a house for the Principal, and the chapel—which, however, was afterwards enlarged by the addition (in 1636) of a sacrarium. He also built a library, "with a walk under," probably a colonnade, to the north of the Hall and west of his new house; but it is doubtful whether he meant this to be a permanent building. He enlarged the foundation, augmented the endowments of the College, and enriched the library with books. He died October 8th, 1630, and was buried in the chapel.

On the death of Sir Eubule Thelwall, Dr. Francis Mansell was again appointed to the Headship.

Encouraged, perhaps, by the example of his predecessor, he, in his second tenure of the office, greatly enlarged the buildings of the College, "for though our Principall had no fonds but that of his owne Zeale, such was the Interest, which his Relation in Blood to the many noble Families and (which was more prevailing) his public and pious Spirit, had procured him, that he had Contributions sufficient in view to finish and perfect his new Quadrangle; Sr George Vaughan of Ffoulkston in Wiltshire having declared that himselfe would be at the whole charge of the west end, which was designed to be the Library; but all these pious designes and contributions were lost by the dispersions and Ruines that by the Warr befell those who intended to be our Benefactors."[292] Notwithstanding, Dr. Mansell was able to effect much, for he pulled down Thelwall's library, which does not seem to have been a satisfactory building, and erected the north and south sides of the inner quadrangle. He also enriched the College with revenues and benefices, some of which appear to have been since alienated.

Dr. Mansell was obliged to leave Oxford in 1643, owing to "the sad newes of his Brother Sr Anthony's decease, who fell with all the circumstances of signall Piety and Vallor in the first Newbury fight; where he commanded as field-Officer under Lord Herbert of Ragland." He had to remain in Wales to settle his brother's affairs, and look after his orphan children for some time; but "the Garrison of Oxon being surrendered in 1646, and the Visitation upon the University coming on, in July 1647, he hastened away from Wales to his station there; and though the Earle of Pembroke (who was chiefe in the Action) owned our Principall as his near Kinsman and had a Favour to the College as the naturall Visitor thereof by Charter, and though the Earles Two younger Sons who had lived severall years Commoners in the College under our Principall's charge, offered him their Service with all Affection possible, yet neither the Propensions of the Earle, nor the Kind offices of his Sons could bring our Principall to fframe himself to any the least evasion, much less to the direct owneing of that Power. Being ejected out of the Headship, which was not actually done by order of the Visitors till the one and twentieth day of May 1648, he Applyed himself to state all Accompts between him and the College; And having delivered the muniments and Goods that belong to it to the hands of the Intruders, he withdrew into Wales and took up his Residence att Llantrythyd, a House of his Kinsman's, Sir John Auberey's K[nt] and Baronett, which house Sequestration having made desolate, while Sir John was in prison for his Adherence to the King, afforded him the Conveniency of a more private retirement and of having severall young Gentlemen of Quality, his Kindred under his eye, while they were taught and Bread up by a young man[293] of his College that he had chosen for that employment."

Here he suffered many persecutions and indignities, "for the Doctor's very Grave and Pious aspect, which should have been a protection to him among Salvages, was no other than a Temptation to those (who reputed themselves Saints) to Act their Insolencies upon him." At last, driven from his retirement, he returned to Oxford, where, "when our Principall came first to Towne, he took up at Mr. Newmans,[294] a Baker in Holy-well; but the good Offices he dayly rendered to the College disposed the then Society so farr to comply with his Inclinations (which had been allway to live and dye in the College) as to invite him to accept of one Chamber for accommodating himself, where he built severall faire ones for the Benefitt of the College. This motion was accepted, and he Lived in the College, near the stoney staires near the Gate, for eight years where he had Leisure to observe many Changes and Revolutions within those Walls, as without them till that happy one of his majestie's Restauration by God's infinite Mercy to the College as well as to the Nation happily came on."

He was restored to his Headship on the 1st of August 1660, but owing to "the decayes of Age, especially dimness of Sight," he resolved to resign once more. His first wish was that Dr. William Bassett, Fellow of All Souls, should succeed him, "who would have added to the Reputation of the College by his Government, and to the Revenew of it in all Probability, by his generous minde and ample Fortune; But Dr. Bassett's want of health not allowing him to accept of the Burthen, it was (by the Unanimous Consent of all the Fellowes at a ffree-election the first of March, 1660,[295] and with the good Liking of Our Common Father) devolved upon

Dr. Jenkins.[296] This being done he had no other thought but for Heaven, nor Leasure but for Prayer; he came by degrees to be confined to his chamber and at last to his Bed and upon the first day of May 1665 he changed this Life for a better of Blisse and Immortality."

The following items from the *Book of Receipts and Disbursements*, in Dr. Mansell's own handwriting, are of interest as showing some of the charges to which a College was put during the Civil War—

"Other various and Extraordinary Expenses, most of them peculiar to the time.

Put uppon Domus by Mr *Evans* for Bread and Beere to the Kinges Souldiers at their first Cominge to *Oxon* from *Edgehill*	(1:	2:	
Payd by him the Taxe layd uppon the Coll: towards the works from the beginninge of it to the 28th of *Jan:* '43	(3:	6:	
More by him for Musquets, Pikes and the like	(3:	4:	
Given by him to the Prince his Trumpetters	(0:	0:	0
Payd by Pole after 12^d a head every weeke for all of	(2:	1:	0

the Coll. towards the fortifications in *Xst Church* Meade from the 17th of *June* to the end of *July*

More towards the same in *Aug. & Sept.*

(2:	:	0

For a little Peece of Plate of another man's, which was in my Study, and by mistake taken out with the Coll. Plate,[297] and lent to his Matie, which weighed some what more than 8 ounces

| (2: | 0: | 0 |

Pay'd uppon his Maj^ties Motion towards the Maintenance of his Foote Souldiers for one Monthe after fower Pounds by the Weeke

|] 6: | 0: | 0 |

The Totall of Receipts

| (5: | : |

The Totall of Disbursments

| 41: | : |

And so the Disbursments doe exceede the Receipts by the Summe of

| 46: | : | 0 |

Which I the Principall have lay'd out of the Coll. Money remayninge in my hands, mine owne, or what I borrowed of others.

And I disbursed the
money lent by Common
Consent to his Matie

```
                           ]
              00:      0:       0"
```

In the interval between Dr. Mansell's ejection in 1648 by the Parliamentary Visitors and his restoration in 1660 by Charles II.'s Commissioners, two Principals ruled the College. Of the first of these, Michael Roberts, Sir Leoline Jenkins uses the words "infamous and corrupt." Perhaps the words are not to be taken literally; but nothing of the kind is said of his successor, Francis Howell, though he also was a Puritan. It is also on record that in 1656 the Fellows deposed Roberts on charges of embezzling the College funds and corrupt dealing in elections; and that although for the time the Parliamentary Visitors refused to endorse the action of the Fellows, he did vacate his Principalship that year or the next, presumably to avoid expulsion. Afterwards he "lived obscurely" in Oxford, dying on 3rd May, 1670, "with a girdle[298] lined with broad gold pieces about him (100£ they say)," and was buried in St. Peter's in the East churchyard. The appointment in his place of Francis Howell, Fellow of Exeter, on 24th October, 1657, marks the ascendancy of the Independents over the Presbyterians in Puritan Oxford. The Fellows of the College had elected Seth Ward (afterwards Bishop of Salisbury), but the Independents persuaded Oliverus Protector to appoint Howell, after the fashion already set in Oxford by Elizabetha Regina, and afterwards followed by Jacobus Rex.

In the *Familiar Letters* of James Howell are some interesting notices of Oxford and of Jesus College during the times of Mansell, Thelwall, and Jenkins. The writer, James Howell, son of Thomas Howell, minister of Abernant in Carmarthenshire, was born about 1594; and entered Jesus College, where he took his B.A. degree, in 1613. During his absence abroad in the diplomatic service he was chosen on the Foundation of his College by Sir Eubule Thelwall; but whether he was actually admitted is not recorded. Space forbids extracting from his letters the entertaining passages about Oxford; but this is the less to be regretted since the letters are found in many editions, the last being issued in 1890.

Some years after Howell had left College, viz. in 1638, Henry Vaughan, "The Silurist," entered. In early life he does not seem to have written much; it was owing to illness and trouble that he was led to imitate and often to excel the devotional poetry of George Herbert. This is not the place to dwell upon his merits. His works have been little read, but have gradually asserted their claim to an enduring place in English literature.

Soon afterwards his twin brother, Thomas Vaughan (Eugenius Philalethes), an eminent writer, philosopher, and chemist, was educated in the College. In 1644, James Usher, Archbishop of Armagh, was resident in and a member of the

College. At a still earlier period (1602), Rees Prichard was a member of the College. He was afterwards Vicar of Llandovery, and became an eminent poet. His book *Canwyll y Cymru*, is the best known and most highly valued collection of devotional and religious poetry in the Welsh language.

The above were all Anglican Churchmen and Royalists, but there was at this period some Puritanism in the College. "The growth of Puritan feeling in the city of Oxford is shown by the formation of the first Baptist Society under Vavasour Powell of Jesus College, in 1618. He made many converts in Wales, and in 1657 we hear of John Bunyan accompanying him to Oxford. Powell died at last in the Fleet Prison."[299]

Among other distinguished members of the College during the sixteenth and seventeenth centuries may be briefly mentioned Dr. John Davies (1573), a Welsh scholar and grammarian; John Ellis (1628), author of *Clavis Fidei*; Edward Lhwyd (1682), a celebrated antiquary, and keeper of the Ashmolean Museum; Henry Maurice (1664), a learned divine and Margaret Professor of Divinity; David Powel (1571), a learned divine and eminent antiquary; his son Gabriel Powel (1592), considered "a prodigy of learning"; John White, M.P. (1607), a well-known character during the Commonwealth; John Williams (1569), Margaret Professor of Divinity, Dean of Bangor, and author; Sir William Williams, a very eminent lawyer and statesman,

Speaker of the House of Commons, Solicitor-and Attorney-General (1688); Owen Wood (1584), Dean of Armagh, a considerable benefactor to the College; with many Bishops, a list of whom is here given:—

Bishops educated in Jesus College.

.	Richard Meredith	Leighlin and Ferns (1589)
.	John Rider	Killaloe (1612)
.	Lewis Bayley	Bangor (1616)
.	Edmund Griffith	Bangor (1633)
.	Morgan Owen	Llandaff (1639)
.	Thomas Howell	Bristol (1644)
.	Hugh Lloyd	Llandaff (1660)
.	Francis Davies	Llandaff (1667)
.	Humphrey Lloyd	Bangor (1673)
0.	William Thomas	St. Davids (1677), Worcester (1683)
1.	William Lloyd	St. Asaph (1680), Lichfield (1698), Worcester (1699)
	Hump	Bangor (1689)

2.	hrey Humphreys	
	John	Ossory (1689)
3.	Parry	
	John	St. Davids (1686)
4.	Lloyd	
	John	Bangor (1701), Meath
5.	Evans	(1715)
	John	St. Asaph (1714), Bath and
6.	Wynne[300]	Wells (1729)

Bishops not educated in Jesus College, but who have been members of the Society. [301]

Lancelot Andrews	Chichester, Winchester	Ely,
Thomas Dove	Peterborough.	

Leoline Jenkins, who succeeded Dr. Mansell in 1661, has been well termed the second founder of the College. He almost completed the buildings, restored discipline, fostered study, augmented the revenues, and at his death left his whole estate to the College. He therefore deserves a somewhat fuller record of his life than any of his predecessors or successors. His charges as a Judge and Commissary of the Archbishop of Canterbury, and his correspondence as an Ambassador were published by William Wynne, Esq., of the Middle Temple, in 1734, in two large folio volumes; to this is prefixed a memoir from which we gather the following facts—

"He was born in the year 1625, in the parish of Llanblithian, in the county of Glamorgan, and was the son of Leoline Jenkins, or Jenkins Llewelyn, of the same place, a man of about £40 a year, and who left behind him in that neighbourhood the character of a very honest, prudent, and industrious man. The first Essays and Foundation of his son's future Learning were laid at Cowbridge School, very near the place of his birth and even then no inconsiderable School, which, as a grateful Acknowledgement of benefits there received, he afterwards liberally endowed.

"He was admitted into Jesus College in the year 1641, not quite 16 years of age. Mr. Jenkins' behaviour from his first appearance in College was so regular and exact that a good Opinion was soon taken of him. But the Troubles of the Nation soon after coming on, Mr. Jenkins took Arms for the Royal Cause. Thus were his tender years seasoned and exercised not only with Learning and Diligence, but also with an equal Mixture of Adversities, the best Preparatives for the succeeding Varieties of his Life. For the Society into which Mr. Jenkins had been admitted, was not only obliged to give way to Strangers, but also the College itself was dismantled, and became Part of a Garrison by Order from Court; and for some time continued to be the Quarters of the Lord Herbert afterwards Marquiss of Worcester, and of other persons of Quality, that came out of Wales on the King's Service. The Garrison of Oxford being surrendred in the year 1646, and the Visitation of the University by the two Houses coming on in the following year, this College, among others, soon felt the fatal Effects of it, for of 16 Fellows and as many Scholars, there remained but one Fellow and one Scholar that was not ousted of their Subsistance. Mr. Jenkins retired to Wales and settled not far from Llantrythyd where Dr. Mansell was living at the House of Sir John Auberey who was an adherent of the Royal Cause. The first employment found for Mr. Jenkins was the tuition of Sir John's eldest son. Being indicted for keeping a Seminary of Rebellion and Sedition, he was forced to leave that Countrey and removed with his Charge to Oxford in May 1651, and settled there in a Town-house belonging to Mr. Alderman White[302] in the High-street, which from him was then commonly called and known by the Name of the Little Welsh-Hall. Mr. Jenkins's regular and orthodox Behaviour at Oxford was not quite so close and reserved, as to escape all Observation, but he began to give Offence to some of the inquisitive schismatical Members of the University and was obliged to retire from thence, with his Pupils as it were in his Arms, and go beyond Sea, for fear of Imprisonment, or of some worse Disaster. Even this was no unlucky Accident, for it helped to add to his former Acquirements the Knowledge of Men as well as Letters. It gave him an Acquaintance with some eminent and learned Men, particularly Messieurs Spanheim and Courtin; it was the Means of acquiring a great Accuracy in the French and other Languages. It appears by a little Diary that he made a Tour over a great part of France, Holland and Germany, and resided at their famous Seats of Learning, especially at Leyden. He returned to England in 1658, and was invited by Sir William Whitmore, a great Patron of the distress'd Cavaliers, to live with him at Appley in Shropshire, where he continued till the year 1660 enjoying the Opportunities of Study, and a well-furnished Library. As soon as the King was restored to his Kingdom and the University to its just rights, Mr. Jenkins returned to Jesus College, about the 35th Year of his Age, and his Reputation among his Countrymen was so considerable that upon his first Appearance and Settlement of the Society, he was chose one of the Fellows, and his Behaviour gained so fast upon them that he was very soon after, upon the Resignation of Dr. Mansell, unanimously chose Principal of the College, and thereupon commenced Doctor of the Civil Law.

"And indeed the College had never more Occasion of such a Ruler than at this Time, when the former Discipline of it had been so long interrupted by the late distracted and licentious Times, and had suffered so much by the Management of his 'infamous and corrupt' Predecessor.[303] Dr. Jenkins did abundantly satisfie the Hopes conceived of him; he made it his first Concern to restore the Exercises, Disputations and Habits, and to review and consider the Body of Statutes. By these prudent Methods he retrieved the Reputation and advanced the Discipline of the College. He busied himself in adding to the Buildings of the College, and completed the Library and part of the western side of the Inner Quadrangle. He was made Assessor to the Chancellor and Deputy

Professor of Civil Law. He was also of singular use to the University in maintaining their Foreign Correspondences by his skill in the French and other Languages. He was also very instrumental to his Friend and Patron Archbishop Sheldon in the Settlement of his Theatre and Printing-House. He not only framed the Draught of that Grant with his own Hand, but also the Statute 'de Vesperiis and Comitiis a B. Virginis Mariæ templo transferendis ad Theatrum,' that the House of God might be kept free for its own proper and pious Uses.

"The University now became too narrow a Field for such an active Mind and too scanty an Employment for those high and encreasing Abilities which exerted themselves in him. He was therefore encouraged by his Friend the Archbishop to remove to London in Order to apply himself to the publick Practice of the Civil Law. So he resigned his Principality in 1673, and was succeeded by Mr. (afterwards Dr.) John Lloyd. The after career of the great Lawyer was successful and distinguished, but it does not lie within the scope of the present work, so it must be very briefly described. He rose to be Judge of the High Court of Admiralty and Prerogative Court of Canterbury, Ambassador and Plenipotentiary for the General Peace at Cologne and Nimeguen, and Secretary of State to King Charles II. He was also made a Knight, and became Member of Parliament for Hythe, one of the Cinque Ports, and afterwards Burgess for his own University. It may, however, be excusable to give the description of his last return to the College he loved so much, when his body was brought to be buried by the side of 'his dear Friend Dr. Mansell in Jesus College Chappel.'

"The Pomp and Manner of his Reception there and of his Interment is thus described by one that was an Eyewitness. When the Corps came near the City, several Doctors, and the principal Members and Officers of the University, the Mayor, Aldermen and Citizens, some in Coaches, some on Horseback, went out to meet it and conducted it to the Publick Schools, where the Vice-Chancellor, Bishop of the Diocese and the whole Body of the University were ready to receive it and placed it in the Divinity-School, which was fitted and prepared for that Purpose, with all convenient Ornaments and Decorations. Two Days after, the Vice-Chancellor, several Bishops, Noblemen, Doctors, Proctors and Masters met there again in their Formalities, as well as many others that came to pay their last Respects to him; and the memory of the Deceased being solemnized in a Latin Oration by the University Orator, the Corps was removed to the Chappel of Jesus College. Where the Vice-Chancellor (who happened to be the Principal thereof) read the Offices of Burial; and another Latin Oration was made by one of the Fellows of the College, which was accompanied with Musick, Anthems and other Performances suitable to the occasion. After which it was interr'd in the area of the said Chappel, with a Marble Stone over his Grave and a Latin Inscription on it, supposed to be made by his old Friend Dr. Fell Lord Bishop of Oxford and Dean of Christ Church."

Among other benefactions Sir Leoline left his valuable library to the College, only reserving forty law-books to begin the library at Doctors' Commons in London.

His portrait, painted by Tuer, at Nimeguen, hangs in the College Hall; of this painting there are two replicas, one in the Principal's Lodgings, the other in the Bursary, both so well executed as hardly to be distinguished from the original. He is represented sitting by the council-table in a chair[304] covered with red velvet and holding a memorial in his hand. His dress is plain, but decorated with rich lace at the neck and wrists; his hair is long and flowing; his features strongly marked and melancholy in expression.

The last Principal of the seventeenth century was Jonathan Edwards, who seems to have been an able man, and was a benefactor to the College. He contributed £1000 to the improvement and decoration of the chapel.

A long list of benefactions might be written down for the sixteenth and seventeenth centuries; but space allows individual mention of one only. King Charles I. gave (1636) divers lands and tenements in trust to the University, that they with the profits of them maintain a Fellow in Jesus College (as also in Exeter and Pembroke Colleges) born in the Isle of Jersey or Guernsey. To these benefactions conditions were generally annexed, the profits to be paid to Fellows or scholars, frequently with preference for the kindred of the donor, or for natives of particular places and counties, or for certain schools in Wales.

The eighteenth century presents a great contrast in interest to its predecessor. In Jesus College it was exceptionally uneventful. The buildings of the College were complete, the north-west corner of the inner quadrangle being finished in 1713. Since then the College has not been altered in form nor enlarged. Several valuable benefactions were received, but there was none of the vigour or enthusiasm of the sixteenth century. The most considerable endowment was what is now called the Meyricke Fund, left in trust to the College by the Rev. Edmund Meyricke. Meyricke was, like the original founder of the College, treasurer of the cathedral church of St. Davids. He was one of the Ucheldre family, a branch of that of Bodorgan, in Anglesey. He declares in his Will—"as for my worldly estate, which God Almighty hath blessed me with above my merits or expectation, I dispose of in manner following: Imprimis, whereas I always intended to bestow a good part of what God should please to bless me withall for the encouragement of learning in Jesus College, in Oxford, and for the better maintenance of six of the junior scholars of the foundation of the said College out of the six counties of North Wales; I doe give devise and bequeath all my real and personal estate," &c. The property thus left became very valuable, and a number of Exhibitions were established, strictly confined to Welshmen, with a preference for natives of North Wales. It has been questioned by some whether this fund has been beneficial to the College. There is no doubt it made a University education possible to many Welshmen who would otherwise not have thought of an Oxford Degree. These new students, drawn from the middle and lower classes in Wales, soon formed a majority of the undergraduates. It therefore became customary for the sons of Welsh gentry to resort to other Colleges in Oxford, and to some extent the old connection was broken. This was a decided loss to the social status and prestige of the College; but it is probable that the compensating gain was greater. The young squires who resorted to the University in the eighteenth century were not as a rule students, and formed an element in a College requiring much discipline and toleration. On the other hand, the students, encouraged by the new endowment, if not intellectually very distinguished, owing to lack of early advantages, generally made good use of the privileges afforded by the University, and did solid work for the Principality in after life. When the endowments of the College were strictly and by statute confined to Welshmen, it is in Wales that we must look for educational results. And it must be confessed that when we do look, we are not disappointed. In every department of civil life, but especially in the Church, we find sons of the College occupying posts of usefulness and dignity. Even for the highest posts in the Church there was no deficiency of native talent, but it was the mistaken policy of the Government under the Georges to make use of the Welsh Bishoprics as rewards for English ecclesiastics, who were ignorant of the language and characteristics of the people whom they were supposed to guide—a policy which is now admitted to have inflicted serious, and it is to be feared permanent, injury on the Church in Wales. Thus in the eighteenth century the College was debarred from furnishing occupants of the four Welsh sees, though many of her sons may be pointed out as worthy of the mitre. Soon after the mistaken policy was discontinued we have seen half the Welsh sees occupied by ex-scholars of the College.[305]

Among the distinguished men of this period may be mentioned Thomas Charles, B.A., 1779, commonly called Charles of Bala, founder of the sect of Calvinistic Methodists, and author of the *Geiriadur*, a book still much used. He was a man of great piety and learning, and did not secede, but was driven out of the Church by the injudicious treatment of his ecclesiastical superiors. His name is still a "household word" in Wales. David Richards (Dafydd Ionawr), an eminent Welsh poet, author of *Cywydd y Drindod*; Thomas Jones, 1760, a painter of considerable merit, a favourite pupil of Wilson; Evan Lloyd, 1755, a poet, and friend of Churchill, Garrick, Wilkes, &c.; Goronwy Owen, a celebrated Welsh poet and scholar, one of the great names in Welsh literature; John Walters, Master of Ruthin School, 1750; James Bandinel, the first Bampton Lecturer (1780); and William Wynne, 1704, a Welsh poet. We may also mention as a contrast to the above, who are chiefly ecclesiastics, Richard Nash, best known as "Beau Nash," for fifty years the celebrated Master of the Ceremonies at Bath, whose smile or frown proclaimed social success or ostracism in fashionable life.

Towards the middle of the eighteenth century the College became in a peculiar degree connected with the Bodleian Library. In 1747 Humphrey Owen, Fellow and afterwards Principal, was elected Librarian. After some years he made John Price, a Fellow of the College, Janitor, and in 1758 Adam Thomas, M.A., Sub-Librarian; when Thomas quitted the Library in 1761 his place was taken by Price, John Jones becoming Janitor. In 1768, on Owen's death, Price was made Librarian, and held office for forty-five years. From 1758 to 1788 all the Sub-Librarians in succession were members of Jesus College, and nearly all the persons who are found otherwise employed in the Library—no full or official list exists—bear Welsh names.

Dr. Johnson in one of his frequent trips to Oxford made Jesus College his head-quarters. This fact has been recently ascertained by Dr. G. Birkbeck Hill, the well-known authority on Johnson and his times, in preparing for publication the great lexicographer's letters. His host was his "convivial friend," Dr. Edwards the Vice-Principal of the College, the editor of Xenophon's *Memorabilia*, who gave up his rooms to his guest. These were, probably, situated in the south-western corner of the outer Quadrangle on the first-floor. It was early in June 1782 that Johnson came into residence in the College, at a time when he was broken in health. Nevertheless, as we learn from Miss Hannah More, who was at the time the guest of the Master of Pembroke College, he did what he could to spread cheerfulness around him. The Fellows of Jesus College were to give a banquet in his honour and hers, to which "they invited Thomas Warton and all that was famous in Oxford." Unfortunately she does not give us any account of the banquet. Doubtless it was held and the old Hall rang with the sound of Johnson's deep voice, but not an echo has been caught. The fact of his residence is curiously confirmed by the Battel-books, which show that at the time when he was in Oxford the Battels of Dr. Edwards and other members of the College were unusually high. In fact, everybody in the College seems to have indulged in hospitality, no doubt being anxious to let his friends see the great man whose sun was now supposed to be so rapidly setting.

Perhaps the first half of the nineteenth century is remote enough from our times to warrant the mention of a few names of distinguished men who have been removed by death. Here, as in the preceding century, we must look chiefly to Wales, where we find among Welsh poets, Daniel Evans (Daniel Ddu); John Jones (Ioan Tegid), a well-known writer and editor of Welsh books; John Blackwell (Alun), one of the most pleasing and attractive of Welsh poets; Morris Williams (Nicander), well known as poet, preacher, and writer in Welsh; and last, but not least, John Richard Green, the brilliant historian. We must not omit to mention the late Principal, Charles Williams, D.D., who was well known in the University for his love of his country, his hospitable social qualities, and his acute and elegant scholarship.

In 1857 the University Commission, which made such changes in Oxford, dealt with Jesus College, but forbore from adopting the sweeping measures at one time threatened. The chief change made was that half the Fellowships were declared for the future to be open to general competition. This declaration did not excite much opposition or remark in Wales, though great indignation was expressed when more than twenty years later another Commission dealt in the same way with the scholarships. It should be remembered that the principle was sacrificed in 1857, and that the opposers of the last Commission could only advance arguments of expediency, on which Commissioners are apt to have their own opinions. Whether the change is likely to be for the good of the College and of Wales is a point much disputed, and this is not a place where it can be discussed.

We have seen that the buildings of the College have not been enlarged in extent since 1713; many structural alterations have, however, taken place. The upper story throughout the College, except on its extreme western side, consisted of attics with dormer windows, which in old pictures gives the College a picturesque appearance. The roof has, however, been raised, and in the outer quadrangle battlements surmount the walls; in the inner quadrangle gables mark the points where the dormer windows formerly existed. The dining-hall, which once had a fine open oak roof, was, in the time of Principal Hoare, fitted with a plaster ceiling, in order that the space above might form attics to increase the accommodation of the Lodgings. Since the enlargement of the Principal's house in 1886 the accommodation is no longer needed, and it is to be hoped that the hall may soon regain its original proportions.

The chapel, which was consecrated in 1621, has been frequently altered, and at least once (in 1636) enlarged. The doorway, with its picturesque porch, bearing the scroll, "Ascendat Oratio, Descendat Gratia," is not the original entrance. When the south wall was being re-faced some years ago, another doorway of older workmanship than the present one, was discovered. The change was probably made when the massive Jacobean screen was put up, which now separates the chapel from the ante-chapel. In 1864 the whole interior was restored. Of the success of the restoration there may be two opinions; but there is no doubt that the widening of the chancel-arch was a mistake, as it has permanently dwarfed the proportions of the building. The woodwork substituted for what existed previously, though good of its kind, presents too violent a contrast with the screen already mentioned. The east window is a painted one of some interest, though not of high artistic merit. In the ante-chapel is an excellent copy of Guido's picture of "St. Michael triumphing over the Fallen Angel." The original is in the Capucini Church at Rome. The picture was presented by Lord Bulkeley of Baron Hill in Anglesey.

In 1856 the whole eastern front of the College was re-faced, and a tower built. The work was carried out under the superintendence of Mr. Buckler, architect, Oxford, and is admitted to be very well done. There are, however, some who think that the old Jacobean gateway was more in harmony with the domestic architecture of the College, and more suitable to its position in a narrow street.

The library contains a considerable number of volumes which are not of great interest to the student of the present day, but is exceptionally rich in pamphlets of the seventeenth and eighteenth centuries, and in works on Canon Law. A valuable and numerous collection of manuscripts has been removed to the Bodleian Library for safety. The best known of these is the *Llyfr Coch*, the famous Red Book of Hergest, containing a collection of Welsh legends and poetry, which is gradually being edited by Professor Rhys and Mr. Evans.

The College is not exceptionally rich in portraits, but possesses two of great merit—a portrait of Charles I. by Vandyke, and of Queen Elizabeth by F. Zucchero.

Like many other Colleges, Jesus College sacrificed its original plate, of which a goodly inventory exists, to the needs of the Royalist cause in 1641; but has since been presented with a fair collection, of which the most remarkable piece is a very large silver-gilt bowl,[306] given by Sir Watkin Williams Wynn in 1732.

Nothing has been said above of the Church patronage of the College, which is considerable, advowsons being a favourite form of bequest with the donors already mentioned, and with others. Unfortunately, few of the livings are situated in Wales. Thus many able Welshmen have been withdrawn from the service of their national Church to their own loss and that of their country.

It is to be remarked that no considerable benefaction has been given to the College during the present century. The history of Jesus College has thus been brought down to living memory, which is the limit of this work. Perhaps more space has been taken up than an existence of little over three hundred years deserves. But the College holds a unique position in Oxford as having a strong connection, notwithstanding much alienation, with a Principality which is not yet English in language or feeling. Such a connection has many advantages, and perhaps some drawbacks. It is to be hoped that the College will be left undisturbed long enough to prove that the latter are altogether outweighed by the former.

XVII.
WADHAM COLLEGE.

BY J. WELLS, M.A., FELLOW OF WADHAM.

Wadham College occupies an interesting position in the history of the University, as having been the last College founded until quite recent times, for both Pembroke and Worcester were but expansions of older foundations. Though actually dating from the reign of James I., it may be said to share with Jesus College the honour of belonging to the days of Elizabeth, as its founder and foundress were well advanced in years at the time when they carried out their long meditated plans, and both in the spirit which animates its statutes and in the architecture of its fabric, Wadham College belongs rather to the sixteenth than to the seventeenth century.

The founder of the College, Nicholas Wadham, of Merifeild, in the county of Somerset, belonged to one of the oldest and wealthiest of the untitled families of the West of England. He married Dorothy, daughter of Sir William Petre, the well known benefactor of Exeter College, but having no children, he resolved to devote his great wealth to some pious use. Antony à Wood tells us that his original intention had been to found a College at Venice for English Romanists, but that he was persuaded to change his plans; the story[307] seems doubtful, and Nicholas Wadham at all events died in the Anglican communion. All his patrimonial estates went to his three sisters, who had married into some of the chief families of the West of England; but he had for some time past been accumulating money for his new foundation; and in two conversations held with his nephew and executor, Sir John Wyndham, very shortly before his death, he had given full directions as to many points in the College. Of these two were especially notable: he desired that the Warden as well as the Fellows should be unmarried; and also that each of them should be "left free to profess what he listed, as it should please God to direct him;" he did not wish them to "live thro' all their time like idle drones, but put themselves into the world, whereby others may grow up under them." He also arranged that the College should be called after his own name, and that the Bishop of Bath and Wells should be perpetual Visitor.

His widow and executors set to work at once to carry out his wishes, and the present site of the College was purchased from the city of Oxford for £600. It had formerly been occupied by the Augustinian Friars, whose name survived in the old phrase for degree exercises,[308] "doing Austins," down to the beginning of this century. The foundation stone was laid with great ceremony on July 31st, 1610, and two years later the foundress, having some time previously obtained a charter from James I., put forth her statutes (August 16th, 1612). In these her husband's wish was carried out by the provision that Fellows should resign their posts eighteen years after they had ceased to be regent masters: this provision remained in force down to the commission of 1854. Originally the Warden was not required to be in orders, but was allowed to proceed to his Doctorate in Law or Medicine as well as in Divinity; but the foundress was persuaded to alter her arrangements on this point, and the two former alternatives were struck out.

There were to be fifteen Fellows and fifteen scholars, the former being elected from among the latter; of these three scholars were to be from Somerset, and three from Essex, while three Fellowships and three scholarships were restricted to "founder's kin." These were originally intended for the children and descendants of the sisters above-mentioned, but in course of time it became frequent to trace kinship with the founder through collateral branches of the Wadham family. The buildings erected by the foundress are remarkable in more ways than one. Their architect, who is supposed to have been Holt[309] of York, the architect of the New Schools, was employed at several other Colleges in Oxford, e. g. at Merton, Exeter, Jesus, University, and Oriel. The resemblance between the inner quadrangle at the first of these and that of Wadham is very marked. Owing to the extent of the original design and the excellence of the building material employed, Wadham has the unique honour among the Colleges of Oxford of having remained practically unaltered since it left its foundress' hands.

Of the various parts of the building the hall and the chapel are the most remarkable; the latter in the shape of its ante-chapel is a combination of the short nave found at New College and of transepts such as are found at Merton; while in the tracery of the windows of its choir it furnishes a continual puzzle to architectural theorists; for though undoubtedly every stone of it was built at the beginning of the seventeenth century, and though the wood-work is pure Jacobean, the windows both in their tracery and in their mouldings belong to a period one hundred and fifty years earlier. In fact the chapel is exactly one of the magnificent choirs with which the churches of Somerset abound, and it is difficult to believe that the resemblance is not more than accidental; for in the building documents of the College we have clear evidence of both materials and workmen coming from the county of the founder. The cost of the whole building was £11,360.

Even before it was finished, the new Foundation received a munificent present in the shape of the library of Dr. Philip Bisse, Archdeacon of Taunton, who dying about 1612 left some two thousand books (valued at £1700?); these books are all distinguished by having their titles carefully inscribed in black letter characters on the sides of their pages, near the top, and may be not unworthily compared to the famous library, the cataloguing of which made Dominie Sampson so happy a man. The foundress made Dr. Bisse's nephew an original Fellow of her College, though he had not yet taken a degree, "Ob singularem amorem avunculi ejus," and also had painted the portrait of the Archdeacon in full doctor's robes, which still adorns the library.

On April 20th, 1613, the first Warden, Robert Wright, formerly Fellow of Trinity College and Canon of Wells, was admitted at St. Mary's, and in the afternoon of the same day he in turn admitted the Fellows and scholars nominated by the foundress. Wright, however, very shortly resigned his position, because (says Wood) he was not allowed to marry.

The foundation of the College seems to have attracted considerable attention elsewhere than in Oxford. Among the State Papers in the year 1613 is calendared (somewhat incongruously) a parody of the statutes of Gotam College, founded by Sir Thomas à Cuniculis,[310] with a license from the Emperor of Morea; and from the first the number of men matriculated was very large, and the class from which they were drawn a wealthy one. This is most clearly proved by the fact that although the College had been in existence less than thirty years when the Civil War broke out, the amount of plate surrendered by it to the King was only surpassed by one other Foundation. The College still possesses an inventory of articles given, which make up "100 lbs. of white plate and 23 lbs. of gilt plate." As might have been expected, a large proportion of the members of the College at this period, and for long after, came from the West country; two-thirds, probably, were from Dorset, Somerset, or Devon; and this connection has happily never been entirely broken. Among these West countrymen was the famous Admiral, Robert

Blake, who graduated from Wadham in 1617 at the age of twenty, and was still in residence six years later. His portrait now hangs in the hall.

During this first period of College life, down to the outbreak of the rebellion, two events deserve a passing notice. The first of these was the fierce controversy[311]waged between James Harrington, one of the original Fellows, and the rest of the Foundation, as to his right to retain his place, although he possessed an annual pension of £40 a year. There are numerous references to this in the Calendar of State Papers; and Laud, as Bishop of Bath and Wells, was put to no small trouble to decide it. In the end Harrington apologized for "having behaved himself in gesture and speeches very uncivilly"; but the quarrel only ended with the expiration of his Fellowship in 1631. Much more important was the attempt of King James, in 1618, to obtain a Fellowship for William Durham of St. Andrews, "notwithstanding anie thing in your statutes to the contrarie." Unfortunately we know very little about this early parallel to James II.'s attempt at Magdalen; but the College clearly was successful in upholding its rights.

It is perhaps not altogether fanciful to trace the feelings of the College as to James I. in the register next year (1619), when its usual dry formality is given up, and Carew Ralegh the son of the King's late victim, is entered as "fortissimi doctissimique equitis Gualteri Ralegh filius."

Wadham, during this same period, completed its material fabric by receiving the gift of the large east window of the chapel from Sir John Strangways, the founder's nephew; it was made on the premises by Bernard van Ling, and the total cost was £113 17s. 5d. (including the maker's battels for ten months and a week—£2 17s. 8d.).

The Civil War affected Wadham as it did the rest of the University. Its plate disappeared as has been said, only the Communion plate ("donum fundatricis") being spared; its students were largely displaced to make room for the King's supporters, among whom the Attorney-General, Sir Edward Herbert, seems to have made Wadham a kind of family residence. After the final defeat of the King, the Warden, Pytt, and the great majority of the Foundation were deprived by the Parliamentary Commissioners. But it may be fairly said that the changes made did far more good than harm to the College. The man appointed to the vacant Wardenship was the famous John Wilkins, divine, philosopher, and mathematician, who enjoyed the almost unique honour of being promoted by the Parliament, by Richard Cromwell, and by Charles II., and to whom the College owes the honour of being the cradle of the Royal Society. Evelyn records in his *Diary* (July 13th, 1654), how "we all dined at that most obliging and universally-curious Dr. Wilkins's, at Wadham Coll."—and speaks of the wonderful contrivances and curiosities, scientific and mechanical, which he saw there. Round Wilkins gathered the society of learned men who had previously begun to meet in London, and who were afterwards incorporated as the Royal Society. The historian of that famous body, Dr. Sprat, afterwards Bishop of Rochester and himself a member of the Foundation of Wadham College, records[312] how "the first meetings were made in Dr. Wilkins his lodgings, in Wadham College, which was then the place of resort for virtuous and learned men," and that from their meetings came the great advantage, that "there was a race of young men provided against the next age, whose minds receiving their first impressions of sober and generous knowledge were invincibly armed against all the encroachments of enthusiasm." The traditional place of these meetings is the great room over the gateway, though this is more than doubtful. Of the original members, there belonged to Wadham College, besides Wilkins— Richard Napier, Seth Ward, afterwards Bishop of Salisbury, the famous mathematician; and last but not least, that "prodigious young scholar, Mr. Christopher Wren," who after being a Fellow Commoner at Wadham College, was elected Fellow of All Souls, and who showed his affection for his original College by the present of the College clock and a beautiful sugar-castor, of which the latter is still in daily use, while the face, at any rate, of the former remains in its old place. The works of the clock are preserved in the ante-chapel as a curiosity.

Warden Wilkins had for two hundred years the distinction of being the only married Warden of Wadham. His wife was a sister of the Lord Protector, with whom he had great influence, which he used for the benefit of the University as a whole, and of individual Royalists. Anthony Wood seems mistaken in saying that Wilkins owed his dispensation to marry to his connection with Cromwell. The original MS. in the possession of the College bears date January 20th, 1652 (four years before Wilkins actually married), and comes from the Visitors of the University of Oxford. Of both Wren and Wilkins there are portraits in the Hall.

The most distinguished undergraduates of this period were John, Lord Lovelace, who took a prominent part in the Revolution (a fine portrait of him by Laroon hangs in the College hall), William Lloyd, afterwards Bishop of St. Asaph, and one of the famous "Seven Bishops," and the notorious Mr. Charles Sedley, a donor of plate to the College, all of whom matriculated in 1655. An even better known member of Wadham was John Wilmot, the wicked Earl of Rochester, who matriculated in 1659, immediately after Warden Wilkins had been promoted to the Mastership of Trinity College, Cambridge; but as he proceeded to his M.A. in September 1661, being then well under fourteen, he probably did not give much trouble to the disciplinary authorities. John Mayow too, the distinguished physician and chemist, who became scholar in 1659, continued the scientific traditions of the College.

Wilkins and three of his four successors all became Bishops; of these the most famous was Ironside, who, as Vice-Chancellor in 1688, ventured to oppose James II. in his arbitrary proceedings against Magdalen. The fall of James saved Ironside, who was made Bishop of Bristol (and afterwards of Hereford) by William III., and was succeeded by Warden Dunster, the object of Thomas Hearne's hatred and contempt. He accuses him[313] of being "one of the violentest Whigs and most rascally Low Churchmen" of the time, and of various other defects, physical and moral, which may perhaps be conjectured to be in Hearne's mind convertible terms with the above.

Wadham as a whole during this period was strongly Whig and Low Church; not improbably this was due to its close connection with the West country, where the suppression of Monmouth's rebellion had taught men to hate the Stuarts; but whatever the reason, the fact is undoubted. Probably there is no other College hall in England which boasts of portraits both of the "Glorious Deliverer" and of George I.

As might be expected, Hearne's account of the College is extremely black. He dwells on the blasphemies[314] for which a certain Mr. Bear of Wadham was refused his degree; and even the distinguished scholar, Dr. Hody, the Regius Professor of Greek and Archdeacon of Oxford, is continually attacked by him, though he admits "he was very useful."[315] Hody, both in his life and by his will, showed himself a loyal son of his College. Dying at the early age of forty-six, he bequeathed the reversion of his property to Wadham, for the encouragement of Hebrew and Greek studies; and the ten exhibitions he founded (now made into four scholarships) have been especially successful in developing the study of the former language. A far greater scholar than Hody belongs in part to Wadham at the same period. In 1687 Richard Bentley was incorporated M.A. of Oxford from St. John's College, Cambridge, and put his name on the books of Wadham. He was in Oxford as tutor to the son of Bishop Stillingfleet.

Almost to the same period belong the buildings erected on the south side of the College (No. IX. staircase), which were begun in 1693, and finished next year; it was intended to build a similar block on the north side, beyond the Warden's lodgings, as is shown in some old prints, but this was never carried out. I am unable to assign a date to No. X. staircase. It certainly belonged to the College before the final purchase of the staircase next the King's Arms (No. XI.), which was made early in the present century: there exists a drawing of it in a much earlier style of architecture than the present, or than that of No. IX.

The only other person worthy of special mention connected with the College at this period, was Arthur Onslow, Speaker of the House of Commons throughout the reign of George II., who matriculated in 1708; his affection for Wadham is illustrated by the splendid service-books presented by him to the chapel, while two excellent portraits show the pride which the College felt in him.

The fifty years which follow the promotion of Warden Baker to the see of Norwich in 1727 were an undistinguished period in the history of Wadham, as in that of the University generally. Of the four Wardens, only one, Lisle, became a bishop, and there is reason to think the College was in a bad state; very few of its members rose to distinction, though James Harris of Salisbury, the author of *Hermes* [316] (whose portrait by Reynolds hangs in the hall), Creech, the translator of Lucretius, and Kennicott, the Hebrew scholar, might be mentioned.

But in Warden Wills, who was appointed in 1783, the College found its most liberal benefactor since the death of the foundress. It was in his time that the present beautiful garden was laid out on the site of the old formal walks, with a mound in the centre, which appear in the prints of the last century. It has been conjectured with some probability that "Capability" Brown had a hand in the laying out of the garden as it now is. Whoever was the gardener, it may be confidently asserted that a finer result was never produced in so small a space. Warden Wills in another way increased the beauty of the College, by buying for the use of the Warden the lease of a large piece of land to the north of the College property; of this the College afterwards bought the freehold from Merton, and it was incorporated with the Warden's garden.

Early in this century too the College received its final extension in the way of rooms, by purchasing from the University the buildings between itself and the King's Arms, which had formerly been used by the Clarendon Press; the old name of No. XI. staircase, "Bible warehouse," long preserved in the books of the College the memory of the old use of the buildings: probably the site had belonged to the College from the first, and it was only the remainder of a lease that was now bought. This purchase was made in the Wardenship of Dr. Tournay, who presided over the College with dignity and success for twenty-five years till 1831, when he resigned. The most distinguished member of Wadham during his time was undoubtedly Richard Bethell, afterwards Lord Westbury, who was elected scholar in 1815, before he had completed his fifteenth year. This fact is duly recorded, at his own especial wish, on his monument in the ante-chapel, as having been the foundation of his subsequent success.

Shortly after the resignation of Warden Tournay, the chapel was taken in hand by the "Gothic Renovators," a new ceiling was put on, and the whole of the east end was recast by the introduction of some elaborate tabernacle work, which, if not entirely appropriate in design, is yet interesting as displaying a careful study of mediæval models most unusual so early as 1834.

Of the history of the College since 1831 there is not space to say much. Under Warden Symons it became recognized as the stronghold of Evangelicalism in the University; so much was this the case that on his nomination to the Vice-Chancellorship in 1844, he was opposed by the

Tractarian party; but this unprecedented step met with no success, as the Chancellor's nomination was confirmed by 883 votes to 183. It was during his tenure of the Vice-Chancellorship (1844-8) that proceedings were taken against Mr. Ward, and against Tract No. XC. But if on the one hand the College produced leading lights of the Evangelical school, like Mr. Fox and Mr. Vores, it also lays claim to Dr. Church, the late Dean of St. Paul's, and Father Mackonochie. It may well be doubted whether there ever was a more brilliant period in the history of Wadham than about the middle of the century, when Dr. Congreve was Tutor and one of the leaders in the University of the "Intellectual Reaction" against the Tractarian movement. With him as Tutor was associated the late Warden, Dr. Griffiths, whose name will be always remembered as that of one whose true interest throughout life was in his College, and who ranks among its benefactors by his bequests, especially that of his collection of prints and drawings illustrative of the history of the College and of those who had been educated at it.

Under them within less than ten years there were in residence as undergraduates the present Bishop of Wakefield, the late Professor Shirley, Dr. Johnson the Bishop of Calcutta, Mr. B. B. Rogers the scholarly translator of Aristophanes, Mr. Frederic Harrison, the present Warden, Professor Beesly, Dr. Bridges afterwards Fellow of Oriel, Dr. Codrington the missionary and philologer, and others who might be mentioned, who have won distinction in ways most various. Wadham carried off three Brasenose

Fellowships in succession within a very short space of time, just as in 1849 its Boat Club had "swept the board" at Henley; these were but the outward signs of the intellectual and physical activity of the College. And here its story must be left, for we are already among contemporaries, while the action of the Commission of 1854-5 has drawn a gulf for good or ill between old and modern Oxford. Enough has been said to show that the sons of Wadham have not been altogether unworthy of a College of which other than her own sons have said that to know her and "to love her was a liberal education."

XVIII.
PEMBROKE COLLEGE.

BY THE REV. DOUGLAS MACLEANE, M.A., FELLOW
OF PEMBROKE.

Pembroke College has its name from William Herbert, Earl of Pembroke, Shakespeare's friend and patron, thought to be "Mr. W. H.," the "onlie begetter" of the Sonnets. Clarendon calls him "the most universally loved and esteemed of any man of that age." This Society, constituted as a College in 1624, is one of the younger Oxford foundations. But there had been a considerable place of religion and learning here from the earliest times, Pembroke College having for centuries previously existed as *Broadgates*, or, more anciently still, *Segrym's* Hall.

Wood calls this Hall "that venerable piece of antiquity." He believes that St. Frideswyde's Priory had here a distinguished mansion, from which the canons received an immemorial quit rent, and that here their novices were instructed. In Domesday it is called Segrim's Mansions, a family of that name then and for generations afterward holding it from the priory in demesne, with obligation to repair the city wall. But in the 38th of Henry III. Richard Segrym, by a charter of quit claim, surrenders for ever to God and the Church of St. Frideswyde, "that great messuage which is situated in the corner of the churchyard of St. Aldate's," the canons agreeing to receive him into their family fraternity, and after his death to find a chaplain canon to celebrate service yearly for his soul, the souls of his father and mother, and the soul of Christiana Pady.

From a very early date this house was occupied by clerks, studying the Civil and Canon Law. It is described as a "nursery of learning," and "the most ancient of all Halls." It retained the name Segrym (sometimes Segreve) Hall till the accession of Henry VI., when, a large entrance being made,[317] it came thenceforth to be called Broadgates Hall, though there were in Oxford several other houses of this name. It was the most distinguished of a number of hostels occupied by legists, and clustered round St. Aldate's Church, then a centre of the study of Civil Law, which had come into vogue in the twelfth century. A chamber built over the south aisle (Docklington's aisle) of that church was used as a Civil Law School and also as a law library, the books being kept in chests, but afterwards chained. Such a library of chained books still exists over one of the aisles of Wimborne Minster. The aisle below was used by the students before and after the Reformation. The "Chapel in St. Eldad's" (Hutten[318] tells us) "is peculiar and propper to Broadgates, where they daily meete for the celebration of Divine Service." The fine monument of John Noble, LL.B., Principal of Broadgates, was formerly in this aisle.

The importance of the Halls dates from 1420, when unattached students were abolished, and every scholar or scholar's servant was obliged to dwell in a hall governed by a responsible principal. After the great fire of 1190 they were built of stone. They contained a common room for meals, a kitchen, and a few bedrooms, each scholar paying 7s. 6d. or 13s. 4d. a year for rent. Every undergraduate was bound to attend lectures. Discipline however was not very strict. One summer's night in 1520, an ever-recurring dispute happening between the University and the city respecting the authority to patrol the streets, certain scholars of Broadgates had an encounter with the town watch, in which one watchman was killed and one severely hurt. The delinquents fleeing were banished by the University, but allowed after a few months to return on condition of paying a fine of 6s. 8d., contributing 1s. 8d. to repair the staff of the inferior bedell of Arts, and having three masses said for the good estate of the Regent Masters and the soul of the slain man.

Broadgates Hall becoming a place of importance, and being obliged to extend its limits, acquired a tenement to the east belonging to Abingdon Abbey, the monks of which owned also a moiety of St. Aldate's Church, the other moiety having passed to St. Frideswyde's, according to a curious story related by Wood.[319] A little further east still was a tenement which the Principal of Broadgates rented from New College (*temp.* Henry VII.) for 6s. 8d. In 1566 Nicholas Robinson[320] mentions Broadgates among the eight leading Halls, and as especially given up to the study of Civil Law. In 1609 Nicholas Fitzherbert[321] says it was a resort of young men of rank and wealth. In 1612 it had 46 graduate members, 62 scholars and commoners, 22 servitors and domestics, in all 131 members, being exceeded in numbers by only five Colleges and one Hall, viz. Christ Church, 240; Magdalen, 246; Brasenose, 227; Queen's, 267; Exeter, 206; Magdalen Hall, 161. A century later Pembroke had only between 50 and 60 residents, and in the preceding century, when Oxford had been for a while almost empty, the numbers must have been few. The zeal of the reforming Visitors in 1550 had left the chamber above Docklington's aisle four naked walls. "The ancient libraries were by their appointment rifled. Many MSS., guilty of no other superstition than red letters in the front or titles were condemned to the fire ... such books wherein appeared angles [angels] were thought sufficient to be destroyed because accounted Papish, or diabolical, or both." We read of two noble libraries being sold for 40*s.* for waste paper.

Henry VIII., in 1546, annexed Broadgates, together with the housing of Abingdon to the new College established by Wolsey under a Papal bull on the site and out of the revenues of St. Frideswyde's—successively Cardinal College, King Henry VIII.'s College, and Christ Church.

Broadgates Hall then had filled no inconsiderable part as a place of learning when it became Pembroke College. The history of the foundation of Pembroke is interesting. Thomas Tesdale, or Tisdall (descended from the Tisdalls of Tisdall in the north of England), was a clothier to Queen Elizabeth's army, and afterwards attended the Court. Having settled at Abingdon as a maltster he there filled the posts of

Bailiff, principal Burgess and Mayor. Finally he removed to Glympton, Oxon, where trading in wool, tillage, and grazing he attained to a very great estate, of which he made charitable and pious use, his house never being shut against the poor. He maintained a weekly lecture at Glympton, and endowed Christ's Hospital in Abingdon. The tablet placed in Glympton Church to his wife Maud records the many parishes where "she lovingly annointed Christ Jesus in his poore members." A fortnight before Tesdale's decease in 1610, he made a will bequeathing the large sum of £5000 to purchase lands, etc., for maintaining seven Fellows and six Scholars to be elected from the free Grammar School in Abingdon into any College in Oxford. This foundation Abbot, Archbishop of Canterbury, sometime Fellow of Balliol (his brother Robert at this time being Master), was anxious to secure for that Society; and the Mayor and burgesses of Abingdon falling in with the plan a provisional agreement was signed, on the strength of which Balliol College bought, with £300 of Tesdale's money, the building called Cæsar's Lodgings, for the reception of Tesdale's new Fellows and scholars, and they for a time were housed there.

Meanwhile, however, a second benefaction to Abingdon turned the thoughts of the citizens in a more ambitious direction. Richard Wightwick, B.D.—descended from a Staffordshire family, formerly of Balliol, and afterward Rector of East Ilsley, Berks, where he rebuilt the church tower and gave the clock and tenor bell—agreed, twelve or thirteen years after Tesdale's death, to augment the Tesdale foundation so as to support in all ten Fellows and ten Scholars. For this purpose he gave lands, bearing however a 499 years' lease (not yet expired), the rents of which amounted at that time to £100 a year. Thereupon, the Mayor, bailiffs, and burgesses of Abingdon, abandoning the previous scheme, desired the foundation of a separate and independent College, for which purpose no place seemed more suitable than Broadgates Hall. An Act of Parliament having been obtained, they presented a petition to the Crown, in reply to which King James I. by Letters Patents dated June 29th, 1624, constituted the said Hall of Broadgates to be "one perpetual College of divinity, civil and canon law, arts, medicine and other sciences; to consist of one master or governour, ten fellows, ten scholars, or more or fewer, to be known by the name of 'the Master, Fellows, and Scholars of the College of Pembroke in the University of Oxford, of the foundation of King James, at the cost and charges of Thomas Tesdale and Richard Wightwicke.'" The better, we are told, to strengthen the new foundation and make it immovable, they had made the Earl of Pembroke, then Chancellor of the University, the Godfather, and King James the Founder of it, "allowing Tesdale and Wightwick only the privileges of foster-fathers." James liked to play the part of founder to learned institutions, and the Earl of Pembroke was a poet and patron of letters— "Maecenas nobilissimus" Sir T. Browne calls him. In his honour the Chancellor was always to be, and is still, the Visitor of the College. Moreover, as a Hall Broadgates had had the Chancellor for Visitor. Wood says that "had not that noble lord died suddenly soon after, this College might have received more than a bare name from him."

On August 5th, 1624, Browne, as senior commoner of Broadgates, now Pembroke, delivered one of four Latin orations in the common hall. The new foundation was described as a Phœnix springing out of the rubble of an ancient Hall, and the right noble Visitor, it was foreseen, would create a truly marble structure out of an edifice of brick. Dr. Clayton, Regius Professor of Medicine, last Principal of Broadgates and first Master of Pembroke, spoke the concluding oration of the four. The Letters Patents were then read, as well as a license of mortmain, enabling the Society to hold revenues to the amount of £700 a year. The ceremony was witnessed by a distinguished assembly, including the Vice-Chancellor and Proctors, many Masters of Arts, a large company of the nobility and gentry of the neighbourhood, and the Mayor, Recorder, and burgesses of Abingdon. Indeed, great and wide interest seems to have been taken in this youngest foundation, carrying on as it did the life of a very ancient and not unfamous place of academic learning. The students of Broadgates were now the members of Pembroke, and the speeches on the day of the inauguration of the College still affectionately style them "Lateportenses." A commission issued from the Crown to the Lord Primate, the Visitor, the Vice-Chancellor, the Master, the Recorder of

Abingdon, Richard Wightwick, and Sir Eubule Thelwall, to make statutes for the good government of the House. The statutes provided that all the Fellows and scholars should proceed to the degree of B.D. and seek Holy Orders. Some were to be of founders' kin, but, with this reservation, the double foundation was to be entirely for the benefit of Abingdon. These provisions have been for the most part repealed by later statutes. But the tutorial Fellows are still bound to celibacy.

Further additions were soon made to the original foundation. In 1636 King Charles I., who in that year visited Oxford "with no applause," gave the College the patronage[322] of St. Aldate's, which had been seized by the Crown on the dissolution of the religious houses. With a view to raising the state of ecclesiastical learning in the Channel Islands, King Charles further founded a Fellowship, as also at Jesus College and Exeter, to be held by a native of Guernsey or Jersey. Bishop Morley, in the next reign, bestowed five exhibitions for Channel islanders. A principal benefactor to this College was Sir J. Benet, Lord Ossulstone. In 1714 Queen Anne annexed a prebend at Gloucester to the Mastership. The Master, under the latest statutes, must be a person capable in law of holding this stall. Other considerable benefactions have from time to time been bestowed.

The new foundation, however, was not disposed to forego any portion of what it could claim. Savage, Master of Balliol, whose "Balliofergus" (1668) contains the account of the opening ceremony called "Natalitia Collegii Pembrochiani," 1624, complains with pardonable resentment: "This rejeton had no sooner taken root than the Master and his company called the Master and Society of our Colledge into Chancery for the restitution of the aforesaid £300" (the £300, viz. of Tesdale's money with which Cæsar's Lodgings had been purchased). Wood says: "The matter came before George [Abbot] Archbishop of Canterbury, sometime of Balliol College, who, knowing very well that the Society was not able at that time to repay the said sum, bade the fellows go home, be obedient to their Governour, and JEHOVAH JIREH, i. e. GOD shall provide for them. Whereupon he paid £50 of the said £300 presently, and for the other £250 the College gave bond to be paid yearly by several sums till the full was satisfied. The which sums as they grew due did the Lord Archbishop pay." Abbot seems to have allowed the agreement between the Mayor and burgesses of Abingdon and Balliol. Yet his attitude towards Pembroke, in whose foundation he was concerned, was one of marked benevolence. It is to be noted that Tesdale's brass in Glympton Church, put up between his death and the new turn of affairs brought about by Wightwick's benefaction, describes him as "liberally beneficial to Balliol Colledge in Oxford." He is represented standing on an ale-cask, in allusion to his trade as maltster. The alabaster monument to Tesdale and Maud his wife was repaired in 1704, as a Latin inscription shows, by the Master and Fellows of Pembroke.

Part of the founders' money was laid out in building. Few Colleges stand within a more natural boundary of their own than Pembroke, and yet that boundary has only been completed within the last two years, and the College itself is an almost accidental agglomeration of ancient tenements. The south side stands directly on the city wall from South Gate to Little Gate, looking down on a lane for a long time past called Brewer's Street, but formerly Slaughter Lane, or Slaying Well Lane, King Street, and also Lumbard[323] Lane. The western boundary of the College is Littlegate Street, the eastern St. Aldate's Street (formerly Fish Street), the northern Beef Lane and S. Aldate's Church, though the College owns some interesting old houses on the south side of Pembroke Street, formerly Crow Street and Pennyfarthing[324] Street. At the time of the transformation of Broadgates Hall into Pembroke College, the "Almshouses" opposite Christ Church Gate were an appendage to Christ Church. Then came the vacant strip of ground called "Hamel," running north and south. Next on the west stood New College Chambers and Abingdon Buildings, which passed with Broadgates into Pembroke. Beckyngton, Bishop of Bath and Wells, was once Principal here. Further west still stood Broadgates Hall, the sole part of which still remaining is the refectory, now the library. As depicted in the large Agas (1578) it seems to have been an irregular cluster of buildings (mostly rented), of which the largest was a double block called Cambye's, afterwards Summaster's, Lodgings (vulgarly Veale

Hall). This in 1626 was altered for the new Master's Lodgings, but in 1695 it was replaced by a six-gabled freestone pile, the outside of which was remodelled with the rest of the frontage in 1829, a storey being added later by Dr. Jeune, afterwards Bishop of Peterborough. Loggan's print shows the old building in 1675, and Burghersh gives its appearance in 1700, as rebuilt by Bishop Hall.

Broadgates Hall (except the refectory), together with Abingdon Buildings and New College Chambers, gave place, when Pembroke College had been founded, to the present *Old Quadrangle*, of which the south and west sides and a portion of the east side were erected in 1624, the remainder of the east side in 1670. Three years later the original north frontage, which had been merely repaired in 1624, was half pulled down and replaced by "a fair fabrick of freestone." The rest of the north front as far as the Common Gate was rebuilt by Michaelmas 1691, the *Gate Tower* in 1694, Sir John Benet supplying most of the cost. This tower of 1694, the last part of the frontage to be built, was more classical than the remainder. The tower shown in Loggan's print (1675) in the *centre* of the front can never have existed. Probably it was projected only. A storey was added in 1829, when the exterior of the College was remodelled in the Gothic revival manner of George IV. The interior of the quadrangle, though less altered than the outside, has lost much of its character by being refaced with inferior stone, and by the substitution of sashes for the quarried lights. Some changes were made in the battlements and chimneys, and in the upper face of the tower by Mr. Bodley in 1879.

The history of the present *New Quadrangle* is as follows: West of the present Master's lodging stood a number of ancient halls for legists, viz. Minote, Durham (later St. Michael's) and St. James' (these two in one) and Beef Halls. The last gives its name to Beef Lane. Dunstan Hall, on the town wall, was (*temp.* Charles I.) pulled down, and the whole space between the city wall and the "*Back Lodgings*," as the halls fringing Beef Lane were called, was divided into three enclosures. That furthest to the west became a garden for the Fellows, having a bowling alley, clipt walks and arbours,[325] and a curious dial. The middle enclosure was the Master's garden, and here were shady bowers and a ball court. That nearest the College was a common garden; but when the chapel was built in 1728 the pleasant borders probably got trampled, and grass and trees were replaced by gravel. Such was, with little alteration, the aspect of the College till 1844. Two woodcuts in *Ingram* (1837) show the picturesque old gabled Back Lodgings still standing. But in 1844 Dr. Jeune took in hand the erection of new buildings. The new hall and kitchens occupy the western side, and the Fellows' and undergraduates' rooms the entire north side of the *Inner Quadrangle* thus formed, a large plat of grass filling the central space, while the chapel and a tiny strip of private garden upon the town wall form the south side. With the irregular range of old buildings on the east, and especially when the luxuriant creepers dress the walls with green and crimson, this is a very pleasing court, though a visitor looking in casually through the outer gateway of the College might hardly suspect its existence. Mr. Hayward of Exeter, nephew and pupil of Sir C. Barry, was the architect. The *Hall*, built in 1848, is a much better example of the Gothic revival than a good many other Oxford edifices, and the dark timbered roof is exceedingly handsome. There is the usual large oriel on the daïs, a minstrels' gallery, and a great baronial fireplace, where huge blocks of fuel burn. As in the ancient halls, the twin doors are faced by the buttery hatches, and the kitchen is below.

The time-honoured hall, much the oldest part of the College, and once the refectory of Broadgates (the kitchen was in the S.W. corner of the Old Quadrangle) was now made the College *Library*. The long room over Docklington's aisle in St. Aldate's was on the foundation of Pembroke repaired at Dr. Clayton's expense, and used once more for the reception of books presented by various donors, though Wood says that for some years before the Great Rebellion it was partly employed for chambers. The books certainly were at first few. Francis Rous, one of Cromwell's "lords" and Speaker of the Little Parliament, who founded an Exhibition, "did intend to give his whole Study, but being dissuaded to the contrary gave only his own works and some few others." But in 1709 Bishop Hall, Master of Pembroke, bequeathed his collection of books to the College, and a room was built over the hall to be the College library. When the hall became the library in 1848 this room, Gothicized, was converted to a lecture-room. From 1709 the "chamber in St. Aldate's" was used no more, and this extremely ancient Civil Law School and picturesque feature of the church has now unhappily been demolished. A Nuremburg Chronicle among Dr. Hall's books is inscribed by Whitgift's hand, and a volume of scholia on Aristotle has the autograph, "Is. Casaubonus." Here also are Johnson's deeply pathetic *Prayers and Meditations*, in his own writing.

The Pembroke library has recently been fortunate enough to acquire by gift from a lady to whom they were bequeathed[326] the unique collection of Aristotelian and other works made by the late Professor Chandler, Fellow of the College, and galleries were added last year (1890). The transverse portion of the room, which is shaped like the letter T, was built in 1620 by Dr. Clayton, four years before Broadgates Hall became Pembroke College. A book of contributors (headed "Auspice Christo") is extant, and has the signatures of Pym and of "Margaret Washington of Northants," kinswoman of the famous Virginian.

In 1824, on the occasion of the "Bicentenary" of the College, when Latin speeches were delivered, the windows were enlarged and filled with glass by Eginton, and the blazoned cornice added at a cost of £2000. But the room is the same one in which Johnson (whose bust by Bacon is here) dined and abused the "coll," or small beer, which he found muddy and uninspiring to Latin themes—

"Carmina vis nostri scribant meliora poetae?
Ingenium jubeas purior haustus alat."

Whitfield carried about the liquor in leathern jacks here as he had done in his mother's inn at Gloucester. In this room they attended lectures. Every Nov. 5th there were speeches in the hall. "Johnson told me that when he made his first declamation he wrote over but one copy and that coarsely; and having given it into the hand of the tutor who stood to receive it as he passed was obliged to begin by chance and continue on how he could, for he had got but little of it by heart; so fairly trusting to his present powers for immediate supply he finished by adding astonishment to the applause of all who knew how little was owing to study" (Piozzi). We read of "a great Gaudy in the College, when the Master dined in public and the juniors (by an ancient custom they were obliged to observe) went round the fire in the hall." Johnson told Warton, "In these halls the fireplace was anciently always in the middle of the room till the Whigs removed it on one side." At dinner till lately the signal for grace was given by three blows with two wooden trenchers, such as were used for bread and cheese till 1848. Hearne laments, "when laudable old customs alter, 'tis a sign learning dwindles." There were four "College dinners" annually, one of which was an Oyster Feast.[327] The Manciple's slate still hangs in this room. An undergraduates' library has lately been established "between quads." Where, by the bye, is Lobo's *Voyage to Abyssinia* (the original of *Rasselas*) which Johnson borrowed from the Pembroke library?

It has already been said that the students of Broadgates used Docklington's aisle for divine service, and the aisle was rented for this purpose by Pembroke College. The pulpit and Master's pew are now at Stanton St. John's. The present College chapel dates from 1728, the year of Johnson's matriculation. It was consecrated July 10th, 1732, by Bishop Potter of Oxford, a sermon on religious vows and dedications being preached by "that fine Jacobite fellow" (as Johnson calls him), Dr. Matthew Panting, then Master, from Gen. xxviii. 20-22. Hearne styles him "an honest gent," and says: "He had to preach the sermon at St. Mary's on the day on which George Duke and Elector of Brunswick usurped the English throne; but his sermon took no notice, at most very little, of the Duke of Brunswick." Bartholomew Tipping, Esq., whose arms are on the screen, contributed very largely towards building the chapel. It was then "a neat Ionic structure," plain and unpretending, but well proportioned and pleasing enough. The picture in the altar-piece was given at a later date by the Ven. Joseph Plymley (or Corbett), a gentleman commoner. It is a copy of our Lord's figure in Rubens' painting at Antwerp, "Christ urging St. Theresa to succour a soul in Purgatory." In 1884 the chapel was elaborately embellished and enriched at an expense of nearly £3000, so as to present one of the most beautiful interiors in Oxford. The work was executed by Mr. C. E. Kempe, M.A., a member of the College. The windows, in the Renaissance manner, are particularly fine. A quantity of silver and silver-gilt altar plate was presented at the same time. The work is not yet finished, and a design for an organ remains on paper. It is worth recording that until twenty-seven years since the Eucharist was administered here, as at the Cathedral and St. Mary's, to the communicants kneeling in their places. Johnson must, as an undergraduate, have attended St. Aldate's (where the College worshipped once again for several terms during the recent decoration of the chapel); but when in later years he visited Oxford, people flocked to Pembroke chapel[328] to gaze at the "great Cham of literature," humblest of worshippers, tenderest and most loyal of Pembroke's sons.

Dean Burgon connects a bit of old Pembroke with Johnson. The summer common room behind the present hall was, before its demolition, the only one left in Oxford, except that at Merton. He writes (1855): "This agreeable and picturesque apartment was in constant use within the memory of the present Master; but, while I write, it is in a state of considerable decadence. The old chairs are drawn up against the panelled walls; on the small circular tables the stains produced by hot beverages are very plainly to be distinguished: only the guests are wanting, with their pipes and ale—their wigs and buckles—their byegone manners and forgotten topics of discourse. It must have been hither that Dr. Adams, Master of Pembroke conducted Dr. Johnson and his biographer in 1776, when the former after a rêverie of meditation exclaimed: 'Ay, here I used to play at draughts with Phil Jones and Fludyer. Jones loved beer, and did not get very forward in the Church. Fludyer turned out a scoundrel, a Whig, and said he was ashamed of having been bred at Oxford.'" The old brazier, which Mr. Lang surmises Whitfield may have blacked, is, I believe, in existence.

The most important modern addition to the College is the Wolsey Almshouse, purchased in 1888 from Christ Church for £10,000, by the help of money bequeathed by the Rev. C. Cleoburey. This is part of "Segrym's houses," held of St. Frideswyde's Priory, and converted after the Conquest into hostels "for people of a religious and scholastick conversation." "With the decay of learning they came to be the possession of servants and retainers to the said priory." They were occupied by Jas. Proctor when Wolsey converted them into a hospital; later, Henry VIII. settled in them twenty-four almsmen, old soldiers, with a yearly allowance of £6 each. Not long ago the bedesmen were sent to their homes with a pension, and the building became the Christ Church Treasurer's lodging till it was heroically purchased by Pembroke, which thus completed her "scientific frontier." There is a fine timber roof here, said to have been brought from Osney Abbey. The building has been a good deal altered. Skelton (1823) shows the south part of it in ruins.

The external history of Pembroke since its foundation in 1624 has been comparatively uneventful. When King Charles was besieged in Oxford in 1642, like other Colleges it armed a company to defend the city. Twice the loyal Colleges had given their cups and flagons for their Sovereign's necessities. Pembroke keeps the King's letter of acknowledgment, with his signature. When the Parliamentary Commissioners visited Oxford in 1647, they ejected the then Master of Pembroke, who had received them with these words: "I have seen your commission and examined it. … I cannot with a safe conscience submit to it, nor without breach of oath made to my Sovereign, and breach of oaths made to the University, and breach of oaths made to my College: et sic habetis animi mei sententiam,—Henry Wightwicke." Henry Langley, an intruded Canon of Christ Church, and "one of six Ministers appointed by Parliament to preach at St. Mary's and elsewhere in Oxon to draw off the Scholars from their orthodox principles," was put in Wightwick's room, but removed in 1660. In 1650 "Honest Will Collier," a Pembrokian, heads a plot to seize the Cromwellian garrison, and is "strangely tortured," but his life spared.

The College pictures include a splendid Reynolds of Johnson,[329] given by Mr. A. Spottiswoode. Two interesting relics of Johnson are to be seen—the small deal desk on which he wrote the *Dictionary*, and his china teapot. It holds two quarts, for Johnson once drank five-and-twenty cups at a sitting. He called himself "a hardened and shameless tea-drinker," who "with tea amuses the evenings, with tea solaces the midnights, and with tea welcomes the mornings." Peg Woffington made it for him "as red as blood."

Pembroke since the seventeenth century has been a small College, though it has a large foundation of scholars. It has not been specially noted as either a "rich man's" or a "poor man's" College, and while winning at least its fair share of distinction in the schools, it has been known perhaps chiefly as a compact, pleasant, and not uncomfortable Society, whose Promus no longer serves "muddy" beer, and whose Coquus no Latin verses satirize. There is a handsome show of plate. It includes several silver "tumblers" or "tuns," which when placed on their side tumble upright again, and a large hammered tankard (lately presented) with the "Britannia" mark, and made after the ancient manner with pegs between its thirteen pints to measure the draught to be taken. The oldest inscribed piece of plate is dated 1653. Pembroke has been usually a rowing College. The Eight was Head of the River in 1872; the Torpid in 1877, 1878, and 1879, the Eight then being second. The "Christ Church Fours" are rowed every year for a challenge goblet given by the Christ Church Club in gratitude for an eight lent by Pembroke in a time of need. The racing colours are cherry and white, with the red rose for badge of the Eight and the thistle of the Torpid.[330] The "Junior Common Room" is the oldest of undergraduate wine clubs. There is a flourishing and old-established literary club called the "Johnson," and there is of course a Debating and a Musical Society. The Master, Fellows, and Scholars of Pembroke are patrons of eight benefices. College meetings are called Conventions.

A few names may be cited from the roll of (Broadgates and) Pembroke worthies—

Edmund Bonner, "Scholar enough and tyrant too much" (Fuller), entered Broadgates in 1512. In 1519 he became Bachelor of Canon and Civil Law; D.C.L. 1535. He was successively Bishop of Hereford and of London, but was deprived and imprisoned under Edward VI. Having been restored by Mary, on Elizabeth's accession he refused the oath of the Supremacy, and was committed to the Marshalsea, where he died September 5th, 1569. *Thomas Yonge*, Archbishop of York, 1560. *John Moore*, Archbishop of Canterbury, 1783, began as a servitor at Pembroke. The Duke of Marlborough had then a house in Oxford, and walking with Dr. Adams one day in the street, asked him to recommend a governor for his son, Lord Blandford. Dr. Adams in reply pointed to the slight figure of a lad walking just in front, and said, "That is the person I recommend." The Duke afterwards brought Moore's merits under the notice of the King, who placed the Prince of Wales under his care, which led to his ecclesiastical elevation. *William Newcome*, Archbishop of Armagh, 1795. The primatial sees of Canterbury, York, and Armagh have thus each been filled from Broadgates or Pembroke. *John Heywoode*, "the Epigrammatist," one of the earliest English dramatic writers. While attached to the Court of Henry VIII. he wrote those six comedies which are among the first innovations upon the mysteries and miracle-plays of the middle age, and which laid the foundation of the secular comedy in this country. His *Interludes*, in which the clergy are satirized, are earlier than 1521. Yet he was favoured by Mary Tudor, and was also the friend of Sir Thomas More. *George Peele*, dramatist. *Charles Fitzjeffrey*, 1572, "the poet of Broadgates Hall" (Wood). *David Baker*, entered 1590, a Benedictine monk, historian, and mystical writer, author of the *Chronicle*. *Francis Beaumont*, the poet, entered February 4th, 1596, as "Baronis filius æt. 12." His father dying April 21st, 1598, he left without a degree. His elder brother, *Sir John Beaumont*, entered Broadgates the same day. He was a Puritan in religion, but fought on the Cavalier side. *William Camden*, the antiquary, called "the Strabo of England," entered 1567, aged sixteen; Clarencieux King of Arms; Head-master of Westminster. He died 1623. The Latin grace composed by Camden to be said after meat in Broadgates Hall is still in use at Pembroke. In 1599 entered *John Pym*, the politician, aged fifteen. Among the contributors to the enlargement of the Hall in 1620 his signature appears, "Johannes pym de Brimont in com. Somerset quondam Aulae Lateportensis Commensalis. 44/. Jo. Pym." *Sir Thomas Browne*, author of that delightful book *Religio Medici*, the quaint thought of which inspired Elia. He entered as Fellow Commoner in 1623. His body lies in St. Peter Mancroft, Norwich. When it was disentombed in 1840 the fine auburn hair had not lost its freshness. *Matthew Turner*, one of the first Fellows, who wrote all his sermons in Greek. It will be remembered that, not many years before, Queen Elizabeth had received an address in Oxford, and *replied* to it, in this learned tongue, and that in the period of Puritan ascendancy (1648-1659) the disputations in the schools for M.A. were often in Greek. Other worthies of this House are Cardinal *Repyngdon*, the Wycliffist; *John Storie*, whose career closed at Tyburn; *Thomas Randolph*, constantly employed by Elizabeth on important embassies; *Timothy Hall*, one of the few London clergy who read James II.'s Declaration. He was made Bishop of Oxford, but in his palace found himself alone, hated, and shunned; *Carew*, Earl of Totnes; *Peter Smart*, Puritan poet, Cosin's assailant; Chief Justice *Dyer*; Lord Chancellor *Harcourt*; *Collier*, the metaphysician; *Southern*, the Restoration dramatist; *Durel*, the Biblical critic; *Henderson*, "the Irish Creichton"; *Davies Gilbert*, President of the Royal Society; *Richard Valpy*; *John Lemprière*; *Thomas Stock*, co-founder of the Sunday School system.

In 1694, Prideaux (whom Aldrich sets down as "muddy-headed") calls Pembroke "the fittest colledge in the town for brutes." But a Mr. Lapthorne, twenty years later, gives a different picture of it. "I have placed my son in Pembroke Colledge. The house, though it bee but a little one, yet is reputed to be one of the best for sobriety and order." It is not till the Georgian time, however, that we get a distinct view of the inner life of Pembroke—the time when Shenstone, Blackstone, Graves, Hawkins, Whitfield, and—towering above all—Johnson, were contemporary or nearly contemporary here.

Samuel Johnson entered as a Commoner October 31st, 1728, aged nineteen. Old Michael Johnson anxiously introduced him to Mr. Jorden, his tutor. "He seemed very full of the merits of his son, and told the company he was a good scholar and a poet, and wrote Latin verses. His figure and manner appeared strange to them; but he behaved modestly, and sate silent, till, upon something which occurred in the course of conversation, he struck in and quoted Macrobius." Johnson told Boswell that Jorden was "a very worthy man, but a heavy man." He told Mrs. Thrale that "when he was first entered at the University he passed a morning, in compliance with the customs of the place, at his tutor's chamber; but, finding him no scholar, went no more. In about ten days after, meeting Mr. Jorden in the street, he offered to pass without saluting him; but the tutor stopped and enquired, not roughly neither, what he had been doing? 'Sliding on the ice,' was the reply; and so turned away with disdain. He laughed very heartily at the recollection of his own insolence, and said they endured it from him with a gentleness that whenever he thought of it astonished himself." Once, being fined for non-attendance, he rudely retorted, "Sir, you have sconced me twopence for a lecture not worth a penny." Dr. Adams, however, told Boswell that Johnson attended his tutor's lectures and those given in the Hall very regularly. Jorden quite won his heart. "That creature would defend his pupils to the last; no young lad under his care should suffer for committing slight irregularities, while he had breath to defend or power to protect them. If I had sons to send to College, Jorden should have been their tutor" (Piozzi). Again, "Whenever a young man becomes Jorden's pupil he becomes his son." Still, when Johnson's intimate, Taylor, was about to join him at Pembroke, he persuaded him to go to Christ Church, where the lectures were excellent. In going to get Taylor's lecture notes at second-hand, Johnson saw that his ragged shoes were noticed by the Christ Church men, and came no more. He was too proud to accept money, and, some kind hand having placed a pair of new shoes at his door, Johnson, when his short-sighted vision spied them, flung them passionately away. His room was a very small one in the second storey over the gateway; it is practically unaltered.

"I have heard," wrote Bishop Percy, "from some of his contemporaries, that he was generally to be seen lounging at the College gate with a circle of young students round him, whom he was entertaining with wit and keeping from their studies, if not spiriting them up to rebellion against the College discipline, which in his maturer years he so much extolled. He would not let these idlers say 'prodigious,' or otherwise misuse the English tongue." "Even then, Sir, he was delicate in language, and we all feared him." So Edwards, an old fellow-collegian of Johnson's, told Boswell half a century later. Johnson, hearing from Edwards that a gentleman had left his whole fortune to Pembroke, discussed the ethics of legacies to Colleges. Edwards has given us a saying we would not willingly lose: "You are a philosopher, Dr. Johnson. I have tried too in my time to be a philosopher; but, I don't know how, cheerfulness was always breaking in." Johnson remembered drinking with Edwards at an alehouse near Pembroke-gate. Their meeting again, after fifty years spent by both in London, Johnson accounted one of the most curious incidents of his life.

Dr. Adams told Boswell that Johnson while at Pembroke was caressed and loved by all about him, was a gay and frolicsome fellow, and passed there the happiest part of his life. "When I mentioned to him this account he said, 'Ah, sir, I was mad and violent. It was bitterness which they mistook for frolick. I was miserably poor, and I thought to fight my way by my literature and my wit; so I disregarded all power and all authority.'" Bishop Percy told Boswell, "The pleasure he took in vexing the tutors and fellows has been often mentioned. But I have heard him say that the mild but judicious expostulations of this worthy man [Dr. Adams, then a junior Fellow] whose virtue awed him and whose learning he revered, made him really ashamed of himself: 'though I fear,' said he, 'I was too proud to own it.'" Johnson was transferred from Jorden to Adams, who said to Boswell, "I was his nominal tutor, but he was above my mark." When Johnson heard this remark, his eyes flashed with satisfaction. "That was liberal and noble," he exclaimed. Jorden once gave him for a Christmas exercise Pope's "Messiah" to turn into Latin verse, which the veteran saw and was pleased to commend highly.

Carlyle has drawn a fancy picture of the rough, seamy-faced, rawboned servitor starving in view of the empty or locked buttery. Dr. Birkbeck Hill has shown that though Johnson was poor, he lived like other men. His batells came to about eight shillings a week. Even Mr. Leslie Stephen introduces the usual talk about "servitors and sizars." Johnson was not a servitor. "It was the practice for a servitor, by order of the Master, to go round to the rooms of the young men, and, knocking[331] at the door, to enquire if they were within, and if no answer was returned to report them absent. Johnson could not endure this intrusion, and would frequently be silent when the utterance of a word would have ensured him from censure, and … would join with others of the young men in hunting, as they called it, the servitor who was thus diligent in his duty; and this they did with the noise of pots and candlesticks, singing to the tune of 'Chevy Chase' the words of that old ballad—

'To drive the deer with hound and horn.'"

Any one who has occupied the narrow tower staircase can imagine the noise of Johnson's ponderous form tumbling down it in hot pursuit. The present balusters must be the same as those he clutched in his headlong descents one hundred and sixty years ago. Amid this boisterousness he read with deep attention Law's racy and masculine book, the *Serious Call*.

Dr. Hill has examined exhaustively the difficult question of the length of Johnson's residence, and proved that the fourteen months, to which the batell books testify, was the whole of his Oxford career. He was absent for but one week in the Long Vacation of 1729. He ceased to reside in December, 1729, and removed his name from the books October 8th, 1731, without taking his degree, his caution money (£7) cancelling his undischarged batells. But, his contemporaries assure us, "he had contracted a love and regard for Pembroke College, which he retained to the last." It has been thought that the College helped him pecuniarily. He loved it none the less that it was reputed a Jacobitical place. In his *Life of Sir T. Browne* he speaks of "the zeal and gratitude of those that love it." Whenever he visited Oxford in after days he would go and see his College before doing anything else. Warton was his companion in 1754. Johnson was highly pleased to find all the College servants of his time still remaining, particularly a very old manciple, and to be recognized by them. But he was coldly received when he waited on the Master, Dr. Radcliffe, who did not ask him to dinner, and did not care to talk about the forthcoming Dictionary. However, there was a cordial meeting with his old rival Meeke, now a Fellow. At the classical lecture in hall Johnson had fretted under Meeke's superiority, he told Warton, and tried to sit out of earshot of his construing. Besides Meeke, it seems, there was at this time only one other resident Fellow. Boswell describes other visits, when Dr. Adams, Johnson's lifelong friend, was Master. He prided himself on being accurately academic, and wore his gown ostentatiously. The following letter from Hannah More to her sister is dated Oxford, June 13th, 1782:—

"Who do you think is my principal cicerone in Oxford? Only Dr. Johnson! And we do so gallant it about! You cannot imagine with what delight he showed me every part of his own College (Pembroke), nor how rejoiced Henderson looked to make one of the party. Dr. Adams had contrived a very pretty piece of gallantry. We spent the day and evening at his house. After dinner Johnson begged to conduct me to see the College; he would let no one show it me but himself. 'This was my room; this Shenstone's.' Then, after pointing out all the rooms of the poets who had been of his College, 'In short,' said he, 'we were a nest of singing birds. Here we walked, there we played at cricket.' He ran over with pleasure the history of the juvenile days he passed there. When we came into the common room we spied a fine large print of Johnson, framed and hung up that very morning, with this motto, 'And is not Johnson ours, himself a host?' under which stared you in the face, 'From Miss More's Sensibility.' This little incident amused us; but alas! Johnson looked very ill indeed; spiritless and wan. However he made an effort to be cheerful, and I exerted myself to make him so."

A few months before his death, his ebbing strength beginning to return, he had a wistful desire to see Oxford and Pembroke once again, and, weary as he was with the journey, revived[332] in spirit as the coach drew near the ancient city. He presented all his works to the College library, and had thoughts of bequeathing his house at Lichfield to the College, but he was reminded of the claims of some poor relatives. "He took a pleasure," Boswell says, "in boasting of the many eminent men who had been educated at Pembroke."

Shenstone, the poet, entered Pembroke in 1732, after Johnson had left. Burns says: "His divine Elegies do honour to our language, our nation, and our species." Johnson writes: "Here it appears he found delight and advantage; for he continued his name in the book ten years, though he took no degree. After the first four years he put on the civilian's gown." *Hawkins*, Professor of Poetry. *Rev. Richard Graves*, junior, admitted scholar, November, 1732—poet and novelist. He was the author of the *Spiritual Quixote*, a satire on the Methodists. He tells us: "Having brought with me the character of a tolerably good Grecian, I was invited to a very sober little party, who amused themselves in the evening with reading Greek and drinking water. Here I continued six months, and we read over Theophrastus, Epictetus, Phalaris' Epistles, and such other Greek authors as are seldom read at school. But I was at length seduced from this mortified symposium to a very different party, a set of jolly, sprightly young fellows, most of them West country lads, who drank ale, smoked tobacco, punned, and sang bacchanalian catches the whole evening.... I own with shame that, being then not seventeen, I was so far captivated with the social disposition of these young people (many of whom were ingenuous lads and good scholars), that I began to think them the only wise men. Some gentlemen commoners, however, who considered the above-mentioned a very *low* company (chiefly on account of the liquor they drank), good-naturedly invited me to their party; they treated me with port wine and arrack punch; and now and then, when they had drunk so much as hardly to distinguish wine from water, they would conclude with a bottle or two of claret. They kept late hours, drank their favourite toasts on their knees, and in short were what were then called 'bucks of the first head.' … There was, besides, a sort of flying squadron of plain, sensible, matter-of-fact men, confined to no club, but associating with each party. They anxiously inquired after the news of the day and the politics of the times. They had come to the University on their way to the Temple, or to get a slight smattering of the sciences before they settled in the country." Graves breakfasts with Shenstone (who wore his own hair), a Mr. Whistler being of the company. This was "a young man of great delicacy of sentiment, but with such a dislike to languages that he is unable to read the classics in the original, yet no one formed a better judgment of them. He wrote, moreover, a great part of a tragedy on the story of Dido." In a later day we may surmise this young gentleman of delicacy of sentiment would have written a Newdigate. The three friends often met and discussed plays and poetry, Spectators or Tatlers.

George Whitfield entered as a servitor, November, 1732. An old schoolfellow, himself a Pembroke servitor, happened to visit Whitfield's mother, who kept a hostelry in Gloucester, and told her how he had not only discharged his College expenses for the term, but had received a penny. At this the good ale-wife cried out, "That will do for my son. Will you go to Oxford, George?" "With all my heart," he replied. He tells us that at College he was solicited to join in excess of riot with several who lay in the same room; but God gave him grace to withstand them. His tutor was kind, but when he joined Wesley's small set he met with harshness from the Master, who frequently chid him and even threatened to expel him. "I had no sooner received the Sacrament publickly on a week-day at St. Mary's, but I was set up as a mark for all the polite students that knew me to shoot at. ... I daily underwent some contempt from the collegians. Some have thrown dirt at me, and others took away their pay from me." Johnson told Boswell that he was at Pembroke with Whitfield, and "knew him before he began to be better than other people" (smiling). But they cannot have been in residence together, nor can Whitfield have been "chevied" by Johnson to the accompaniment of candlestick and pan.

To the pictures of Pembroke life supplied by Graves and Whitfield, Dr. Birkbeck Hill adds a sketch of a gentleman commoner of this time. Mr. Erasmus Philipps, of Picton Castle, (afterwards fifth baronet), entered in 1720. He is a youth of fashion, but not, as he would probably be in the present day, a dunce and a fool. He attends the races on Port Mead, where the running of Lord Tracey's mare Whimsey, the swiftest galloper in England, brings to his mind the description in Job. He goes to see a foot-race between tailors for geese, and another day to see a great cock-match in Holywell between the Earl of Plymouth and the town cocks, which beat his lordship. He attends the ball at the "Angel"—a guinea touch—and gives a private ball in honour of the fair Miss Brigandine. He writes an Essay on Friendship set him by his tutor, who the same evening goes with the young man to Godstow by water with some others, taking music and wine. Or he attends a poetical club at the "Tuns," with Mr. Tristram,[333] another of the Fellows, drinks Gallician wine there, and is entertained with two masterly fables of Dr. Evans' composition. Pembrokians meet at the "Tuns" to motto, epigrammatize, etc. Mr. Philipps has literary tastes and attends the Encaenia, not to make a poor noise, but to criticize the Proctor's oration. He presents a curious book to the Bodleian, and Mr. Prior's works in folio to the Pembroke library. He cultivates the society of men of learning and taste, among them an Arabic scholar from Damascus. "On leaving Pembroke he presented one of the scholars with his key of the garden, for which he had on entrance paid ten shillings, treated the whole College in the Common Room, and then took up his Caution money (£10) from the bursar and lodged it with the Master for the use of Pembroke College."

When Graves went to All Souls as Fellow (which many Pembroke students of law did), his friend Blackstone went with him. *Sir William Blackstone*, the great jurist, entered in 1738, aged fifteen. He is buried at Wallingford.

Westminster Abbey has received the ashes of at least four members of this House, viz. Francis Beaumont and his brother Sir John, Pym the parliamentarian, and Johnson the champion of authority. Pym's body was cast out at the Restoration.

Nisi Dominus aedificaverit Domum in vanum laboraverunt qui aedificant eam.

XIX.
WORCESTER COLLEGE.

BY THE REV. C. H. O. DANIEL, M.A., FELLOW OF
WORCESTER COLLEGE.

Gloucester College, 1283-1539.

The beginnings of the history of Gloucester
College anticipate by nine years the establishment of
Merton College upon its present site and under
statutes which had assumed their final shape, by
three years the code of rules drawn up by the
University for the University Hall, and by one year
the date of the statutes of Balliol College, statutes
which preceded the establishment of students upon
the present site of that College. It was in 1283 that
John Giffarde, Baron of Brimsfield, on St. John the
Evangelist's day, being present in St. Peter's Abbey
at Gloucester, founded Gloucester College, "extra
muros Oxoniæ," as a house of study for thirteen
monks of that abbey, appropriating for their support
the revenues of the church of Chipping Norton. This
was the first monastic College established in Oxford.
It differed from the Hall which not long after was
built for the Benedictines of Durham, in that, while
Durham College admitted secular students,
Gloucester College was limited to monks of the
Benedictine Order. It was not long before the other
great English Benedictine Houses, whose students
when sent to Oxford had hitherto been placed in

scattered lodgings, recognized the advantage of bringing them together under common discipline and instruction and a common Head. They obtained permission therefore of the Abbey of Gloucester to share with them their house at Oxford, and to add to the existing buildings several lodgings, each appropriated to the use of one or more of the Benedictine Houses. The building made over in the first place by Giffarde had been originally the mansion of Gilbert Clare earl of Gloucester, for whom it had the advantage of being close to the Royal palace of Beaumont, in Magdalen Parish. His arms were in Antony Wood's day still to be seen "fairly depicted in the window of the Common Hall." It subsequently passed into the hands of the Hospitallers of St. John of Jerusalem, and was exempt from Episcopal and archidiaconal jurisdiction "a tempore cujus memoria non existit." It was from the Hospitallers that Giffarde bought the house which he made over to Gloucester Abbey. In 1290 or 1291, upon the agreement to admit other Benedictine Houses to a joint use of the College, the founder purchased four other tenements, and, obtaining a license in mortmain from Edward I., conveyed the whole to the Prior and monks. Thereupon was held at Abingdon a General Chapter of the Abbots and Priors of the Order, at which provisions were made for regulating the new buildings to be erected and for providing contributions towards the expenses, while rules were drawn up for the conduct of the College. All Benedictines of the Province of Canterbury were to have right of admission to "our common House in Stockwell Street," and all the students were to have an equal vote in the election of the Prior. The strife and canvassing which took place over these popular elections in time arose to such a head as to create a scandal in the order, to remedy which it was decreed by a General Chapter that the author of any such disturbance should be punished by degradation and perpetual excommunication. The monks themselves, differing in this respect from the subsequent foundation of Durham College, were not permitted to study or be conversant with secular students; they were bound to attend divine service on solemn and festival days; to observe disputations constantly in term-time; to have divinity disputations once a week, and the presiding moderator was endowed with a salary of £10 per annum out of the common stock of the Order, which provided also for the expenses of their Exercises and Degrees in the matter of fees and entertainments. It was the duty of the Prior to enforce all regulations and to see that the monks preached often, as well in the Latin as in the vulgar tongue. It was further jealously stipulated that in their exercises they should "answer" under one of their own Order, a trace of the struggle between the religious orders and the University which arose to such a height in the case of the various orders of Friars.

Few structures carry their history and their purpose upon their face in a more obvious or more picturesque manner than do the still surviving remains of the old Benedictine colony. Each settlement possessed a lodging of its own "divided (though all for the most part adjoining to each other) by particular roofs, partitions, and various forms of structure, and known from each other, like so many colonies and tribes, (though one at once inhabited by several abbies,) by arms and rebuses that are depicted and cut in stone over each door." These words of Antony à Wood are a perfect description of the cottage-like row of tenements which still form the south side of the present quadrangle, and partially apply to the small southern quadrangle, though many of the features have been in this case obliterated. But on the north side all that now remains of what is represented in Loggan's well-known print is the ancient doorway of the College, surmounted by two shields, (there used to be three, bearing respectively the arms of Gloucester, Glastonbury and St. Alban's,) and the adjoining buildings, which are of the same character as the tenements on the south side. The first lodgings on the north side were allotted, we are told, to the monks of Abingdon: the next were built for the monks of Gloucester. These in later days became the lodgings of the Principal of Gloucester Hall, an arrangement followed in the position of the present lodgings of the Provost of the College. On the five lodgings of the south side one may see still in place the shields described by A. Wood. Over the door at the S.W. corner is a shield bearing a mitre over a comb and a tun, with the letter W (interpreted as the rebus of Walter Compton, or else in reference to Winchcombe Abbey). Another shield bears three cups surmounted by a ducal coronet. Between these is a small niche. The chambers next in order were assigned by tradition to Westminster Abbey; and the central lodgings of the five were "partly for Ramsey and Winchcombe Abbies." Over the doors of the easternmost lodgings again are shields, the first bearing a "griffin sergreant," the other a plain cross. Another plain shield remains *in situ* in the small quadrangle; one has been removed and built into the garden wall of the present kitchen.

A. Wood gives a list of the abbies which sent their monks to Gloucester College. These were Gloucester, Glastonbury, St. Alban's, Tavistock, Burton, Chertsey, Coventry, Evesham, Eynsham, St. Edmondsbury, Winchcombe, Abbotsbury, Michelney, Malmesbury, Rochester, Norwich. It may be presumed that other Houses of the Order made use of the place, among those whose representatives were present at the Chapter held at Salisbury the day after the interment of Queen Eleanor, 1291, when the Prior for the time being, Henry de Helm, was invested with the government of the College, and provision was made for the election of his successor.

We do not at this early date find any mention of Refectory or Chapel. The parish church was, no doubt, as in other cases, frequented by the student-monks for divine services, but they also had licence to have a portable altar. It was not till 1420, in the prioralty of Thomas de Ledbury, that John Whethamsted, Abbot of St. Alban's, formerly Prior, contributed largely to the erection of a chapel, which stood upon the site of the present chapel. Its ruins are figured in Loggan's sketch. He built also a Library on the south side of the chapel, at right angles to it, the five windows of which, giving upon Stockwell Street, are also depicted in Loggan's sketch. Upon this Library he bestowed many books both of his own collection and of his own writing; and at his instance Humphrey Duke of Gloucester, besides other benefactions, gave many books to the Library. The benefits conferred by Whethamsted were such that a Convocation of the Order styled him "chief benefactor and second founder of the College." One other name, a name of local interest, we find associated with the place as its benefactor—that of Sir Peter Besils, of Abingdon. Thus a century of dignified prosperity was assured to the College, during which period it numbered among its *alumni* John Langden, Bishop of Rochester; Thomas Mylling, Abbot of Westminster and afterwards Bishop of Hereford; Antony Richer, Abbot of Eynsham, afterwards Bishop of Llandaff; Thomas Walsingham the chronicler.

The dissolution of the monasteries of course involved the suppression of the Benedictine College; Whethamsted's Chapel and Library were reduced to a ruin; and the books "were partly lost and purchased, and partly conveyed to some of the other College Libraries," where Wood professes to have seen them "still bearing their donor's name."

Bishop of Oxford's Palace, **1542-1557(?)**.

The College, its buildings and grounds, remained in the hands of the Crown till the thirty-fourth year of Henry's reign, when, upon his founding the Bishoprick of Oxford, the seat of which was at Osney, it was allotted to the Bishop for his palace, and was for a certain time occupied by Bishop King, who had been the last Abbot of Osney. On the transfer of the See within three years to the church of St. Frideswyde, the endowments which had been attached to the Bishoprick and temporarily resigned to the Crown were conveyed to the new foundation, the intention of Henry VIII., who had died in the meantime, being carried out by Edward VI. But there is no mention among the endowments thus re-conveyed of Gloucester College, which remained in the possession of the Crown until it was granted by Elizabeth, in the second year of her reign, to William Doddington. He at once made it over to the newly-founded College of St. John Baptist, for whom it was purchased by the founder. The legend runs that Sir Thomas Whyte was inclined for a while to Gloucester Hall as the site of his new College, but that a dream directed him to the selection of St. Bernard's College.

The Bishop of Oxford in 1604 revived his claim to the Hall, maintaining that the surrender to the Crown had not been acknowledged by Bishop King, nor duly enrolled in Chancery, and to try his rights he "did make an entry by night and by water, and did drive away the horses depasturing on the land belonging to the said Hall." He failed however to make good his claim against St. John's College.

Gloucester Hall, 1559-1714.

Sir Thomas Whyte effected considerable repairs in his new purchase, and converted it into a Hall with the name of the Principal and Scholars of St. John Baptist's Hall: the Principal was to be a Fellow of St. John's College, elected by that Society and admitted by the Chancellor of the University. On St. John Baptist's day, 1560, the first Principal, William Stock, and one hundred Scholars took their first commons in the old monks' Refectory. It was in the September of this same year that the body of Amy Robsart, Robert Dudley's ill-fated wife, was secretly brought from Cumnor to Gloucester College, and lay there till the burial at St. Mary's, "the great chamber where the mourners did dine, and that where the gentlewomen did dine, and beneath the stairs a great hall being all hung with black cloth, and garnished with scutcheons."[334] Before long the patronage of this Hall passed with that of others into the hands of the Chancellor, this same Robert Dudley, then become Earl of Leicester, so that the restriction to Fellows of St. John's College was no longer observed.

There are but few notices of the Hall to be found in the Register of St. John's College. Under date 1567 there is entry of the lease of a chamber, formerly the Library, to William Stocke, Principal of the Hall. In 1573 it was ordered that at the election of a Principal to succeed Mr. Stocke it be covenanted that Sir Geo. Peckham may quietly enjoy his lodging there. And again in 1608 there is entered a grant of six timber trees out of Bagley Wood towards building a chapel. This was in the principalship of Dr. Hawley, in whose time it was that the old Hall for a second time, if the legend of Sir Thomas Whyte be credited, won the regard of an intending Founder; Nicholas Wadham selected it as the site of his projected College, and his widow, Dorothy, sought to carry out his intention, and purchase it. But the scheme went off; for the Principal, Dr. Hawley, refused to resign his interest in the Hall, except upon the Foundress naming him as the first Warden of her College.

In Principal Hawley's time it may be inferred that the Hall was at a low ebb in point of numbers; but among its students was one whose quaint, adventurous career had its fit commencement in those picturesque ruins. Thomas Coryate the Odcombian—that strange amalgam of shrewdness, buffoonery, learning, and adventure—became a member of the Hall in 1596. He passed his life in wandering afoot—a pauper pilgrim—through the East. He was so apt a linguist as to silence "a laundry woman, a famous scold," in her own Hindustani. From the Court of the Great Mogul he dated epistles, which were the amusement of the wits, and are now the treasures of the collector of literary curiosities. These, and the "Crudities hastily gobbled up," a record of his earlier wanderings in Europe, will preserve his memory, when men of more serious consequence have passed into oblivion.

At this low ebb of the Hall's chequered existence, it seems to have been a common practice to let lodgings to persons not necessarily connected with the Hall. We have already seen how Sir George Peckham occupied a lodging in Principal Stocke's time; the famous Thomas Allen again in the reign of Elizabeth and James found a refuge here for many years; and now Degory Whear, who had been, with Camden, a member of Broadgates Hall, and then Fellow of Exeter, retiring with his wife to Oxford upon his patron's death, had rooms allotted to him in Gloucester Hall. In 1622 he was, through Allen's interest, appointed by Camden the first Professor on his History Foundation, and retained this chair, together with the Principalship of the Hall to which he was nominated in 1626, until his death in 1647. Degory Whear, though the friend and *protégé* of so good antiquaries as Allen and Camden, finds amusingly scant favour in the eyes of Antony Wood, who bestows upon him the faint praise that "he was esteemed by some a learned and genteel man, and by others a Calvinist. He left behind him a widow and children, who soon after became poor, and whether the Females lived honestly, 'tis not for me to dispute it."

The fame or vigour of Degory Whear, with the reputation of Thomas Allen, revived the decaying fortunes of the Hall; for we are told that "in his time there were 100 students: and some being persons of quality, ten or twelve met in their doublets of cloth of gold and silver." Among other noticeable names Christopher Merritt, Fellow of the Royal Society, was admitted in 1632, and Richard Lovelace in 1634. At that date there were ninety-two students in the Hall (Wood's *Life*, ii. 246). Degory Whear not only filled his Hall with students, but carried out many much-needed repairs of the buildings. The chapel, for instance, to the erection of which we have seen that St. John's contributed six timber trees from Bagley Wood, was now by his exertions completed; the Hall and other buildings were repaired; books were purchased for the Library, plate for the Buttery. In a MS. book preserved in the College Library are set forth the names of donors to these objects between the years 1630 and 1640. Among the entries are the following—"*Kenelmus Digby* Eques auratus 2 li. *Johannes Pym* armiger 20s. *Rogerus Griffin* civis Oxon. e Collegio pistorum donavit 2 millia scandularum ad valorem 22 solid. *Johannes Rousæus* publicæ Bibliothecæ præfectus 1 li. 2s. *Samuel Fell* S. Th. Doctor 5 li. *Thomas Clayton* Regius in Medicina Professor 2 li. *Guil. Burton* LL. Baccalaureatus gradum suscepturus 2 li. 10s." This last was at first a student at Queen's, where he was the contemporary and friend of Gerard Langbaine, but, his means failing him, Mr. Allen brought him to Gloucester Hall, and conferred on him the Greek Lecture there. As the friend of Langbaine it may be supposed he would have a friendly leaning to the plays which at this time, Wood says, were acted by stealth "in Kettle Hall, or at Holywell Mill, or in the Refectory at Gloucester Hall" (*Life*, ii. 148). He subsequently became the Usher to the famous Thomas Farnaby, and at last

Master of the School of Kingston-on-Thames. His "Græcæ Linguæ Historia; sive oratio habita olim Oxoniis in Aula Glevocestrensi ante XX & VI annos," was published in 1657 with a laudatory letter of Langbaine's, and a dedication to his pupil Thomas Thynne.

We next have an account of the expenditure upon the chapel—"Imprimis fabro murario sive cæmentario 25 li 10s. Materiario sive fabro tignario 38 li 10s. Gypsatori et scandulario 10 li. 11s. Vitriario 4 li 6s. fabro ferrario 7 li 10s. pictori 1 li 4s. storealatori 00 9s."

The Hall too was put into repair; for this Thomas Allen's legacy of £10 was employed, as also for the purchase of an *armarium* or bookcase, "parieti inferioris sacelli affixum." But in spite of this safeguard, the books, Wood says, with pathetic simplicity, "though kept in a large press, have been thieved away for the most part, and are now dwindled to an inconsiderable nothing." Under the date 1637 there is an entry of a contribution of 40 shillings to the expenses of the University in the reception of the King and Queen. It may be noted that these disbursements seem to have required the assent of the Masters of the Hall as well as of the Principal.

There are two papers in the University Archives bearing the signature of Degory Whear as Principal, which give some information as to fees and customary observances of the Hall. Commoners upon admission paid to the House 4*s.*, to the College officers (Manciple, Butler and Cook) 4s. Semi-commoners or Battlers, to the House 2s., to the officers 1s. 6d. A "Poor Scholar" paid nothing. Every Commoner paid weekly to the Butler 1d., towards the Servitors of the Hall a halfpenny. He also paid quarterly 1s. for wages to the Manciple and Cook, besides a varying sum for Decrements, a term which covered kitchen fuel, table-cloths, utensils, &c. This item sometimes amounted to 5s. a quarter, never more. On taking any Degree 10s. was paid to the Principal, and another 10s. to the House, or else there was given a presentation Dinner. The Principal further received only the chamber rents, out of which he kept the chambers in repair, and paid quarterly to two Moderators or Readers the sum of £1 6s. 8d. It appears that it was the custom for every Commoner to take his turn as Steward, go to market with the Manciple and Cook, see the provisions bought for ready money, apportion the amount for each meal, attend to oversee the divisions at Dinner and Supper, and be accountable for any Commons sent to private chambers. At the end of every quarter the accounts were inspected by the Principal and such of the Masters as he pleased to send for. On Act Monday it had been customary for the proceeding Masters to keep a common supper in the Hall, but this charge had of late years been turned to the building of an Oratory, the flooring of the Hall, the purchase of plate and of books.

In Whear's time then the Hall must be regarded as having attained its highest prosperity, due no doubt partly to the energy and distinction of the Principal, but due also in great measure to the influence and reputation of Mr. Thomas Allen, to whom the Principal himself had owed his promotion. This distinguished mathematician and antiquary, "being much inclined to a retired life, and averse from taking Holy Orders,"[335] about 1570 resigned his Fellowship at Trinity College, and took up his residence in Gloucester Hall, where he remained until his death in 1632. His intimate relations with the Chancellor, the Earl of Leicester, at once marked and increased his distinction, while it exposed him to the attacks of Leicester's enemies. Leicester would have nominated him to a Bishoprick, and the malignant author of "Leycester's Commonwealth" stigmatizes him as one of Leicester's spies and intelligencers in the University, and couples him with his friend John Dee as an atheist and Leicester's agent "for figuring and conjuring." Indeed his reputation as a mathematician ("he was," says his pupil Burton, "the very soul and sun of all the Mathematicians of his time") caused him to be regarded by the vulgar as a magician. Fuller says of him that "he succeeded to the skill and scandal of Friar Bacon," and that his servitor would tell the gaping enquirer that "he met the spirits coming up the stairs like bees." Indeed in those days when horoscopes were in fashion the mathematician merged into the astrologer; the friend of John Dee not unnaturally was supposed to have dealings in magical arts, and Leicester's patronage of both would give countenance to the reputation. But the friendship of the most learned men of the time—of

Bodley, Saville, Camden, Cotton, Spelman, Selden—is an indication of Allen's genuine attainments. Bodley by his will bequeaths to Mr. Wm. Gent of Gloucester Hall "my best gown and my best cloak, and the next gown and cloak to my best I do bequeath to Mr. Thomas Allen of the same Hall." Camden also leaves him in his will the sum of £16.[336] Allen's valuable collection of MSS. passed into the hands of his eccentric pupil, Sir Kenelm Digby, by whom they were placed in Sir Thomas Bodley's newly-founded library.

On Whear's decease in 1647 Tobias Garbrand, of Dutch descent, was made Principal by the Earl of Pembroke as Chancellor. He was ejected at the Restoration in 1660. From this date the fortunes of the Hall seemed to have reached their lowest depth.[337] If a stray gleam of fortune lit upon the place, it was only to suffer immediate eclipse. Thus, when John Warner, Bishop of Rochester, left a foundation in 1666 for the maintenance of four Scotch scholars to be trained as ministers, and the Masters and Fellows of Balliol College were unwilling to receive them, as being not in any way advantageous to the House, they were for a time placed in Gloucester Hall. But when Dr. Good became Master of Balliol in 1672, Gutch remarks with quiet humour, "he took order that they should be translated thither, and there they yet continue."

The fortunes of the Hall sank lower and lower, till a time came when it remained for several years entirely untenanted by students. It shared in the general depression of the University, to which Wood bears evidence. "Not one Scholar matric. in 1675, 1676, 1677, 1678, not one Scholar in Gloucester Hall, only the Principal and his family, and two or three more families that live there in some part to keep it from ruin, the paths are grown over with grass, the way into the Hall and Chapel made up with boards."

Prideaux, writing to Ellis (Sept. 18, 1676), says— "Gloucester Hall is like to be demolished, the charge of Chimney money being so great that Byrom Eaton will scarce live there any longer. There hath been no scholars there these three or four years: for all which time the hall being in arrears for this tax the collectors have at last fallen upon the principal, who being by the Act liable to the payment, hath made great complaints about the town and created us very good sport; but the old fool hath been forced to pay the money, which hath amounted to a considerable sum."

Loggan's picturesque view, taken in 1675, suggests a mournful desolation, and the pathetic motto which it bears—"Quare fecit Dominus sic domui huic?"—is eloquent of decay. Dr. Byrom Eaton, Archdeacon of Stow, and then of Leicester, had held the Principality for thirty years, when in 1692 he resigned it to make way for a younger and more vigorous man. Such was found in Dr. Woodroffe, one of the Canons of Christ Church, whose nomination to the Deanery by James II. in 1688 had been cancelled at the Revolution in favour of Dean Aldrich. Woodroffe is described by Wood as "a man of a generous and public spirit, who bestowed several hundred pounds in repairing (the place) and making it a fit habitation for the Muses, which being done he by his great interest among the gentry made it flourish with hopeful sprouts." The hopeful sprouts, however, do not seem to have been so very numerous after all, since we find the entry in Wood's *Life* under date Jan. 1694—"I was with Dr. Woodroffe, and he told me he had six in Commons at Gloucester Hall, his 2 sons two." Prideaux's letters to Ellis contain several references to Dr. Woodroffe, the reverse of complimentary— ludicrous accounts of sermons, which he confesses to be hearsay accounts, accusations of heiress hunting, of whimsical ill-temper, of want of dignity. "Last night he had Madam Walcup at his lodgings, and stood with her in a great window next the quadrangle, where he was seen by Mr. Dean himself and almost all the house toying with her most ridiculously and fanning himself with her fan for almost all the afternoon." But Prideaux's gossip was probably inspired by personal antipathies and College jealousies. Woodroffe was no doubt a keen, bustling, pushing man.[338] He was shrewd enough, at any rate, to marry a good fortune; but became involved in difficulties, which led to the sequestration of his canonry. He seems to have lost no opportunity of advertising himself and combining "public spirit" with private advantage. Such was the man who became associated with one of the most interesting though short-lived experiments in the history of the University—the establishment of a Greek College. Some seventy years had passed since Cyril Lucar, Patriarch first of Alexandria and then of Constantinople, had sent to England a Greek youth, Metrophanes Critopylos, whom Abp. Abbott placed at Balliol College, of which his brother had not long before been Master. Here Critopylos remained as a student till about 1622, when he returned to the East, and subsequently became Patriarch of Alexandria in the room of Cyril Lucar. Nothing more seems to have come of this particular overture, but the English Chaplains of Constantinople, Smyrna, and Aleppo, kept open to some extent the communications with the Eastern Church. At last, upon the representations of Joseph Georgirenes, Metropolitan of Samos (a man who subsequently took refuge in London, and had built for him as a Greek church what is now St. Mary's, Crown St. Soho), Archbishop Sancroft and others who favoured the hope of reunion with the Eastern Church promoted a scheme for the education of a body of Greek youths at Oxford, and the establishment of a Greek College there. Foremost amongst Oxford sympathizers was Dr. Woodroffe, the newly appointed Principal of Gloucester Hall. In a letter to Callinicos, the Patriarch of Constantinople, he suggests that twenty students, five from each of the four patriarchates, should be sent over to the Greek College now founded at Oxford (Gloucester Hall), which had been placed "on the same rank footing and privilege which the other Colleges enjoy there." He explains the course of study to be pursued, and suggests the advantage of a reciprocity of students, as also of books and manuscripts. He designates the three English chaplains named above as convenient channels of communication. The scheme contemplated an annual succession of students, who were to be of two classes. For two years they were to converse in Ancient Greek, and then to learn Latin and Hebrew. They were to study Aristotle, Plato, the Greek Fathers, and Controversial Divinity. The services were to be in Greek, and public exercises were to be performed in Greek, as directed by the Vice-Chancellor. Their habit was to be "the gravest worn in their country," and finally they were to be returned to their respective Patriarchs with a report of the progress made. Trustees were to manage the funds of the College, which was to be supported by voluntary contributions. This bold scheme was but partially attempted, and before long came to a disastrous end. Mr. Ffoulkes, who first claimed attention in the "Union Review" for the Greek College, which, as he observes, had been strangely ignored by Wood's continuators, quotes from Mr. E. Stevens, a nonjuror, and enthusiastic advocate of "Reunion," his account of the experiment and its breakdown. Five young Grecians were in 1698 brought from Smyrna and placed in Gloucester Hall. Three of them were, according to Mr. Stephens, lured away by Roman emissaries: two of these, brothers, after various adventures, took refuge with Mr. Stephens, and were at last sent home "with their faith unscathed." The third was decoyed to Paris, to the Greek College lately established there, presumably in rivalry of the

Oxford scheme. There appears too to have been another establishment set up in friendly rivalry at Halle in Saxony. But the most fatal blow was the mismanagement of the College itself. "Though they who came first were well enough ordered for some time; yet afterwards they and those who came after them were so ill-accommodated both for their studies and other necessaries, that some of them staid not many months, and others would have been gone if they had known how; and there are now but two left there."[339] Add to these drawbacks the temptations of London, and it is not surprising that the Oxford College received its quietus in a missive from Constantinople. "The irregular life of certain priests and laymen of the Eastern Church, living in London, is a matter of great concern to the Church. Wherefore the Church forbids any to go and study at Oxford, be they ever so willing." This was in 1705. From that moment, as Mr. Ffoulkes picturesquely says, the Greek College "disappears like a dream." Of its students one name only is preserved to us. We find in *Hearne* (March 15th, 1707)—"Francis Prasalendius, a Græcian of the Isle of Corcyra, lately a student in the Public Library, and of Gloucester Hall, has printed a book in the Greek language (writ very well as I am informed by one of the Græcians of Glouc. Hall) against Traditions, in which he falls upon Dr. Woodroffe very smartly."

Worcester College, founded 1714.

But while the Greek College was still perishing of inanition, its principal was engaged in a scheme of a more ambitious though less interesting nature. A Worcestershire Baronet, Sir Thomas Cookes, had made known his desire through the Bishop of Worcester of founding a College at Oxford; £10,000 was the sum he proposed for an endowment. There was competition for the prize. Dr. Woodroffe wanted to secure it for Gloucester Hall, Dr. Mill for St. Edmund Hall, Dr. Lancaster for Magdalen Hall; Balliol College was at one time the favourite object, at another a workhouse for his county. The choice inclined to Gloucester Hall, but was well-nigh lost; for Woodroffe had inserted in the charter a clause providing that the King should have liberty to put in and turn out the Fellows at his pleasure. With the recent experience of Magdalen fresh in men's minds, such intervention of the crown was not likely to find favour, and Bishop Stillingfleet drily observed that "kings have already had enough to do with our Colleges." The hopes of Edmund Hall rose high; for indeed the Bishop had, according to Hearne, nominated that Hall in the first place. However Dr. Woodroffe prudently withdrew his clause, and in 1698 a charter passed the great seal for the incorporation of the Hall under the title of the Provost, Fellows, and Scholars of Worcester College, with Dr. Woodroffe for the first Provost.[340] This was followed by a Ratification dated November 18th, naming the Bishop of Worcester as Visitor, and the Bishop of Oxford as his assessor in difficult cases, and making elaborate provision for the organization, conduct, and educational system of the College. There were to be twelve Fellows, six Senior Tutors, six Junior Sub-Tutors, and eight Scholars, chosen from the Founder's schools of Bromsgrove and Feckenham, or, failing them, from Worcester and Hartlebury. Each Fellow and Scholar was to have £14 per annum, the Provost double that amount. There were to be Lectureships, two "solemnes" in Theology and History, three ordinary in Mathematics, Philosophy, and Philology; the Lecture in Theology to be catechetical, on the model of that at Balliol, and to be given in the chapel. The Prælector of History was to lecture from seven to nine on Sundays on Biblical history. The others were to lecture at the discretion of the Provost five or at least four times a week. An elaborate scheme of medical and other studies was prescribed. There was a carefully-graduated scale of payments "obeuntibus cursus et acta," ending with 13*s*. 4*d*. for the speech in commemoration of the Founder. The Provost was to allot a cubiculum to one or at the most to two occupants. In winter the afternoon chapel service was to be at three, the morning service at seven, but in summer at six. This was to consist of a shorter Latin form "ad usum Ecclesiæ Xti," with a chapter of the Bible in Greek. Private prayers and Bible-reading were enjoined for each day, and two hours specified for Sunday. A chapter in Greek or Latin was to be read at meal-times in Hall. Offenders against rules were to be "gated" or sent into seclusion, "quasi minor quædam excommunicatio," or else to be exiled to the ante-chapel. As regards the cook, butler, &c. the Aularian Statutes were to be observed.

After all the Charter remained a dead letter. Sir Thomas Cookes, anxious to find excuses for putting off Dr. Woodroffe's importunities, claimed for his heirs the nomination to the Headship; and after two years the Chancellor conceded this point. It was objected that the Chancellor had not the power to make this concession without the consent of Convocation: which was never asked; and if it had, would not have been given. Sir Thomas found fresh reasons for hanging back. The fact that Gloucester Hall was a leasehold and that St. John's were supposed to have been forbidden by their Founder to part with the fee simple was one of these difficulties. Then there were the Statutes, which Sir Thomas Cookes persistently refused to sign, "nor would he pay one farthing for passing the Charter." In 1701 he died, leaving his £10,000 in the hands of certain Bishops, with the Vice-Chancellor and the Heads of Houses, for the carrying out his intentions. The money was left to accumulate for some years till it amounted to £15,000. In the meantime Dr. Woodroffe tries to obtain an Act in 1702 for settling the money on Gloucester Hall, the lease of which he proposed St. John's College should make perpetual at the then rent of £5 10s. The Bill, however, was thrown out on the second reading. At Oxford, it is clear, there was a powerful opposition to Dr. Woodroffe and his claim for Gloucester Hall. On Nov. 22, 1707, nineteen out of the thirty Trustees met in the Convocation House, and on the ground that "the erecting of Buildings would make the charity of less use than endowing some Hall in Oxford already built," determined "to fix the Charity at Magdalen Hall, and to endow Fellows and Scholars there." On the other hand the Archbishop of Canterbury, the Bishop of Worcester, the Bishop of Oxford and others were in favour of carrying out what they believed to be in spite of all his vacillation the final determination of Sir Thomas Cookes in favour of Gloucester Hall. They deposed moreover[341] that "the ground Plats of Gloucester Hall and the Gloucester Hall buildings Quadrangles and Gardens are 3 times as much as Magdalen Hall, and the ground on which the buildings of Gloucester Hall stand is twice as much as that of Magdalen Hall, and there are large and capacious chambers in Gloucester Hall to receive 20 scholars, and 9 are inhabited, and the principal's lodgings are in good repair and fit for a family of 12 persons, and there is a large Hall, Chapel, Buttery and Kitchen, and a large common room lately wainscoted and sash windows, and in laying out about £500 in repairs there will be good conveniency for 60 scholars, and the place is pleasantly situated and in a good air." Dr. Woodroffe dies in 1711, his ambition still unfulfilled, and a Fellow of St. John's, Dr. Richard Blechynden, succeeds to the Principalship of an empty Hall. There was, according to Hearne, hardly one Scholar in the place. At last the trustees saw their way to carrying out the will of Sir Thomas Cookes. St. John's College in 1713 agrees to alienate Gloucester Hall for the sum of £200, and a quit-rent of 20*s*. per annum. In the following year, two days only before the Queen's death, a Charter of Incorporation, for the second time, passes the great seal, and Gloucester Hall or College is finally merged in Worcester College. The foundation was now to consist of a Provost, six Fellows, and six Scholars, whose emoluments were to be on a somewhat more liberal scale than that of the original statutes. Fellows and Scholars were to be allowed sixpence a day for commons, the Fellows to have £30 per annum, the Scholars 13*s*. 8*d*. a quarter, the Provost £80 per annum, but no allowance for commons. Among the other "ministri" was to be a Tonsor, receiving an annual salary of 20*s*. This important official lingered on in diminished importance till the present generation. The Bishops of Worcester and Oxford and the Vice-Chancellor were appointed Visitors. In other respects the provisions of the new Statutes were much simplified. The scheme of Lectureships was omitted; so were the elaborate directions as to studies, private devotions, &c., as well as the scale of payments on the performance of exercises. Latin was to be the ordinary speech, "so far as might be convenient," except at College meetings. Undergraduates were to "dispute" every day, and write weekly Themes; Bachelors to "dispute" twice a week, and make a Terminal "Declamation." Candidates for Degrees were to oppose or respond on a problem set by the Provost in the College Hall, while candidates for the M.A. Degree had the option of commenting on a passage of Aristotle. On the Degree Day a Bachelor was to give a supper, or pay 20*s.* for the College uses. The supper given by an M.A. was not to exceed 40*s.*

Of the new College Principal Blechynden was named as the first Provost; of the six Fellows, one, Roger Bouchier, was already a member of the Hall—"a man of great reading in various sorts of learning, the greatest man in England for Divinity."[342] The others were Thomas Clymer of All Souls', Robert Burd of St. John's, William Bradley of New Inn Hall, Joseph Penn of Wadham, and Samuel Creswick of Pembroke, who was afterwards Dean of Wells.

It was not till 1720, that with the modest sum of £798 0*s.* 3*d.*, the remnant of a disputed bequest of Mrs. Margaret Alcorne, the newly-founded College was enabled to commence the "restoration" of its buildings. Had the designs of Dr. Clarke, illustrated by the Oxford Almanack of 1741, which were similar in character to those of Hawkesmoor and other architects for the reconstruction of Brasenose, All Souls', and Magdalen, been carried out, the picturesque history of the place would have been entirely effaced, and a quadrangle of "correct" and "elegant" monotony would have satisfied the taste of Dean Aldrich and the amateurs of the day. Fortunately the means were wanting; all that was put in hand at first were the Chapel, Hall, and Library. By the liberality of Dr. Clarke the interior of the Library was completed in 1736, its exterior in 1746. The Hall was at last finished in 1784, while the

Chapel still remained incompleted in 1786, the date of Gutch's account—nor does the College Register give any indication on the point. But in the meantime two considerable benefactors arose, who contributed new Foundations to the corporation. Dr. Clarke, Fellow of All Souls' and Member for the University, left an endowment for six Fellowships and three Scholarships, together with his valuable library, while Mrs. Sarah Eaton, daughter of the former principal, bequeathed an endowment for seven Fellowships and five Scholarships to be held by the sons of clergymen. These new Foundations were incorporated by Charter in 1744. For lodging Dr. Clarke's Foundation the demolition of the old buildings on the north side of the quadrangle was begun, and nine sets of rooms erected by his trustees, 1753-9, while in 1773 the remainder of the old north side was swept away, and twelve sets of rooms built for Mrs. Eaton's Foundation, together with the present Provost's lodgings. Meanwhile the College was providently with such resources as it possessed enlarging its borders. In 1741 it purchased of St. John's College for £850 the garden ground on the south side of the College, and in 1744 the gardens and meadows to the north and west, "together with the house called the Cock and Bottle." In 1801 it bought for £1330 the "King's Head," opposite to the front of the College, and in 1813 enfranchised the premises on the east front held under lease of the City; while in 1806 it cleared away "Woodroffe's Folly," a building erected by that Principal opposite the front of the College, for which St. John's received a valuation of £401 16*s.* The College thus became surrounded with an open belt, destined to be an incalculable boon in the modern days of building extension. The garden ground on the south side was in 1813 ordered to be kept in hand for the use of the Fellows, and it was about the year 1827 that the late Mr. Greswell signalized his Bursarship by laying out the ornamental grounds, as they now exist. These gardens, falling to a piece of water, together with the fortunate preservation of an open quadrangle, a mode of construction for the merits of which Sir Christopher Wren contended at Trinity,[343] secured to the College the sanitary as well as the picturesque advantages of a *rus in urbe*—a "*rus*" so rural that, the tradition runs, a tutor of the last generation would take his gun, and slip down between his lectures to the pool for a shot at a stray snipe.

William Gower, upon Dr. Blechynden's death, was nominated Provost in 1736. He had been admitted Scholar in 1715, the year after the incorporation of the College. He rivalled Thomas Allen in the length of his connection with the College. For 62 years he was borne upon its foundations, as Scholar, Fellow, or Provost. Longevity has been a characteristic of the Provosts of this College. One only, Dr. Sheffield, held his office for so short a period as 18 years. The other three, Gower, Landon, and Cotton, were Provosts respectively for 41, 44, and 41 years—collectively 126 years, and Dr. Cotton kept 70 years of unbroken residence. Dr. Gower was a man of great literary attainments. He left many valuable books to the

College Library. Dr. King[344] says that he was "acquainted with three persons only who spoke English with that eloquence and propriety that if all they said had been immediately committed to writing, any judge of the English language would have pronounced it an excellent and very beautiful style." The other two were Atterbury and Johnson. It was in his second year's Provostship that Samuel Foote of Worcester School claimed and established a right to a Scholarship as Founder's kin. His student life was brief and stormy. In 1740 the College passes sentence that "Samuel Foote having by a long-continued course of ill-behaviour rendered himself obnoxious to frequent censure of the Society public and private, and having while he was under censure for lying out of College insolently and presumptuously withdrawn himself and refused to answer to several heinous crimes objected to him, though duly cited by the Provost by an instrument in form, in not appearing to the said citation, for the above reasons his Scholarship is declared void, and he is hereby deprived of all benefit and advantage of the said Scholarship." This entry gives an interest to the opening of Gower's Provostship; another of a different character occurs near its close. In 1775 is recorded an injunction of the Visitors of the College "as to the use of napkins in the Common Hall."

The Provostship of Dr. Landon, 1795-1835, witnessed the commencement of that growth of Oxford, of which our own generation has seen so remarkable a development. The opening up of Beaumont St., as to which the College was in treaty with the city in 1820, materially assisted in drawing Worcester within the comity of Colleges.[345] It was still—and for many years to come—unrecognized upon the Proctorial rota. The first Proctor it nominated in its own right held office in 1863. The College could only be approached either by George St. and Stockwell St., or more directly by the narrow alley called Friar's Entry; and an amusing picture is given of the stately Vice-Chancellor—"Old Glory" was his soubriquet—preceded by his Bedels, with their gold and silver maces, ducking beneath the fluttering household linen suspended across the alley on washing day. This must have been a trying test of the dignified deportment which had distinguished Dr. Landon as host of the Allied Sovereigns, and gained for him—so it is said—from the Prince Regent the Deanery of Exeter.

The College, thus drawn more directly within the influences of University life, began to feel the impulse given to academical resort by times of peace. New rooms were added; sets long vacant were fitted up for occupants. In 1821 three additional sets were constructed "in the space afforded by the old College chapel." In 1822 it was ordered that all such apartments not at present inhabited, as shall be found capable of accommodating undergraduates, be immediately prepared for their reception. In 1824 the roof of part of the old building was raised, so as to give six additional sets of rooms. Finally in 1844 a new and handsome kitchen was built and seven additional sets constructed.[346]

The most distinguished inmate of the College in Landon's time was Thomas de Quincey, of whom his old servant on No. 10 staircase—Common Room man till 1865—retained many memories. He lived a somewhat recluse life. He was always buying fresh books, and was sometimes at a loss how to find money for them. In those days men dressed for Hall: and De Quincey having one day parted with his one waistcoat for the purchase of a book went into Hall hiding his loss of clothing as best he could. But concealment was in vain, and he was promptly sconced for the deficiency. De Quincey crowned the peculiarities of his College career by suddenly leaving Oxford before the close of a brilliant examination.

In 1826 another member of the College—Francis William Newman—received the unique distinction of a present of books (now in the College Library) from his mathematical examiners. Bonamy Price, Arnold's favourite pupil, shed a lustre upon the next generation of undergraduates. Both of them were subsequently Honorary Fellows of the College, and were present at the celebration of its six hundredth anniversary. Dr. Bloxam, a contemporary of the two, preserves some interesting recollections of the customs of the day. The Bachelors who resided for their M.A. Degree used to appear in Hall in full evening dress, breeches and silk stockings. Undergraduates had left off attending dinner in white neckcloths and evening costume. The table on the right was occupied by the gay men of the College, and was called the "Sinners' Table." These formed a class by themselves. The table on the left was called the "Smilers' Table," who also formed a distinct set between the "Sinners" and the "Saints," the latter being the more quiet men, who occupied the table nearest the High Table, on the left. The Fellow Commoners, an institution retained at the present day for the convenience of older men resorting to the University, were at that time young men of fortune, who desired an exemption from the stricter discipline of undergraduate life. They dined at the High Table, and were members of the Common Room. But their affinities lay rather with the occupants of the "Sinners' Table," and their existence must have been a perpetual difficulty to a sorely-tried Dean. "Bodley" Coxe, a member of the College in those days, subsequently one of its Honorary Fellows, would tell of the formidable muster of "pinks" in Beaumont St. after a champagne breakfast, and of the excuse which satisfied a simple-minded tutor that the delinquent would not offend again during the whole of the summer.

There has been a great change too in the habits of the Seniors. The tutors, as elsewhere, gave their lectures or rather lessons, consisting of translations by the class, with questions and answers, without form or ceremony in their own rooms. After an early dinner they would retire to an uncarpeted Common Room. There after wine long clay pipes were a regular indulgence. An evening walk or other interlude was succeeded by a hot supper at nine, and the evening finished with a rubber. Dr. Cotton in his time was singular in retiring to his rooms after Common Room without joining the whist and supper party. All these customs have dropped away with the barbers and knee-breeches of our fathers. The Latin form of Morning Prayers was abolished by an excess of reforming zeal, and the Statutes of the College are no longer recited in annual conclave. Ordinances have succeeded statutes, and statutes succeeded ordinances. One ancient custom lingers on—the Porter still makes his morning rounds, and hammers upon the door of each staircase with a wooden mallet. This is a Benedictine usage, an echo of the thirteenth century continuing to haunt the old Benedictine walls.

XX.
HERTFORD COLLEGE.[347]

BY THE REV. H. RASHDALL, M.A., FELLOW OF
HERTFORD.

Although Hertford is the youngest College of the University, it stands close to the very centre of the University's most ancient home, on a site which has been the scene of Academical life from the earliest times. What the Oxford Local Board has chosen to call S. Catherine's Street, has been known from the earliest times onwards as "Catte-Street" (Vicus Murilegorum). Lying just outside School Street, the scene of the Arts lectures, Cat Street was in the twelfth century the especial home of the Writers, Bookbinders, Parchment-makers, and Illuminers, for whose wares the growth of the University had created a demand. In the following century, it was partly occupied by University Halls or Hospices. At least four were comprised within the limits of the present College: Cat Hall, near the present Principal's Lodgings; Black Hall, at the corner of New College Lane; Hart Hall, and Arthur Hall, the two latter occupying the Library corner of the Quadrangle. Hart Hall eventually swallowed up all its neighbours as well as the ground between them. The history of this process want of space forbids me to trace. I must confine myself to the Hall which has given its name to the present College.

Hart Hall, 1280(?)-1740.

The house is first known to have been a residence for scholars when it had passed into the possession of one Elias de Hertford, from whom it got its name of Hert Hall (*Aula Cervina*). This was between 1261 and 1284. A Hall was then simply a boarding-house, hired by a party of students as a residence. One of them, called a Principal, paid the rent and collected the amount from the rest. From the first the Principal possessed a certain authority, but it was not necessary that he should be a Master or even a Graduate. Eventually the University required that he should be a Graduate, and a new Principal had to be admitted by the Chancellor. When, after the Reformation, the Colleges absorbed the greater part of the now greatly reduced Academic population, most of the old Halls disappeared and no new ones were created. Hence the few that remained divided the monopoly of University education with the Colleges, and their Principalships became not unimportant pieces of patronage, which after a long struggle the Chancellor succeeded in appropriating to himself, except in the case of S. Edmund Hall. To a very late period, however, there remained traces of the old democratic *régime*, under which the students claimed the right to elect their own Principal, that is to say, to consent to the transfer of the house by the landlord from one Principal to another. Since, prior to the Laudian statutes, there was nothing to prevent a scholar freely transferring himself from one Principal to another, the necessity of their acceptance of the landlord's new tenant is obvious. Even after the right of the Chancellor to nominate was fairly acknowledged, it was considered necessary that the students (graduate and undergraduate) should be solemnly assembled in the Hall and required to elect the Chancellor's nominee, a formality which at Hart Hall lasted as long as the Hall itself. The present Fellows of Hertford enjoy less autonomy than the ancient students, and the Chancellor still enjoys an absolute right to appoint the Principal.

In 1312 the Hall, after some intermediate transfers, passed to Walter de Stapeldon, Bishop of Exeter. For some years before the acquisition of their present site, it was the habitation of the Rector and Scholars of Stapeldon Hall, now known as Exeter College. After this, Hart Hall continued to belong to them and was let to a Principal, usually one of their own Fellows. The rent varied from time to time till 1665, after which a fixed sum of £1 13s. 4d. continued to be paid, and it became a question whether prescription had not extinguished any further rights on the part of the College.

Among the "Principals" appear the first three Wardens of New College, Richard de Tonworthe (1378), Nicolas de Wykeham (1381), and Thomas de Cranleigh, afterwards Archbishop of Dublin (1384).[348] During these years (probably 1375-1385) Hart and Black Halls were occupied by William of Wykeham's New College, while their own buildings were in course of erection. There is, indeed, in the New College book of "Evidences" what purports to be a conveyance (dated 1379) of Hart Hall to William of Wykeham, under a quit-rent, by the Prioress and Convent of Studley. But from the documents of Exeter College it is clear that the "capital lords" in actual possession were the Prior and Convent of S. Frideswyde's.[349] Hence it would seem that the astute Bishop of Winchester was outwitted for once by the Nuns of Studley (who were really proprietors of the adjoining Scheld Hall), and bought land with a bad title.[350] Nuns had a great reputation as women of business.

Later on the Hall was tenanted by a body of scholars supported by Glastonbury Abbey. At the dissolution a pension of £16 13s. 4d. was paid for the support of five scholars to Hart Hall, or rather to the University on its behalf. The amount was at first a rent-charge payable, but not always paid, by the grantee of certain Abbey lands. At the Restoration these lands were resumed by the Crown. The pension was still paid at the end of the last century, but has now disappeared.

The most distinguished man who can be fairly claimed as an *alumnus* of Hart Hall is the learned Selden (1600-1603), then "a long scabby-pol'd boy but a good student." Ken, the saintly Bishop of Bath and Wells, was apparently a member of the Hall for a few months while waiting for a vacancy at New College. Sir Henry Wotton, one of the seventeenth century worthies immortalized by Izaac Walton, resided here, though it would seem that he was not a member of the Hall but a Gentleman-Commoner of New College.

Richard Newton was born in the year 1675 or 1676, being a son of the squire of Laundon, Bucks, a moderate estate to which he eventually succeeded. He came up to Christ Church as a Westminster Student in 1694. After being for a time a Tutor of that House, he became tutor to the two Pelhams, the future Duke of Newcastle and his brother. In 1704 he was presented to the Rectory of Sudbury, Northants, by Bp. Compton. He was admitted Principal of Hart Hall, and took his D.D. in 1710, continuing to hold Sudbury. He made his mark as a preacher; and a number of pamphlets testify to his zeal as a University Reformer. In 1726 he wrote against an undoubted abuse, the evasion of the statute against unauthorized migration, though it must be admitted that his zeal on that occasion was stimulated by a recent desertion from his own Hall. Another of his pamphlets is on the perennial subject of University expensiveness. It is clear that in his own Hall he attempted to practise what he preached. In the pamphlets against him there are sneers against "a regimen of small-beer and apple-dumplings"— which (it is possible) had something to do with the frequent migrations of which the Doctor had to complain, though we are told that in one case the attraction was a Balliol Scholarship, and in another the "fine garden" of Trinity which the deserter "hoped would be to the advantage of his health." Eventually he even stopped the small-beer, holding that (as he explains) more beer was drunk when it was got both in the Hall and out of it than when it could only be obtained outside. Newton was the "active" Head of his day, the "Monarch of Hart Hall" as the scoffers put it. He had pupils to travel or stay with him in "the Long," usually "young gentlemen of fortune" in his College. He lamented the indolence and inactivity, and was pained to observe "the secular views and ambitious schemes" of other Heads. He held what was then accounted the eccentric opinion that "a gentleman-Commoner has a soul to be saved as well as a servitor, and is under the same obligations to religion and virtue." In confidential moments he would declare himself in favour of "Common-sense and Reason in matters of Religion"; and he appears to have practised a somewhat latitudinarian mode of meditation. "He[351] would, a little before bed-time, desire his young friends to indulge him in a short vacation of about half-an-hour for his own private recollections. During that little interval they were silent, and he would smoke his pipe with great composure, and then chat with them again in a useful manner for a short space, and, bidding them good night, go to his rest." When resident on his living, he had daily service at seven p.m. He was a Church Reformer as well as a University Reformer, and wrote on "Pluralities Indefensible." After his call to Oxford, he held his living as an absentee, but "never pocketed a farthing of the profits thereof"; and eventually succeeded in resigning in favour of his curate. Altogether the life of Dr. Newton exhibits an example of independence, honesty, and disinterestedness, rare indeed among the Churchmen of his time. Pelham gave it as his only reason for not preferring his old tutor, that he could not do it "because he never asked me." A man whom Pelham actually employed to write King's Speeches for him might certainly have been a Bishop for the asking. It was only in the year before his death (1752) that he got a Canonry at Christ Church.

Hertford College, 1740-1816.

Newton had one ambition, and that was a disinterested one. "Dr. Newton is commonly said to be Founder-mad," wrote the malicious Hearne; "Dr. Newton is very fond of founding a College," wrote another, in 1721. The patronage which he would not stoop to ask for himself, he sought to use for his College. But his grand friends did little for him; nearly all that he spent came out of his own pocket. He spent about £1500 on building a Chapel for the Hall (consecrated in 1716) and the adjoining corner of the present Quadrangle. He published an edition of Theophrastus by subscription for the benefit of his College, but it did not appear till after his death. His proposals for the foundation of a College were made public in 1734 in a Letter to the Vice-Chancellor, though he had already "made a noise" about it "many years." Considering the slenderness of the means at his disposal, it is not surprising that the project encountered some ridicule. Hearne had at first been much impressed by the Doctor's sermons, and styled him "an ingenious honest man," but on the appearance of his pamphlet on migration pronounced him "quite mad with pride and conceit," and the book a "very weak, silly performance." Now he laments that "'tis pitty Charities and Benefactions should be discountenanced and obstructed; but it sometimes happens when the persons that make them are supposed to be *mente capti* and aim at things in the settlement which are ridiculous, which seems to be the case at Hart Hall, as 'tis represented to me. However, after all," the charitable critic concludes, "'tis better not to publish the failings of persons, especially of clergymen, on such occasions, least mischief follow, the enemy being always ready to take advantage." The grant of the charter was long opposed by Exeter College: but the opinion of the Attorney-General was unfavourable to the claim on the part of that College to anything but the accustomed rent. In 1740 Dr. Newton got his Charter of Incorporation, and his Statutes approved by George II.

Dr. Newton was not at all disposed to lose by his elevation to the Headship of a College the autocracy which he had so long enjoyed as Head of a Hall. Hence, although he styles the four Tutors of the new Foundation "Senior Fellows" and their eight "Assistants" "Junior Fellows," the whole government of the College seems to be ultimately vested in the Principal, who was to be a Westminster student and Tutor of Christ Church nominated by the Dean of that House. There were to be no "idle fellowships" on Newton's foundation: all were "official," and lasted, the Senior Fellowships till the completion of eighteen years from Matriculation, the Junior only from B.A. to M.A. The College was designed for thirty-two "Students," who enjoyed a modest endowment of £6 13*s.* 4*d.* for the first year and £13 6*s.* 8*d.* for four years more, with commons. There were also four "Scholars" who were to act as Servitors to the four Tutors, and to perform such functions as ringing the bell and keeping the gate. Commoners and Gentleman-Commoners were expressly excluded: but wealthier men might become honorary Scholars, with leave to wear a "tuft" as well as the Scholar's gown. Each Tutor was to take charge of the freshmen of one year, who remained his pupils throughout their course. This division of the College into four classes must have been suggested by the Scotch University system, or by the arrangement of the French Colleges on which the Scotch system was based. It was, at all events, vastly superior to the old "Tutorial system," under which every Tutor played the polymathic Professor to Undergraduates of every year simultaneously.

Dr. Newton's Statutes are very curious reading. He aimed at perpetuating the "system of education" which he had himself introduced. They are full of wise provisions, some of them rather crotchety, and others excellent in themselves but perhaps hardly practicable even then. Each Tutor lived in a different "Angle" of the Quadrangle, and was responsible for its discipline. His post must have been no sinecure, if he was really to keep men out of each others' rooms during the hours of work, from Chapel (6.30 or 7.30 a.m. according to season) till the 12 o'clock dinner, and from 2 to 6 p.m. Supper was at 7 instead of the usual 6 p.m., to limit the time available for compotations. The gate was shut at 9 p.m., and after 10 the key was to be taken to the Principal's bedroom and no egress or ingress permitted. As an "educationist," the Founder apparently believed in Disputations and insisted much on English composition, but disbelieved in verse-making except for "Undergraduates having a genius for Poetry." The sumptuary regulations are somewhat severe, including the requirement that no bills shall be "contracted without their Tutor's knowledge and consent." Allowances from parents were to be sent to the Tutor, who was to pay his pupils' debts before transmitting the remainder to their destination. "Dismission" was the penalty for contracting a debt of more than 5s. "with any person keeping a Coffee-house or Cook's-shop or any other Public House whatsoever."

Newton's first two successors were men of mark in their day. William Sharp (1753-1757) was Regius Professor of Greek. David Durell (1757-1775) was eminent as a Hebraist. But the Principalship depended for its endowments entirely upon room-rent, and the Studentships could never have been really paid out of Newton's slender endowment of less than £60 *per annum*. The existence of the College depended upon the reputation of its Tutors. During the Tutorship[352] of Newcome, afterwards Archbishop of Armagh, the College was still prosperous. His "pupils were for the most part men of family," says Sir George Trevelyan; among them,

Charles James Fox (1764-1765). For a Gentleman-Commoner (Dr. Newton's Statutes were defied) Fox read hard, and found Mathematics "entertaining." "Application like yours," the Tutor found it necessary to write to him, "requires some intermission, and you are the only person with whom I have ever had any connexion, in whom I could say this." He read so hard in fact, that his father, Lord Holland, sent him abroad without taking his degree, to the no small injury of his mind and character. It appears, however, that Fox's life had a lighter side even while at Oxford. In Lockhart's story of Reginald Dalton, we read: "Although Hart Hall has disappeared, we trust the authorities have preserved the window from whence the illustrious C. J. Fox made the memorable leap when determined to join his companions in a Town and Gown row." Alas! the window has disappeared not only from the world of reality but (what does not always follow) from that of tradition!

It was in the time of the fourth Principal, Dr. Bernard Hodgson, that the College collapsed. On his death in 1805 no one would accept the almost honorary headship; but at last in 1814 the one surviving Fellow,[353] who was (we are told) considered "half-cracked," announced that he had "nominated, constituted, and admitted himself Principal"! At this time the place was all but deserted. It became a sort of no man's land in which a score of "strange characters" ("as if being 'half-cracked' were a qualification for admission") squatted rent free. Eventually the University took upon itself to close the building. In 1820 the building adjoining Cat Street actually fell down "with a great crash and a dense cloud of dust."

Magdalen Hall (on this site), 1820-1874.

On January 9th, 1820, a fire deprived Magdalen Hall of its local habitation.[354] The old Hall stood upon the site of the existing S. Swithin's buildings, and belonged to the College from which it took its name. In 1816 the President and Fellows had procured an Act of Parliament transferring the site and buildings of Hertford Society to Magdalen Hall, *i. e.* technically, to the University in trust for the Hall. With part of the small property of the College, the Hertford Scholarship was founded: the rest passed to the Society of Magdalen Hall, which in 1822 took possession of its new home. A word must be said as to the traditions of which Hertford College thus became the inheritor.

About the year 1480 the Founder of Magdalen College built some rooms near the gate of his College for the accommodation of the officers of his Grammar School. To these other rooms were added, and the building occupied by students and called S. Mary Magdalen Hall. This Society had at first the closest connection with the College, the Principal being always a Fellow. It was not till 1694 that the Chancellor of the University finally established his right to nominate the Principal of Magdalen Hall.

It was in this Hall that the Ultra-Protestant traditions of Magdalen lingered after they had died out in the College itself. It had been within the walls of Magdalen Hall that the English Reformation had its true beginning in certain meetings for Bible-reading started by William Tyndale, afterwards the translator of the Bible; and in the seventeenth century, when the Laudian movement had got the upper hand in the Colleges at large, it became a refuge for the oppressed Puritans. At one time it boasted three hundred members. In 1631 its Principal John Wilkinson, and Prideaux, Rector of Exeter, were summoned before the King in Council at Woodstock and received "a publick and sharp reprehension for their misgoverning and countenancing the factious partie!" Soon after, Oxenbridge, one of its Tutors,[355] was convicted of a "strange, singular, and superstitious way of dealing with his Scholars by perswading and causing some of them to subscribe as votaries to several articles framed by himself (as he pretends, for their better government)," for which presumption he was "distutored." In 1640 Henry Wilkinson (also of the Hall) was suspended for preaching in a very bitter way against some of the ceremonies of the Church.[356] But the day of vengeance came. When the Parliamentary Visitors came to Oxford the suspended Tutor, Henry Wilkinson, senior, commonly known as "Long Harry," was the most prominent and zealous of the Visitors. The students of Magdalen Hall and New Inn submitted to a man, and the places of the ejected Fellows and Scholars were largely recruited from their numbers. A very large proportion of the eminent Puritans of the seventeenth century came from these two Halls. A few of the distinguished Magdalen Hall men, whom Hertford College now claims as a sort of step-mother, may be added. John L'Isle, President of the High Court of Justice; John Glynne, Lord Chief Justice of England under Cromwell; William Waller, the Cromwellian Poet (afterwards at Hart Hall); Sir Matthew Hale, the most famous of English Judges; Sydenham, "the English Hippocrates"; Sir Henry Vane; Pococke, the Orientalist; and Dr. John Wilkins, the Mathematician, afterwards Warden of Wadham, then Master of Trin. Coll. Cambr., and later Bishop of Chester. Few Colleges in the University ever sent out so many distinguished men within so short a time. But the greatest name that Magdalen Hall can boast figures oddly in this list of Puritan Worthies. Thomas Hobbes of Malmesbury entered when not quite fifteen in 1603, and went down in 1607 with the B.A. degree. It is curious that it should have been by the Puritan Principal, John Wilkinson, that the Philosopher of Erastian Absolutism was introduced as tutor or companion into the Devonshire family with which he remained connected for the rest of his life. In spite of the Puritan *régime*, which was, however, hardly established in his day, Hobbes describes the place of his education as one "where the young were addicted to drunkenness, wantonness, gaming, and other vices." Clarendon was also a member of the Hall for a short time while waiting for a Demyship at

Magdalen College. Swift, whose Undergraduate life was passed at Dublin, took his Oxford B.A. from Magdalen Hall in 1692, and proceeded M.A. a few weeks later, during which interval we may perhaps assume that he resided in the Hall.

Hertford College, founded 1874.

The last of the many vicissitudes which this venerable site has experienced remains to be recorded. In 1874 the defunct Hertford College was recalled to life by the munificence of Mr. T. C. Baring, M.P., who endowed it with seventeen Fellowships, and thirty Scholarships of £100 per annum, limited to members of the Church of England.[357] An Act of Parliament gave the new foundation "all such rights and privileges as are possessed or enjoyed or can be exercised by other Colleges in the University of Oxford;" and Dr. Richard Michell, the last Principal of Magdalen Hall, became the first Principal of the present Hertford College.

While future ages will feel towards the name of Baring all the loyalty that is a Founders due, it is a fortunate circumstance that the accidents which have been related enabled him to give to his new foundation the only thing which money could not buy—a slight flavour of antiquity. The existing foundation is substantially the creation of Mr. Baring, but enough remains of its predecessors—the Elizabethan hall now transformed into a Library, the Jacobean Common-rooms which represent the pre-

Newtonian Hart Hall, Newton's Chapel with the adjoining "angle," the plate and pictures of Magdalen Hall and its ten Scholarships[358]—to give us a link with the past, a not uninteresting past, of which, however glorious its future, the College need never be ashamed. In one sense, notwithstanding the newness of its foundation, the College belongs to the past more than its more venerable sisters. It is untouched by recent legislation, its Statutes are constructed upon the old model, and it still rejoices in Fellowships which are tenable during life and celibacy.

XXI.
KEBLE COLLEGE.

BY REV. WALTER LOCK, M.A., SUB-WARDEN OF
KEBLE COLLEGE.

This, the most recent of the Oxford colleges, was opened in 1870, the foundation of it being due to a combination of three different but cognate causes: the first was a widespread desire to make University education more widely accessible to the nation, and especially to those who were anxious to take Holy Orders in the Church of England; the second, the desire to ensure that this education should be in the hands of Churchmen; and the third, the desire to perpetuate the memory of the Rev. John Keble, formerly Fellow and Tutor of Oriel College, Professor of Poetry in the University (1832-1841), Vicar of Hursley (1836-1866), and author of *The Christian Year*, *Lyra Innocentium*, *A Treatise on Eucharistical Adoration*, &c.

Of these motives the first had been stirring in Oxford for many years. In 1845 the following address was presented to the Hebdomadal Board—

"Considerable efforts have lately been made in this country for the diffusion of civil and spiritual knowledge, whether at home or abroad. Schools have been instituted for the lower and middle classes, churches built and endowed, missionary societies established, further Schools founded, as at

Marlborough and Fleetwood, for the sons of poor clergy and others; and, again, associations for the provision of additional Ministers. But between these schools on the one hand, and on the other the ministry which requires to be augmented, there is a chasm which needs to be filled. Our Universities take up education where our schools leave it; yet no one can say that they have been strengthened or extended, whether for Clergy or Laity, in proportion to the growing population of the country, its increasing empire, or deepening responsibilities.

"We are anxious to suggest, that the link which we find thus missing in the chain of improvement should be supplied by rendering Academical education accessible to the sons of parents whose incomes are too narrow for the scale of expenditure at present prevailing among the junior members of the University of Oxford, and that this should be done through the addition of new departments to existing Colleges, or, if necessary, by the foundation of new Collegiate bodies. We have learned, on what we consider unquestionable information, that in such institutions, if the furniture were provided by the College, and public meals alone were permitted, to the entire exclusion of private entertainments in the rooms of the Students, the annual College payments for board, lodging, and tuition might be reduced to £60 at most; and that if frugality were enforced as the condition of membership, the Student's entire expenditure might be brought within the compass of £80 yearly.

"If such a plan of improvement be entertained by the authorities of Oxford, the details of its execution would remain to be considered. On these we do not venture to enter; but desire to record our readiness, whenever the matter may proceed further, to aid, by personal exertions or pecuniary contributions, in the promotion of a design which the exigencies of the country so clearly seem to require.

"Sandon, Ashley, R. Grosvenor, W. Gladstone, T. D. Acland, Philip Pusey, T. Sothron, Westminster, Carnarvon, T. Acland, Bart., W. Bramston, Lincoln, Sidney Herbert, Canning, Mahon, W. B. Baring, J. Nicholl (Judge Advocate), W. T. James, S. R. Glynne, J. E. Denison, Wilson Patten, R. Vernon Smith, S. Wilberforce, R. Jelf, W. W. Hall, W. Heathcote, Edward Berens, J. Wooley, Hon. Horace Powys, W. Herbert (Dean of Manchester), G. Moberley, A. C. Tait."[359]

In spite of this influential list of signatures no action was taken by the Board, but the subject gave rise to many pamphlets, one of which, by the Rev. C. Marriott, deserves a special notice. In it he propounded a definite scheme for the foundation of a college either in or out of Oxford, which should contain about one hundred students living "a somewhat domestic kind of life," which should be shared in close intercourse by their tutors. Mr. Marriott received considerable promises of help towards the endowment of such a college, but his early death cut short the scheme.[360] The University Commission of 1854 tended to stimulate the desire to make University education more national; but it was not until 1865 that any definite step was taken. On Nov. 16 of that year a meeting of graduates was held at Oriel College, "to consider the question of University Extension with a view especially to the education of persons needing assistance and desirous of admission into the Christian ministry." The conveners of this meeting were chiefly influenced by the belief that the education of the national clergy was the unquestionable duty of the Universities, but that it was to a large extent passing out of their hands. They recognized, however, that this was far from the sole ground of University Extension, and especially urged that the system of Local Examinations required as its natural complement some further movement which should enable the successful candidates to follow out their studies at the University itself. At this meeting six sub-committees were formed to consider various methods of such extension. The history of Keble College is concerned only with the first of these, of which Dr. Shirley, the Professor of Ecclesiastical History, was Chairman, the other members being Professors Bernard, Burrows, Mansel, Pusey, and the Revs. W. Burgon, R. Greswell, W. Ince, and J. Riddell.

The instructions given to them were to consider the suggestion of extending the University "by founding a college or hall on a large scale, with a view not exclusively but especially to the education of persons needing assistance and desirous of admission into the Christian ministry." The substance of the report was to the effect that, without interfering with either the moral and religious discipline or the social advantages of an academical life, it would be possible very considerably to reduce the average of expenditure. With this purpose they suggest the building of a new Hall, by private subscription, large enough to hold one hundred undergraduates; for the sake of economy the rooms should be smaller than in most colleges, they should be arranged along corridors instead of by staircases, and be furnished by the College; breakfast as well as dinner should be taken in common, caution-money and entrance fees abolished, and all necessary expenditure included in one terminal payment. By this means it was hoped that the University would be opened to a class of men who cannot now enter, but without placing them apart from the classes who now avail themselves of it. The Hall was not to be "such an eleemosynary establishment as would be sought only by persons of inferior social position, less cultivated manners, or of attainments and intellect below the ordinary level of the University, but rather one which is adapted to the natural tastes and habits of gentlemen wishing to live economically."[361]

In the following year (on March 16, 1866) the Rev. John Keble died, and on the day of his funeral it seemed to his friends that the most fitting memorial to him would be to build such a college as had been contemplated by this committee. Mr. Keble had himself joined in the movement which led to the appointment of the committee; he had seen and approved the Report. This report was accordingly taken as the basis of action. The details were, in the main, arranged upon its lines; perhaps the chief difference was that from the first the preparation of candidates for Holy Orders was less insisted upon, and more emphasis was laid upon the duty of providing a suitable education for all Churchmen, whatever their vocation might be. To quote the words of the appeal which was issued, "The College was intended first to be a heartfelt and national tribute of affection and admiration to the memory of one of the most eminent and religious writers whom the Church of England has ever produced, one whose holy example was perhaps even a greater power for good than his *Christian Year*; secondly, to meet the great need now so generally felt of some form of University Extension, which may include a large portion of persons at present debarred through want of means from its full benefits; while, thirdly, it is hoped that it will prove, by God's blessing, the loyal handmaid of our mother Church, to train up men who, not in the ministry only but in the manifold callings of the Christian life, shall be steadfast in the faith."[362] The aims of the promoters of Keble College were, in a word, exactly the same as those of the munificent founders of the earlier colleges, viz. to extend University education to those who could not otherwise enjoy it, to extend it in the form of collegiate life, and in loyalty to the English Church.

A public appeal for subscriptions was at once made, and these amounted in a very short time to more than £50,000. The building of the College was intrusted to Mr. Butterfield. On St. Mark's Day (the anniversary of Mr. Keble's birthday), 1868, the first stone was laid by the Archbishop of Canterbury (Dr. Longley); and rooms for one hundred undergraduates and six tutors were ready for occupation in 1870, and at Commemoration the first Warden, the Rev. E. S. Talbot, senior student of Christ Church, was formally installed by the Chancellor of the University. A council had already been elected by the subscribers: this constitutes the Governing Body of the College, and perpetuates itself by co-optation as vacancies arise. The Council elect the Warden, who nominates the Tutors. On June 6th a Royal Charter of Incorporation was granted. This, after reciting that the subscribers had joined together to give public and permanent expression to their feeling of deep gratitude for the long and devoted services of the Rev. John Keble to the Church of Christ, and with that intent had resolved to establish a college or institution in which young men now debarred from University education might be trained in simple and religious habits, according to the principles of the Church of England, created the Warden, Council, and scholars into a corporate body with power to hold lands not exceeding the value of five thousand pounds (A subsequent amendment of the Mortmain Act, passed by Parliament in August 1888, extended to Keble College the exemption of the Mortmain Act, by which persons are enabled to bequeath property to it.) This Royal Charter carried with it no academical privileges. It left the Council free to move the College elsewhere, or even to wind up the Corporation; at the same time it authorized them, if they saw fit, to obtain the incorporation of the College within the University of Oxford.

This was not, however, the course actually adopted; the question of formal incorporation was not free from difficulties, as in previous cases such incorporation had been generally effected either by Royal Charter or by an Act of Parliament, and so it has never been raised. What actually happened was as follows. On June 16th, 1870, a decree was passed by Convocation, authorizing the Vice-Chancellor to matriculate students from Keble College pending further legislation. On March 9th, 1871, a new statute dealing with New Foundations for Academical Study and Education was passed, and on April 8th Keble College was admitted to the privileges granted by it. By this statute all its members have in relation to the University the same privileges and obligations as if they had been admitted to one of the previously existing Colleges or Halls, and the Warden has with regard to the members of his society the same obligations, rights, and powers as are assigned to the heads of existing Colleges or Halls, though the statute does not impose upon him any other obligations or confer any other right, privilege, or distinction. Any other statutes in which Colleges are mentioned by name, such as those respecting the University sermons or the election of Proctors, would not apply to any such new foundations, unless so amended as to include them expressly. The statute affecting the Proctorial cycle was so amended in 1887, and Keble College was for that purpose placed on a level with other colleges. The further question whether the head of such a society possesses the rights possessed by the heads of the earlier colleges has never been decided.[363]

Meanwhile the College had been opened successfully in Michaelmas Term 1870. At that time the north, east, and west blocks were completed, with a temporary chapel and hall on the south. The rooms were arranged in corridors, but subsequent experience has since partly modified this arrangement. The quadrangle south of the gateway was commenced in 1873, and finished on the eastern side in 1875, on the western in 1882. In 1873 W. Gibbs, Esq., of Tynterfield, laid the foundation of the permanent Chapel, of which he was the sole and munificent donor. This was formally opened on St. Mark's Day, 1876, and on the same day the foundation-stone of the Hall and Library was laid, these being the scarcely less munificent gifts of his sons, Messrs. Antony and Martin Gibbs. The architect of these buildings also was Mr. Butterfield. In the Chapel, the general aim of the decoration is to set forth the Christ as the sum and centre of all history, to whom all previous ages pointed, from whom all subsequent ages have drawn their inspiration. In the main body of the Chapel the mosaics represent typical scenes from the lives of Noah, Abraham, Joseph, and Moses, while the great prophets and kings of the Old Testament are portrayed in the windows. Around the Sanctuary the ornament is richer as it attempts to do honour to the fact of the Incarnation—alabaster and marble take the place of stone. On either side in the mosaics are seen the Annunciation, the Birth, the Baptism, the Crucifixion, the Resurrection of the Lord; in the windows the leading Apostles and Doctors of the Christian Church. The Ascension is given in the east window; while in the quatre-foil mosaic, the centre of the whole decoration, appears a vision of the Lord Himself as described by St. John in the Apocalypse, seated in the midst of the candlesticks, with the stars in His hand, and the sword coming out of His mouth. Around the Living Lord are grouped saints of all the Christian centuries and of every vocation in life. The western mosaic closes the series with the Last Judgment.

In one respect the arrangement differs from that of all the other College chapels—all the seats are ranged eastwards, not north and south. This results from the change which has passed over college life in Oxford. The earlier chapels were built for colleges in which every one was in theory a life-member on the foundation, and had his permanent seat as in a cathedral body; but a modern college chapel, containing almost exclusively a large passing congregation of undergraduates, presents conditions much more like that of an ordinary church, and alike for purposes of worship and of preaching it seemed better that the whole body should face eastward in the usual manner. It should also be mentioned that the chapel has not been formally consecrated, it being a question whether such consecration might not limit the powers conferred upon the Council by the Charter.

The Hall and Library were formally opened in 1878, Mr. Gladstone being among the speakers on the occasion. Since then the Hall has been enriched with a beautiful oil painting of the Rev. J. Keble, painted by G. Richmond after Mr. Keble's death from a crayon drawing which he had made in his lifetime; by portraits of Archbishop Longley, who laid the foundation stone of the College; of Dr. Shirley, Chairman of the Committee on whose report the College was based; of Earl Beauchamp, the senior member of the Council, from the first one of the most strenuous and munificent friends of the College; of the Rev. E. S. Talbot, the first Warden (1870-1888); of W. Gibbs, Esq., the donor of the Chapel; and of J. A. Shaw Stewart, Esq., the treasurer of the original Memorial Fund and resident Bursar of the College (1876-1880). To these is to be added soon a portrait of Dr. Liddon, member of the Council (1870-1890), and of the Rev. Aubrey L. Moore, Tutor (1881-1890). In addition to these, all of which are connected with the College history, Earl Beauchamp has presented a portrait of Archbishop Laud.

In the Library the nucleus of the collection was formed by the gift of the majority of Mr. Keble's own books and many of his MSS., presented mainly by his brother, partly also by his nephew. Among these are the original drafts of the *Lyra Innocentium* and many of the *Miscellaneous Poems* (written on stray scraps of paper or on backs of envelopes), of the *Eucharistical Adoration*, the sermons on Baptism, and the translation of St. Irenæus; and, most interesting of all, a fair copy made by himself of the greater part of the *Christian Year*, written in an exquisitely clear and delicate hand in seven small note-books. Other relics of Mr. Keble, including his study-table and the candelabrum presented to him by his pupils on leaving Oxford, are preserved in the common room. The Library has also received large donations or legacies of books from Cardinal Newman, Archbishop Trench, Lord Richard Cavendish, Miss Yonge, &c. Quite recently there has been added to it Dr. Liddon's library, rich especially in historical, liturgical, and theological books, and containing also an excellent collection of Dante literature. Mr. Holman Hunt's picture, *The Light of the World*, presented by Mrs. Combe of the University Press, at present hangs in the Library, though it will probably be ultimately transferred to the chapel.

Of the history of the internal working of the College there is little to say. From the opening till the present its rooms have always been full; and clear proof has thus been given of the reality of the demand for University extension on such a plan. The annual charge to each undergraduate is £82 a year, which includes tuition, board, and rent of furnished rooms; groceries, wines, &c. have been supplied from the College stores; and a special common room is open to undergraduates, serving both for entertainment and as a reading-room. Two of those who have worked as tutors in the College have already been raised to the Episcopate—Dr. Mylne, the Senior Tutor in the first years of the College, now Bishop of Bombay, and Dr. Jayne, now Bishop of Chester.

In academical distinction the College has quite held its own with many of the older Colleges, and has specially gained distinction in the Honour Schools of Theology, Modern History, and Natural Science. Several private benefactions, notably those of Miss Wilbraham (1872), Mrs. William Gibbs (1875), A. J. Balfour, Esq., M.P. (1875), Lady Gomm (1878), Miss Chafyn Grove (1879), H. O. Wakeman, Esq. (1882), and a subscription raised to found a "Caroline Talbot" Scholarship in memory of the first Warden's mother, have enabled the College to offer several scholarships for open competition to members of the Church of England, or to aid those who are already members of the College to complete their career. There are also special prizes to encourage the study of theology, such as the Wills and Phillpott's prizes for undergraduates, the Liddon prize, and the "Edward Talbot" studentship, founded to commemorate the services of the first Warden, for graduates; but these are all the endowments that the College has, and they are not sufficient to enable it to compete on equal terms with the other colleges in the offer of scholarships.

The College has also received many advowsons, and is likely to do useful service to the Church of England as patron of livings.

FOOTNOTES

[1] From the old printed copy in Bodl. Bibl. MSS. Tanner 338, fol. 216.

[2] *Annals of University College*, p. 339.

[3] I have used Mr. William Smith's rendering of these passages of Matthew Paris.

[4] This, as Mr. William Smith says, to whose printed volume and MSS. preserved in the College archives, my obligations are so profuse that henceforth I will not mention them in detail, was the sum allowed to the Merton scholars also, and would in an ordinary year purchase twelve and a half quarters of the best wheat.

[5] This writ of King Richard is only entered on the back of the ancient roll containing the French Petition, and is not upon Record. (W. Smith's *Annals*, p. 311.)

[6] Mr. Wm. Rogers of Gloucestershire, a member of the College. The speech spoken by Mr. Edw. Hales upon ye setting up of it was printed by Dr. Charlett. Mr. Hales was afterwards killed at ye Boyne in Ireland most couragiously fighting for his master King James. (Hearne by Doble, II. p. 143.)

[7] In the earlier part of this chapter I have been under constant obligations to the old College history entitled *Balliofergus, or, a Commentary upon the Foundation, Founders, and Affaires of Balliol Colledge, Gathered out of the Records thereof, and other Antiquities. With a brief Description of eminent Persons who have been formerly of the same House.* By Henry Savage, Master of the said Colledge (Oxford 1668). I am also considerably indebted to Mr. Maxwell Lyte's *History of the University of Oxford* (1886), and to the somewhat perfunctory and ill-informed

account of the College muniments given by Mr. H. T. Riley in the appendix to the Fourth Report of the Historical Manuscripts Commission (1874). The Statutes of the College are cited from the edition prepared for the University Commission of 1850, and published in 1853. In dealing with later times I have had the advantage of a number of references kindly furnished me by Dr. G. B. Hill of Pembroke College, Mr. C. E. Doble of Worcester College, and Mr. C. H. Firth of Balliol College. Mr. Rashdall, of Hertford College, has been so good as to look over the proof-sheets of this chapter; and, although he is not to be held chargeable with any errors that may have escaped him, I have to thank him for many corrections and suggestions.

[8] The identification seems certain, though the name is suppressed in the *Chronicon de Lanercost* (ed. J. Stevenson, 1839), p. 69.

[9] *Chron. de Mailros*, s. a. 1269.

[10] *Statutes of Balliol College*, pp. v.-vii.

[11] In this document we have for the first time the mention of the *Master* and Scholars of the House: Savage, p. 18.

[12] See extracts from the deeds in Riley, p. 446.

[13] 13 July 1293: ibid., p. 443.

[14] See Savage, pp. 29 f.; Wood, *Hist. and Antiqq. of the Univ. of Oxford* (ed. Gutch), *Colleges and Halls*, pp. 73, 86 f.

[15] In this document the head of the College is styled *Warden* (Riley, p. 443), a title which occurs in 1303 (Wood, *Colleges and Halls*, p. 81), and which alternates with that of Master for some time later. *President* occurs in 1559; *Statutes*, p. 25.

[16] Wood, *Hist. and Antiqq.* ii. 731-733.

[17] Ibid., pp. 774 f.

[18] Riley, pp. 442 f.; Wood, *Colleges and Halls*, p. 73.

[19] *English Historical Review*, vi. (1891) 152 f.

[20] *Dict. of Nat. Biogr.* xix. (1889) 194-198.

[21] *Statutes of Balliol College*, pp. viii-xix.

[22] It may be remarked that a grant of the year 1343 is noted by Savage, p. 52, as the first among the College muniments in which the name *Balliol* is spelled with a single *l*.

[23] See the extract from a letter of the Rectors, one a Doctor of Divinity and the other a Franciscan, of 1433, given by Riley, p. 443 *a*.

[24] In 1433: Savage, pp. 64 f.

[25] In 1477: ibid., p. 66.

[26] *Statutes of Balliol College*, pp. 1-22; cf. Lyte, pp. 415 ff.

[27] The eightpence a-week assigned them by the Statutes of Dervorguilla had been raised to twelve pence so early as 1340, by Sir William Felton's benefactions, which also provided funds for clothes and books (Savage, p. 38). It was now ordered that the sum should not exceed 1*s.* 8*d.* Besides this Masters were to receive an annual stipend of 20*s.* 8*d.*; Bachelors, of 18*s.* 8*d.* (*Statutes*, p. 14).

[28] Compare Savage, p. 74.

[29] *Statutes*, pp. 38 f.

[30] *Queen's College Statutes*, p. 14.

[31] We may remember that "between the years 1485 and 1507, Oxford was visited by at least six great pestilences" (Lyte, p. 380). In 1486 we find the Fellows of

Magdalen sojourning at Witney and Harwell (not far from Wantage) "tempore pestis." Rogers, *Hist. of Agric. and Prices*, iii. (1882) 680.

[32] See W. W. Shirley, *Fasciculi Zizaniorum* (1858), intr., pp. xi-xv, 513-528; P. Lorimer, notes to Lechler's *John Wiclif* (ed. 1881), pp. 132-137; R. L. Poole, *Wycliffe and Movements for Reform* (1889), pp. 61-65.

[33] *Dict. of Nat. Biogr.*, xi. (1887) 157 f.

[34] Lyte, p. 321.

[35] W. D. Macray, *Ann. of the Bodl. Libr.* (2nd ed., 1890), pp. 6-11.

[36] *Comment. de Scriptt. Brit.* (ed. A. Hall, Oxford 1709), p. 442.

[37] *Scriptt. Brit. Catal.* (Basle 1557), viii. 2.

[38] Leland, p. 460.

[39] Wood, *Hist. and Antiqq. of the Univ. of Oxf., Colleges and Halls*, p. 89; who notices (vol. ii. 107) that though Balliol Library lost much in 1550, it also gained some of the spoils of Durham College at the time of its dissolution.

[40] The substance of the foregoing account is borrowed from the writer's article on Grey in the *Dict. of Nat. Biogr.* xxiii. (1890) 212f.

[41] See, on the buildings and inscriptions, Savage, pp. 67-72, Wood, *Coll. and Halls*, pp. 90-98.

[42] Lyte, p. 326.

[43] Savage, pp. 105-108.

[44] Leland, pp. 475-481; Lyte, pp. 385 f.; *Briefwechsel des Beatus Rhenanus* (ed. A. Horawitz & K. Hartfelder, 1886), p. 72.

[45] Lyte, p. 322.

[46] Nevill supplicated for his B.A. degree in 1450: Anstey, *Munim. Acad. Oxon.* (1868), p. 730 f.

[47] *Reg. of the Univ. of Oxford,* i. (ed. C. W. Boase, 1885) 1.

[48] Leland, pp. 466-468, 476; Lyte, pp. 384 f.

[49] Tanner, *Bibl. Brit. Hib.* (1748), p. 598; Le Neve's *Fast. Eccl. Angl.* (ed. T. D. Hardy, Oxford 1854) i. 141.

[50] Leland, p. 462 f.

[51] *Dict. of Nat. Biogr.*, xxiii. 351.

[52] Already by Anthony Wood's time "the old accompts" were lost; "So A. W. was much put to a push, to find when learned men had been of that coll." *Life* (ed. Bliss, Eccl. Hist. Soc., Oxford 1848), p. 144. So too *Athen. Oxon.* (ed. Bliss) iii. 959.

[53] Savage, pp. 74-77; Wood's *City of Oxford,* ed. A. Clark, ii. 3; P. Heylin's *Cyprianus redivivus* (1668), p. 208; Wood's *Hist. and Antiqq.* (ed. Gutch), ii. 677.

[54] *Statutes*, p. 30.

[55] P. 33.

[56] P. 35.

[57] Savage, p. 56. After 1718 the payment was made out of the College revenues: *Statutes*, p. 36.

[58] *Statutes*, p. 31.

[59] Humphrey Prideaux, *Letters to John Ellis* (ed. E. M. Thompson, Camden Society, 1875), pp. 12 f., under date 23 August 1674.

[60] *Statutes*, pp. 61-66.

[61] In 1677 the library was increased by the gift of "one of the best private librarys in England" (Prideaux, p. 61), from the bequest of Sir Thomas Wendy of Haselingfield, sometime gentleman commoner of the College. In 1673 these books were valued at £600: Wood, *Colleges and Halls*, p. 90.

[62] *Statutes*, pp. 25-28.

[63] Ibid., pp. 45-50.

[64] Savage, pp. 85-87.

[65] See Wood, *Colleges and Halls*, pp. 616-619.

[66] *Statutes*, pp. 40-45, 50-56. In 1676 the number was increased to two Fellows and two Scholars.

[67] Ibid., pp. 57-61. The endowment provided for the erection of lodgings for the Periam Fellow and Scholars, and the foundress's name is still remembered in connection with one of the buildings of the College.

[68] The College benefactors, down to John Warner, are enumerated by Wood, *Colleges and Halls*, pp. 75-80.

[69] *Scotland and Scotsmen in the Eighteenth Century*, from the MSS. of John Ramsay of Ochtertyre (ed. A. Allardyce, 1888), ii. 307 note.

[70] See above, pp. 26 f., 37.

[71] Savage, p. 77; Wood, *Colleges and Halls*, p. 99.

[72] *Life*, p. 143.

[73] Savage, p. 68.

[74] See an account of them by the Rev. C. H. Grinling in the *Proceedings of the Oxf. Archit. and Hist. Society*, new series, iv. 137-140. The windows in their original situation are described by Savage, pp. 77 f., and Wood, *Coll. and Halls*, pp. 100-102.

[75] Wood's *Coll. and Halls*, p. 88, and *City of Oxford*, ed. A. Clark, i. (1889) 634 note 8.

[76] Savage, pp. 61, 79-81; cf. Wood's *City of Oxford*, i. 372.

[77] P. V[ernon], *Oxonium Poema*, 18.

[78] Wood, *Coll. and Halls*, p. 87, with Gutch's note.

[79] See Wood, p. 99, and the plan in W. Williams' *Oxonia Depicta* [1732].

[80] *Reg. Univ.*, i. (ed. Boase), pref., p. xxiii.

[81] *Reg. Univ.*, ii. (ed. Clark) pt. ii. pp. 30, 31.

[82] Gutch, *Collect. curiosa* (Oxford, 1781), i. 200.

[83] *Reg. Univ.*, ii. pt. ii. 412.

[84] Wood, *Hist. and Antiqq.* ii. 365.

[85] In these last two totals Commoners of more than four years' standing have been omitted. The lists in the Calendar are moreover always slightly in excess of the truth, since they take no account of occasional non-residence. An unofficial census taken by the *Oxford Magazine* of 4 February, 1891, gives the number of undergraduates in residence as 158.

[86] Savage, pp. 119-121; Evelyn, *Memoirs* (ed. W. Bray, 1827), i. 13 f.

[87] See above, p. 42.

[88] Savage, pp. 85 f.; *Calendar of State Papers*, Domestic Series, 1623-1625 (1859), p. 383.

[89] Heylin, p. 215.

[90] *Memoirs*, i. 12-16.

[91] Gutch, *Collect. cur.*, i. 227; Wood's *Life*, p. 14 note, where the editor observes that the College retained a chalice of 1614.

[92] *Register of the Visitors* (ed. M. Burrows, Camden Society, 1881), pp. 167, 188, and introd. pp. cxxv, cxxvi.

[93] See the list, ibid., pp. 478 f., and the references there given.

[94] Riley (p. 444) dismisses this book as "a vapid and superficial production"; but there is little doubt that Savage had the assistance in it of no less an antiquary than Anthony Wood. See his *Life*, pp. 104-108, 143 f., 157. When Wood speaks disparagingly of Savage, it must be remembered that he had himself proposed to write a work on a similar plan: *Athen. Oxon.* (ed. Bliss, 1817), iii. 959.

[95] *Reg. of Visit.*, p. 4.

[96] *Athen. Oxon.*, iii. 1154.

[97] *Letters*, pp. 12 f.

[98] The sign of the house is understood to have been a double-headed eagle.

[99] Dr. Bathurst, President of Trinity, Vice-Chancellor, 1673-1676.

[100] *Letters*, pp. 13 f., under date 23 August, 1674.

[101] *Life of Ralph Bathurst* (1761), p. 203.

[102] Gutch, *Collect. cur.*, i. 195.

[103] The Master at this time was Good's successor, John Venn, who married "an ancient maid," niece to the first Earl of Clarendon.

[104] W. D. Christie, *Life of Shaftesbury* (1871), ii. 390-401.

[105] Riley, p. 451.

[106] *Reliqq. Hearn*, iii. 308.

[107] *Terrae Filius*, 1733 (2nd ed.), pp. 5f.

[108] J. R. M'Colloch, *Life of Dr. Smith*, prefixed to the *Wealth of Nations* (ed. Edinburgh, 1828), i. p. xvi.

[109] *Scotland and Scotsmen in the Eighteenth Century*, ii. 307 note.

[110] J. Pointer, *Oxoniensis Academia* (1749), i. 11. Hearne mentions a custom which had been given up at Merton since Wood's time, but which partially survived "at Brazenose and Balliol coll., and no where else that I know of. I take the original thereof to have been a custom they had formerly for the young men to say something of their founders and benefactors, so that the custom was originally very laudable, however afterwards turned into ridicule:" *Reliqq. Hearn*, iii. 76.

[111] R. Blacow, *Letter to William King*, 1755. The whole story is told by Dr. G. B. Hill, *Dr. Johnson, his Friends and his Critics* (1878), pp. 68-72.

[112] *Life and Correspondence* (ed. C. C. Southey, 1849), i. 164, 170, 177, 203, 211 f., 215, 176 note.

[113] G. V. Cox, *Recollections of Oxford* (1868), p. 191.

[114] Letter of 15 November 1807, in J. Veitch's *Memoir of Sir W. Hamilton* (1869), p. 30.

[115] Letter of J. Traill, quoted, ibid., p. 44.

[116] Letter of G. R. Gleig, quoted, ibid., p. 53.

[117] *Discussions*, p. 750, quoted, ibid., p. 52.

[118] *Memoir*, p. 30.

[119] *Statutes*, pp. 38 f.

[120] Ibid., p. 39.

[121] W. Ward, *William George Ward and the Oxford Movement* (1889), pp. 429-431; cf. p. 343, &c.

[122] Quoted in Wood's *City of Oxford* (ed. A. Clark), i. 632. Cf. C. Wordsworth, *University Life in the Eighteenth Century* (1874), p. 161.

[123] The writer of this chapter is, of course, indebted to his own *Memorials of Merton College*, published in 1885, in the Oxford Historical Society's series; but has revised afresh the results of his former researches, with the aid of new materials.

[124] Subsequently called Cornwall Lane, from its proximity to the Western College. It is now inclosed within the site of the College.

[125] From the *Life of Conant*, by his son.

[126] The "moderator" presided over the disputation, seeing that the disputants observed the rules of reasoning, and giving his opinion on the discussion, and on the arguments which had been advanced in it, in a concluding speech.

[127] John Conybeare, Fellow of Exeter, 1710; Rector, 1730; Dean of Christ Church, 1733; Bishop of Bristol, 1750.

[128] The pre-eminence of Merton, its conspicuous buildings, and its wealth, seem to have distinguished it as "the College," until it found a rival in the "New College" of William of Wykeham.

[129] The seal at present in use is believed to be the original seal of the College. The upper part represents the Annunciation; below under an arcade is the kneeling figure of Adam de Brome. Round the edge is the legend "Sy. Comune Domus Scholarium Beate Marie Oxon."

The only other memorial of its foundation which the College possesses is its founder's cup, given to it, according to the College tradition, by King Edward the Second; though an entry in the Treasurer's accounts recording the purchase in December 1493 for £4 18s. 1d., of a standing gilt cup marked with E and S, and a cover to the same, is in favour of its belonging to a later date.

[130] The Hospital itself was also intended to be a place to which members of the Society could remove, in case of sickness or pestilence, into a purer air than that of Oxford.

[131] To enable the College to take these additional endowments, a further license in mortmain to the extent of ten pounds a year was granted, 14th March, 1327.

[132] See page 94.

[133] Hawkesworth was one of the first Fellows of Queen's, nominated by the original Statutes in 1341; but as the ground on which his election was annulled is expressly stated to be its informality and not any defect in the person chosen, he was probably also connected with the College either as Fellow or ex-Fellow. He appears as acting on the College behalf in 1341.

[134] It has been printed in the Oxford Historical Society's *Collectanea*, vol. i. p. 59.

[135] In Wood's list, both Symon and Byrche are entered as of University College; but there is little doubt that they both belonged to Oriel.

[136] These two manors adjoin one another, but are entirely independent and in distinct parishes; they appear, however, as held together at the time of the Domesday Survey, and never to have parted company since that date.

[137] In his account of this building Wood must for once have fallen asleep, or he would not have suggested that the letters O. C. (Oriel College) were inscribed by "the Saints,

in honour of their great Commander." But such is the vitality of error that this absurd blunder is copied without correction into every guide-book for Oxford, and actually reappears in the note prefixed to a very careful account of the Hospital, published by the Oxford Architectural Society.

[138] *I. e.* take this, and prosper. To "grow thrifty" in the sense of to thrive seems to have been used in America as late as 1851, (Dr. Smith's Latin Dictionary, preface, p. vii.)

[139] *State Papers, Domestic*, Elizabeth xvii. p. 57. *Letter of Francis and others to Cecill*, 11 May, 1561.

[140] See Carleton's *Life of Gilpin.*

[141] On the election of Joseph Browne, who succeeded Provost Smith in 1756. See *Letters of Radcliffe and James* (Oxford Historical Society, ix.), p. xxiii.

[142] *I. e.* to an ecclesiastical benefice.

[143] See *State Papers, Domestic*, Elizabeth, vol. 271, 49, March, 1601.

[144] P. 129.

[145] Sir Richard Richards, 1776; Sir William Carpenter Rowe, 1827; William Basil Tickell Jones, 1848; Thomas William Lancaster, 1809; James Garbett, 1824; Adam Storey Farrar, 1852; Edward Feild, 1825; Samuel Thornton, 1859; Robert Gaudell, 1845. The dates are of election to Fellowship. Sir William Wightman, Justice of the Court of Queen's Bench, and Henry John Chitty Harper, Metropolitan of New Zealand, were also on this foundation, but never Fellows.

[146] Those reading "Logic," termed "sophistae."

[147] "Artista," a student (here probably a Master) in the faculty of Arts.

[148] Students not yet advanced to the study of Logic.

[149] The study of theology began two years after the attainment of the M.A. degree.

[150] See Tobie Matthew's letter to Lord Burghley in *State Papers, Addenda*, Elizabeth, xxxii. 89, Oct. 16, 1593, and Boast's life in *Dict. of Nat. Biog.*

[151] Except to the grammar-boys at Merton, and the "poor boys" at Queen's.

[152] The following details are from Anstey's *Munimenta Academica*, pp. 241, *seqq.*

[153] Anstey's *Munimenta Academica*, p. 286.

[154] In the fifteenth century Cicero or a classical poet might be substituted. Some other alternatives are omitted.

[155] See Wood's *Annals* (edit. Gutch), ii. p. 292; Ayliffe, ii. p. 316.

[156] See Professor Montagu Burrows' delightful *Memoir of Grocyn* in the Oxford Historical Society's *Collectanea*, vol. ii.

[157] A few Gentleman-commoners educated at Winchester had been admitted to the College earlier. Among these, but only for a very short time, was the Sir Henry Wotton who still lives in Izaac Walton's *Lives*.

[158] G. V. Cox, *Recollections of Oxford* (1870), p. 50.

[159] These "Sunday pence" were paid in all Oxford parishes. In 1525 payment was disputed; and in the test case between Lincoln College, as rector of All Saints church, and William Potycarye alias Clerke of All Saints parish, payment was enforced under penalty of "the greater excommunication." Several tenements in Oxford continue to this day to pay to their parish church quit-rents of 4s. 8d. representing these old "Sunday pence." Their owners have

the satisfaction of knowing that these tenements represent the most ancient holdings in Oxford.

[160] On 13th Dec., 1432, in the time of the first rector, the celebrated Thomas Gascoigne gave twelve MSS. to the library.

[161] Mr. Maxwell Lyte, in his *History of the University of Oxford*, has taken for the original the seventeenth century copy on the south side of the quadrangle, which was put there by a married Head to cloak his annexation of College rooms.

[162] In memory of this occasion the vine was probably planted which in Loggan's picture (1675) is seen spreading over the west front of the hall; the successors of which in the chapel quadrangle and the kitchen passage still in sunny years bear plentiful clusters.

[163] Robert Parkinson, *ut supra*. Rotheram's arms are carved on the north wall of this building. In the herald's certificate of 1574, they are given as "vert, three stags trippant two and one or." They are nowadays generally blazoned wrongly.

[164] The final deed of incorporation is dated 20th Nov., 1478.

[165] Among the rest Dagville's Inn (now the Mitre), which was already an ancient inn when Dagville inherited it from his uncle.

[166] The provocation was both wanton and fatuous. On 24th Aug., 1717, Crewe began to execute in his lifetime the provisions of his will, viz. to pay to the Rector £20 per annum, to each of the twelve Fellows and to each of the four Chaplains £10 per annum, to the bible-clerk and eight Scholars together £54 6*s.* 8*d.* per annum; and to each of twelve Exhibitioners founded by him £20 per annum. On the 27th June, 1719, the Rectorship fell vacant; the Fellows

asked Crewe to state who he wished to succeed. He twice refused; but on being asked the third time said, "William Lupton," Fellow since 1698. On 18th July, 1719, the Fellows, by nine votes to three, elected into the Rectorship not Lupton but John Morley!

[167] In 1537 the full number of Rector, twelve Foundation and three Darby Fellows is found; again in 1587; and again in 1595. In 1606 the Visitor allows the number of Fellows to be twelve only, and thereafter that number is never exceeded.

[168] Of the three persons nominated by Darby in 1538 as his first Fellows, two, William Villers (his kinsman) and Richard Gill, were undergraduates. One nomination of this kind was eminently unsuccessful; Walter Pitts, nominated by the Visitor in 1568 to the Darby Fellowship for Oxfordshire, was removed in 1573 because he had repeatedly failed to get his degree. The Parliamentary Visitors in 1650 put undergraduates into Fellowships in Lincoln College; one of these, John Taverner, in 1652 was fined 13s. 4d., "for swearing two oaths, as did appear upon testimony."

[169] When the number of Fellowships was reduced by treating the three Darby Fellowships not as additional to, but as taking the place of three of, the Foundation Fellowships, the Stowe Fellowship was substituted for one of the Lincoln county Fellowships, the other two for two of the Lincoln diocese Fellowships. With this modification the regulations about counties and dioceses were very faithfully observed in elections to Fellowships, until these limitations were all swept away by the Commission of 1854.

[170] The Visitor (John Williams, who had built the new chapel), in 1631, discontinued this (except the procession on All Saints day). The procession on All Saints day has

been discontinued under another Visitor's Order of 6th Feb., 1867.

[171] These two services were changed at the Reformation to a sermon; the appointment of a preacher for this sermon was discontinued about 1750.

[172] The first of these sermons was assigned to the Rector by statute, the second by custom.

[173] The earliest College duty assigned to John Wesley, after his election to a Fellowship at Lincoln, was to preach the St. Michael's sermon on Michaelmas Day 1726.

[174] B.A. Fellows might not have theological works, but only works in philosophy and logic.

[175] Rectors, suffering under the despotism of too efficient Subrectors, have accused this officer of mis-spelling his alternative title and regarding himself as *Co-rector*.

[176] The barber's duties were at first to supply the clean shave, the tonsure, and the close crop which became "clerks." In later ages more extravagant fashions in hair added to his labour. At the close of the eighteenth century he had to dress for dinner the heads of all the College in the pomp of powder and the vanity of queue. Beginning about noon with the junior Commoner, he concluded with the senior Fellow on the stroke of three, when the bell rang for dinner. The higher, therefore, you were in College standing, the longer was the time available for your morning walk, and the ampler the gossip of the day with which you were entertained.

[177] If any one wishes a modern parallel, he may note how Oxford became filled with Jacobites ejected from their country cures within two or three years of the imposition of the Oath of Allegiance to William and Mary.

[178] Their Catholic sympathies are evident from the Colleges to which they made their benefactions. Neither in Lincoln College under John Bridgwater, nor in Caius College under John Caius, was a young Romanist in any danger of being converted to Protestantism.

[179] Several entries show that their position was inferior to that of a Commoner, and involved menial service in College. In 1661 we have an entry—"Whereas Henry Rose, a scholar, did lately officiate as porter, and had no allowance for his pains," he is to be excused the College fee for taking B.A. In Feb. 1661-2 these Traps' exhibitioners were exempted from some College charges on consideration of their waiting at the Fellows' table.

[180] As "Commissary," *i. e.* Vice-chancellor, of the University from 1527 to 1532, Cottisford had been set to several painful pieces of duty, in the discovery and arrest of Lutheran members of the University. Thus in 1527 Thomas Garret was arrested by the Proctors and imprisoned in Cottisford's rooms: but his friends stole into College when Cottisford, with the rest of the College, was in chapel at Evening Prayers, and enabled him to effect his escape. This "Lollard's" ghost, oddly enough, was at one time supposed to haunt the gateway-tower.

[181] On only two other occasions is this silence broken; the next is in 1633, when the register notes that the King was at Woodstock, and that the Rector had forbidden undergraduates to go there; the latest is a notice of the grief of the nation on the death of the Princess Charlotte, and of the services in the College chapel on the day of her funeral.

[182] There is some suspicion that about this time the Government had a paid spy in College. In Sept. 1566 an Anthony Marcham, of Lincoln College, writes to Cecil asking money, otherwise he will be unable to stay on in Oxford (*Calendar of State Papers, Domestic Series*).

[183] There is, of course, the usual legend that Rotheram built this addition as "conscience-money" for his defalcations as Bursar.

[184] The Rotherams of Luton in Bedfordshire were descended from the Archbishop's brother, to whom he had bequeathed that estate.

[185] Baker's *History of St. John's, Cambridge* (edit. Mayor), p. 208.

[186] The intrusive dog occurs several times in College orders. The most noteworthy entry is perhaps that of 30th June, 1726:—"No gentleman-commoner, or commoner, whether graduate or undergraduate, shall keep a dog within the College. The Bursar is required to see that all dogs be kept out of the Hall at meal-times."

[187] Previously, the College meetings had been held in the Rector's lodgings.

[188] The rooms which Wesley occupied in College are said, by tradition, to be those over the passage from the first quadrangle into the chapel quadrangle.

[189] This sermon, esquire-bedell G. V. Cox notes, was "two and a half hours long," and the sitting it out made a vacancy in the headship of a College.

[190] Tatham's broad Yorkshire dialect gave a tone of vigorous rusticity to his speech.

[191] I understand that it was not destroyed, but passed into private possession. The recovery, after so many years, of the Brasenose "brasen nose" forbids Lincoln to despair of yet getting back its overseer.

[192] Throughout this chapter I must acknowledge my indebtedness to Professor Burrows' invaluable *Worthies of All Souls*. I must also mention that both the Warden of All Souls and Professor Burrows have been good enough to

look through these pages, and have kept me from many pitfalls. The Warden furnished me with much information in the later pages of this chapter which would have been quite inaccessible without his help.

[193] *Worthies*, p. 32.

[194] Capi-tolium. A horrible derivation!

[195] See page 226.

[196] The effigy on Richard Patten's monument has been described as showing the dress of a merchant; but there does not seem to be anything in the costume which would indicate unmistakably the status of the wearer. The monument, formerly in the old Church of All Saints at Wainfleet, was removed to Oxford by the Society of Magdalen College to preserve it from destruction on the demolition of the church, in 1820. It is now placed in the little oratory on the north side of the choir of the College chapel.

[197] This Hall is of course to be distinguished from the later society of the same name, which was at first a dependency of Magdalen College, and afterwards became a separate foundation.

[198] Another duty incumbent upon the members of the Hospital was the preaching of a sermon *ad populum* on St. John Baptist's Day. This, with certain other duties, was transferred to the College. The sermon was at one time preached as a rule from the stone pulpit in the corner of what is now called St. John's Quadrangle; but the stone pulpit was not always employed even in early times. Thus in 1495 there is a record of a payment of 4*d.* to "four poor scholars" for bringing a pulpit from New College for St. John Baptist's Day, and taking it back again. In the early part of the eighteenth century the sermon was preached in

the chapel if the day chanced to be wet; and what was then the exception has become the rule.

[199] This name was given to the scholars who received half the allowance given to Fellows. It appears to have been in current use at the time when the founder's statutes were drawn up.

[200] This priory, originally a dependency of St. Florence at Saumur, was made "denizen" in 1396, before the alien priories were suppressed.

[201] An Augustinian Priory, founded by Peter des Roches, Bishop of Winchester, in 1233. It was suppressed by Waynflete, after several attempts had been made to reform it.

[202] Neither the benefaction of Henry VII. nor his annual commemoration has any connection with the custom of singing a Latin hymn on the Tower at sunrise on May-day. Two accounts of the origin of this custom, which allege such a connection, have often been repeated and sometimes confused: (1) That Mass was formerly said at an early hour on May 1st upon the top of the Tower for Henry VII., and that the hymn is a survival from this service. (2) That the sum paid by the Rectory of Slymbridge to the College was intended for the maintenance of the custom of singing on the Tower. Of the first of these accounts it may be said that there is no evidence of any celebration of Mass on the Tower (a thing *à priori* highly improbable) at any time; and that the hymn, which now forms part of the College "Grace," is probably a composition of the seventeenth century, and is certainly not part of the Requiem Mass according to the rite of Sarum, or any other rite. Of the second account it may be said that the deeds relating to Slymbridge show clearly that the payment was not intended for this purpose, to which it was never applied. The present custom of singing the hymn from the "Grace"

originated, it is believed, in the last century on an occasion when the former custom of performing secular music on the Tower was interrupted by bad weather. The hymn was probably chosen as a substitute because the choir were perfectly familiar with its words and music. The details of the ceremony as it is at present performed were arranged about fifty years from the present time.

[203] The Tower was begun in 1492, and finished in 1507. The theory which ascribes to Wolsey the credit of being its designer rests on no secure foundation. At the time when it was begun he was not more than twenty-one years of age. The legend that he left Oxford in consequence of some misapplication of the College funds in connection with this work, is perhaps still less trustworthy. He was twice bursar during the progress of the building, being third bursar in 1498 and senior bursar in 1499-1500. In the former year he also held the post of Master of the College School, and was for some time absent from Oxford, acting as tutor to the sons of the Marquis of Dorset. The accounts for this year are preserved, and show no sign of any transaction of the kind alleged. The accounts of 1499-1500 are now lost; but it may be remarked that in 1500 Wolsey was appointed to the office of Dean of Divinity, which would hardly have been the case if the College had had reason to complain of his conduct as bursar.

[204] Some members of the College, including apparently several of those who had withdrawn at the accession of Mary, were ejected by Bp. Gardiner at a Visitation in 1553.

[205] There is an interesting brass in the College chapel bearing the effigy of President Cole, now concealed by the steps at the lectern.

[206] The elms now in the grove were planted soon after the Restoration, in 1661 or 1662. The walks round the meadow were laid out in their present shape rather later.

[207] Frewen was one of the few bishops who outlived the Commonwealth period. He was afterwards Archbishop of York. Warner, Bishop of Rochester, another of the bishops who returned from exile, was also a member of Magdalen College, and a considerable benefactor to its library.

[208] This organ is now, or was till quite lately, in the Abbey Church at Tewkesbury. Cromwell has left a curious memorial of his presence in a note written on the fly-leaf of a copy of Bp. Hall's Treatises, still in the College Library.

[209] *Spectator*, No. 494.

[210] The names of those who returned are engraved on a cup known as the "Restoration Cup," which is used as a "Grace-cup" in the Hall on the 29th of May. The same cup is used on the 25th of October to commemorate the Restoration of the President and Fellows, who were ejected in 1687, and restored just before the Revolution, on Oct. 25th, 1688. The same "toast" is employed on both occasions—*Jus suum cuique.*

[211] It has been related with some picturesque detail, but with substantial accuracy, by Macaulay: and it is more completely treated in the sixth volume of the publications of the Oxford Historical Society.

[212] Oxf. Hist. Soc. *Collectanea*, II. (1890), pp. 147-8; see the *English Historical Review*, Apr. 1891.

[213] In like manner the position of the head of the earliest College (Merton) was rather that of a Bursar than a Master, a *gardianus bonorum* more than *scholarium.*

[214] Wood's *History of the University of Oxford*, ii. 755-7. The name of Brasenose occurs in the well-known forged charter which professes to be of the date 1219.

[215] Wood's *History*, ii. 756.

[216] See Peck's *History of Stamford*, which contains an engraving of the gateway and knocker. The latter is perhaps more accurately described as a door handle.

[217] See the Proceedings of the Oxford Architectural and Historical Society for November 18th, 1890. The site of the Hall with the gateway and knocker was purchased by Brasenose College in 1890, and the eponymous Brazen Nose itself is now fixed in a place of honour in the College hall.

[218] Until 1827 every candidate for a degree at Oxford took an oath "Tu jurabis, quod non leges nec audies [deliver or attend lectures] Stanfordiæ, tanquam in Universitate, Studio vel Collegio generali."

[219] *Register of the Visitors*, ed. Burrows (Camd. Soc. N.S. xxix.), 1881, p. cxxi.

[220] *Life of Scott*, 1837, i. 374.

[221] The printed editions run—

> "No workman steel, no ponderous axes rung;
> Like some tall palm the noiseless fabric sprung."

[222] *Odds and Ends*, 1872, p. 108: F. G. Lee's *Glimpses of the Supernatural*, 1872, vol. ii. p. 207. The story there told of a sudden death at a club meeting, and a simultaneous appearance in Brasenose of a fiend dragging a man out of the window through the bars, is probably a mixture of two incidents, the death of a woman who had been given brandy out of a Brasenose window on Dec. 5, 1827, and the death of the President of the H. F. Club in 1834, which closed the career of that society, between

which and the Phœnix there was no connection whatever. The story has now become a commonplace of fiction, to judge by the way in which it occurs dressed up in Maltese surroundings in *Blackwood's Magazine*, Feb. 1891.

[223] Printed incorrectly in *Blackwood's Magazine*, vol. liv. (1843).

[224]

The Eights.

Brasenose has started head boat since 1837, when the Eights records become complete:—

- *1839 (1 day)
- *1840 (9)
- 1841 (4)
- *1845 (6)
- *1846 (8)
- 1847 (7)
- *1852 (7)
- *1853 (8)
- *1854 (8)
- 1855 (7)
- *1865 (2)
- *1866 (7)
- *1867 (8)
- 1868 (2)
- *1876 (7)
- 1877 (2)
- *1889 (5)
- *1890 (6)
- *1891 (6)

* In these years it left off Head of the River.

In all 110 days; the next highest number being 63 (University). The boat has never held a lower position than ninth. Of the earlier years between 1815 and 1836, B.N.C. left off head at least in 1815, 1822, 1826, 1827.

The Torpids.

Brasenose has started head boat since 1852, when the Torpids were first rowed in the Lent Term:—

- *1852 (3 days)
- 1853 (5)
- 1854 (4)
- 1859 (2)
- *1861 (5)
- *1862 (6)
- 1863 (5)
- *1866 (5)
- 1867 (2)
- *1874 (2)
- *1875 (6)
- 1876 (1)
- 1882 (2)
- 1883 (3)
- *1886 (4)
- *1887 (6)
- *1888 (6)
- *1889 (6)
- *1890 (6)
- *1891 (6)

* In these years it left off Head of the River.

In all 85 days; the next highest number being 59 (Exeter). The boat has never fallen lower than the eighth place. Between 1839 and 1851, when the Torpids were rowed after the Eights, B.N.C. left off head at least in 1842, 1845, 1850 and 1851.

[225] In Parker's *Handbook to Oxford* is noticed the singularly beautiful effect of the sun shining on summer evenings through both the west and east windows, when viewed from Radcliffe Square.

[226] The reputed founder of Little University Hall: it is believed that the "King's Hall" in the formal title of B.N.C. is a reference to Alfred; but he, Henry VIII., and Victoria may be regarded as equally claiming the Royal Arms which face the High Street.

[227] A Life of Foxe, prefixed to his episcopal register at Wells, by Mr. Chisholm Batten, passed through the press simultaneously with my article. The two lives are perfectly independent of one another, and neither had been seen by the author of the other, though Mr. Batten and I had interchanged information on certain points. I am glad to say that I believe there is no material fact in Foxe's Life in regard to which we differ.

[228] See the chapter on Trinity College.

[229] This word = "kissing," alluding to the amatory propensities of some of the monks of the time. It is often wrongly printed "buzzing."

[230] Thus, in speaking of the three readers of Theology, Greek, and Latin, he says:—"Decernimus igitur intra nostrum alvearium tres herbarios peritissimos in omne aevum constituere, qui stirpes, herbas, tum fructu tum usu praestantissimas, in eo plantent et conserant, ut apes ingeniosae e toto gymnasio Oxoniensi convolantes ex eo exugere atque excerpere poterunt."

[231] And yet there are, in the College Library, two copies of Horace, and one each of Homer, Herodotus, and Plato (see above), all given by the Founder himself.

[232] Ac caeteros, ut tempore, ita doctrina, longe posteriores.

[233] "Ut intus operentur mellifici nec evocentur ad vilia, decernimus ut sint quidam ab opere mellifico liberi et aliis obsequiis dediti. Verumtamen, si quispiam eorum mellifico voluerit imitari, duplicem merebitur coronam"; Statut. cap. 17. In cap. 37 the lecturers are required to admit the "ministri Sacelli" and "famuli Collegii" to their lectures, without charge.

[234] There can be no doubt that, at this period and subsequently, the College servants were often matriculated and proceeded to their degrees. And, as they were entered in the College books not by their names but by their offices, this is one reason why it is often so difficult to trace a student of those times to his College.

[235] In the years 1649-52, there are several entries in the "Register of Punishments" to the effect that scholars or clerks are "put out of commons" for refusing to wait in hall. At that time, therefore, there must have been a feeling that the practice was irksome or degrading.

[236] See the Statutes of Jesus College, Cambridge, chap. xx., where they are limited to two in a day, and, on each occasion, to a pint of beer and a piece of bread.

[237] In a list of Greek Readers given by Fulman (Fulman MSS., Vol. X.), David Edwards is mentioned as preceding Wotton, but, possibly, he held the appointment only temporarily, or there may be some confusion in the matter.

[238] Both these dials have now disappeared. The large and very curious dial now in Corpus quadrangle was constructed by Charles Turnbull, a native of Lincolnshire, in 1605.

[239] In addition to the assistance he received from his College (as an academical clerk), from his uncle, and (in the earlier part of his career) from Bishop Jewel, who died

in 1571, we find that Hooker, on no less than five occasions, was assisted out of the benefaction of Robert Nowell, who had left to trustees a sum of money to be distributed amongst poor scholars in Oxford. One of these entries is peculiarly touching:—"To Richard hooker of Corpus christie college the xiith of februarye Anno 1571 to bringe him to Oxforde iis vid." This date is probably that of his return to Oxford after a visit to his parents at Exeter on recovering from a serious illness, the circumstances of which, including his affecting interview with Jewel at Salisbury, are so feelingly told in Walton's Life. *The Spending of the Money of Robert Nowell* (brother of Alexander Nowell, Dean of St. Paul's), which contains some most curious and interesting entries, is one of the Towneley Hall MSS., and was edited, for private circulation only, by the Rev. A. B. Grosart in 1877.

[240] Wood's *Annals, sub anno* 1568.

[241] The Visitors.

[242] From a table in Burrows' *Register of the Visitors* (Camden Society), pp. 494-6, it may be calculated that the proportion of those who were expelled to those who remained was probably about four to one.

[243] My attention was directed to the rare book, which contains this account, by Mr. C. H. Firth of Balliol College. It is entitled *The Private Memoirs of John Potenger, Esq., edited by C. W. Bingham,* and was published by Hamilton, Adams & Co. in 1841.

[244] And yet, at the date of his admission, he was more than 16 years old. Even in the early part of the present century, there were many admissions of scholars younger than Potenger. John Keble, when admitted, was only 14 years 7 months old; his brother, Thomas Keble, 14 years 5 months; Thomas Arnold, 15 years 8 months; and R. G. Macmullen, who was admitted in 1828, was actually under

14, his age being 13 years 11 months. During the first thirty or forty years of this century, 15 and 16 were not uncommon ages for the admission of scholars at Corpus; and, in addition to the cases cited above, there were occasional instances of admission at 14. Even then, however, the age was most frequently 17 or 18.

[245] *Memoirs of R. L. Edgeworth, Esq.*, in two vols., 1820. My attention was kindly directed to this book by the Rev. R. G. Livingstone of Pembroke College.

[246] That, in 1665, Monmouth resided in Corpus is distinctly stated by Wood [MS. D. 19 (3)]: "Sept. 25, 1665, the king and duke of Monmouth came from Salisbury to Oxon. ... The king lodged himself in Xt Ch. ... and the duke of Monmouth and his dutchess at C. C. Coll." They probably continued in Corpus till Jan. 27 following, when "the king with his retinue went from Oxon to Hampton." I am indebted to the Rev. A. Clark for this reference to Wood's MS.

[247] *Life of Archdeacon Phelps*, Hatchards, 1871.

[248] The story of St. Frideswide and of the convent built in her honour is very fully and quaintly told by Anthony à Wood. See Wood's *City of Oxford* (edit. Clark), vol. ii. p. 122.

[249] See Boase, *Oxford*, p. 3.

[250] See, however, the note at the end of this chapter.

[251] Boase, p. 48.

[252] Sir Gilbert Scott is convinced that this is the original design, and no alteration. However, Dr. Ingram should be read (at p. 18 of his *Memorials of Oxford*), where he asserts a Norman superposition of the upper arches, and the Saxon construction of the lower shafts up to the half-capitals. His writings are founded on careful personal study of the structure in his time.

[253] The hall staircase, with its palm-shaped column (which is, in fact, more like a banyan-tree, as it is virtually a pendant from the vaulted roof), is the principal architectural addition of the seventeenth century; and, with Wadham College, is its most beautiful work in Oxford.

[254] The lower portion only; the upper part, containing the great bell ("Great Tom"), is Wren's.

[255] Late in Elizabeth's reign; confirmed by private Act of Parliament, A.D. 1601.

[256] The organ must have been placed between the nave and choir, in the old order so well remembered and regretted by old Christ Church men, who must still acknowledge the great improvement of these latter days.

[257] John Cottisford, Rector of Lincoln College; not the Bishop of Lincoln ordinary of the University, and executioner of Clark.

[258] John London, Warden of New College; who, however, behaved with sense and kindness during the later proceedings of Wolsey's persecution.

[259] See Wood's *City of Oxford* (edit. Clark), vol. ii. p. 220. Twenty shillings was paid for its conveyance from Oseney to Christ Church in Sept. 1545, with the rest of the peal (*ibid.* p. 228). Their names are contained in the following hexameter; and many Latin verses of equal melody have been composed in their immediate vicinity—

"Hautclere, Douce, Clement, Austin, Marie, Gabriel et John."

[260] Now Bishop of Peterborough.

[261] His mind on the matter is fully given in *Stones of Venice*, vol. ii. p. 158 *sqq.* A new volume by Mr. Cooke, New College, on Professor Ruskin's work in Oxford, is said to contain an excellent account of his later University work. See also his many published lectures.

[262] Note by Professor Westwood. "The age of a particular MS. being ascertained, we are able approximately to determine also the age of the stone or ivory carvings or metal chasings whose art is completely identical with the designs in the MS." See *Pentateuch of Ælfric*, full of architectural detail; and the *Benedictional of Bp. Æthelwulf*, reproduced by the Society of Antiquaries, vol. xxiv. See also *The Pre-Norman Date of the Design and some of the Stone-work of Oxford Cathedral*, by J. Park Harrison (H. Frowde, 1891).

I have to thank my friend the Rev. T. Vere Bayne, Senior Student of Christ Church, for some valuable corrections of this paper.—R. St. J. T.

[263] *S. John's College MSS.*

[264] The statue of S. Bernard over the great gate still remains.

[265] Joseph Taylor, D.C.L., *Hist. of College*, dated 1666. *College MSS.*

[266] *Ibid.* It is mentioned also in *Terrae Filius.*

[267] Royal Patent of Foundation, 1 and 2 Phil. & Mar.

[268] 5th March, 4th and 5th Phil. and Mar.

[269] Statutes as revised under Dr. Willis; Jos. Taylor's MS. *Hist.*

[270] The lease had been made during the last years of the founder's life, at his request, and was especially excepted from the Acts 18 Eliz. cap. 6 and 18 Eliz. cap. 11 against long leases of corporate property.

[271] This letter was soon printed, and every Fellow and scholar may still receive a copy of it.

[272] "A.M. 1572. M.D. 1590. Cujus scripta extant logica, ethica, œconomica, in 8°. libb: physicorum

encomium, musicae encomium, apologia Academiarum, rebellionis vindiciae, quae tamen nondum in luce prodierunt." *Coll. MSS.*

[273] *Oxoniana*, i. 133.

[274] Laud's *Works*, vol. v. p. 152 *sqq.*

[275] It was called "Love's Hospital," and was written by George Wilde, who in 1661 became Bishop of Derry.

[276] Laud's *Works*, vol. v. pp. 82, 83.

[277] Jos. Taylor, *Coll. MS.*

[278] *Terrae Filius*, p. 181. The room was built in Charles II.'s reign, and was the first room built in an Oxford College for use by the Fellows in common.

[279] J. R. Green in *The Druid* (College Magazine), 1862.

[280] Printed in Wood's *City of Oxford* (edit. Clark), i. 640.

[281] See Wood's *City of Oxford*, i. 586, 587.

[282] In that year its members were three graduates and eighteen undergraduates, with a manciple and cook.

[283] Clark's *Register of the University of Oxford*, II. ii. 7.

[284] *Ibid.* p. 36.

[285] Thus, it would seem, leaving the buildings of White Hall untouched for the present.

[286] On the north side of the gateway the following distich was carved—

"Breconiæ natus patriæ monumenta reliquit,
Breconiæ populo signa sequenda pio."

[287] His father was Maurice Johnson of Stamford, M.P. for Stamford in 1523; but his mother was a Welsh heiress and had property in Clun. This was perhaps the connection with Wales that made him be chosen on the Foundation. He had been of Clare Hall and Trinity College, Cambridge.

[288] Principal Hoare (1768-1802) may seem to be an exception, but the College books record that he was born in Cardiff.

[289] The Indenture by which Sir Leoline Jenkins assigned definite Fellowships and Scholarships to North or South Wales is dated 1685.

[290] See Clark's *Register of the University of Oxford*, II. i. 291-293.

[291] Printed (but not published) in 1854. This contemporary Memoir has therefore been largely used in the present sketch.

[292] *The Life of Francis Mansell, D.D.*, by Sir Leoline Jenkins, p. 45. Sir George Vaughan is said to have been of Fallesley, Wilts.—not of Ffoulkston—his family was a branch of the Breconshire Vaughans.

[293] Presumably Leoline Jenkins.

[294] The house and business still remain, No. 66 Holywell.

[295] 1661, as we now reckon the year.

[296] The letter of thanks to Mansell, in which Jenkins acknowledges that he owed his election entirely to Mansell's influence, came into the hands of Anthony Wood, who had the art of "acquiring" stray papers, and the habit of preserving them; and it is now in Wood MS. F. 31. It may be noted that Jenkins' good services to his College, and many personal kindnesses to Wood himself, compel the Oxford antiquary for once to give the lie to his

reputation that he "never spake well of any man"; the terms in which he speaks of Sir Leoline are always handsome.

[297] The plate "lent" by Jesus College to the King is stated by Bishop Tanner to have weighed 86 lb. 11 oz. 5 dwt.

[298] Wood's (MS.) Diary, under that date.

[299] Boase's *Oxford*, p. 140.

[300] Principal, 1712. His portrait is in the College Hall.

[301] To this list may be added:—

Francis John Jayne, Chester (1889).

See also p. 383, note.

[302] Afterwards Mayor, and knighted. Sir Sampson White's house was opposite University College.

[303] Michael Roberts.

[304] This chair was made the pattern of the chairs in the Bursary.

[305] Alfred George Edwards, Bishop of St. Asaph, 1889. Daniel Lewis Lloyd, Bishop of Bangor, 1890.

[306] There is a trivial but well-known story that the College is to present this piece of plate to whoever first fairly encircles it at its widest with his arms, but that from the shape and actual girth (5 ft. 2 in.) this feat has rarely been accomplished. A second task has, however, been kept in reserve; that the winner should drain it filled with the strong punch for which it was designed, and then be able himself to remove it; it holds ten gallons.

[307] Wood quotes no authority, and his story of the founder's intentions is inconsistent in one or two points with the curious old (though not contemporary) MS. account of the last wishes of the founder, which is among

the papers of Wadham College. Dorothy Wadham, however, was certainly a Recusant not long before her death (cf. *Calendar of State Papers*, 1619-1623, p. 330); it may perhaps be conjectured that the atrocity of the Gunpowder Plot alienated her husband from his co-religionists, and induced him to conform to the National Church.

[308] A statute of 1268 directed that every B.A. should dispute against the Austin Friars once a year in the interval between his taking that degree and proceeding M.A. Although these disputations were removed to St. Mary's Church, and afterwards to the Natural Philosophy School, they retained the name "Austin Disputations." See Wood's *City of Oxford* (edit. Clark), ii. p. 465. From *Oxoniana* we learn that the name and some shadow of the disputations remained as late as 1812 among the exercises for M.A.

[309] Of this man an excellent account is given in the *Portfolio* for 1888. But there is some difficulty in attributing the buildings to Holt, for in the very full MSS. accounts for the buildings possessed by the College, his name only occurs as that of a working carpenter, receiving ordinary wages. Perhaps the founder's servant Arnold may have been the real architect.

[310] Vol. 1611-1618, p. 217.

[311] A full account of this controversy may be read on pp. 6-8 of the Rev. R. B. Gardiner's *Registers of Wadham College*, Oxford, to which most valuable and interesting book I wish to acknowledge my constant obligations throughout this chapter. At present only the first volume is out (down to 1719); it is the earnest desire of all interested in the history of the College that Mr. Gardiner may soon be able to complete his work.

[312] P. 53.

[313] I. 291.

[314] II. 106.

[315] I. 318.

[316] "A philosophical inquiry concerning Universal Grammar." Johnson disputes his title to be an "eminent Grecian."

[317] Fuller gives us a proverb current in Oxfordshire, "Send farthingales to Broadgates Hall in Oxford," adding that the gowns not only of the gadding Dinahs but of most sober Sarahs of a former age were so penthoused out far beyond their bodies with bucklers of pasteboard, that their wearers could not enter at any ordinary door, except sidelong.

[318] Leonard Hutten's *Antiquities of Oxford* (1625), Oxf. Hist. Society's reprint, p. 88.

[319] Wood's *City of Oxford* (edit. Clark), ii. 35.

[320] *Queen Elizabeth in Oxford*, 1566—

"Candida, *Lata*, Nova, studiis civilibus apta,
Porta patet Musis, Justiniane, tuis."

[321] Nicolai Fierberti *Oxoniensis Academiae Descriptio*, Romae, 1602:—"Divitum nobiliumque plerumque filiis, qui propriis vivunt sumptibus, assignata *Broadgates*." (Oxford Hist. Society's reprint, 1887, p. 16.)

[322] The patronage of this rectory, usually held by a Fellow, was alienated rather more than thirty years ago.

[323] The slaughter-houses were replaced by a brew-house, to the use of which the old well beneath the wall was in 1672 diverted. Lumbard was a Jew who lived here. It is odd that the only shop in this lane still exhibits the arms of Lombardy, and perhaps carries on the business of this mediæval Jew: the Jewry was elsewhere.

[324] From a family named Penyverthing. A physician named Ireland who lived here in this century, and whose patients made believe to think his fee was 1¼d., got the name changed to Pembroke Street.

[325] Between 1675 and 1700 a new style of gardening seems to have come into vogue. Compare Loggan and Burghersh.

[326] Mrs. Evans, wife of the Rev. Dr. Evans, Master of the College.

[327] This is the meaning of the entry "pro ostreis" in the Bursar's accounts.

[328] The late Bishop Jeune told Mr. Burgon that aged persons in his time remembered this.

[329] "Johnson could not bear to be painted with his defects … 'He [Reynolds] may paint himself as deaf as he pleases, but I will not be *Blinking Sam*'" (Piozzi).

[330] It is curious that the College arms have almost from the first been blazoned wrongly, the argent and or fields of the chief having changed places. The argent should be on the dexter side.

[331] As it seems with a key; possibly a relic of the "wakening-mallet" of religious houses.

[332] Contrast Gibbon's spiteful words: "To the University of Oxford I acknowledge no obligations; and she will as cheerfully renounce me for a son as I am willing to disclaim her for a mother."

[333] This Mr. Tristram is abused by Hearne. He had caricatured some of Hearne's plates.

[334] Dugdale MSS.

[335] Wood.

[336] Whear, in his funeral oration over Camden, bears testimony to the lifelong intimacy of the two.—Camden's *Insignia*.

[337] It had fared roughly in the Civil Wars "in gladiorum Bombardarumque fabricas mutata, quasi Vulcano magis quam Palladi imposterum sacranda prorsus desolata jacuit."—Patent of 1698.

[338] Though Hearne calls him "a man of whimsical and shallow understanding"—"of a strange, unsettled, whimsical temper, which brought him into debt."

[339] V. also "the case of Gloucester Hall, rectifying the false stating thereof by Dr. Woodroffe," p. 40. "The poor Greek boys, whom he used in such a manner that they all or most of them ran away from him."

[340] "The Doctor's precipitation was so violent that he forgot all the Corporation which should have been incorporated but himself—as if he intended by the power of this charter to turn his Body Natural into a Body Politick."—*Case of Gloucester Hall*, p. 24.

[341] Vide *Case for the Attorney-General* (College MS.).

[342] Hearne ed. Bliss, anno 1723.

[343] Willis and Clark's *Cambridge*, iii. 279.

[344] "Anecdotes of his Own Times," p. 174.

[345] Matthew Griffith of Gloucester Hall, absent from St. Mary's when his grace was asked, was excused because "ob distantiam loci et contrarios ventos campanae sonitum audire non potuit!"—Reg. Univ. Oxon. (edit. Clark), II. i. 33.

[346] College Register.

[347] I have to acknowledge the great kindness of our present Principal and Vice-Chancellor, the Rev. Henry Boyd, D.D., in placing at my disposal the materials collected by him for a History of the College which, I hope, may yet see the light.

[348] Gilbert Kymer, M.D., afterwards well known as Chancellor of the University, became Principal in 1412.

[349] A quit-rent continued to be paid by Exeter to S. Frideswyde's and afterwards to Christ Church as long as Hart Hall existed.

[350] Unless the name Hart Hall covered some adjoining tenement.

[351] Nicholls, *Literary Anecdotes*, v. 708.

[352] Newcome became Tutor about 1750.

[353] G. V. Cox's *Recollections of Oxford*, p. 190.

[354] Except the picturesque building now remaining.

[355] Laud's *History of his Chancellorship*, ed. Wharton, 1700, p. 70.

[356] *Ibid.*, p. 209.

[357] With the exception of the five original Fellowships created by the Act.

[358] The Founder of one of these, Dr. William Lucy (1744), provides that his scholars "whilst Under-Graduates shall wear open-sleeved Purple Gowns, with Square Capps, black Silk and white Silver Tuffs equally mixt, as a Mark of Distinction, to dispose others to the like or greater Charity." The Court of Chancery ordered that every Scholar should express in writing his willingness to wear the prescribed garb if it were permitted by the University Statutes. Of the remaining Scholarships four were founded by the Rev. John Meeke in 1665, three by Mr. Henry Lusby

(who divided his estate between this Hall and Emmanuel College, Cambridge) about 1832, and one in memory of Dr. Macbride, Principal 1813-1868. There are also benefactions, now paid to three Bible-clerks, by Dr. Thomas Whyte (founder of the Moral Philosophy Professorship) in 1621, and Dr. Brunsel.

[359] *Oxford University Herald*, Nov. 8, 1845. Reprinted in an anonymous pamphlet entitled "Six Letters addressed to the Editor of the *Oxford Herald* on the subject of an address presented to the Heads of Colleges, &c. Oxford, 1846."

[360] University Extension and the Poor Scholar Question. A Letter to the Rev. E. C. Woollcombe by C. Marriott. Oxford, 1848. Esp. pp. 10-14. Compare also *University Extension*, by C. P. Eden, M.A., Oxford, 1846; and *University Extension and the Poor Scholar Question*, a letter by E. C. Woollcombe, M.A. Oxford, 1848.

[361] Oxford University Extension. *Reports*, pp. 1-20. London, 1866.

[362] *Proceedings* at the laying of the First Stone of Keble College, pp. 2, 3. London, 1868.

[363] Vide *Oxford University Gazette*, Nov. 29th, 1870.